Portsmouth Record Series
Book of Original Entries
1731-1751

*Fig 1* MEETINGS OF 21 AND 28 DECEMBER 1747 (nos 142, 143).
CE6/1, p. 149

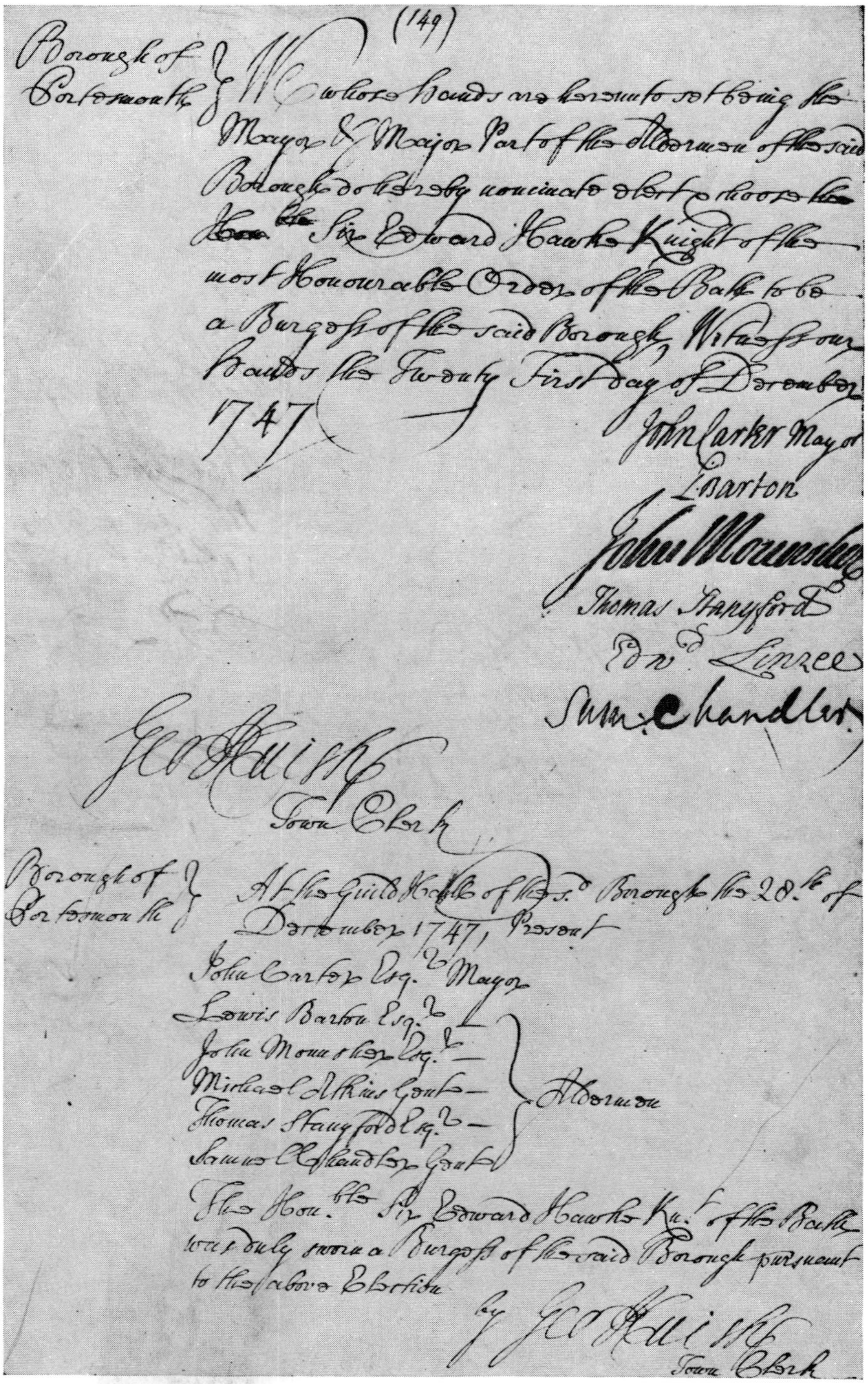

(149)

Borough of Portsmouth } We whose hands are hereunto set being the Mayor & Major Part of the Aldermen of the said Borough do hereby nominate elect & choose the Hon.ble Sir Edward Hawke Knight of the most Honourable Order of the Bath to be a Burgess of the said Borough, Witness our hands the Twenty First day of December 1747

John Carter Mayor
L Barton
John Mounsher
Thomas Stanyford
Edw.d Linzee
Sam. Chandler

Geo Huish
Town Clerk

Borough of Portsmouth } At the Guild Hall of the s.d Borough the 28.th of December 1747, Present

John Carter Esq.r Mayor
Lewis Barton Esq.r
John Mounsher Esq.r
Michael Atkins Gent
Thomas Stanyford Esq.r
Samuel Chandler Gent
} Aldermen

The Hon.ble Sir Edward Hawke Kn.t of the Bath was duly sworn a Burgess of the said Borough pursuant to the above Election

by Geo Huish
Town Clerk

# Portsmouth Record Series
# Book of Original Entries
# 1731-1751

## Edited by
## N. W. Surry and J. H. Thomas

Published by the City of Portsmouth

Published by the City of Portsmouth, Guildhall, Portsmouth PO1 2AL
ISBN 0 901559 30 X
Bound in Black Reliance Cloth No. 73. Text set in 'Monotype' Baskerville
and printed letterpress on Basingwerk White Parchment 100 g/m², by
Eyre & Spottiswoode (Portsmouth) Ltd, Grosvenor Press

# General Editor's Preface

It is appropriate to record here the great debt that the Portsmouth Record Series owes to Mr S. G. Kerry, who died in October 1975 while this volume was in proof. He had been Technical Adviser and Art Editor of the Series since its inception, and he planned and designed its volumes not only with the meticulous craftsmanship of an expert typographer but also with an artistry and vision that were peculiarly his own. The inclusion of the first volume of the Series in the National Book League's exhibition of British Book Production 1972 – a most unusual distinction for a local-record publication – was a fitting tribute to him. The standards of design and production that he set for the Record Series will form a lasting memorial to someone whom all concerned in this work remember with admiration and affection.

P. D. A. HARVEY
*University of Southampton*

# Preface

The editors wish to thank the staffs of the British Library, the National Maritime Museum, the Public Record Office and Her Majesty's Customs and Excise Library, Museum and Records for their valuable assistance. Acknowledgment is also made to these institutions for permission to reproduce documents in their possession.

We are also indebted to Miss M. E. Cash, County Archivist of Hampshire, Mrs P. Gill, County Archivist of West Sussex, Mr E. G. Earle, County Archivist of the Isle of Wight, and Miss S. D. Thomson, Archivist of Southampton. We must also particularly thank Mr E. Banks, Town Clerk of Chichester, Mr W. R. Wilks, Chief Executive Officer of Medina Borough Council, Mr G. F. Smith, Chairman of the Yarmouth Town Trust, and Mrs E. Lang, Clerk to the Trust, who very kindly made their records available to us for examination.

We are grateful to Mrs J. Craig, Archivist to the Hudson's Bay Company, Mrs M. Draper, Archivist to the Bedford Estates, Mr C. P. Finlayson, Keeper of Manuscripts in Edinburgh University Library, Mr E. L. C. Mullins, former Secretary to the History of Parliament Trust, and Mr L. M. Payne, Librarian of the Royal College of Physicians, for help with a number of specific problems.

Acknowledgement is made to the Marquess of Cholmondeley for permission to quote from the letters and papers of Sir Robert Walpole, at present on deposit in Cambridge University Library; to the trustees of the Bedford Estates to quote from the naval papers of John, fourth Duke of Bedford; to the directors of the Goodwood Estates Co. Ltd for allowing us to use the manuscripts of Charles, second Duke of Richmond; and to the Hon. Victor Montagu for giving us similar privileges with the papers of John, fourth Earl of Sandwich. The staff of Sheffield City Library kindly gave us full access to the Wentworth Woodhouse muniments, while Capt. A. J. Pack, RN, and Mr W. B. Windsor were equally generous in making available to us the papers in the Victory Museum, Portsmouth Dockyard, and the Ordnance manuscripts at Priddy's Hard, Gosport, respectively. The Reference Librarian, Salisbury City Library, kindly lent us microfilm copies of the *Salisbury Journal and Devizes Mercury*, for which we are very grateful. Thanks are also extended to the many private individuals who answered our enquiries.

For permission to quote from published works we are grateful to the Delegates of the Clarendon Press (J. S. Watson, *The reign of George III* (1960), pp. 55–6), the Controller of Her Majesty's Stationery Office (R. Sedgwick, *The House of Commons 1715–1754* (2v., 1970), i, p. 243), Messrs Macmillan and Co. (J. H. Plumb, *The growth of political stability in England 1675–1725* (1967), p. 119), Leicester University Press (R. W. Greaves, *The Corporation of Leicester, 1689–1836* (1939), p. 1), and Princeton University Press (D. A. Baugh, *British naval administration in the age of Walpole* (1965), p. 92).

Particular thanks must be expressed to the Earl of Rosse for his efforts to locate Hawke family papers for us; to Miss V. Stokes, Archivist of Messrs Coutts and Co., bankers, and Mr R. F. Mackay of St Andrews University for the time and trouble they have expended on our behalf; to Sir Edward Warner, at present calendaring the papers of John, fourth Earl of Sandwich, for his courtesy and invaluable help on the Sandwich manuscripts; to Mrs M. Guy, of Portsmouth Central Library, and her staff; to Mr D. Francis and the staff of Portsmouth Polytechnic Library, with special thanks to Mrs F. Littlefield; to Professor J. S. Bromley and Dr P. D. A. Harvey of Southampton University, whose useful comments on the draft typescript saved us from many errors; and to Professor P. Mathias of All Souls College, Oxford, who also kindly read the Introduction in draft. We must also thank Mr M. J. W. Willis-Fear, former Portsmouth City Archivist, for his untiring efforts on our behalf over the years, and his staff for their patient and valuable assistance.

It would be discourteous not to acknowledge the provision of research facilities by Dr W. Davey, President of Portsmouth Polytechnic, and Dr G. C. Millard, Head of the Department of Historical and Literary Studies, as well as the timely assistance of Mrs P. Johnson, Mrs M. Pickett and Mrs P. Parsons of the same Department for their valuable help in typing various sections of the book.

N.W.S.
J.H.T.

# Contents

A*

# Contents

ix

A*

# List of Illustrations

# List of abbreviations

| | |
|---|---|
| Baugh | D. A. Baugh, *British naval administration in the age of Walpole* (1965) |
| B.L. | British Library, Reference Division (formerly British Museum) |
| Bonham-Carter | V. Bonham-Carter, *In a Liberal tradition: a social biography 1700–1950* (1960) |
| *Burke's Peerage* | *Burke's Peerage baronetage and knightage* (105th edn, 1970) |
| *Cal.S.P.Dom.* | *Calendar of State Papers, Domestic Series, preserved in the Public Record Office* |
| *Cal.T.B.* | *Calendar of Treasury Books preserved in the Public Record Office* |
| *Cal.T.B.&P.* | *Calendar of Treasury Books and Papers preserved in the Public Record Office* |
| *Cal.T.P.* | *Calendar of Treasury Papers preserved in the Public Record Office* |
| C. & E. | records of the Department of Customs and Excise |
| C.C.A. | Chichester Corporation archives |
| C(H) | Cholmondeley (Houghton) manuscripts |
| Charnock | J. Charnock, *Biographia navalis; or, impartial memoirs of the lives and characters of officers of the Navy of Great Britain, from the year 1660 to the present time* (6v., 1794–8) |
| C.U.L. | Cambridge University Library |
| Defoe | D. Defoe, *A tour thro' the whole island of Great Britain* (edn of 1927) |
| *D.N.B.* | *Dictionary of national biography*, ed. L. Stephen and S. Lee (63v., 1885–1900) |
| East | R. East, *Extracts from records in the possession of the Municipal Corporation of the Borough of Portsmouth and from other documents relating thereto* (2nd edn, 1891) |
| Everitt, 'Church notes' | A. T. Everitt, 'Church notes and other memoranda relating to Hampshire' (typescript, 2v., n.d.; copy in P.C.L.) |
| Everitt, 'Misc. collns' | P.C.R.O. 67A/13: A. T. Everitt, 'Miscellaneous collections' (2v.) |
| Everitt, 'Pedigrees' | P.C.R.O. 67A/13: A. T. Everitt, 'Hampshire pedigrees' (4v.) |
| *F.R.M.C.C.* | *First Report of the Commissioners appointed to inquire into the municipal corporations in England and Wales* (2v., 1835; in British Parliamentary Papers 1835, no. 116, vols xxiii, xxiv) |
| G.E.C. | G. E. Cockayne, *The complete peerage* (2nd edn, 13v., 1910–59) |
| *Geese* | *The geese in disgrace, a tale* (1751). Printed in Appendix II. |
| *Gent. Mag.* | *The Gentleman's Magazine* |
| *Hants. Allegns* | *Hampshire Allegations for Marriage Licences granted by the Bishop of Winchester. 1689 to 1837*, ed. W. J. C. Moens (Harleian Soc., vols xxxv, xxxvi; 1893) |
| Hants.R.O. | Hampshire Record Office, Winchester |

| | |
|---|---|
| Hawke MSS. | papers of the Hawke family belonging to the Earl of Rosse |
| I.W.R.O. | Isle of Wight Record Office, Newport |
| *Life of Martin* | *Life of Captain Stephen Martin 1666–1740*, ed. C. R. Markham (Navy Records Soc., vol. v; 1895) |
| Linzee | J. W. Linzee, *The Lindeseie and Limesi families of Great Britain* (privately printed, 2v., 1917) |
| *List of sheriffs* | *List of sheriffs for England and Wales from the earliest times to A.D. 1831* (P.R.O. Lists and Indexes, vol. ix; 1898) |
| *Lond. Mag.* | *The London Magazine* |
| Mackay | R. F. Mackay, *Admiral Hawke* (1965) |
| Murrell & East | R. J. Murrell and R. East, *Extracts from records in the possession of the Municipal Corporation of the Borough of Portsmouth and from other documents relating thereto* (1884) |
| Namier & Brooke | L. Namier and J. Brooke, *The House of Commons 1754–1790* (History of Parliament; 3v., 1964) |
| N.B.A. | Newport (I.W.) Borough archives |
| N.M.M. | National Maritime Museum |
| P.C.L. | Portsmouth Central Library |
| P.C.R.O. | Portsmouth City Record Office. The following classes of records are cited: |

| | |
|---|---|
| CCR | Reports of committees of the Borough Council |
| CD | deeds of Corporation property |
| CE1 | Election and Sessions Books |
| CE3 | Election or Mayor's Files |
| CE5 | Book of Constitutions |
| CE6 | Books of Original Entries |
| CF1 | Chamberlain's Accounts |
| CF2 | Chamberlain's Vouchers |
| CF3 | Court Leet Fines |
| CF5 | Rent Rolls of Town Rents |
| CF20 | Registers and Particulars of Grants and Leases |
| DD | deeds of Corporation property |
| L1 | Court Leet Views of Frankpledge |
| L2 | Court Leet Presentments |
| PE2 | papers relating to parliamentary elections |
| PL1 | Overseers' Accounts |
| PL12 | Workhouse Day Books |
| S1 | Sessions Oaths Rolls |
| S2 | Sessions Sacramental Certificates |
| S3 | Sessions Files |
| 3A | miscellaneous deposited papers |
| 11A | apprenticeship indentures |
| 16A | papers of the Hewlett family of Titchfield |
| 22A | parish records of St Thomas's (Portsmouth Cathedral), St Michael's Landport, St George's Portsea and St John's Portsea |
| 67A | miscellaneous manuscripts transferred from P.C.L. |
| 81A | records of the City Treasurer |
| 83A | parish records of Widley and Wymering |
| 100A | parish records of St Mary's and other churches in Portsea |
| 169A | parish records of Portchester |
| 210A | parish records of Holy Trinity Gosport |

| | |
|---|---|
| | 257A  records of John Pounds Memorial Church (Unitarian) |
| | 381A  parish records of South Hayling |
| | 570A  papers of the Ordnance Board |

P.H.  records of the Ordnance Depot, Priddy's Hard, Gosport

*Poll, 1705*  *A true copy of the poll, for the electing of Knights of the Shire for the County of Southampton* (1705)

*Poll for Suss., 1734*  *A poll taken by Henry Montague Esq; (Sheriff of the County of Sussex) . . . for the election of two Knights to serve the said County* (1734)

*Poll for Hants., 1734* *An exact list of the names of the gentlemen and other freeholders that voted for Knights of the Shire for the County of Southampton* (1736)

*Poll, 1779*  *County of Southampton. A true copy of the Poll Book for the election of one Knight in the room of Sir Simeon Stuart, Bart. deceased* (1780)

P.R.O.  Public Record Office. The following classes of records are cited:

| | |
|---|---|
| Adm.3 | Admiralty Minutes |
| Adm.49 | Admiralty, Accounting Departments, Miscellanea, Various |
| Adm.110 | Admiralty, Victualling Departments, Out-letters |
| C.108 | Chancery Masters' Exhibits (Farrar) |
| Prob.11 | Prerogative Court of Canterbury, Registered Copy Wills |
| T.70 | Treasury Expired Commissions, African Companies |
| W.O.30 | War Office Miscellanea |
| W.O.46 | Ordnance Office Out-letters |
| W.O.49 | Ordnance Office Accounts, Various |
| W.O.55 | Ordnance Office Miscellanea |

Rogers  J. C. Rogers, *A history of our family* (1902)

St Barbe  C. St Barbe, *Records of the Corporation of the Borough of New-Lymington* (privately printed, 1848)

*Salis. Journ.*  *The Salisbury Journal and Devizes Mercury*

Sandwich  papers of the fourth Earl of Sandwich belonging to Mr Victor Montagu

Sedgwick  R. Sedgwick, *The House of Commons 1715–1754* (History of Parliament; 2v., 1970)

Slight  H. and J. Slight, *Chronicles of Portsmouth* (1828)

Trail & Steer  R. R. Trail and F. W. Steer, *Dr John Bayly of Chichester* (Chichester Papers, no. 34; 1963)

*Turnpike Minute Book*  *Portsmouth and Sheet Turnpike Commissioners' Minute Book 1711–1754*, ed. W. Albert and P. D. A. Harvey (Portsmouth Record Series, vol. ii; 1973)

*V.C.H. Hants.*  *Victoria History of Hampshire and the Isle of Wight* (5v. and index, 1900–14)

V.M.  Victory Museum, Portsmouth

Webb  S. and B. Webb, *English local government from the Revolution to the Municipal Corporations Act*, vols ii, iii: *The Manor and the borough* (1908)

White  L. F. W. White, *The story of Gosport* [1964]

Wilkins  R. Wilkins, *The borough: being a faithful, tho' humorous, description, of one of the strongest garrisons, and sea-port towns, in Great-Britain* (1748). Printed in Appendix I.

Woburn  naval papers of the fourth Duke of Bedford belonging to the Trustees of the Bedford Estates

| W.Suss.R.O. | West Sussex Record Office |
| Y.T.T. | Yarmouth (I.W.) Town Trust |

For abbreviations used only in Appendices V and VI see the notes at the beginning of each.

# Introduction

## 1  Portsmouth, 1731–1751

### THE TOWN AND ITS SURROUNDINGS

Visitors to eighteenth-century Portsmouth were all struck by certain characteristics of the town: the harbour's magnificence, the elaborate nature of the fortifications, the dock-yard's complexity. Early in 1704 Queen Anne expressed to the Duke of Somerset her anxieties about the King of Spain's health while he waited in Portsmouth to return to his country, hoping his health would not suffer as the town 'has no very good reputation as to the wholesomeness of the air'.[1] Some years later, in January 1729, Stephen Martin, a clerk in the Navy Pay Office, described the town as having

> two principal streets from east to west, from the land gate to the sea, besides some other smaller and a great many cross streets and alleys or lanes. . . . The buildings are tolerably good, but none remarkable.[2]

Portsmouth had been described in rather more glowing terms by that inveterate traveller Daniel Defoe, who a few years previously had pointed to its basic strengths:

> As to the Strength of the Town by Land, the Works are very large and numerous, and besides the Battery at the *Point* aforesaid, there is a large Hornwork on the South-side, running out towards *South-Sea Castle*; there is also a good Counterscarp, and double Mote, with Ravelins in the Ditch, and double Pallisadoes, and advanc'd Works to cover the Place from any approach, where it may be practicable: The Strength of the Town is also consider-ably augmented on the Land-side, by the Fortifications raised in King *William*'s Time about the Docks and Yards, which are now perfected, and those parts made a particular Strength by themselves; and tho' they are indeed in some Sense independent one of another, yet they cover and strengthen one another, so as that they cannot be separately attack'd on that side, while they are both in the same Hands.[3]

In the 1750's the town was the subject of comments by the inventor of the umbrella, Jonas Hanway, who wrote in raptures to a lady friend:

> Portsmouth had been now, for many months, the rendezvous of the fashionable world; every gay young man of fortune, and woman also, in their circle of joyous amusements, took a transient view of it; whilst those who have a relish of one of the noblest sights, which art or industry has yet produced, considered our fleet of capital ships, at this time in particular, with delight and exultation.[4]

And yet such statements mask the important fact that during these years the town of Portsmouth occupied but a small corner of the flat, marsh-rimmed island of Portsea. The majority of the inhabitants led a somewhat cramped existence behind the fortifications,

---

[1] *Cal. S. P. Dom. 1703–4*, p. 510: letter from Sir Charles Hedges to the Duke of Somerset, 26 Jan. 1703/4.
[2] *Life of Martin*, p. 206.
[3] Defoe, i, pp. 137–8.
[4] J. Hanway, *A journal of eight days journey from Portsmouth to Kingston upon Thames* (2nd edn, 2v., 1757), i, p. 16: letter to Mrs D., 9 Aug. 1755.

remodelled by De Gomme in 1665 and subsequently by other engineers.[1] Those on the seaward side have survived while the remainder were demolished on the orders of an enlightened War Office during the years 1870–8. During the eighteenth century the town boundaries virtually coincided with those of Portsmouth parish. The remainder of the island consisted of the parish of Portsea, thinly populated and given over in great part to agriculture, part of the parish of Wymering in the north and east, and the extra-parochial area known as Salterns. The boundaries of the unreformed municipal borough covered the western third of the island and the whole of the harbour from the entrance of Fareham Creek to the harbour mouth.[2]

The main entrance to the town was through the Landport Gate on the old London road, while other gates provided access to the Point and the Town Quay. The street pattern conformed roughly to that of a square, and *The borough*, a pamphlet by Robert Wilkins published in 1748, gives a vivid impression of the living conditions then obtaining:

> The Town, consisting of about Six Hundred Houses, is enclosed within a Stone-Wall, several Feet thick and deep; and upon that, a very thick Mud-Wall, as high, or rather higher, than the Tops of the Houses; so that the Inhabitants are constantly buried in Smoak: But as the greatest Part of them are Natives of the Place, and upon that Account inured to it, they seldom mention it as an Inconvenience. They are badly supplied with Water, having none but what partakes of a saline Quality; and even this so very scarce, that were it not for Showers of Rain, which is most industriously catched by every Body, the People could not possibly subsist.[3]

An ambitious attempt a few years earlier by Thomas Smith, lord of the manor of Farlington, to provide the town with fresh water had met with failure,[4] and no further schemes came to fruition until the beginning of the next century.

A reasonably accurate picture of Portsmouth during these years can be gleaned from guide-books and histories published from 1775 onwards. In the centre of the High Street, and opposite the medieval parish church of St Thomas, stood the Guildhall. Rebuilt in 1738, during the mayoralty of John Vining, it represented the major civic achievement of the years covered by the text.[5] The building had an impressive appearance, being described in 1828 as

> a market-place, with arches on the sides and end, a noble hall of fine proportions, with a vaulted ornamental ceiling, fourteen feet high; and at the western end, the Record-room, . . . and above, several small rooms and stores. The Hall is lighted by a large Venetian window at the end, and five on either side. Above the large entrance is placed an emblazonment of the armorial crest of the Borough, with the date and Mr. Vining's name. . . . Above the roof was a small cupola and dome . . . and there is much taste and architectural knowledge displayed in the building.[6]

The High Street was the town's main thoroughfare, and in 1716 it contained some thirty public houses, brandy shops and coffee-houses,[7] intermingled with the houses of Aldermen, Burgesses and Corporation officials. At the street's southern extremity stood the

---

[1] A report of 1708 suggested expenditure of £62000 or more on the fortifications (P.R.O. W.O.55/148/10). Under Acts of 1708 and 1709 for fortifying Portsmouth, Harwich and Chatham more than £100000 was spent on Portsmouth (K. W. Maurice-Jones, *The history of coast artillery in the British Army* (1959), p. 16, where the Act is dated 1704). See Appendix VI for the full titles and citations of Acts of Parliament mentioned in the Introduction.

[2] *V.C.H. Hants.*, iii, pp. 183–4, 191–2.

[3] Wilkins, p. 1 (see Appendix I).

[4] This was embodied in an Act of 1740, 'to enable Thomas Smith, esq., . . . to supply the town of Portsmouth . . . with good and wholesome water at his own proper costs and charges.' For a late Stuart enterprise see East, p. 17.

[5] No. 59; P.C.R.O. CE1/13, p. 266 (14 Mar. 1738/9).

[6] Slight, p. 18. An earlier description of the building is in Wilkins, p. 6 (see Appendix I).

[7] East, pp. 729–34. As a rough indication of urban growth, the returns to the War Office of inns providing bedding and stabling in Portsmouth show 164 beds and space for 87 horses in 1686, and 256 beds and space for 293 horses in 1756 (P.R.O. W.O. 30/48, p. 164; W.O.30/49, p. 17).

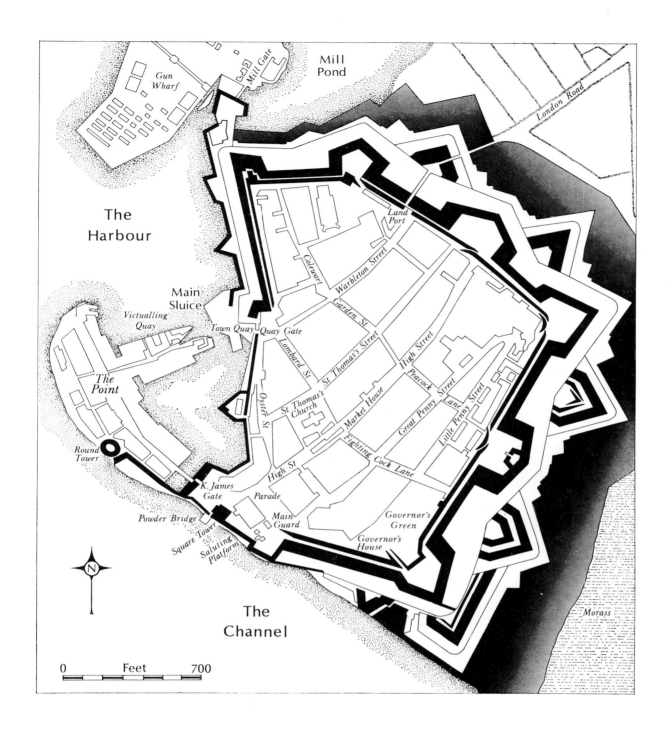

The Harbour

Mill Pond

Gun Wharf

Mill Gate

London Road

Land Port

Colewort

Warbleton Street

Garden St

Main Sluice

Victualling Quay

Town Quay

Quay Gate

St Thomas's Street

High Street

Lombard St

The Point

Oyster St

St Thomas's Church

Market House

Peacock Lane

Great Penny Street

Little Penny Street

Round Tower

Fighting Cock Lane

High St

K. James Gate

Parade

Powder Bridge

Square Tower

Saluting Platform

Main Guard

Governor's Green

Governor's House

The Channel

Morass

N

0    Feet    700

*Fig 2*   RECONSTRUCTED MAP OF PORTSMOUTH based on a version of J. P. Desmaretz's General Plan of the Fortifications 1745

Parade, leading to the ancient hospital of Domus Dei. Following the Dissolution this building had been turned into a residence for the Governor of the Garrison since when 'great alterations and modern additions have been made to it'.[1] While the new Guildhall was being constructed the Corporation used the building for its meetings and courts, paying money to the military authorities for this purpose.[2]

Parallel to the High Street lay King Street, site of the victualling stores, while towards the Camber Dock in Broad Street lay the Customs House, a former public house that was subsequently used as a store by the Board of Ordnance.[3] To the east of the High Street ran Penny Street, site of an almshouse endowed for eight widows, where a new poorhouse was built in 1725, and where lived Alderman William Smith, M.D. who 'left his Dwelling House to be a Charity School for Grammatical Learning'.[4]

Point Gate, at the southern end of the High Street, provided access to the Point. At high tide this was cut off from the rest of the town, communications being maintained by a drawbridge. By the closing years of the seventeenth century the Point contained houses and at least one storehouse and a quay,[5] while one eighteenth-century Alderman, Michael Atkins, had his block-making premises there.[6] The Point's chief importance, however, was as a rendezvous for the more disorderly elements of the population. During his visit Stephen Martin lamented:

> Here the Johns carouse, not being confined to hours, and spend their money for the good of the public, which makes ale houses and shops thrive mightily upon this spot. Some have compared it to the Point at Jamaica that was swallowed by an earthquake (*i.e. Port Royal, 1692*), and think, if that was Sodom this is Gomorrah; but it is by no means so bad as some would make it, though bad enough.[7]

Adjacent to the Point lay the Camber, harbour for merchant ships, dominated by the Town Quay. And from here, through Key Gate, lay the road to the suburb of Portsea, whose growth dates from about 1700.[8] The process of growth, hastened in great part by frequent conditions of war, took place in a healthier part of the island and one that was unencumbered by the confines of town walls and the restrictions of garrison life, a feature not unnoticed by Defoe:

> Since the encrease of Business at this Place, by the long continuance of the War, the Confluence of People has been so great, and the Town not admitting any enlargement for Buildings, that a kind of Suburb, or rather a New Town has been built on the Healthy Ground adjoining to the Town, which is so well built, and seems to encrease so fast, that in time it threatens to outdo for Numbers of Inhabitants, and beauty of Buildings, even the Town it self; and particularly by being unconfin'd by the Laws of the Garrison, as above, and unencumbered with the Corporation Burthens, Freedoms, Town Duties, Services, and the like.[9]

The suburb's independence and prosperity were demonstrated in 1751 when the more influential residents were successful with a petition for a chapel of ease.[10]

---

[1] L. Taswell, *The Portsmouth guide* (1775), p. 9.

[2] No. 69; P.C.R.O. CE1/13, p. 271. P.C.R.O. CF2/2, no. 7, 11 Sept. 1739, records payment of £5.5s. 'to be distributed among the servants of Major Generall Campbell Lieut. Governor of Portesmouth for the use of the Great Hall att Gods House . . . employed by us for Keeping our Courts during the time of Building the New Town Hall'.

[3] Slight, p. 24.

[4] Obituary in *Gent. Mag.*, iii (1733), p. 101.

[5] P.C.R.O. CF5/6.

[6] P.R.O. Prob.11/792, f. 27: will of Michael Atkins, 25 Dec. 1751.

[7] *Life of Martin*, p. 210.

[8] The returns of 1686 show the inns of Portsea as having only six beds and no provision for stabling (P.R.O. W.O.30/48, p. 164).

[9] Defoe, i, p. 139.

[10] Nos 171, 172; the chapel was the future St George's, Portsea. Cf. B. F. L. Clarke, *The building of the eigheetnth century church* (1963), p. 218.

For the visitor to Portsea Island in the eighteenth century, however, the most striking features were without doubt the ever-increasing dockyard facilities and the presence, in enormous numbers, of members of the armed forces. A handbook of 1723 described Portsmouth as 'a fortify'd town and Harbour, and Royal Arsenal'.[1] The Navy by this time had become 'the largest in Europe, and it employed more workers than any other industry in the country',[2] and the martial expansion of the first half of the eighteenth century was responsible in no small way for the expansion and development that took place on Portsea Island. The relationship that developed between the town and the armed forces, while complex and intriguing, can be seen on two levels. Economically there were problems of labour opportunities and of supply, while at a social level there were the issues surrounding civil relationships with the military and naval personnel, and in particular the links between the Corporation and the armed forces. But these issues, of fundamental importance in the understanding of Portsmouth's development, have hitherto been but scantily examined.

During and after the period of Walpole's domination the Dockyard was easily the largest employer of men in the whole of Portsea Island. With a history stretching back to the early Tudor period the Dockyard had not undergone rapid expansion until after 1660, and during the reign of William III an ambitious programme was set in motion.[3] The reign of Dutch William had witnessed the construction of a new dry dock and two wet docks and the inauguration of a policy of harbour reclamation, carried out with such effect that 10½ acres had been added to the Yard by 1710.[4] In the following year the wooden fence surrounding the Yard was replaced by a brick wall, the prelude to an extensive building programme that lasted for the next forty years or more. During the reign of George I the rope-house facilities were extended, an additional 23 acres were enclosed within the Dockyard compound and piping was laid on so that long-boats could restock with water from the jetties with minimum inconvenience.[5] In the 1730's the North Dock was enlarged,[6] and a further enclosure of land took place in 1747, after which there was a lull of about four decades. The growth of the earlier years was such as to impress Defoe, who commented:

> These Docks and Yards are now like a Town by themselves, and are a kind of Marine Corporation, or a Government of their own kind within themselves; there being particular large rows of dwellings, built at the publick Charge, within the New Works, for all the principal Officers of the Place; especially the Commissioner, the Agent of the Victualling, and such as these; the Tradesmen likewise have Houses here, and many of the Labourers are allow'd to live in the bounds as they can get Lodging.[7]

As to the officers who manned the Yard, the author of *The borough* had the following pertinent remarks to make:

> The Officers here are generally sent by the Government; and are such as by their Services at Sea have very well merited the pleasant, comfortable Subsistence, they enjoy for Life; which is never disturbed, but when a Favourite creeps in, who always distinguishes himself, by his haughty and supercilious Deportment. Most of these Gentlemen, by their constant

---

[1] J. Chamberlayne, *Magnae Britanniae notitia* (26th edn, 1723), p. 11.
[2] J. H. Plumb, *The growth of political stability in England 1675–1725* (1967), p. 119.
[3] Baugh, pp. 272–3.
[4] F. M. Pope, 'A historical review of the fortifications of Portsmouth' (typescript, 1961; copy in P.C.L.), p. 33.
[5] *V.C.H. Hants.*, v, p. 388.
[6] No. 22.
[7] Defoe, i, p. 138.

Attendance on, and Application to their several Duties, very justly acquire the Advantages they make; and I doubt not, but the Government are highly satisfied, as well with their Integrity as Ability; or otherwise we should not hear so much of their prudent Conduct in the Management of publick Affairs.[1]

While the numbers of men employed in the Yard were subject to fluctuation they were nevertheless of impressive size. In 1754 Dr Pococke thought that the Yard employed between 1000 and 1500 men, marvelling 'it is curious to see them go out at the toll of a bell at noon and night'.[2] Labour opportunities also extended across the harbour to Gosport, where the victualling service operated in Clarence Yard. There the number of coopers rose from 11 to 32 between October 1736 and summer 1740, and in the three-month period after July 1741 no fewer than 45 extra labourers were taken on. In June 1740 a bake-house started operations, doubling in size within two years and employing 28 hands at the latter date.[3] In addition there was a small private shipyard at Gosport employing about 50 men in July 1749 and engaged in the construction of East Indiamen and other vessels.[4] But though opportunities abounded pay was not always forthcoming in a regular fashion. In June 1733, for example, Viscount Torrington, Treasurer of the Navy, was informed that employees in the victualling service were nearly a year in arrears with their pay.[5]

The naval presence was also emphasised by the provision of hospital facilities and the creation of the naval academy. Hospital facilities for wounded servicemen date from 1713 when Nathaniel Jackson was running the Fortune Hospital in Gosport, equipped with 700 beds.[6] Thirty years later, in September 1744, the Navy Board presented George II with proposals for building naval hospitals in Portsmouth, Plymouth and Chatham, arguing that

the want of such hospitals is so sensibly felt, and Your Majesty's service suffers so greatly from the loss of seamen, either by death or desertion who are sent onshore for the cure of their distempers.[7]

Building operations for Haslar spanned the years 1746–62, though the hospital opened for the reception of patients in 1754.[8] Allied with this development was the attention paid to the recruitment and education of future officers. In 1729 the Royal Naval Academy was set up in the town, important as the forerunner of Dartmouth and Greenwich. In 1733 it had its first intake of 'forty young gentlemen, sons of noblemen and gentlemen', who were to learn a variety of disciplines including French, Latin, fencing and the use of the firelock. But the boys soon, and inevitably, became objects of resentment in the town being scorned as 'Academites' or 'College Volunteers'.[9] Construction of the Academy brought more money to the town, though the costs, in excess of £6000, were subsequently given as one of the reasons for the rise of the naval debt during the period 1721–32.[10]

---

[1] Wilkins, pp. 16–17 (see Appendix I).
[2] *The travels through England of Dr. Richard Pococke*, ed. J. J. Cartwright (Camden Soc., new ser. vols xlii, xliv; 1888–9), ii, p. 115.
[3] V.M. Clarence Yard Pay Book no. 4 (1736–44), passim.
[4] P.R.O. C.108/286 (pay book, 1745–50), passim. The Yard drew some of its timber supplies from Egham in Surrey.
[5] P.R.O. Adm.110/11, p. 87: letter from the Victualling Commissioners, 22 June 1733.
[6] W. Tait, *A History of Haslar Hospital* (n.d.), p. 8.
[7] Ibid., p. 9.
[8] Ibid., p. 15.
[9] C. Lloyd, 'The Royal Naval Colleges at Portsmouth and Greenwich', *Mariner's Mirror*, lii (1966), pp. 145–56. By 1736 the boys were learning 'the use and Exercise of the Cannon' once a month in a ship in ordinary (P.R.O. W.O.55/1988: letter from the Ordnance Board to Portsmouth, 23 Mar. 1735/6).
[10] C.U.L. C(H) Papers 20/44 gives construction costs as £6675. 5s. 3¾d. while Wilkins maintained that it cost £8000 (Wilkins, p. 17 (see Appendix I)).

Important as the Dockyard was as an employer of men and impressive though the numbers of seamen in the town always were, they have tended to overshadow the importance of the military presence. Indeed, until the Victorian development of Aldershot, Portsmouth was of key military importance. By the mid-eighteenth century the town contained four barracks, the largest of which could hold over 1000 officers and men;[1] regiments marching into and out of Portsea Island, either for service on the island or en route for service overseas,[2] were quartered there or in the town. As with the Yard, the Garrison was virtually a town within a town. The Governor, usually a high-ranking military figure, enjoyed a salary of £700 in the early 1730's, at which time the entire Garrison was costing nearly £2000 per year in wages.[3] The presence of troops brought both advantages and disadvantages, as Defoe was quick to point out:

> The Government of the Place is by a Mayor and Aldermen, &c. as in other Corporations, and the Civil Government is no more interrupted by the Military, than if there was no Garrison there, such is the good Conduct of the Governors, and such it has always been, since our Soveraigns have ceas'd to encourage the Soldiery to Insult the Civil Magistrates: And we have very seldom had any Complaint on either side, either of want of Discipline among the Soldiers, or want of Prudence in the Magistrates: The Inhabitants indeed necessarily submit to such Things as are the Consequence of a Garrison Town, such as being Examin'd at the Gates, such as being obliged to keep Garrison Hours, and not be let out, or let in after Nine a Clock at Night, and the like; but these are Things no People will count a Burthen, where they get their Bread by the very Situation of the Place, as is the case here.[4]

### THE CORPORATION AND CONTRACTS

For labour, opportunities obtained in working for the Garrison and the Board of Ordnance, the body that kept both Army and Navy supplied with all kinds of essential equipment. There were always opportunities for recruiting civilians to carry out tasks, though the Board naturally strove to hire at the going terms, as explained in a letter written in spring 1738, about the hiring of scavelmen[5] and labourers

> as the Office pay is as regular and punctual as that of private persons we can see no reason why they should not work as well and as Cheap for the King, as for them, and we are determined to give no more than what the Gentlemen in the Neighbourhood of Portsmouth give.[6]

Indeed, the two most prominent characteristics of the presence of the Ordnance in Portsmouth are the constant concern over expenditure and the extremely tight grip on affairs in the town that was kept by the Office of Ordnance in the Tower of London. Witness, for example, the plight of Robert Eddowes, Ordnance storekeeper at Portsmouth, who was ordered to account for £1.1s. paid to a rat-catcher, being told to report to the Surveyor-General

> by whose Order you employ'd and paid the Ratcatcher, as it does not appear by any of the Books or Minutes of this Office, that you ever received any Orders either upon one or t'other.[7]

---

[1] L. Allen, *The history of Portsmouth* (1817), pp. 146–7.
[2] E.g. *Cal. T. P. 1720–8*, p. 493; *Cal. T. B. & P. 1735–8*, p. 540; *Cal. T. B. & P. 1739–41*, pp. 364, 374, 577.
[3] Sheffield Central Library, Wentworth Woodhouse muniments, M. 25 ('Establishment of his Majesty's Guards and Garrisons', 1734), f. 34. A second estimate, giving the same figures, is in C.U.L. C(H) Papers 117/1.
[4] Defoe, i, pp. 138–9. When Tate Wilkinson, the actor, visited Portsmouth in June 1758 he was subjected to questioning by the military 'at each gate and drawbridge' as the road 'from Hillsey Barracks to Portsmouth, is a continued chain of draw-bridges' (T. Wilkinson, *Memoirs* (4 v., 1790–1), i. p. 214; for Wilkinson, see *D.N.B.*
[5] 'The scavelmen are a description of labourers who attend to clean and pump the docks, and in general assist the shipwrights' (*The Naval Chronicle*, xv (1803), p. 58). A scavel was, in fact, a small spade.
[6] P.R.O. W.O.55/1988: letter from the Ordnance Board to Portsmouth, 14 Apr. 1738.
[7] P.R.O. W.O.55/1996: letter from the Ordnance Board to Portsmouth, 8 Dec. 1750.

Within another month he was asked to inform the Office whether any of the six buckets missing since a fire in Portsmouth had actually been recovered.[1] The degree of control exerted by London is suggested by two incidents, each almost farcical. In August 1728 the Ordnance Office in Portsmouth was informed

> I have this day laid before Sir Charles Willis (*i.e. Sir Charles Wills*) your Letter of the 6: inst: who was pleas'd to Order that the Hay rick in the new Barrack Yard be remov'd of which you are to give notice to Mr Wm. Penford Owner thereof.[2]

Some years later, in December 1751, a desperate overseer of works wrote from Portsmouth about the theft of half a ton of lead from the flat guardhouse roof at Landport Ravelin, asking for directions as to 'what method to take in order to discover the persons concerned in the said Robbery'. As the reply and instructions were six days in coming back, it is to be wondered if the villains were ever apprehended.[3]

While there was this close degree of control from London the very nature of the contracts awarded to the townsfolk led to power for some men and conflict for others. The result was a situation in which patronage and influence could be exerted to their full. John Vining is an example. As early as 1718 he was contracting with the Navy for supplies of salt, to be followed within two years by supplies of peas.[4] During the 1730's and until his death he was in a position of real power. Not only did he secure twelve contracts during these years for a whole variety of products, ranging from laths and charcoal to 'culm' (i.e. soot or coal dust), but these twelve were far more than were secured by any other contractor. At the same time, the wages of some labourers and two 'hoymen' employed by the Clarence Yard were also being paid over to him.[5] Alternatively there are the examples of Henry Friend and the members of the Ridge family. Friend, a vinegar merchant,[6] applied with Vining's widow to take on her late husband's contracts, and by the closing years of the 1740's had gained naval contracts for slates, tiles and plantation pitch. In the following decade he turned his attention more to the Board of Ordnance, supplying soap even though, as the Portsmouth storekeeper was informed, 'the Soap is Charged at 2/6 Firkin more than it Costs here by the Single pound'.[7] By now he was a man of some standing, having been admitted a Burgess in late October 1750, one of the massive creation of that date.[8]

In contrast to the widespread interests of both Vining and Friend, the members of the Ridge family concentrated on naval contracts, for beer in the 1730's and for teams of horses in the 1730's and 1740's. Perhaps they were prudent men seeking to allay the notoriety attached to their brewing ancestor Sir Thomas Ridge. The scandal surrounding the Ridge episode illustrates the untold opportunities provided by the lucrative gains to be made from contracting, and though the incident dates from Anne's reign it is nevertheless worthy of mention. By the middle years of Anne's reign Thomas Ridge, a prominent Portsmouth brewer, was sitting at Westminster as Member for Poole. In September 1708 he was respectable and affluent enough to entertain the Queen of Portugal, on her arrival

---

[1] P.R.O. W.O.55/1996: letter from the Ordnance Board to Portsmouth, 29 Jan. 1750/1.
[2] P.C.R.O. 570A/2: letter from the Ordnance Board to Portsmouth, 20 Aug. 1728.
[3] P.R.O. W.O.55/1996: letter from the Ordnance Board to Portsmouth, 19 Dec. 1751.
[4] V.M. Weekly Accounts, 1718.
[5] V.M. Clarence Yard Pay Book no. 4 (1736–44). A hoy was a small vessel used for coastal voyages.
[6] In January 1741/2 Friend, described as vinegar merchant, petitioned the Treasury for repayment of duty on cider made into vinegar (*Cal. T. B. & P. 1742–5*, p. 109).
[7] P.R.O. W.O.55/1996: letter from the Ordnance Board to Robert Eddowes, 29 Mar. 1751.
[8] No. 164.

from Holland, at his house in the town.[1] Within three years, however, his standing had slumped. Early in January 1710/11 he appeared before the parliamentary committee enquiring into victualling abuses in the fleet, and a month later had been expelled from the Commons, with the fear of prosecution hanging over him.[2] His misdemeanour was of no mean proportions. Having accepted payment bills for 8217 tuns of beer, he had in fact brewed only 4482 tuns, and his explanation to the committee had implicated his brother, 'the Officer that Gauges the casks at Portsmouth'.[3]

Yet Ridge's shortcomings, serious though they were, pale into insignificance beside those of the elder Thomas Missing, merchant prince of Titchfield and a Portsmouth Alderman. From at least 1715 he was contracting with the government for supplying the garrison at Gibraltar,[4] and from at least 1718 with the Navy for the supply of biscuits.[5] In the 1720's and 1730's he broadened his areas of interest to include Canso and Annapolis Royal in Nova Scotia and Placentia in Newfoundland.[6] Member of Parliament for Southampton in 1722, he was described at his death eleven years later as 'an eminent Merchant, and Contractor for the Victualling of Gibraltar'.[7] Within two years of his death his executors were petitioning the Treasury for money owing to their recently departed relative, asserting that this amounted to more than £2700.[8] But then the tide turned and the Treasury started demanding money back from them, and as late as June 1740 restitution was still being made for Missing's short deliveries of bread at Canso in 1727.[9] And such a course of action makes rather ironic nonsense of the monumental inscription in Titchfield church which states that he died of a large fortune 'acquired by honest abilities'.

One very noticeable feature about the distribution of contracts was the number that went to Portsmouth Aldermen. Mention has already been made of Vining and Missing. Two other equally prominent contractors were Henry Stanyford and William Rickman. The Stanyford family had connections with government contracts that extended back to the reign of James II,[10] and when he was in his late thirties Henry Stanyford began supplying the Board of Ordnance with various materials. Between 1701 and 1710 he provided ordnance and ropes for the Garrison, wheelbarrows and pulleys, carried out floor repairs to a magazine, as well as repairing the flagstaff at Calshot Castle.[11] In the 1720's he made gun-carriages and standing carriages, rented a house to the Board for the use of their storekeeper, stood as security for a smith employed in the Board's service,[12] and acted as the major channel of communication between the Board and Portsmouth.[13] Thus it is by no means an exaggeration to say that he enjoyed a position of monopoly with the Board. Very different in character were the activities of Rickman, marked by their very diversity. Brewer and merchant, Rickman gained contracts for Portland stone for the docks at Portsmouth and Plymouth, supplied beer to the Portsmouth Yard

[1] N. Luttrell, *A brief historical relation of state affairs* (6 v., 1857), vi, p. 355.
[2] Ibid., vi, pp. 674, 675, 691.
[3] C.U.L. C(H) Papers 44/78: report on activities of Ridge and Dixon, n.d.
[4] *Cal. T. P. 1714–19*, p. 139.
[5] V.M. Weekly Accounts, 1718.
[6] *Cal. T. B. & P. 1735–8*, passim.
[7] Obituary, *Gent. Mag.*, iii (1733), p. 380; *Lond. Mag.*, ii (1733), p. 370, also carried his obituary.
[8] *Cal. T. B. & P. 1735–8*, pp. 63, 185.
[9] *Cal. T. B. & P. 1739–41*, p. 382.
[10] In August 1687 Ambrose Stanyford secured a contract for the house-carpenter's work on ten boat-houses 'to be Built in the Feild behind the Anchor Sm[i]th Shopp att £36 for each house' (P.R.O. Adm.49/27, f. 53).
[11] P.H. Ordnance MS. 32 (account of materials provided, 24 Dec. 1701); Ordnance MSS. 8, 133, 5, 16 (letters from the Ordnance Board to Portsmouth, 1 Mar. 1700/1, 24 Apr. 1702, 21 Mar. 1703/4, 29 June 1709).
[12] P.C.R.O. 570A/2: letters from the Ordnance Board to Portsmouth, 30 May and 2 June 1722, 3 Jan. and 19 Feb. 1722/3.
[13] P.C.R.O. 570A/2: letter from the Ordnance Board to Portsmouth, 28 Mar. 1729.

smithy and contracted for pitch. His activities extended to the colonies as well. In May 1736, for example, he complained to the Treasury about the importation of beaver skins via Gibraltar and not directly from America,[1] which suggests that he had connections of some sort with the fur trade. In the following decade his agile and acquisitive mind turned to proposals for supplying bread to the troops in the Austrian Netherlands.[2] No doubt one of the ace-cards in the early stages of his career was that he was Missing's son-in-law. This certainly helped with victualling contracts. Thus on Missing's death Lord Lymington approached Walpole about the possibility of Rickman and Benjamin de la Fontaine, a second son-in-law, succeeding to the victualling contracts for Gibraltar and Minorca garrisons. As he explained to Walpole it was the 'Mayor and some honest and hearty friends of the Gouvernents at Portsmouth' that had sought his intercession. Besides forwarding their letter he enclosed a second recommendation on behalf of the two men from Lord Harry Paulet and James Crosse, Recorder of Portsmouth, pointing out that the two were

> zealously affected to his Majesty's person and Government and being well recommended to us by several of the principal Gentlemen and Inhabitants of Portsmouth

and adding that if the two men were to succeed to the contract this would be 'of great Benefitt to the Town of Portsmouth in general'.[3]

Such a situation obviously bred factions amongst the town's leading inhabitants. While the Navy exerted the strongest hold, the Board of Ordnance attempted to build up a rival interest.[4] Several Aldermen had dealings with the Board, and contracts are known to have been awarded to Henry Stanyford, Daniel Smith, John Mounsher, Michael Atkins and others. Here the chief figure with Stanyford was Lewis Barton, Clerk of the Cheque to the Ordnance. Barton, in the Board's employ for many years and frequently absent from his post,[5] was accused in October 1750 of being unjustly negligent.[6] The distribution of interests can be seen by considering contracts involving Aldermen between 1700 and 1750.

ALDERMEN AND CONTRACTS, 1700–1750

| Name | Service | Commodity |
| --- | --- | --- |
| Atkins, Mic. | Navy and Ordnance | Blocks |
| Belfield, Henry | Navy | Tallow and candles |
| Carter, John | Navy | Salt |
| Missing, Tho. | Navy and Ordnance | Bread and biscuits |
| Mounsher, John | Ordnance | Rope |
| Rickman, Wil. | Navy and Treasury | Stone, bread, etc. |
| Smith, Dan. | Navy and Ordnance | Beer and — (?) |
| Stanyford, Henry | Ordnance | Gun-carriages, etc. |
| Vining, John | Navy | Salt, stone, etc. |
| White, John | Navy | Timber |

[1] *Cal. T. B. & P. 1735–8*, p. 218.
[2] *Cal. T. B. & P. 1742–5*, pp. 445, 454.
[3] C.U.L. C(H) Correspondence 2010: 8 July 1733, with enclosure of 6 July 1733. Missing died on 6 July.
[4] Similar rivalry between the Admiralty and the Ordnance Board existed at Queenborough, Kent (L. B. Namier, *The structure of politics at the accession of George III* (2nd edn, 1957), pp. 141–2).
[5] During 1735–7 Barton sought and obtained leave of absence for six weeks, while during the period 1749–53 he applied for and obtained leave of absence on a total of eleven occasions, for a period in excess of thirty weeks (P.R.O. W.O.55/1988, 1996, passim).
[6] Barton, Eddowes and Bowerbank were accused of making a false return for 10 000 excess copper rivets for the March quarter 1750 (P.R.O. W.O.55/1996: letter from the Ordnance Board to Portsmouth, 24 Oct. 1750).

The overall picture is that one-third of the Aldermen engaged in contracts, either with the Navy Board or the Ordnance or with both, and on occasion with the Treasury. It is important to note that while the Navy interest was dominant, it by no means excluded the interest of the Board of Ordnance.

Vital though such contracts obviously were to the economic well-being of Portsmouth, they were by no means the exclusive preserve of Portsmouth people. Witness the success of Thomas Till, in December 1735, in obtaining a contract for supplies of beech plank on behalf of his master the Duke of Richmond.[1] A second example of noble enterprise was that of the Earl of Scarborough, who gained contracts for supplying timber from Stansted Park through the endeavours of his agent Desborow Cathray.[2] Among contractors outside Portsmouth one of the most prominent and powerful was Thomas Bowerbank. His connections with the town stretched back to Anne's reign, when he was described as Overseer of the Gun Wharf.[3] Admitted a Burgess in 1732,[4] he was by the middle years of that decade contractor for barrack bedding and Clerk of the Survey at Portsmouth,[5] while in the following two decades he was variously described as barrack master and contractor for barrack bedding and utensils at Portsmouth and adjacent forts.[6] Add to this his services at the time of rebuilding the Guildhall, and he was obviously a figure to be reckoned with in the day-to-day running of Portsmouth. \

### THE CORPORATION AND THE ARMED FORCES

And lastly, what of relations between the armed forces and the Corporation? The hitherto accepted view has been that the Corporation lay snugly in the Admiralty's grip, and a recent reference work stated that as an Admiralty borough 'Portsmouth was managed by channelling local patronage through the corporation, who controlled the representation by their power to create freeman'.[7] Such a statement, while in great part true, masks some aspects of the nature of the relationship. The fact that most of the town's Members of Parliament were serving sea-officers would appear to confirm it, though the author of *The borough* offered another reason:

> having, therefore, no Men of Property among us, it is but small Wonder, that no sort of Improvements have ever been thought of; and truly . . . I could never hear of any properly qualified for Members of Parliament; which doubtless is the true Reason, why our Representatives are always sent us from a-loft.[8]

Such views apart, naval control was very evident, as was seen in April 1734 when Sir John Norris informed Walpole of his decision to stand for Parliament as Member for Rye: 'I will decline standing for Portsmouth and with pleasure see my selfe succeeded there by any body ye shall apoint'.[9] But there were other elements in the relationship between

---

[1] N.M.M. POR/F/5: 20 Dec. 1735. Till was recommended to Walpole for a Customs post, presumably at Chichester (C.U.L. C(H) Correspondence 3323: letter from Richmond to Walpole, n.d.).

[2] N.M.M. POR/F/5, 6, 7, passim. Scarborough had been admitted a Burgess of Portsmouth on 17 Apr. 1731 (East, p. 379).

[3] P.C.R.O. S2/17: 7 July 1708. Correspondence about building a new gun wharf and storehouses, 27 May 1704, is in B.L. Add. MS. 33278, f. 83.

[4] No. 10.

[5] Bowerbank's original securities for the first post were William Sewell of London, gentleman, for £1000 and Thomas Ridge of Portsmouth for £300 and for the second post they were Robert Heart of Forton and Christopher Bowerbank, incumbent of Weyhill, Hants., for £500 (P.R.O. W.O.55/1988: letters from the Ordnance Board to Portsmouth, 28 Nov., 16 Dec. 1735). Heart was admitted a Burgess in 1711 (East, p. 375).

[6] P.R.O. W.O.55/1988, 1995, 1996, passim.

[7] Sedgwick, i, p. 253.

[8] Wilkins, p. 2 (see Appendix I).

[9] C.U.L. C(H) Correspondence 2152: 9 Apr. 1734.

the civic authorities and the armed forces. By no means the least of these was the clash, occasionally violent, between the areas of civic and naval jurisdiction. In May 1697, for example, the civic authorities broke down the Dockyard gates which they found closed against them during their annual perambulation of the urban boundaries.[1] The Admiralty visitation of 1749, the first since the Navy Board's review of 1686,[2] was not without effect upon the town and the Corporation. The visit to Portsmouth in August 1749 of the Earl Sandwich, Lords Anson and Barrington and Thomas Villiers, while the occasion for the admission of three of them as Burgesses,[3] was also the occasion for fears. Suggestions for a manpower reduction in the Yard would obviously not have been well received by the town. Forty-eight rigger's labourers were ordered to be discharged, warrant officers were considered to be absent too frequently and abuses were found in the appointment of the storekeeper's clerks, while the whole tenor of the visitation was one in which:

> The Lords then Acquainted the Officers with the Occasion of their Visitation, as they had done at the other Yards, Recommended Activity Diligence and Oeconomy to them, in a very particular Manner, with an Assurance of Encouragement to such as Exerted themselves in the Publick Service; And took their Leave.[4]

The visitation, with Sandwich's avowed aim of eliminating dockyard graft and corruption, would obviously have encountered the antipathy and even the hostility of the Corporation, and the gravity of the situation may perhaps be illustrated by the fact that when, two decades later, Sandwich invited the Corporation to dine with him as First Lord, he could prevail on only two Aldermen to attend, the main reason for refusal being that his actions 'had provoked resentment'.[5]

Important though the naval hold was in the town, it was not exclusive, for there was an equal, if not greater, hold by the military. Here the main evidence is to be seen in the election of military personnel as Burgesses, such as Edward Strode, Town-Major of Portsmouth, Thomas Gore, Muster-Master General of Great Britain, and the Duke of Montagu, Master General of the Ordnance, and of men such as the Earl of Kildare and John West, Earl De La Warr.[6] At a second level the influence is to be discerned in the important role of the town Governor. The election methods of Governor Gibson in the 1690's, for example, left much to be desired:

> And, anno 1695, in an election for Portsmouth, Gibson the Governour, standing against Admiral Aylmer, came to a private house and Mooday the master-gunner, with trumpets sounding before him, and bid the mobb turn the man upside down, and broke his windows, and several windows besides, and other houses were threatned.[7]

Significantly, Harley in February 1704/5 listed the 'Governor &c for patronage'[8] while three Governors during the eighteenth century were important military figures: Sir Charles Wills and the Duke of Argyle as Masters General of the Ordnance and General Philip Honywood as a distinguished soldier. As the Corporation was frequently dined

[1] M. Beloff, *Public order and popular disturbances 1660–1714* (1938), p. 112.
[2] J. M. Haas, 'The royal dockyards: the earliest visitations and reform, 1749–1778', *Historical Journal*, xiii (1970), p. 193.
[3] Nos 148, 149. Anson had been admitted a Burgess on 14 Aug. 1746 (no. 128).
[4] P.R.O. Adm.3/61, passim. The Portsmouth visitation was carried out between 1 and 6 Aug. 1749.
[5] *A short state of the conduct of administration towards the Borough of Portsmouth* (1780). The two Aldermen were Edward Linzee and Philip Varlo.
[6] Nos 35, 95, 121, 136.
[7] *Memoirs of the life of Mr. Ambrose Barnes*, ed. W. H. D. Longstaffe (Surtees Soc., vol. l; 1867), p. 225.
[8] B.L. MS. Loan 29/9/12, f.2: pre-electoral survey, 7 Feb. 1704/5.

by the Governor, this relationship must obviously be borne in mind, for this may have been a case where a declining military interest was superseded by a naval one.

## 2  The government of the Borough

### CHARTER AND CONSTITUTION

Eighteenth-century England has been characterised as

> not a unitary state but a collection of corporations and groups, each with a life of its own, cohabiting with ease of long experience within the framework of the Revolution Settlement.[1]

Within what was still a largely rural society with a strong sense of continuity and order, the cities and towns, protected by their charters and peculiar jurisdictions, stood out as islands of relative independence. Town corporations in England

> tended to become, in varying degrees, exclusive political clubs, concerned chiefly with the upholding of their civic dignity, the disposal of their patronage, the increase of their civic properties and revenues, the maintenance of their independence, if it were not already lost, against the local aristocracy, and the promotion of the correct political opinions, 'whig', or 'tory', or merely 'corporation party', as the case might be, at parliamentary elections.[2]

It has been argued that what distinguished the genuine municipal corporation from the highly developed manorial borough was the existence in a town of a system whereby members of the corporation were automatically appointed to serve as Justices of the Peace for the borough.[3] In Portsmouth the Corporation enjoyed an exclusive criminal jurisdiction, co-extensive with the boundaries of the Borough, under the terms of the ruling Charter of 1627. In 1684 Portsmouth's Charter was surrendered to Charles II and a fresh Charter issued, in accordance with general royal policy to make the boroughs more subservient to the Crown. The town was governed in accordance with the terms of this document until 1689, when it was discovered that the surrender of the earlier Charter had not been officially enrolled. The Corporation successfully appealed for the return of their Charter of 1627, and until the passing of the Municipal Corporations Act of 1835 the form, if not always the spirit, of this earlier document dictated the government of the Borough. And thus it was under the aegis of this authority that courts and markets were held, by-laws passed and representatives elected to Parliament.[4]

The Corporation was empowered to hold its own Quarter Sessions, Court Leet, Court of Record and Petty Sessions.[5] Over the first of these, Quarter Sessions, presided the Mayor, ex-Mayor, Recorder and three Aldermen, while only the Mayor, three Aldermen and Town Clerk attended the Court Leet.[6] To facilitate matters the petty jury of Quarter Sessions was sworn in as the Leet jury,[7] the chief duty of the Court Leet being to supervise weights and measures, make presentments and impose fines. In contrast the Court of Record, whose judges were the Mayor, Recorder and three Aldermen, exercised jurisdiction over all personal actions, including unlimited jurisdiction over debts and damages.

---

[1] J. S. Watson, *The reign of George III* (1960), pp. 55–6.

[2] R. W. Greaves, *The Corporation of Leicester, 1689–1836* (1939), p. 1.

[3] Webb, i, pp. 266–7; Greaves, op. cit., p. 20.

[4] Webb, i, p. 270n. Following the Revolution of 1688 there were similar petitions to the Privy Council concerning the charters of many towns, including Winchester, Coventry, Plymouth, Nottingham and Deal.

[5] There had also been a Court of Pie Powder, but this had died out by the seventeenth century (*F.R.M.C.C.*, ii, p. 811).

[6] The Court Leet met twice yearly, on the same day as Easter and Michaelmas Sessions.

[7] Such was also the case at Southwold, Suff., and Newport, I.W. (Webb, i, p. 355n).

Petty Sessions, held three times a week, were presided over by two magistrates and dealt mainly with minor offences.[1]

## THE CORPORATION AND ITS OFFICERS

Within the same framework of the Charter, the Mayor was elected by the retiring Mayor, the remaining eleven Aldermen, and the Burgesses, who nominated candidates for that office from amongst the Aldermen.[2] It is scarcely surprising that in a town where the Admiralty and Board of Ordnance wielded so much influence the Mayors of these years were invariably merchants, contractors or officials. Michael Atkins, Mayor in 1737–8 and again in 1743–4, was a block maker by profession, dealt in timber and made regular contracts with Commissioner Hughes on behalf of the Navy Board; John White, attorney, was Mayor on three occasions, in 1724–5, 1731–2 and 1739–40, and John Arnold, a leading Customs official, was Mayor in 1729–30.[3] In the event of a contest – and there were many – the unsuccessful candidate stood over until the following election day (invariably between 14 and 29 September), when one other candidate was proposed on a majority vote of the Burgesses, Aldermen and Mayor.[4] Election was by secret ballot, and in the event of deadlock the Mayor had the casting vote. It is ironical that an Alderman whose election was forced on the Corporation – Samuel Chandler – should have presented the Borough with a ballot box that was still in use in 1769.[5]

In recognition of the Mayor's wide powers and civic responsibilities, he had since 1682 been receiving an annual stipend of £20 together with

> all other perquisites belonging to the Mayoralty (vidzt), the Seale money, Clarke of the marketts dues, Releifes, opening of shoppe windowes groundage & Anchorage the Capon booke, Bushelage Court Fees and Fynes at the Sessions

which it was later claimed amounted to £300 a year.[6] Whether or not the figure is accurate, the Mayor of Portsmouth was certainly more fortunate than either his colleague at Leeds, whose allowance was fixed at £5 a year in 1764, or his contemporary at Arundel, who in 1744 drew a salary of £100 a year from similar perquisites.[7] But, in view of the frequent visits to the town of high officers of state and even members of the royal family[8] and foreign rulers, it is clear that despite this income personal expenditure would be heavy and that only a man of sound financial standing could afford the prestigious and often advantageous role of Mayor. This may explain why Cornelius Colliss 'joyner' was Mayor merely for the year 1735–6, and unlike his contemporary Lewis Barton, Clerk of the Cheque to the Ordnance Board, was unable to reap comparable advantages from the office.[9]

---

[1] For further discussion of the Borough courts see *F.R.M.C.C.*, ii, pp. 811–12.

[2] The madness of James Blackley, Mayor in 1728–9, combined with his longevity, meant that throughout the period 1731–51 one seat on the aldermanic bench remained in effect unfilled. The Mayor's Election Papers of 29 Sept. 1746 dismiss him succinctly as 'lunatick' (P.C.R.O. CE3/18). Blackley died in 1761 (Everitt, 'Pedigrees', i, p. 92).

[3] N.M.M. POR/F/5, passim; B.L. Add. MS. 33283, f. 173; East, p. 317.

[4] *F.R.M.C.C.*, ii, pp. 803–4.

[5] P.C.R.O. CE3/21: 29 Sept. 1769.

[6] P.C.R.O. CE5, f. 7*: 5 Sept. 1682. The figure of £300 is quoted by the Commissioners of 1835 (*F.R.M.C.C.*, ii, p. 807) and may be optimistic for this earlier period. Contemporary comment on the Mayor's income is made by Wilkins, p. 4 (see Appendix I).

[7] Webb, ii, p. 416; i, p. 177.

[8] George III and his Queen visited Portsmouth in May 1778, and created a baronetcy and a knighthood as a result. A second knighthood would have gone to Edward Linzee, but 'the Mayor desired to be excused the honour' (Linzee, ii, p. 471).

[9] P.C.R.O. S1/31 (17 Oct. 1715); East, p. 317. Barton was Clerk of the Cheque in 1727 and Mayor in 1721 when George I visited the town. An undated petition from him to the King is amongst Sir Robert Walpole's papers, and in the same collection his name appears in 'Mr Chetwynd's List of Pensions, 14 September 1728' (B.L. Add. MS. 33283, f. 322; C.U.L. C(H) Papers 53, f. 24; C(H) Papers 80, f. 93). He was Mayor again in 1726–7 and 1740–1 (East, p. 317).

The Mayor was the leading magistrate in the town, and as such was expected to preside over the Borough courts and the aldermanic bench. He was Clerk of the Market, though the responsibility of this office was delegated to the two Sergeants-at-Mace appointed partly for this purpose. It was his job to affix the town seal to all official documents and to examine the Chamberlain's accounts of the Corporation finances. He was responsible for the maintenance of the gaol and appointed prison officers,[1] and had a voice in the election of scholars to the Grammar School. In his absence a Deputy Mayor was expected to perform most of the mayoral duties.

The twelve Aldermen were all in turn Justices of the Peace, although only the Mayor, ex-Mayor, Recorder and three Aldermen performed this function at a given time.[2] All were elected for life, from among Burgesses and the remaining Aldermen. In 1690 it was decided that in the event of deadlock the Mayor should not have a casting vote but instead a fresh election should be held.[3] The part played by the Aldermen in the government of the town was of vital importance, chiefly to be seen in the election of Mayors and Burgesses, the management of Corporation property, and the administration of justice.[4] In addition some held important posts in the County. They were to be numbered among the trustees of the Portsmouth and Sheet Turnpike Trust (set up by an Act of 1711),[5] whilst two, James Deacon and John Carter, were wealthy and astute enough to attract the favourable attention of the Lord Lieutenant, the Duke of Bolton, to be made Justices of the Peace.[6]

Portsmouth's Recorder was usually a professional barrister, whose chief duty was to attend at Quarter Sessions. The appointment was for life, and he was elected by the Mayor and Aldermen.[7] Although his fee was a mere 15 guineas per session, this in no way reflected the importance of his office.[8] If not always 'a member of one of the great families of the district' – a characteristic of the Recorders of Liverpool in this century[9] – all the Recorders of Portsmouth in these years had strong connections elsewhere in Hampshire, with all the accompanying political and social ramifications. James Crosse of Southampton (Recorder from 1726 to 1741) and Francis Chute of the Vyne (1743–5) had both been students of the Inner Temple.[10] Chute had in 1741 aspired to become Solicitor-General.[11] William Pescod, who was chosen Recorder to succeed Chute (1745–60), also held in 1747 the recordership of Winchester.[12] Clearly such men were well equipped to fill the general role of legal adviser to the Corporation, and also to further the particular interests of various members and of local people in general.[13]

---

[1] Extensive repairs were carried out to the gaol in the mayoralty of William Rickman, 1742–3 (P.C.R.O. CF3/2, nos 21, 23: 21 July and 9 Aug. 1743).

[2] There were twelve under the terms of the governing Charter. In 1744 there were eleven, but the number who regularly attended Council meetings rarely amounted to more than eight; in 1835 there were ten. See no. 111 and *F.R.M.C.C.*, ii, p. 804.

[3] P.C.R.O. CE5, f. 8 (7 Aug. 1690), quoted in East, p. 14.

[4] In Penzance they played a similar role; there, under the Charter of 1614, there were eight Aldermen and twelve Assistants (Webb, ii, pp. 406–8).

[5] *Journals of the House of Commons*, xvi, p. 498. When the Act was renewed in 1726, Thomas Missing senior, Henry Stanyford and Dr Brady were all named as trustees, as were nine future Aldermen.

[6] B.L. Add. MS. 35603, f. 130: letter from the Duke of Bolton to Lord Hardwicke, 19 Jan. 1747/8. Under an Act of 1732, Justices of the Peace had to be owners of an estate of at least £100 a year.

[7] *F.R.M.C.C.*, ii, pp. 805, 808.

[8] At Dorchester he received £2. 14s. and at Bristol 100 guineas with a hogshead of port or sherry annually (Webb, i, p. 323n).

[9] Ibid.

[10] *Register of Admissions to the Honourable Society of the Inner Temple*, ed. H. A. Sturgess (1949), i, pp. 246, 271; East, p. 421.

[11] Sedgwick, i, pp. 553–4; B.L. Add. MS. 35586, f. 345 (letter from Chute to Lord Hardwicke, 8 Apr. 1741). In December 1733 Chute had written to Walpole reminding him of a promised appointment as King's Counsel and successor as Solicitor to the Queen (C.U.L. C(H) Correspondence 2092: letter from Chute to Walpole, 4 Dec. 1733).

[12] B.L. Add. MS. 32710, f. 369: letter from Pescod to the Duke of Newcastle, 15 Mar. 1746/7.

[13] In May 1733 Crosse recommended Richard Aubery to Walpole for the new saltern 'making in Hayling Island' (C.U.L. C(H) Correspondence 1978: 11 May 1733).

The Town Clerk was appointed in the same fashion, not by the Mayor as at Huntingdon, nor by a popular vote of the Freemen as at Bedford and Cambridge.[1] His appointment was vital to the successful running of the Corporation as he served as clerk to the Borough courts, compiled the Corporation minutes, acted as Coroner and was in addition the attorney and solicitor to the Corporation.[2] His responsibilities were great, particularly in a town such as Portsmouth where there were always liable to be clashes over jurisdiction with the Admiralty or the Garrison.[3] His salary of £10 a year was supplemented by the fees paid by Burgesses on their election to the Corporation.

The Chamberlain, or Treasurer, was elected annually by the Mayor and Aldermen, but in practice the office throughout this period was held by two men: Hugh Grove, who filled the post from 1731 until 1747, and his successor, John Shepherd, who retained it until 1771.[4] Almost the whole of the Corporation income and disbursements passed through the Chamberlain's hands, and he was assisted by four auditors (the ex-Mayor and three Aldermen), who were also the town cofferers, in the task of presenting and auditing his accounts. He received £5 for every £100 received by the Corporation, exclusive of all expenses or deductions.[5]

Other officials of the Corporation included two Sergeants-at-Mace, appointed annually by the Mayor. In practice the office was held by the same men for many years. Richard Clapham was from 1711 until 1742 first junior then senior Sergeant; Samuel Beven was for many years his junior and held one or other rank from 1727 until 1753.[6] Their duties were to attend as officers at the Court of Record, to serve all processes, execute all writs and summonses made by the Corporation, summon juries (except for the Court Leet) and to serve notices of Corporation meetings. The Sergeants-at-Mace also collected the market tolls and rents from the butchers' standings. The senior Sergeant received £10 a year, but in the case of Richard Clapham this was supplemented with his perquisites as town gaoler.[7] The junior Sergeant, however, received only 2s. 6d. on each writ and summons served and the rents collected from the fair and markets, as well as fees from persons elected into the Corporation.[8] In Beven's case the Corporation supplemented his meagre stipend with a pension.[9] The two Sergeants were also the Town Water Bailiffs, an unpaid office in the Mayor's patronage and renewable annually. Their role was to protect the foreshore from ship-owners who illegally took on ballast and generally to assist the Harbour Master in his duties.[10]

The Town Crier, or Beadle, was likewise appointed by the Mayor, in theory annually, but in practice the Crier retained his office for many years. John Edwards held the post for several decades before 1743, when he was succeeded by Abraham Stallard.[11] His chief tasks were to collect the market tolls and certain small rents, and for this he was paid

---

[1] Webb, i, p. 327n.
[2] *F.R.M.C.C.*, ii, pp. 805, 806.
[3] No. 52; *F.R.M.C.C.*, ii, p. 810 (the case of Rex v. Solgard, 1738).
[4] P.C.R.O. CE1/13, p. 210 (29 Sept. 1731); CE1/14, pp. 64, 221 (21 Sept. 1747, 22 Apr. 1771, when he was succeeded by Timothy Pike). Grove was a stationer by occupation (P.C.R.O. S2/25, passim).
[5] *F.R.M.C.C.*, ii, pp. 805–9.
[6] P.C.R.O. CE1/13, pp. 23, 177 (29 Sept. 1711, 29 Sept. 1727); CE1/14, pp. 22, 174 (29 Sept. 1742, 29 Sept. 1753).
[7] N.M.M. POR/F/5: letter from Commissioner Hughes to the Navy Board, 27 Mar. 1736.
[8] *F.R.M.C.C.*, ii, pp. 805, 808; East, p. 736 (a 'Table of Fees', 30 June 1738).
[9] No. 1.
[10] At Queenborough, Kent, there were a Land Bailiff and a Water Bailiff with similar functions (Webb, i, p. 319n); cf. *F.R.M.C.C.*, ii, pp. 805, 810.
[11] P.C.R.O. CE1/14, p. 25: 7 June 1743. In November 1745 Abraham Stallard was assaulted during the course of his duties by one Berkeley Morris, receiving several broken ribs, as a result of which he was confined to his home '& in a Surgeon's hands for near a Fortnight' (P.C.R.O. S3/125: complaint to Borough Sessions, 13 Jan. 1746/7).

£10 a year and 6s. 8d. for every £1 he collected.[1] There were six Constables for the town, and three for Kingston and Buckland. There were two Searchers of Markets, appointed annually by the Mayor and magistrates, who were required to see that market regulations were being obeyed.[2] James Lipscombe junior held this post from 1731 to 1738, whilst Daniel Grigg was one of the Searchers from 1732 to 1742.[3] Their work, controlled and supervised by the High Constable,[4] was complemented by that of the Searchers of Leather, an office that tended to remain securely in the hands of certain individuals – often from the same family for many years. William Ragget junior was a Searcher of Leather from 1737 to 1753, and George Roach from 1728 to 1737.[5]

The Mayor and magistrates also appointed the Measurer and the Town Hayward. The former's main duty was to attend the Leet jury on their examination of weights and measures, for which he was paid 7s. for each day of attendance.[6] During the years 1733–42 the post was held by James Goodeve.[7] The second official was responsible for the town pound and collected the usual poundage fees,[8] and between 1719 and 1735 the post was held by Roger Hyde.[9]

Lastly, one small group of Corporation officers was concerned with the town's function as a port. The Harbour Master was appointed under the Mayor's seal; this too was an annual appointment, but differed from the others in this category in that such a post was not mentioned in the governing Charter.[10] The Harbour Master's jurisdiction was confined to merchant vessels, the Navy having its own Harbour Master.[11] The civil officer's task was to collect the harbour dues of groundage, anchorage and bushelage, and his salary was 15s. for every £1 collected.[12] The Wharfinger was chosen by the Mayor and Aldermen, his job being to superintend the arrangements for vessels at the Town Quay and to take cognisance of all goods loaded and unloaded there. In addition he was made responsible for collecting the wharfage dues owed to the Corporation.[13] During the first half of the eighteenth century the wharfage was leased out to private individuals, as happened at Lymington,[14] whereas in contrast the small port of Wisbech set a vigorous example in the direct management of its affairs.[15]

### THE BURGESSES

It was rare for any Corporation official below the rank of Chamberlain to be made a Burgess. This reinforces the view of Portsmouth as a closed Corporation, in that the number of Burgesses was entirely subject to the electoral policy of the Mayor and

---

[1] F.R.M.C.C., ii, pp. 805, 810.
[2] P.C.R.O. CE1/13, pp. 201, 219, 265 (29 Sept. 1731, 29 Sept. 1732, 29 Sept. 1738); CE1/14, p. 22 (29 Sept. 1742).
[3] F.R.M.C.C., ii, pp. 805, 810.
[4] F.R.M.C.C., ii, p. 806.
[5] P.C.R.O. CE1/13, pp. 186, 259 (29 Sept. 1728, 29 Sept. 1737); CE1/14, p. 114 (29 Sept. 1753). The Searchers of Leather are not specifically mentioned in F.R.M.C.C.
[6] F.R.M.C.C., ii, pp. 806, 810–11.
[7] P.C.R.O. CE1/13, p. 228 (29 Sept. 1733); CE1/14, p. 29 (29 Sept. 1743).
[8] At Berkeley, Glos., these amounted to 2d. for every stray animal collected (Webb, i, p. 39).
[9] P.C.R.O. CE1/13, pp. 107, 237: 29 Sept. 1719, 29 Sept. 1735.
[10] F.R.M.C.C., ii, p. 805.
[11] F.R.M.C.C., ii, p. 810.
[12] Between 1830 and 1832 his average salary amounted to £50–£60 per annum (F.R.M.C.C., ii, p. 810). There are no surviving accounts of wharfage dues before 1799.
[13] The appointment was 'during pleasure', but in practice was for a term of years (F.R.M.C.C., ii, pp. 805, 810).
[14] From 1711 onwards Lymington Corporation let out the fishing, with a reservation to themselves of the privilege 'to set a moderate price on all such oysters' (Webb, i, p. 179n).
[15] By the early eighteenth century Wisbech had its own Harbour Master and crane (Webb, i, p. 146).

B

Aldermen.[1] In addition the retiring Mayor had the privilege of nominating a special or peremptory Burgess, whose election in this period was never formally opposed.[2] In the decades after 1688, when political feelings ran high, it was inevitable that factional interests should govern the elections of Burgesses. In 1681 there were 332 Burgesses, but by 1773 the number had fallen to 43.[3] In practice in the years 1731–51 there was an average of about a hundred politically active Burgesses,[4] and the involvement of the Admiralty and Board of Ordnance in the town's affairs and the prejudices of the Mayor and Aldermen are vividly reflected in the persons chosen to be Burgesses.[5] Affluent men like Sir Thomas Ridge, the brewer who married off his daughter to Captain William Hervey, third son of the first Earl of Bristol, with a dowry of £8000[6] are to be found as Burgesses along with lesser worthies such as Robert Turvin, Deputy Controller of Customs,[7] Thomas Appleford, tallow-chandler, and Richard Andrews, farmer.[8] In 1694 the Mayor and Aldermen had decided that every son of an Alderman should automatically become a Burgess – as was the case in Boston[9] – but in 1697 this was revoked.[10] In practice, however, the majority of sons of Aldermen did become Burgesses in the fullness of time. In September 1700 the Mayor and Aldermen ruled that all Burgesses would forthwith be expected to pay an admission fee of £5. 10s. or take an oath to attend the Borough courts. Honorary Burgesses – that is to say members of the royal family, the government or high-ranking civil or ecclesiastical dignitaries – had their admission paid out of the town chest.[11]

The chief privilege of the Burgesses lay in their power to elect the Mayor and two Members of Parliament, but in medieval times they appear to have been granted certain trading rights. The right to form a gild merchant is confirmed in the Charter of Charles I, but no records of its activities have survived.[12] Regulations against irregular trading are certainly in evidence; Quarter Sessions records indicate some of the difficulties of enforcement,[13] although some of the difficulties faced by the Corporation clearly emerge in this volume.[14] The whole scope of these problems and the general incapacity of corporations to deal with them reflect the general dislocation in social attitudes brought about by the Civil War, and the widespread decay of old trade gilds, even in towns where they had been far more firmly established, such as Winchester, Newcastle and Ludlow.[15]

Portsmouth's Burgesses were exempt from wharfage dues until 1832, and possessed certain grazing rights on the town common lands. George Huish transcribed these privileges from an older document that he discovered in 1728, writing that

---

[1] *F.R.M.C.C.*, ii, p. 807.
[2] *F.R.M.C.C.*, ii, p. 806.
[3] Bonham-Carter, p. 15.
[4] Sedgwick, i, pp. 252–3.
[5] For those elected in the period covered by the present text see Appendix V. Burgess Rolls for the period 1713–73 have not survived.
[6] *Augustus Hervey's Journal 1746–1759*, ed. D. Erskine (1953), p. xv; *Letter Books of John Harvey, first Earl of Bristol, 1651 to 1750*, ed. S. H. A. Hervey (Suffolk Green Books, no. 1; 3v., 1894), iii, pp. 54–6 (letters from Bristol to Ridge, 22 and 31 Oct. 1729).
[7] B.L. Add. MS. 33283, f. 160. In 1739 Turvin was Controller of Customs at Portsmouth (*Cal. T.B. & P. 1739–41*, p. 65).
[8] N.M.M. POR/F/5, 6, passim; East, p. 380.
[9] Webb, i, p. 296n.
[10] P.C.R.O. CE5, f. 15 (9 Feb. 1697/8), quoted in East, p. 18; *F.R.M.C.C.*, ii, p. 806.
[11] P.C.R.O. CE5, f. 16 (3 Sept. 1700), quoted in East, pp. 19–20.
[12] *F.R.M.C.C.*, ii, p. 811; *V.C.H. Hants.*, iii, p. 185.
[13] E.g. proclamation against forestalling and regrating, 20 Nov. 1705, regulations governing the sale of vegetables, etc., 4 Oct. 1715 (East, pp. 713, 715–6) and, above all, orders of 16 May 1690 to enforce the statutory seven-year apprenticeship regulations (P.C.R.O. CE5, f. 8, quoted in East, p. 13). The only such presentments to survive from this period date from 1751–3 and are in P.C.R.O. L2/8/1–3; only one presentment for illegally keeping shop occurs. But a few years earlier in 1741 Commissioner Hughes was forced to intervene when a shipwright using false indentures was severely beaten up by his workmates (N.M.M. POR/F/6: letter from Commissioner Hughes to the Navy Board, 14 Feb. 1740/1).
[14] No. 39.
[15] Webb, i, p. 297n.

> Every Burgesse of this Corporacon has a Right to the feed of one Horse, dureing the time the Feilds are open as appears by Antient Presentments.[1]

Similar rights over the common lands existed at Gateshead and Manchester.[2] The Burgesses of Portsmouth were also exempt from county jury service in common with all the Borough's inhabitants.


### FINANCES OF BOROUGH AND OFFICERS

When the Municipal Corporations Commissioners made their report in 1835, the town's chief source of revenue derived from wharfage, cranage and petty Customs, based on prescription and ratified in the governing Charter,[3] amounting to an average annual income of £1043 in the years 1830–2. As the collecting of these dues was leased in Portsmouth for most of the eighteenth century, the sums collected per year were far lower. In addition, leases were sometimes cancelled, or tenants fell into arrears.[4] On paper the total yielded amounted to £983 between 1731 and 1752. This compares favourably with surviving accounts for the borough of Penzance, where between 1694 and 1750 the pier and quay produced between £40 and £100 per year.[5] However, the royal great Customs from Portsmouth were said in 1696 to have increased from £800 to £6000 a year, the chief import being French wines.[6] In the early eighteenth century the coal trade expanded and more cattle were imported from the West Country and Ireland. There were also links between the town and the North American trade going back to the first half of the seventeenth century.[7] Closely associated with this expansion of commerce was the Corporation's right to levy and collect harbour dues of anchorage (or groundage) and bushelage, claimed by prescription but also confirmed by the Charter.[8] The Corporation's second source of income came from land. But it was low, owing to the practice of letting on long leases – leases for a thousand years are not uncommon – while many of the rents 'were trifling quit rents'.[9] Rent from land amounted to a mere £119. 5s. in 1726–7 and even for the period 1790–3 the average annual sum from rents amounted to only £200.[10] Minor sources of revenue included market tolls on goods sold there, and these were collected by the Town Crier and handed over to the Chamberlain.[11] Similarly, property rents on the standings for the sale of meat were collected by the Sergeants-at-Mace, who also collected the fair tolls.[12] By the end of the eighteenth century fines levied by the Leet jury scarcely amounted to £10 a year, the remaining courts and improvement commissioners having absorbed most of the Leet jury's traditional functions.

Figures covering these sources do not exist for the period 1731–51, but even by 1790–3 market tolls, standings and fair tolls were only bringing in respectively £26, £65 and £39 a year on average.[13] The surviving general accounts of the Chamberlain for 1738–47

---

[1] East, p. 735.
[2] Webb, i, pp. 102n, 201n.
[3] F.R.M.C.C., ii, p. 816.
[4] Nos 87, 111.
[5] This calculation is based on the leases shown in the text. For Penzance see Webb, ii, p. 409n.
[6] Portsmouth did not rank as a separate port until the end of the eighteenth century; therefore the great Customs were collected with and accounted for by Southampton (V.C.H. Hants., iii, p. 175).
[7] V.C.H. Hants., iii, p. 175; Proceedings and debates of the British Parliaments respecting North America, ed. L. F. Stock (5v., 1924–41), iv, pp. 4–5.
[8] F.R.M.C.C., ii, p. 816. For the years 1790–3 the average annual amount collected was £20.
[9] F.R.M.C.C., ii, pp. 816–17.
[10] P.C.R.O. CF5/8 (25 Mar. 1727); F.R.M.C.C., ii, pp. 816–17.
[11] F.R.M.C.C., ii, p. 817.
[12] F.R.M.C.C., ii, p. 816.
[13] F.R.M.C.C., ii, pp. 814, 816.

show that in the first year Hugh Grove accounted for sums amounting to £173. 11s. 0½d., while in the last year of his office this had risen to £207. 13s. 2½d.; the audited accounts for his successor John Shepherd show a figure of £211. 8s. 7d. for the year 1751–2.[1] On the basis of these figures (including those of wharfage), but ignoring those resulting from fines for the reasons given, the Corporation's average income for the period 1731–52 would amount to approximately £250 a year. This, however, excludes the main irregular source: gifts from the town's Members of Parliament. Sir Charles Wager gave £100 in 1730, Thomas Lewis contributed £100 to Corporation funds in 1735, and his fellow Member, Rear-Admiral Stewart, gave £200 in 1737.[2] There would also be irregular income from sales of land and successful lawsuits.

Expenses for the years 1731–52 were heavy. The rebuilding of the Town Hall necessitated loans of £700[3] and there were legal costs to be met in various cases, the most notable being Rex v. Solgard in 1738 and Portsmouth Corporation v. Goven in 1749.[4] At the same time there were Corporation officers to be paid, property to be kept in repair, the fee-farm rent to the Crown and payments to charity.[5]

Clearly the personal wealth of Mayors and Aldermen was an important factor in helping to retain corporate dignity. Thus on 29 September the election of the Mayor and officers was celebrated by a procession to St Thomas's where a special sermon was delivered to the assembled dignitaries. On these occasions the ringers of St Thomas's were paid £2 and the gunners of the garrison 10s. to sound off at the appropriate moments.[6] The ceremony of beating the bounds in May and August 1719 was marked by expenditure to guards and ringers of sums amounting to £8. 11s. 6d.[7] The Chamberlain's Accounts are marked by regular items of expenditure to keep the uniforms of the Sergeants-at-Mace up to standard, and even such minor matters as 'paid Mr Hunt for cleaning ye Beadles Badge 0.2.0' are recorded.[8] When honorary Burgesses were created there was a formal ceremony followed by a feast.[9] On 25 March 1718 Lord George Berkeley was met at Kingston in a coach hired for the occasion, to convey him with the Mayor and Aldermen into the town. There he travelled in state to the house of 'Mr Reynolds' where the ceremony of admission took place.[10] In equally formal style, the Recorder was officially met at Cosham and led into the town before Quarter Sessions or other formal business.[11] It was clearly desirable for the Corporation to pay attention to the outward niceties of civic display to maintain its sense of dignity and identity in a town that in so many respects was over-shadowed by the presence of the armed forces.

[1] P.C.R.O. CF1/8 (17 Apr. 1739, 21 Sept. 1748); CF1/5 (18 Oct. 1752).
[2] Nos 31, 51; P.C.R.O. CE1/13, p. 196 (15 Sept. 1730).
[3] Nos 59, 147. In September 1730 the Corporation could not decide how to discharge its debt of £200 to Elizabeth, widow of John Bird, a Dockyard official (P.C.R.O. CE1/13, pp. 196–7: 15 Sept. 1730).
[4] Nos 52, 159.
[5] F.R.M.C.C., ii, p. 817, gives salaries as amounting to £119.11s.6d, repairs £42.16s.4d., charities £35.5s. and permanent outgoings £71.16s.6d. for the years 1830–2 inclusive.
[6] P.C.R.O. CF1/8, passim. On the wealth of Aldermen see below, pp. xl-xli.
[7] P.C.R.O. CF2/25: 15 Oct. 1719.
[8] P.C.R.O. CF1/8: 22 Dec. 1723.
[9] The Municipal Corporations Commissioners commented acidly in their Report on the high level of expenditure on feasting (F.R.M.C.C., ii, p. 818), a point gleefully taken up by Sir Robert Peel in the House of Commons debates on municipal reform.
[10] P.C.R.O. CF1/8: 25 Mar. 1718. Such ceremonies did not invariably take place in the Guildhall; for example Lord Chancellor Hardwicke was admitted an honorary Burgess at the King's Arms, one of the principal inns of the town (no. 66; cf. no. 12n).
[11] P.C.R.O. CF1/8, passim.

## 3  The Aldermen

Under the terms of the ruling Charter the government of Portsmouth was to be entrusted to a group of twelve Aldermen. By means of the wisdom of these men, it was hoped, the affairs of Portsmouth would be competently administered. Hitherto little work has been done on the economic and social composition of the aldermanic bench, and beyond the names and a few brief biographical details of the more prominent little has been known about the men whose responsibility it was to conduct the public life of Portsmouth. Life-spans, social standing, inter-relationships, business and financial interests, even what the Aldermen looked like – all has remained shrouded in obscurity. Quite clearly urban history cannot be looked at in a fruitful and meaningful manner unless attention is given to such matters, for in many cases social standing and economic interests help to explain a particular line taken by a particular alderman.

The first and perhaps least obvious note is that not all the Aldermen were Portsmouth born and bred. Admittedly there were some natives of Portsmouth who achieved aldermanic status, men such as Edward Linzee and Henry Stanyford, but there were others who came from outside the town. When Michael Atkins's parents were married at St Thomas's in June 1665 they were both described as being 'of Wickham',[1] while in 1750 John Leeke, the goldsmith Alderman, was described as having been born in Ashbourne, Derbyshire, and as having resided in Portsmouth for the previous fifty years or more.[2] Dr William Smith, physician to the Garrison under William III, came from Newport, Isle of Wight, where at least one of his two brothers practised as a surgeon,[3] while John Mounsher was the son of a man described as 'a french Emigrant gentleman'.[4] Samuel Chandler's father was minister to the Congregational chapel at Fareham and to another at Andover,[5] while possibly the most colourful in origin was Dr Samuel Brady. He is thought to have hailed from Berwick-upon-Tweed, and his family claimed descent from King Miletus of Ireland.[6]

Knowledge of the educational backgrounds of the various men who served as Aldermen during the period covered by the text is scant. Indeed, details are known for but three men. Thomas, eldest son of Henry Stanyford, practised as a sergeant at law and therefore must have received legal training. The only Aldermen whose education can be fully reconstructed are Dr Samuel Brady and Dr William Smith. In 1697 Brady matriculated at Edinburgh University, graduating Master of Arts in 1699.[7] From there he entered the Navy and under the patronage of Admiral Sir Charles Wager became a physician in 1702, obtaining in September of that year the degree of Doctor of Medicine at Utrecht with a thesis entitled '*De renum et vesicae calculo*'.[8] Dr Smith, some years older than Brady, had an educational pattern that conformed to the fashions of the age. From Christ Church, Oxford, he went, at the age of 22, to complete his education at Leyden, returning to

---

[1] P.C.R.O. 22A/2/1/1/1: Parish Register, 1654–67.
[2] Hants.R.O. C/10/A/456: Consistory Court deposition, 1 Feb. 1749/50.
[3] E. C. Bloomfield in the *Portsmouth Evening News*, 9 Feb. 1939.
[4] P.C.R.O. 67A/13: H. Slight, 'Parliamentary history of Portsmouth'.
[5] B.L. Add. MS. 40001, f. 317.
[6] Correspondence about the family origins is to be found in *Notes and Queries*, 2nd ser., iv (July–Dec. 1857), p. 475; v (Jan.–June 1858), p. 176; vii (Jan.–June 1859), p. 33.
[7] *A catalogue of graduates in the Faculties of Arts, Divinity and Law, of the University of Edinburgh, since its foundation*, ed. D. Laing (Bannatyne Club, vol. cvi; 1858), p. 165.
[8] R. W. Innes-Smith, *English-speaking students of medicine at the University of Leyden* (1932), p. 29.

England at some point in the 1680's or early 1690's.[1] To improve his professional standing as a physician, he obtained the degree of Doctor of Medicine from Oxford in June 1696.[2] With the post of physician to the Garrison and fully accredited medical papers, Smith now devoted himself to medicine and local politics.

In contrast, much more is known about the degree of intensity of family relationships and whether there was any feature that could be described, if only arbitrarily, as an 'age pattern'. The list of Aldermen who served during the years 1731–52 numbers twenty-five, including the lunatic James Blackley, and shows predominance of service to the bench by four families: the Stanyford, White, Carter and Missing families with two members each. The fact that so many Aldermen were closely related is perhaps the most remarkable feature of the bench during this period. Besides the eight instances already mentioned, no fewer than half of the remainder were related by marriage. Michael Atkins, professional block maker and part-time brewer, was father-in-law to Philip Varlo, and sufficiently wealthy to provide his daughter with a portion of £1000 at the time of her marriage to Varlo;[3] while Edward Linzee's daughter married the naval leader Hood, Linzee himself was the son-in-law of his fellow-Alderman Robert Newnham.[4] John Carter was a first cousin of John White, while Thomas Missing the elder was father-in-law to William Rickman.[5] Lastly there was a distant link between Leeke and Vining, as the former's daughter married John Vining Heron, the latter's grandson. All in all, therefore, roughly 65 per cent of the bench were linked by either blood or marriage. Moreover these links were in some cases reinforced and supplemented by others in the way of their business or profession.[6]

Interesting as these facts are, they have to be set in the context of age-patterns and length of service to the local community. Was there anything approaching a 'normal age' for election as a Portsmouth Alderman? Were the majority of Aldermen senior citizens, or was there a liberal sprinkling of men from all age groups? At least four Aldermen could claim a wealth of experience that stretched back many years. John Vining and Henry Stanyford were both elected Burgesses in the 1690's,[7] as was Henry Belfield,[8] who had been supplying the Navy with tallow and candles as early as 1688.[9] John Leeke, though admitted a Burgess in 1713, had to wait until 1749, when in his seventies, before becoming an Alderman, while two men – Vining and Linzee – served as members of the Corporation when they were active octogenarians. Vining, an Alderman at 31, amassed wealth, power and influence during his years on the bench, died on 1 June 1743 aged 84, and was 'buried by torchlight (the whole corporation following), in his own vault opposite the north porch of St. Thomas Church Portsmouth'.[10] Linzee outlived many of his fellow-Aldermen and died in the mayoral parlour in mid-May 1782, also aged 84.[11] Alongside these older men worked younger ones. John Carter, for example, was only in his mid-thirties at the time of his election to the aldermanic bench.

---

[1] E. C. Bloomfield, loc. cit. It is curious that E. Peacock, *Index to English speaking students who have graduated at Leyden University* (Index Soc., vol. xiii; 1883), makes no mention of either Brady or Smith.
[2] *A catalogue of all graduates in Divinity, Law and Medicine . . . in the University of Oxford 1659–1814* (1815) p. 353.
[3] P.R.O. Prob.11/792, f. 27: will, 25 Dec. 1751.
[4] Linzee, ii, p. 467.
[5] W. G. Gates, *Illustrated history of Portsmouth* (1900), p. 679; P.R.O. Prob.11/660, f. 204 (will, 25 Jan. 1731/2).
[6] See below, p. xliv.
[7] East, pp. 329, 371.
[8] East, p. 371.
[9] P.R.O. Adm.49/28, f. 19: abstract of contracts in the 1680's.
[10] Rogers, p. 8.
[11] Linzee, ii, p. 467. His obituary appeared in *Gent. Mag.*, lii (1782), p. 263.

The Aldermen, like all good leading citizens, were not averse from practising charity and subscribing to good causes. Ten of them had contributed to repairing the gallery in St Thomas's Church in 1706,[1] thirteen gave towards the new organ erected in the same building in 1718,[2] while no fewer than seventeen contributed to the Association of 1745.[3] In addition, a small number made donations to the Corporation itself. Henry Stanyford gave 'One large Table (called a horseshoe) and one small Table' and John White gave the third volume of *The Statutes at large*.[4] A fatal flaw appears in their testamentary generosity. From the wills so far located only three Aldermen remembered the poor. Cornelius Colliss was by far the most generous, leaving £100 'to such poor persons protestant Dissenters . . . Objects of Charity Inhabitants of the parish of Portsmouth', John White left £10 to the poor of the town, while Thomas Missing the elder, whose total monetary bequests amounted to over £15 500, managed to leave £10 to be distributed in money and bread to the Portsmouth poor not in receipt of parish alms and an identical bequest for the poor of Titchfield. The only other bequest worthy of note in this respect was Vining's generous legacy of £5 to each of his servants living with him at the time of his death, so that they could buy suitable mourning attire.[5]

Many of the Aldermen served the local community, particularly as Justices of the Peace. Belfield, Vining, Henry Stanyford, Carter and several others fulfilled such duties during these years,[6] while some of the wealthier sought and attained higher status at the county level. Henry Stanyford and the elder Thomas Missing served as Sheriffs of Hampshire in 1722 and 1740 respectively,[7] while William Rickman was described in November 1745 as 'one of the Deputy Lieutenants of the County of Southampton', serving as Sheriff two years later in 1747.[8] Jacobite scares and involvement in European conflict led to service of a rather different nature. In 1715 the Governor of the town, Thomas Erle, raised a new regiment in which no fewer than eleven commissions were held by Aldermen,[9] while nearly thirty years later there was an element of aldermanic participation in a regiment of foot raised in the Dockyard by Commissioner Hughes.[10] Assured social prestige, in the form of a grant of arms, eluded all of them, however, with just one exception: Dr William Smith was granted the right to bear arms on 17 September 1711, when he was described as physician to the Garrison at Portsmouth.[11] In addition there were at least three instances of Aldermen taking part in the public life of other communities. In December 1724 Dr William Smith, founder of the Grammar School, was described as Mayor 'of the Burrough of Frankville alias Newtown in the Isle of Wight';[12] the elder Thomas Missing was Member of Parliament for Southampton, and his son was Member

---

[1] Hants.R.O. C/10/A/456: Consistory Court papers in George Huish v. Philip Varlo. The Aldermen's contribution amounted to £43.7s. 6d.

[2] Everitt, 'Church notes', ii, p. 135. The contribution in this instance was £128 of a total £628.7s.6d.

[3] S.C.R.O. S.C.19 (T.C. Box 5/3/26). The range of Aldermen's subscriptions was from £100 downwards.

[4] P.C.R.O. CE3/15: 29 Sept. 1733.

[5] P.R.O. Prob.11/746, f. 144; Prob.11/753, f. 60; Prob.11/660, f. 204; Prob.11/727, f. 215.

[6] The service of Aldermen as Justices is shown in Appendix III.

[7] *List of sheriffs*, p. 57; M. Portal, *The Great Hall, Winchester Castle* (1899), p. 184; P.C.R.O. S2/25 (15 Apr. 1740). On Missing's activities as Sheriff see *Cal. T.B.&P. 1739–41*, pp. 373, 596.

[8] P.C.R.O. S2/25 (4 Nov. 1745); *List of Sheriffs*, p. 57.

[9] P.C.R.O. S2/20, passim.

[10] P.C.R.O. S2/25, passim.

[11] J. Foster, *Grantees of arms named in Docquets and Patents between the years 1687 and 1898* (Harleian Soc., vols lxvi–lxviii; 1915–17), ii, pt ii, p. 337, citing B.L. Add. MS. 14830, f. 159.

[12] P.C.R.O. S2/23: 7 Dec. 1724.

for the Dorset borough of Poole.[1] Service in these many different ways led to a modicum of local cohesion though such acts of service obviously did not imply identity of political views.

The fact that Portsmouth was a walled naval and military town reinforced this local social cohesion. Several Aldermen lived directly on or close to the High Street. Atkins had widespread property interests which included a house in the High Street,[2] Belfield owned a house on its south side,[3] and the elder Missing had a house on the north side.[4] Henry Stanyford was also a near neighbour,[5] while James Deacon owned a 'Messuage . . . in the High Street of Portsmouth . . . known by the Name or Sign of the three Tons Tavern'.[6] John Leeke and John Vining also resided in this area.[7] As early as the 1690's four Aldermen had been renting property from the Corporation,[8] while there was an instance of one Alderman letting property to another.[9] Important though the link was between the town and its resident Aldermen, there were many who were sufficiently wealthy to live outside Portsmouth, or at least to own extensive tracts of land in other parts of Hampshire, in the Isle of Wight and Sussex, and even further afield. While the elder Missing owned a house in Portsmouth, he also possessed properties in Shedfield and Stubbington and described himself in his will as being of the latter village.[10] When William Rickman made his will he described himself as 'late of Portsmouth and now of Posbrooke in the parish of Titchfield',[11] while Daniel Smith held manors, messuages and lands in the Isle of Wight.[12] John Vining had lands and tenements in the parish of Westbourne in Sussex, farm lands in Boldre and messuages in Sandown and Brockenhurst. James Deacon also owned freehold property at Findon and at Inlands in Westbourne, Sussex, and held messuages and farm lands in Emsworth and at Whitwell in the parish of Godshill, Isle of Wight.[13] Those Aldermen with property interests that extended furthest afield were Henry Belfield with a tenement in Cecil Court, St Martin's Lane, London,[14] and John Leeke who, despite years away from his native Derbyshire, had retained links in the form of two tenements and extensive tracts of land in and around Ashbourne in that county.[15]

The bulk of the Aldermen of course enjoyed a good deal of comfort and an impressive life-style. Among the bequests made to Elizabeth Colliss by her father were ready money, plate, diamond and other rings, gold buttons, gold and silver studs, and a 'Deer's Foot with a Gold Ferril'.[16] Henry Belfield left his widowed grand-daughter £100, twelve silver spoons, twelve silver forks, his largest silver tankard bar one and a silver mug.[17] Thomas Stanyford's possessions included a gold watch with a gold case, pictures, plate, rings and

---

[1] *Return of the name of every Member of Parliament* (2 v., 1878; in British Parliamentary Papers 1878, no. 69, vols lxii, lxiii), ii, p. 55; Sedgwick, ii, pp. 260–1.
[2] P.R.O. Prob.11/792, f. 27.
[3] P.R.O. Prob.11/685, f. 217.
[4] P.R.O. Prob.11/660, f. 204.
[5] P.R.O. Prob.11/673, f. 193.
[6] P.R.O. Prob.11/767, f. 37.
[7] P.R.O. Prob.11/909, f. 225; Prob.11/727, f. 215.
[8] P.C.R.O. CF5/6.
[9] In the 1730's Henry Stanyford was letting a house on the south side of the High Street to Cornelius Colliss (P.R.O. Prob. 11/673, f. 193).
[10] P.R.O. Prob.11/660, f. 204.
[11] P.R.O. Prob.11/916, f. 74.
[12] P.R.O. Prob.11/680, f. 254.
[13] P.R.O. Prob.11/767, f. 37.
[14] P.R.O. Prob.11/685, f. 217.
[15] P.R.O. Prob.11/909, f. 225.
[16] P.R.O. Prob.11/746, f. 144.
[17] P.R.O. Prob.11/685, f. 217.

watches,[1] while those of Vining included plate, a gold watch, jewels and an assortment of items studded with diamonds.[2] Many Aldermen owned horses and carriages, while some had extensive and expensive literary tastes. As a serjeant at law, Thomas Stanyford would have owned copious books, even though his will does not specify them in detail.[3] John Carter had a deep interest in both history and theology and owned volumes by such authors as Dr Saul Clarke, Dr James Foster and Archbishop Tillotson, Burnet's *History of his own times*, works on Roman history, three volumes of Locke's works, a history of the Emperor Charles V, and many others.[4]

In only a few instances are there any indications of what the Aldermen actually looked like. Portraits exist of Linzee and Carter, the former as a youngish man with slender features and sharp eyes, and the latter as what may only be called a 'knowing man'. There was also a three-quarter-length portrait, now sadly lost, of Vining in his official robes, showing a 'somewhat stern, hard-featured man'.[5]

### THE ALDERMEN IN THEIR ECONOMIC SETTING

The shape of the Corporation's economic fabric has not yet been dealt with. The occupational structure of the bench during this period reveals that the majority of members enjoyed professional or near-professional status, as shown below:

OCCUPATIONS OF ALDERMEN, 1731–1751

| *Name* | *Occupation* | *Source* |
|---|---|---|
| Arnold, John | Merchant and Customs official, Portsmouth and Southampton | *Cal. T. B. 1716*, pp. 129, 144; J. Chamberlayne, *Magnae Britanniae notitia* (26th edn, 1723), pp. 514, 516. |
| Atkins, Mic. | Block maker and brewer | P.R.O. Prob.11/792, f. 27. |
| Barton, Lewis | Clerk of Cheque and Stores to Ordnance Board, Portsmouth | P.C.R.O. S2/21. |
| Belfield, Henry | Tallow-chandler | P.R.O. Adm.49/28, f. 19. |
| Blackley, James | Gentleman (?) | P.C.R.O. S2/21. |
| Brady, Sam. | Doctor and surgeon | P.C.R.O. S2/21; Baugh, p. 80. |
| Carter, John | Merchant and contractor | N.M.M. POR/F/6, 7, 8, passim. |
| Chandler, Sam. | Attorney | Hants.R.O. C/1/A8/7; Historical MSS. Commission, *MSS. of the late R. R. Hastings* (4v., 1928–47), iii, p. 62. |
| Collis, Cornelius | Joiner | P.C.R.O. S1/31. |
| Deacon, James | Wine merchant | P.R.O. Prob.11/767, f. 37. |
| Leeke, John | Goldsmith | East, p. 376. |
| Linzee, Edw. | Apothecary | Sandwich MS. 380; P.R.O. Prob.11/1092, f. 299. |
| Missing, Tho., senior | Government contractor | *Cal. T.B., Cal. T.B.&P.*, passim. |
| Missing, Tho., junior | Gentleman | P.R.O. Prob. 11/980, f. 302. |

---

[1] P.R.O. Prob.11/908, f. 160.
[2] P.R.O. Prob.11/727, f. 215.
[3] P.R.O. Prob.11/908, f. 160.
[4] P.R.O. Prob.11/1242, f. 128. John White had an equally wide range of literary and historical interests (P.R.O. Prob.11/753, f. 60).
[5] Rogers, p. 9. P.C.R.O. 67A/13 states that in 1852 a copy of this portrait was in the possession of C. Longcroft, esq., of Havant, a descendant. It was the work of 'Mr. Shalders the Son of an Actor at the Portsmouth Theatre'. We are indebted to Dr D. R. Hodges of Croydon for drawing our attention in January 1973 to a portrait he has recently acquired, described as 'A Mayor of Portsmouth attributed to Hogarth: half length c. 1760'; the identity of the sitter remains uncertain.

B*

| Name | Occupation | Source |
|------|-----------|--------|
| Mounsher, John | Rope maker and postmaster | *Geese*, p. 9 (see Appendix II); P.H. Ordnance MSS., passim. |
| Newnham, Rob. | Surgeon | East, p. 377. |
| Rickman, Wil. | Merchant, brewer and (1739–48) agent for Spanish prisoners | P.C.R.O. S2/24; P.R.O. Adm.110/12; N.M.M. ADM/F/3–10. |
| Smith, Dan. | Brewer | P.R.O. Adm.110/11, p. 62. |
| Smith, Wil. | Doctor | *Gent. Mag.*, iii (1733), p. 101. |
| Stanyford, Henry | Timber merchant and contractor, carriage maker and house-carpenter | P.C.R.O. 570A/2. |
| Stanyford, Tho. | Serjeant at law | P.R.O. Prob.11/908, f. 160; P.R.O. W.O.55/1988. |
| Varlo, Phil. | Grocer and contractor for ships' blocks | Hants.R.O. A Wills, 1742; Sandwich MS. 380. |
| Vining, John | Joiner, merchant and contractor | Rogers, p. 2; Hants.R.O. 1M.49/20–29. |
| White, John | Attorney | East, p. 373. |
| White, Tho. | Attorney | East, p. 379. |

Classification of the members of the bench by occupation reveals a pronounced dominance of merchants, as is only to be expected in a thriving port. Besides the frequent coming and going of naval vessels, there were the arrivals of prize ships in time of war and a busy coastal trade dealing in timber, provisions, wheat and other commodities,[1] as well as vessels plying to and fro between the Isle of Wight and Portsmouth. Quite obviously, therefore, the opportunities for the merchant were both many and varied. But although the bench was dominated by merchants, whether dealing in timber, wine or a variety of commodities, other callings were also represented. In some cases there was only a single representative, such as John Leeke, the solitary goldsmith, or John Mounsher, the only rope maker to sit as an Alderman during this period. Brewers and medical men were also present, while the law was heavily and richly represented.

In all four legal figures had connections with the Corporation during these years. Examination of their activities is important because contemporary opinion held that their presence had done much for the Corporation:

> This Right Worshipful Body, till within these few Years, would have been puzzled to produce one Man among them, that could both write and read in a tolerable Manner; but having introduced some of the learned in the Law among them, they are really greatly improved; and I believe more than half have given over setting their Mark. And it is to be hoped, with the Assistance of the aforesaid Gentlemen, they will be enabled, in Time, to make a further Progress in what has been so happily begun; if they don't chance to fall into the same Dilemma with the Sheep in the Fable, who chose the Wolves for their Keepers: how literally the whole may be applied, both to one and the other, I leave other People to determine.[2]

Among the most colourful personalities, though in many ways an outsider, was Samuel Chandler, an attorney with a flair for penning frivolous verse. Practising as an attorney

---

[1] W. G. Hoskins, *Industry, trade and people in Exeter 1688–1800* (1935), passim. For further details see T. S. Willan, *The English coasting trade 1600–1750* (1938), passim.
[2] Wilkins, p. 5 (see Appendix I). All the aldermanic wills gathered so far have been signed with a name rather than a cross, with the exception of James Deacon's.

by 1731,[1] Chandler was Mayor in 1746 and a Justice and Deputy Mayor in 1750.[2] His importance as an outsider rested on his service as an election agent to the Duke of Richmond,[3] though perhaps his chief claim to distinction is the part he took in the legal proceedings following the activities of Lord Lovat and the Earl of Cromartie in 1745.[4] Very different were the remaining legal figures connected with the bench: John White and his brother, Thomas, and Thomas Stanyford. John White had been admitted to Clement's Inn as early as 1709; by the 1720's he had ceased to attend regularly to legal affairs in London, and by the early months of 1734 was described as being 'lame and infirm so as to be incapable to practice'.[5] At his death he was described as 'an eminent and wealthy Attorney at Law, reckoned one of the best Conveyancers in this County'.[6] His brother Thomas was in partnership in 1775 with George Binsteed and was described as 'independent with a moderate Fortune'.[7] And lastly there was Thomas Stanyford, eldest son of Henry, the Ordnance contractor. A Burgess in 1726 and an Alderman nine years later, Stanyford served as Mayor on two occasions, in 1744 and 1749. Though he described himself as a serjeant at law in his will there are suggestions that he in fact partially carried on his father's business as contractor.[8] Henry Stanyford left his business premises in the first instance to his widow and then to Thomas, and *The geese in disgrace*, published long after the death of Henry Stanyford, made reference to the fact that

> ONE of the *Aldermen*, 'tis true,
> Had much of Meat and Honour too;
> But to his Credit be it said,
> He labour'd for his daily Bread;
> He hew'd and chopt great *Oaken-Blocks*
> To make the *Eagle's Pop-Gun* Stocks;[9]

To substantiate such a suggestion, it is known that a Mr Stanyford travelled from London to Portsmouth carrying Ordnance business with him and was providing axle-trees and trucks for the Board in 1738,[10] perhaps the same Mr Stanyford who was making naval gun-carriages in 1758.[11] This was almost certainly Thomas: in 1752 Thomas Stanyford was described as Solicitor to the Board of Ordnance[12] while of his two brothers Eli had predeceased him by many years and George was not twenty-one by 1735.

In some instances, an Alderman's income was supplemented by shrewd investment. In all, eight out of twenty-five men are known to have been making investments, as shown below.

---

[1] C. & E. 58/143, p. 32.

[2] P.C.R.O. S2/25 (25 Oct. 1746); S2/26 (9 Oct. 1750).

[3] B.L. Add. MS. 32698, ff. 357, 377: letters from Chandler and Richmond to the Duke of Newcastle, 22 and 25 Nov. 1741.

[4] Historical MSS. Commission, *MSS. of the late R. R. Hastings* (4v., 1928–47), iii, p. 62 (letter from Henry Hastings to the Earl of Huntingdon, 19 Aug. 1746); B.L. Add. MS. 32711, f. 128 (letter from Chandler to — Graham, 25 May 1747).

[5] *Pension Book of Clement's Inn*, ed. C. Carr (1960), pp. 269, 150–1, 179. At a pension held 3 July 1721 White claimed that he was 'not in Town ten of the Terms charged to his Account' (ibid., p. 89).

[6] *Salis. Journ.*, 9 Feb. 1746/7.

[7] Sandwich MS. 380: list of Portsmouth voters, 1775.

[8] W. G. Gates, *Illustrated history of Portsmouth* (1900), p. 683.

[9] *Geese*, p. 6 (see Appendix II).

[10] P.R.O. W.O.55/1988: letter from the Ordnance Board to Portsmouth, 4 July 1738.

[11] P.C.R.O. 570A/2: letter from the Ordnance Board to Portsmouth, 19 May 1758.

[12] P.C.R.O. S2/26: 25 Sept. 1752. It is interesting to note that a sacrament certificate, 9 Oct. 1750, makes no reference to this office (P.C.R.O. S2/26).

| Name | Investment | Amount |
|---|---|---|
| Atkins, Mic. | Public stocks or funds | — |
| Carter, John | 4% Consolidated Annuities | £1250 |
| Colliss, Cornelius | Old South Sea Company annuities plus government and private securities | — |
| Deacon, James | 'Interest in ships' | — |
| Leeke, John | Public funds | — |
| Linzee, Edw. | 3% Consolidated Annuities | £3300 |
| Vining, John | South Sea Company stock and annuities, Bank of England stock, Navy Board and Victualling Board bills and Ordnance Board debentures | — |
| White, John | Royal Africa Company stock | £6.5s. – £6.17s.6d. |

SOURCES: P.R.O. Prob.11, passim; T.70/182 (balance of Royal Africa Company stocks, 1731–43), pp. 113–14.

Some Aldermen had joint financial interests, such as Michael Atkins and William Rickman, who operated a brewing concern together with a Mrs Elizabeth Smith.[1] Others drew income from several sources. John Arnold, in business as a merchant dealing in liquor, was also a Customs official at Southampton from 1716 onwards[2] and Collector of Customs in Portsmouth from at least 1720.[3] As a Customs official his methods were somewhat high-handed[4] and in the summer of 1725 his activities were the subject of a Treasury enquiry.[5] James Deacon, wine merchant, may also have been a Customs official.[6] In other instances, Aldermen worked together on a professional basis. Thus in July 1727 Dr Brady had his four children inoculated against smallpox by a local apothecary, possibly Robert Newnham, but refused to supervise similar treatment for other Portsmouth residents; as he informed a fellow physician, 'I have declin'd promoting what so many are disposed to find fault with'.[7] In still other instances there were very close commercial links, such as between the elder Missing and his son-in-law William Rickman, or professional ones, as happened when Missing stood as one of the two securities for Barton's post as Clerk of the Cheque to the Ordnance.[8]

In conclusion, it is a sad indictment of Portsmouth that even at this date few of its leading inhabitants chose to invest any of their money in the town. Certainly the Town Hall was rebuilt at great expense but, as a contemporary noted, 'not without Hopes of being one Day reimbursed, by the large Contributions of our present, and future Members of Parliament'.[9] Yet the prosperity which abounded in the town[10] was not matched by improvements there. In all the years covered by the text Dr Smith's endowment of the

---

[1] P.R.O. Prob.11/792, f. 27.

[2] The Treasury warrant for Arnold's appointment as a Customer in Southampton port is dated 2 Mar. 1715/6, at a salary of £62. 13s. 4d. per annum (Cal. T.B. 1716, pp. 129, 144). In 1718 he was named amongst a list of merchants permitted to reduce imported brandy and rum to proof in order that single duty could be paid for the commodity – a curious conflict of interests (Cal. T.B. 1718, pp. 244–5).

[3] P.H. Ordnance MS. 16: letter from John Arnold to — Baxter, 13 Nov. 1721.

[4] An example involving the Norton family of Southwick is preserved in the Daly family archives (Hants.R.O. 5M.50/843).

[5] C.U.L. C(H) Papers 44/20/1–3.

[6] P.H. Ordnance MS. 16 refers to 'Mr. Deacon the Tide Surveyor'.

[7] G. Miller, The adoption of inoculation for smallpox in England and France (1957), pp. 107, 131 (letter to — Jurin, 18 Jan. 1722/3).

[8] Missing and Robert Reynolds of Portsmouth stood as securities for £500 in February 1720/1. In December 1735 Barton nominated as his two securities 'for faithful performance of his duty' Edward Barton of Portsmouth, mercer, and Thomas Barton of London, goldsmith (P.R.O. W.O.55/1988). Both men were admitted Burgesses of Portsmouth, in 1732 and 1726 respectively.

[9] Wilkins, p. 6 (see Appendix I).

[10] At least six Aldermen made wills whose monetary bequests totalled more than £2000. In two cases they were over £10000.

Grammar School was the only act of aldermanic munificence, an atoll in a sea of rising aldermanic wealth. Moreover, it was one thing to endow a grammar school and another to have it run efficiently and economically.[1] Rather was the pattern one of amassing wealth by various, and on occasion devious, means, investing in lands and buildings outside the town, and then moving completely away from Portsmouth when the opportunity arose. Thus for a select few, the town merely provided the opportunity for making copious quantities of money and little else. It was perhaps not without good cause that the author of *The borough* referred to the 'low, sordid Spirit'[2] of the people who lived in Portsmouth.

## 4  Portsmouth and Politics

### RELIGION AND PARTY IN THE CORPORATION

The accession of George I broke up the Tory party and led to the eventual consolidation of those interests amongst the magnates and the commercial elements of society whose aspirations were summed up in the policies of Sir Robert Walpole. Politics in Portsmouth during the half century after 1715 in many ways followed the dominant mood of the country; for here, as in many boroughs, the bitter party strife that marked the last four years of Queen Anne's reign had divided the Corporation against itself.[3] The struggle was all the more harsh because the Borough contained powerful dissenting groups, well represented among the Aldermen and Burgesses.[4]

At the time of the Compton census of 1676 there were few dissenters in Portsmouth, a mere 2 to 2½ per cent of the population.[5] The remainder of the seventeenth century and the early years of the eighteenth saw this small proportion grow in size and significance. By 1694 the Corporation was renting a meeting-house to dissenters,[6] and two more were set up in the years 1700–60. A certificate was granted in August 1729 for a meeting-house at Queen Street, Portsmouth Common, and another in October 1754 for an entirely new building in Orange Row, Portsea Common.[7] Periodic bequests helped the dissenters, as in 1743, when the will of Thomas White, a Portsmouth gentleman, left £40 to the meeting-house trustees to be put out at interest and the proceeds to be paid to the minister for the time being;[8] the bulk of meeting-house funds were invested in the stock of the South Sea Company.[9] As an indication of the strength of the dissenting element, nine Aldermen were registered as dissenters during the years 1716–35 while about thirty Burgesses were of the same disposition.[10]

---

[1] The trustees felt that the annual income of £200 was insufficient to either build or maintain a school and thus the rental of the farm at East Standen, I.W., was allowed to accumulate for eighteen years, after which land was purchased in Penny Street and 'a school of sorts built at the rear of his (*i.e. Smith's*) house'. The trustees were the Dean and Canons of Christ Church, Oxford, and the school was eventually opened in 1750. The cost of the project was estimated at £300 but alterations and additions swallowed up a further £700 (W. Durman, 'Portsmouth education' (typescript, n.d.; copy in P.C.L.), ch. 22, pp. 1–2.

[2] Wilkins, p. 2 (see Appendix I).

[3] East, pp. 762–82.

[4] They were described as Presbyterians by contemporaries, themselves included.

[5] Hants.R.O., abstract of Compton census returns.

[6] Slight, p. 81.

[7] A. J. Willis, *Dissenters' meeting house certificates in the diocese of Winchester 1702–1844* (*A Hampshire Miscellany*, pt 3; 1965), pp. 118, 120. Orange Row was later Orange Street.

[8] A. T. Everitt, 'Hampshire wills' (typescript, n.d.; copy in P.C.L.), pp. 93–4.

[9] P.C.R.O. 257A/1/9/3: General Account Book of High Street Chapel, 1718-40.

[10] Ibid.

And yet the established Church was still a powerful force in the town. The Corporation maintained its dignity by having a separate church pew, a fact that was resented by some of the town's inhabitants,[1] and many Aldermen were buried in the church, on occasion in an impressive style. The Bishop of Winchester's presence was felt as patron of the living of St Thomas's while the Dean and Chapter of Windsor also owned land in the town.[2] In the early part of the period the incumbent of St Thomas's church was Anthony Bliss, later Dr Bliss, who in 1731 published *Observations on Mr Chubb's discourse concerning reason*.[3] His successor to the living, William Langbaine 'went into retirement and refused to see anyone for many years'; he was succeded by Henry Taylor, Fellow of Queens' College, Cambridge, and described as 'an Arian'.[4] As with any other community, leading local personages made bequests and donations to St Thomas's. Governor Gibson presented a large branch of brass candlesticks, while two branches came from Captain John Suffield together with brass sconces for the pulpit and a reading-desk. From the profits accrued by his brewing concern Thomas Ridge gave a large velvet communion table cloth and two cushions.[5] But there is a notable absence of donations of this type by Aldermen, though admittedly they contributed to repairs to the church fabric. And yet care is needed to avoid exaggerating the hostility between Anglicans and and Presbyterians at this time, given the latitudinarian views of Benjamin Hoadly, Edmund Gibson and the majority of the episcopal bench.[6]

While there were religious differences, the political rivalries were far stronger. In 1715, the Tory Aldermen on the Corporation were left unscathed in a purge that involved the dismissal of the Governor of the Garrison, Lord North,[7] and the creation of 59 new Burgesses. But the reinstatement of the Whig Aldermen lost them their majority on the bench, so that the quarrels of the next decade emphasised their growing isolation and became increasingly parochial in character. Two of the prominent surviving Tories, John Vining and Henry Belfield, voted against the election of Cornelius Colliss as Alderman on 22 March 1732/3; a few years earlier, on 28 September 1727, the same men, together with Sir John Suffield and Dr William Smith, had unsuccessfully contested the election of George Huish as Town Clerk, to replace the dead Tory, Charles Bissell.[8] But in 1735 only Belfield protested against the election of Thomas Stanyford as an Alderman.[9] The significance of these quarrels must be seen against the national political background. It is a truism that in the decades after 1715 political in-fighting was increasingly not between Whigs and Tories, but between Whigs and Whigs, the majority of the old Tory party having been first split by the Jacobite issue and then reconciled by Walpole's policies. In Portsmouth the Admiralty and Ordnance loomed large as providers of contracts and preferments. So it is not surprising that the voices of criticism were relatively silenced when it came to the election of Members of Parliament, particularly as for some years Sir Charles Wager was not only an Alderman of the town, but one of its two Members and

---

[1] Hants.R.O. C/10/A/642: Consistory Court papers in Portsmouth Corporation v. John Goven, 1749.
[2] P.R.O. Prob.11/727, f. 215.
[3] P.C.R.O. 67A/13: copy of Slight annotated by Sir Frederic Madden, p. 74.
[4] Ibid.
[5] L. Allen, *The history of Portsmouth* (1817), p. 138n.
[6] It was in such an atmosphere that the dissenting congregation at Kidderminster had no scruples of conscience in attending their parish church until 1782 (R. V. Holt, *The Unitarian contribution to social progress in England* (1938), p. 295).
[7] Sedgwick, i, p. 253.
[8] No. 11; P.C.R.O. CE1/13, p. 173. In the county election of 1734 the then Aldermen voted solidly for the official Whig candidates Lord Harry Paulet and Anthony Chute of the Vyne. The future Alderman John Leeke voted for the opposition candidates, which may help to explain why he was not elected Mayor until 1750 (*Poll for Hants.*, *1734*).
[9] No. 32.

also First Lord of the Admiralty.[1] Certainly the same men who had voted against Colliss, Huish and Stanyford gave their support to the administration, whatever inward doubts they may have had in the matter.[2]

Conflict between Whig and Tory had not died out – it was its underlying character that quickly changed. The Municipal Corporation Commissioners of 1835 pointed out that

> The whole management of the affairs of the corporation is in the hands of the mayor and aldermen. . . . It can hardly be necessary to point out the complete closeness of this system.[3]

At this time closeness sharpened the conflict, for the fewer the contestants the more valuable were the prizes to be obtained. Every year witnessed a struggle in the election of the Mayor – the expense being generally well worth the power and prestige it could command. Lewis Barton stood for the office ten times, though the prize only fell to him twice, but he savoured his pension and his place at the Board of Ordnance. John Vining was nominated on six occasions after 1715, was elected Mayor three times, and until his death in 1743 commanded more Admiralty contracts than any of his fellow-Aldermen. Luckier than either in one sense was Thomas Stanyford, who stood for Mayor three times and was elected twice, although the glittering prize of Recorder to the Borough eluded him to the end.[4] Surviving records of mayoral elections show vigorous participation by Aldermen and Burgesses alike. On 17 September 1733 Samuel Brady was elected Mayor with 74 votes against 63 given to Henry Stanyford; in 1741 Lewis Barton secured 50 votes against William Rickman who obtained a mere 16. The most easily won election was in 1746–7, when Samuel Chandler gained 34 votes to the one cast for John Carter.[5]

The known religious allegiance of Mayors reveals almost a balance between Anglican and dissenter; likewise there was a balance between known office-holders as opposed to contractors. Of the contractors, William Rickman, a Presbyterian, was put up for nomination on four occasions and chosen Mayor three times. Among the office-holders, Brady, another Presbyterian, was also nominated four times and was elected twice. Connections with the meeting-house and contracts in the Dockyard no doubt played their part in forming the prejudices and loyalties of the resident Burgesses, just as kinship and marriage may have done, but it is of significance that, as far as can be judged, the administration gave its confidence most of all to two men on the aldermanic bench with broad interests outside the town: Thomas Missing and Samuel Chandler.[6]

GOVERNMENT AND CORPORATION: PEACE AND WAR, 1731–1748

Relations between the Admiralty and the Corporation, the Board of Ordnance, the Governor and the Aldermen were delicate and complex. Given the oligarchic structure of the town's constitition, the administration constantly needed to review its relationship with the Corporation and to take such steps as were necessary to ensure the goodwill and support of the majority of Aldermen and Burgesses, particularly when a parliamentary

---

[1] Sedgwick, ii, pp. 502–3.
[2] In the one disputed election of this period, that of May 1741, nine Burgesses voted for the unofficial candidate, Admiral Vernon, but not one of the Aldermen did so.
[3] *F.R.M.C.C.*, ii, p. 807.
[4] Nos 98, 119; P.C.R.O. CE1/13, 14; East, pp. 330–1.
[5] P.C.R.O. CE3/15, 16, 18: 29 Sept. 1733, 29 Sept. 1741, 29 Sept. 1746.
[6] These conclusions are based on evidence drawn from the period 1715–52 only, and thus take less account of those who were dead by 1730 or who were only made Aldermen in the 1740's. Daniel Smith, James Deacon, William Smith M.D. and Sir John Suffield were not nominated during these years. Nevertheless clear relationships between office, affluence and dissent emerge, together confirming the increasing irrelevance of the terms 'Whig' and 'Tory' after 1715.

election or by-election drew near.[1] Thus, the election of an Alderman might be of more than local importance, as in 1733. In 1731–2, the proposed election of Cornelius Colliss[2] precipitated a crisis between his group, which had the backing of the Admiralty and Wager, and a more fluid combination centred around the ambitions of Lewis Barton and connected with the Board of Ordnance, whose former Master General, John, second Duke of Argyll, was now military Governor of Portsmouth. The Duke, described by Swift as 'an ambitious, covetous, cunning Scot, who has no principle but his own interest and greatness',[3] was a trial to his colleagues, and his interference in the town's affairs was all the more resented for his eccentric display of national fervour in a flag of his own choosing, where 'the St Andrew's or Scotch Cross was much broader, and the St George's Cross much narrower than they ought to have been'.[4] However, on this occasion, regardless of his usual propensity for intrigue, Argyll appears to have exercised restraint on his supporters in the interests of preserving unity against the surviving Tory Aldermen, Vining and Belfield. The situation was explained by Wager, who wrote to Thomas Missing in February 1732/3:

> I am sorry to find there is still so much difficulty in agreeing amongst our selves, about chusing an Alderman; As it has been represented to me, our freinds in Towne did agree to chuse Mr Collis, and hop'd that you, and Mr Barton, would have joyn'd with them, for which purpose, I suppose, they came over to you: and the only reason as I apprehend, that they were not willing to chuse Mr Rickman, was, what has allways been a reason, that they are not willing to have two in a family,[5] but I wonder Mr. Barton, should propose to joyn with them, for Mr Rickman, because I have seen his letter to the Duke of Argyle, wherein he proposes Mr Eadow[6] should be sett up for an Alderman, and that if His Grace would write a Letter to Dr. Brady, & another to Mr Stanyford it might, at least, prevent any other from being chosen, tho' a Majority might not be got presently for Mr Eddow.
>
> You will not wonder at Mr Barton's writing such a letter, because you know him, and I cannot but think, that his insisting for Mr Rickman, was for no other reason but to prevent any Election at all: but I have told Mr Barton, that if he don't think fitt to Vote for Mr Collis, that I shall make no scruple to go down to Portsmo on purpose to give my vote with my Freinds, not doubting but you will joyn with them, for the good & quiet of the Corporation, after that, you can do whatever you shall agree on, without any of these disagreable difficulties.[7]

Colliss was eventually elected Alderman on 22 March 1732/3, having been opposed solely by Vining and Belfield. But the 'disagreeable Difficulties' were by no means over, as Wager was to inform Walpole in September of the same year, when the general election was at hand:

> I am told from Portsmouth that Sr John Norris had an Agent there, when the Court met about Mr Lewis, who told the Mayor and many others that Sr John Norris hop'd he had done nothing to forfeit their favour, and desir'd their Votes for him; but no notice was taken of it in publick, but Lewis & Cavendish, recommended, and agreed to. . . . My Corespondent says he (i.e. Norris) requires all the weight of the Government to carry his Election at Portsmouth; for the Whigs have a dislike of him but(?) perhaps he may hope for the help of the Duke of Argyle, who has allways been his Friend.[8]

---

[1] B.L. Add. MS.32687, f. 549: letter from John Mounsher to the Duke of Newcastle, 15 Dec. 1732. Mounsher unsuccessfully petitioned Newcastle for the stewardship of the nearby Southwick estates, formerly the property of the wealthy eccentric, Richard Norton. Nevertheless Mounsher remained a consistent supporter of the ministerial interest, only faltering in 1750. He may have been consoled by succeeding Joseph Gardner as Postmaster of Portsmouth. Besides the general elections of 1733, 1741 and 1747 there were eight by-elections in Portsmouth between 1731 and 1752.
[2] See no. 11 for the election of Colliss.
[3] D.N.B. Argyll was Master General of the Ordnance 1725–30 and Governor of Portsmouth 1730–7.
[4] Life of Martin, p. 310.
[5] William Rickman was Thomas Missing's son-in-law.
[6] Robert Eddowes, elected Burgess 27 Nov. 1732, was listed as Storekeeper to the Ordnance Board at Portsmouth in 1735 at an annual salary of £180 (B.L. Add. MS. 33283, f. 322).
[7] B. L. Add. MS. 19030, f. 171: 27 Feb. 1732/3.
[8] C.U.L. C(H) Correspondence 2040: 7 Sept. 1733.

Lewis, a wealthy landowner with estates at Soberton, had been recommended to stand for Portsmouth by Wager himself,[1] and Philip Cavendish was also returned there on the Admiralty interest.[2] Both Wager and the two Members for the town made efforts to restore good relations.[3] Lewis and his successor Admiral Stewart, a protégé of Argyll,[4] played an active part in encouraging the Corporation in their project to rebuild the Town Hall, and provided an officer of the Board of Ordnance, Thomas Bowerbank, to act as architect.[5] In addition, Stewart gave £200 towards the cost on 14 March 1737/8.[6]

Nevertheless, relations between ministers and Corporation remained highly ambivalent. The election of Burgesses showed a preponderance of outsiders favourable to the government, but it was not without considerable pressure from Henry Pelham and the Duke of Richmond that a majority of the Aldermen could be induced to favour the election of the Duke's protégé Samuel Chandler. That Wager was reluctant to assist in the matter may be gleaned from Thomas Hill's letter to his master dated 29 August 1741:

> The Duke of Montagu with whom I dined this day at Greenwich, bid me tel you that he had talk'd with S$^r$ Charles about M$^r$ Chandler's affair, but found him as he thought rather cool upon the matter. That he told him he believ'd the election would not come on in some time yet, which his Grace takes to be don, because the party that opposes Sam have no other way yet of preventing him from being chosen. But his Grace bid me assure you that he had engaged all his friends to be for him, whenever the election shall be, & that he may depend upon their being firm in his interest.[7]

But the government did not achieve its objective until 13 September 1744;[8] the event was celebrated by Chandler in characteristically bad verse, not calculated to smooth his way to further preferment:

> Promotion cometh from the East
> Chandler Subscribes Probatum est
> This certain truth deny who dare
> When you know who his Patrons Are.[9]

The difficulties experienced by Chandler and the Duke of Richmond, together with the involvement of both Wager and Pelham, shed light on the problem of achieving a successful working relationship in an Admiralty borough. Relationships were never clear-cut, as Admiral Vernon explained to Newcastle when recounting his efforts to secure the election of his colleague Admiral Mathews for Rochester:

---

[1] Sedgwick, ii, p. 216.

[2] Sedgwick, i, p. 538.

[3] Nos 28, 34. Lewis went even further and in his will, 6 May 1735, bequeathed £1000 to the Portsmouth poor 'to be disposed of as Sir Charles Wager shall direct' (C.U.L. C(H) Papers 91/85).

[4] Sedgwick, ii, p. 448.

[5] No. 45.

[6] No. 51. Several important contracts associated with the rebuilding operation went to local Burgesses.

[7] W.Suss.R.O. Goodwood MS. 103, f. 236: letter to the Duke of Richmond, 29 Aug.1741. On the same day Henry Pelham assured the Duke of his support for Chandler, indicating that he was writing to John Mounsher with the same end in view (Goodwood MS. 107, f. 718: Pelham to Richmond, 29 Aug. 1741).

[8] No. 105.

[9] W.Suss.R.O. Goodwood MS. 146, f. 146: September 1744–July 1749. An illuminating comment on Chandler's verses comes from Emilia, Countess of Kildare and first Duchess of Leinster, second daughter of the second Duke of Richmond, in a letter to her father, 8 Oct. 1747: 'I find the fate of all the unlucky animals that come to Goodwood is to be, burying them in the Catacombs and an Epitaph by Sam Chandler' (C. H. Gordon-Lennox, Earl of March, *A duke and his friends* (2 v., 1911), ii, p. 630).

As they are a Port, in which a great Part of the Royall Navy is laid up; the Electors judged it more for the Service of their Corporation and likewise for paying a decent Regard, to the Crown, for the Advantages accruing to them, from such their situation to mak choice of two of his Majesties Admyralls to be their Representatives in Parliament: Who may I think be as justly Esteemed to Understand their True Interests, as a Gentleman who has no Relation to the Sea; Either as a Seaman or a Merchant.[1]

As far as Portsmouth was concerned, these 'True Interests' were further clarified in the war years 1739–48, which provided fresh opportunities for Admiralty and Corporation in the ceaseless search for profit, place and power. The town was the chief reception centre for sick and hurt seamen and for prisoners of war. The hospital at Haslar was still being completed, and by 1747 Portchester Castle was holding 3500 prisoners, mainly French and Spanish. As physician to the Garrison and hospital at Forton Dr Samuel Brady was paid £200 a year, but still sought extra for 'his being Obliged to go on board Ships upon such services (*i.e. to inspect medical chests with the surgeon of the Dockyard*) without a gratuity for it'.[2] Moreover Brady had condoned the behaviour of William Butler, agent for sick and wounded seamen at Gosport, whose fraudulent practices resulted in dismissal in 1746.[3]

William Rickman and Pusey Brooke were the government agents for Spanish and French prisoners respectively at salaries of £50 a year.[4] These posts provided considerable financial opportunities as the agents also acted as contractors to feed and care for the men in their charge. There were official protests when Brooke presented a claim for £300 as the cost of transporting a group of French prisoners from Gosport to Salisbury via Winchester and back in 1747, 'under the management of Mr William Rickman'[5] on the outward journey; Rickman acted as subordinate to Brooke who combined his post with that of Commissioner for Customs in the area.[6] But whatever Brooke's shortcomings, he resigned as agent in December 1747, when Rickman's revised contract for feeding prisoners at 4½d. a day was accepted by the Navy Board;[7] Brooke protested to Anson that

> upon his (*i.e. Rickman's*) Terms I can not take it without being a Loser, for I would neither be unjust to the Crown, nor ⌐unkind⌐ (*underlined*) to the Prisoners.[8]

The War of the Austrian Succession brought prosperity both to other members of the Corporation and to the town in general. Among the Aldermen, John Carter in partnership with James White contracted on behalf of cordage manufacturers at Poole, Michael Atkins for blocks and John Vining for a variety of commodities. William Rickman, assisted by his son John, dealt in Portland stone, beer for the Dockyard smithy, and hired at least one transport to the government, while Thomas Stanyford, acting as

---

1 B.L. Add. MS. 32700, f. 23: 5 Feb. 1742/3.
2 N.M.M. ADM/F/3 (23 Aug. 1743); ADM/F/8 (16 Jan. 1746/7).
3 N.M.M. ADM/F/7: 10 Mar. 1745/6.
4 N.M.M. ADM/F/8: 16 Jan. 1746/7.
5 N.M.M. ADM/F/10 (3 Nov. 1747); ADM/M/400 (5 Nov. 1747). The party comprised 70 common prisoners and 33 officers and their servants, and the bill included such items as £5. 1s. for 'a Dinner at Waltham', £8. 2s. 6d. 'For the Entertainment of the Prisoner at Winton in the Road to Salisbury', £10. 18s. 2d. for further 'Entertainments at Stockbridge at Dinner' as well as £25. 15s. for the hire of horses, wagons and guides.
6 Brooke was appointed Surveyor of Customs for Hampshire and Dorset on 19 Feb. 1729/30 at £100 a year for himself and £30 for a clerk; that his counterparts for Sussex and Kent received £350 and £250 respectively led Brooke to petition for an increase in Jan. 1740/1 (C.U.L. C(H) Papers 62/60a).
7 The previous contract stood at 5d. per day for a healthy prisoner and 10d. for one under medical care. The Commissioners had made a previous unsuccessful attempt to reduce expenditure in Sept. 1745. Rickman's tender is quoted in N.M.M. ADM/F/10 (14 Dec. 1747); it was accepted by the Navy Board on the following day (N.M.M. ADM/M/400).
8 B.L. Add. MS. 15955, f. 197: 19 Dec. 1747. Compare Brooke's comment with those of Rickman: 'I shall come to Town as soon as possibly I can, but I imagine my Presence here will now be absolutely necessary for some days in Order to receive over the prisoners from Mr Brooke, and to put the Hospital again in a Method of being enlarged, for I shall really always from Conscience endevour to accomodate Them with Room and every Thing else fit for Creatures of the same make with myself' (N.M.M. ADM/F/10: 14 Dec. 1747).

counsel on behalf of the Admiralty, negotiated on matters affecting the land on which the new hospital at Haslar was sited.[1] But widespread prosperity did not silence opponents of the Admiralty, nor merely those who were denied their fair share of the loaves and the fishes. The suggestion that a 'Combination' for supplying teams of horses to work in the Dockyard was being organised by Thomas Ridge with the connivance of John Monday and others was described by Commissioner Hughes as 'Malicious, Infamous and Scandelous' and 'is looked on by the several persons pointed at, with the utmost contempt'.[2] But more detailed refutation of a further series of allegations made in spring 1748 was felt necessary, since these touched in varying degrees of seriousness all the major officers of the Yard from Hughes downwards. The Commissioner, it was said, 'has Four Labourers to Work everyday in his Garden'. Worse than that, 'The Master Shipwright . . . has a scavenger in his Garden . . . & all the rest in proportion their Grandeur'. The Board of Admiralty was warned to look into the affairs of Winter the master bricklayer, since in his garden 'you will find Barrows, Shovels, Pick Axes, and all Utensils of the Government'. More serious still was a charge involving various contractors, including Henry Friend, accused by inference of fraud, if not theft, with the connivance of Samuel Twilford and others.[3] Later allegations (also anonymous) suggested bribery and theft amongst the Dockyard sawyers, and widespread fraud and loss, 'in the laying apart and delivery of Old Stores'.[4]

These charges touched Admiralty and Corporation alike, but more prolonged disputes affecting jurisdiction recurred throughout this period, tending to divide the Admiralty from the town. Inevitably the majority centred on the harbour, where questions of concurrent jurisdiction were most likely to arise. On 26 October 1736, George Snook of Portsmouth charged a certain John Uphill, master of a sand hoy,[5] with illegally throwing his ballast into 'the Channel of this Harbour'. Hughes informed the Mayor, 'in order as the Corporation apprehends the Harbour to be in their Liberties or Royalty, to enquire into the Abuse and put a Stop to the like ill Practices for the future'.[6] Charges were preferred at the expense of the Admiralty, and Uphill was fined 40s. Hughes's annoyance may be imagined when the Corporation invoked its Charter 'to claim all such fines' whilst refusing to bear the expenses of the case, and going so far as to successfully deny they were conservators whilst claiming their right to the liberty and freedom of those waters.[7] Feeling in the town clearly ran against the Admiralty, for as Hughes later wrote, 'Yet as the Man (*i.e. Uphill*) was One of the Town the Mayor (*i.e. Michael Atkins*) returned him the Money again'.[8] Further complaints from Admiral Cavendish about the same problems brought a fresh outburst from Hughes against the Corporation:

> The Royalty of the Harbour is Claim'd by the Mayor and Corporation of Portsmo who by their Charter are Oblig'd to Maintain or keep a Water Bailiff: but this necessary & useful officer, whose Sole duty would be, to Watch after and prevent all those that would be guilty of these offences (if ever One was appointed) have been Long since laid aside, and wholly Neglected.[9]

[1] N.M.M. POR/F/7, 8, 9, passim.
[2] N.M.M. POR/F/8: 21 Apr. 1747.
[3] N.M.M. POR/F/8: letters from Hughes to the Navy Board, 12 and 21 April 1747, 2 and 8 May 1748.
[4] N.M.M. POR/F/8, 9: letters from Hughes to the Navy Board, 6 Oct. 1749, 21 Feb. 1750/1.
[5] See p. xxivn.
[6] N.M.M. POR/F/5: letter from Hughes to the Navy Board, 26 Oct. 1737.
[7] N.M.M. POR/F/5: letters from Hughes to the Navy Board, 29 Oct., 11 and 21 Nov. 1737, 20 Jan. 1737/8.
[8] N.M.M. POR/F/6: letter to the Navy Board, 7 Aug. 1742.
[9] Ibid.

*Fig 3* SIR PHILIP HONYWOOD, GOVERNOR OF PORTSMOUTH 1741–52, a mezzotint by J. McArdell after a painting by B. Dandridge

Quite clearly, relations were not always smooth. Nor did the Corporation enthusiastically support the Admiralty's attempts to keep the harbour free from encroachments in the shape of private wharves at Gosport or Fareham. The case against John Gringo of Fareham was abandoned by the Admiralty in 1736 even though the Corporation's privileges were involved, a fact that was pointed out to Hughes by Richard Champneys who built another wharf there in 1747.[1] Unfortunately the Commissioner's zeal in this instance was ill-directed since Champneys' daughter Elizabeth was married to Thomas Missing the younger, the 'independent' candidate that one aldermanic faction threatened to set up against the Admiralty at the general election of that year.[2] Nevertheless, with the legal backing of the Admiralty a prosecution was launched against Gringo, Champneys and others similarly engaged at Gosport.[3]

The question of jurisdiction arose in another sphere in 1734 when, as a result of a large-scale theft of lead from the Dockyard, officials attempted to secure a warrant from the town magistrates to search several houses; but the warrants were withheld as the magistrates argued the circumstantial evidence did not justify their acceding to the Commissioner's request.[4] Conversely in 1736 a Dockyard watchman, Richard Young, was bound over by the Mayor charged with assaulting John Thomas, a waterman who attempted to steal wood from the ship that Young was guarding, much to the annoyance of Hughes, who was forced to solicit the Admiralty for proper counsel to defend the man.[5] The case of Rex v. Solgard in June 1738 therefore comes as no surprise in the light of the many strains between the naval and civil authorities.[6]

GOVERNMENT AND CORPORATION: THE CRISIS OF 1747–1751

Attempts by the Admiralty and the administration to maintain a majority for their interest within the Corporation, and thus their own pre-eminence, were liable to periodic breakdowns or crises of confidence. Sir John Norris's 'pride', together with his friendship for the Duke of Argyll, precipitated such a crisis in 1734,[7] but fear of the opposition group within the Corporation, together with renewed attention by the Admiralty to its interests, averted a major confrontation. A minority of strong-minded Burgesses supported Vernon at the by-election of May 1741, but even these nine voters prudently divided their votes between Vernon and the official candidate, Cavendish.[8]

But the phase of renewed bad relations between 1747 and 1750, whilst having certain features in common with previous crises, had a definite character of its own. Unlike his predecessors at the Admiralty the new First Lord, the fourth Duke of Bedford, was determined on a policy of change:

---

[1] N.M.M. POR/F/8: letter from Hughes to the Navy Board, 7 Aug. 1747. The Commissioner was so incensed at the building of Carver's Wharf at Gosport in 1742 that he had suggested the Admiralty should encourage, and later defend, 'four or half a Dozen of the Freeholders at Gosport who belong to this yard. . . . There are many of them, whose fingers itch to pull it down, and would gladly do it, they were sure of an indemnity' (N.M.M. POR/F/7: letter to the Navy Board, 15 Feb. 1743/4).
[2] Everitt, 'Pedigrees,' ii, pp. 933-4; Woburn MS. XVIII, f. 30 (letter, incomplete, from H. Legge(?) to the Duke of Bedford, n.d. 1747, interleaved with letter from Anson to Bedford, 6 Oct. 1747). Cf. no. 14.
[3] N.M.M. POR/F/8: letters from Hughes to the Navy Board, 5 Dec. 1747, 6 Jan. 1747/8. The Commissioner obtained at least one victory, since on 12 Mar. 1752 he was able to report that the additions to Carver's Wharf were partially demolished (POR/F/9: 12 and 18 Mar. 1752).
[4] N.M.M. POR/F/5: letters from Hughes to the Navy Board, 22, 25 and 30 Aug. 1734.
[5] N.M.M. POR/F/5: letters to the Navy Board, 5 and 10 Dec. 1736.
[6] Nos 52, 54. But Hughes could champion the town by supporting those who petitioned the Admiralty for the repair of the roads adjacent to the Dockyard (N.M.M. POR/F/8: letter from Hughes to the Navy Board, 31 Dec. 1746.)
[7] Baugh, pp. 68, 126, comments on Norris's tendency towards 'opposition', a characteristic that he readily shared with Vernon.
[8] No. 81n.

the men who took their seats at the Admiralty in December 1744 were bent on reform and innovation. They were confident, youthful, and impatient, and their leader was a headstrong nobleman who, up to this time, had cast himself as a critic of the government's naval policies.[1]

In practice Bedford leaned heavily on Anson for advice in naval matters, but in overall policy he had not only the latter's approval, but also that of his able young subordinate the Earl of Sandwich. The reform programme was designed to assert the administrative supremacy of the Admiralty Board over permanent officials at the Navy Board, traditionally conservative in outlook. To do this the First Lord relied heavily on the Commander-in-Chief at the major ports, and was initially prepared to by-pass the resident Commissioner and other officials to counteract the Navy Board's slowness and relative caution. Portsmouth felt the brunt of this zeal when the Admiralty in March 1745/6 ordered the Dockyard officers in future to take their orders directly from Vice-Admiral James Steuart and not Commissioner Hughes, who was quick to make a vigorous protest:

> Great things, I presume are Expected to Arise from this Practice; but, if disorder and disappointment don't in the End, I am much mistaken.[2]

The widespread resentment that this provoked was felt by all those with a vested interest in the current system, and not only by Dockyard officials but also by the Corporation.[3] Although policy had been modified by August 1746, the Admiralty was far from popular:

> For by the Description Your Grace lately gave me of the Genius & Temper of Portsmouth, I believe the proper person to represent them would be One whom they only don't dislike, and your Grace absolutely names. . . . A Landsman I think it is agreed ought not to be brought in there.[4]

But from an account of the Corporation's political state in 1747 it is clear that certain of its members were even prepared to raise the spectacle of a landsman rather than a sea officer representing their interests:

> Carter is I hear, one of that Faction who were for Setting up Missen (*i.e. Missing*) – But the Causes which bred that discontent I had the Honour to explain to Your Grace. And they were principally Mr Stewarts being made the Channel of Communications between Your Grace & the Corporation, And – the diable boiteux having, (as they conceived) assumed to himself a certaine Superiority over the rest of the Company.[5] As your Grace's Letter is calculated to cure both those Causes of dissatisfaction,[6] and as I remember, contains in it no particular Confidence to the Mayor of Portsmouth, perhaps it may be as proper for Carter as it would have been for Chandler.[7]

---

[1] Baugh, p. 88.

[2] N.M.M. POR/F/7 (20 May 1746), quoted in Baugh, p. 91. The relationship between the two Boards and the implications of Bedford's reform programme are dealt with brilliantly by Baugh, pp. 83–92. The previous Commander-in-Chief at Portsmouth was Cavendish, who was succeeded by Steuart in 1742.

[3] 'Unless their Lordships were prepared in the midst of a war to demolish and reconstruct the entire civil administration of the navy, they could only choose to relent. . . . But the price of good relations was the postponement of reform in the dockyards' (Baugh, pp. 91–2).

[4] Woburn MS. XVII, f. 70: letter from H. Legge to Bedford, 4 Aug. 1747.

[5] The 'lamed devil' referred to is Thomas Stanyford; cf. 'Justice Bodens, alias Young Pope to Chandler' (W.Suss.R.O. Goodwood MS. 146, f. 3), composed in 1746 when Chandler was Mayor:
Whilst crippled Staniford Sneers & Swears that you
Are in your feet the lamer of the two.
Stanyford's ambition for the recordership has already been alluded to. The Duke of Richmond, writing to Hardwicke about an unspecified petition Stanyford had left with him, enclosed Stanyford's letter that he had had 'nine months in my pockett', but said 'I wish extreamly well to Mr Stanyford, butt I really am doubtfull whether the favor he askes is not to great' (B.L. Add. MS. 35589, f. 358: 24 Nov. 1747). *Geese*, pp. 6–7 (see Appendix II), refers to 'the Carpenter' in strikingly similar words.

[6] B.L. Add. MS. 15955, f. 157: letter from Bedford to Anson, 7 Oct. 1747. Woburn MS. XVIII, f. 42 (letter from Anson to Bedford, 10 Oct. 1747) confirms that the letter had been sent to the Mayor, John Carter.

[7] Woburn MS. XVIII, f. 30: letter from H. Legge(?) to Bedford, n.d. (see above, p. liiin). Missing had been elected an Alderman in 1749.

Thomas Missing's connection with Portsmouth, together with his experience as Member of Parliament for Poole from 1741 to 1747, meant that the threat of his nomination could not be taken lightly, particularly since Bedford's tight control of patronage led to a further slight being given to Missing's friends on the bench in autumn 1747. Even before Samuel Brady's death in April 1747 there had been canvassing for his successor as physician to the Garrison and hospital at Forton. The most popular contender was John Carter's brother-in-law, George Bayly, M.D., of Chichester.[1] The Duke of Richmond had solicited Newcastle on the subject as early as November 1746,[2] but the latter had prevaricated saying that the aged and infirm Governor of Portsmouth, Sir Philip Honywood, 'had thoughts of another' – the place of physician to the Garrison being traditionally in the patronage of the Crown and at the disposal of the Governor.[3] In April 1747 Richmond blamed Bedford and Anson for intervening on behalf of Dr George Cuthbert, backing their candidate and ruling out any compromise based on a straight-forward division of the spoils.[4] Cuthbert subsequently obtained both posts and held them until his death in 1772.[5]

However, the Corporation accepted Admiral Sir Edward Hawke on Bedford's recommendation, and at the by-election of 25 December 1747 he was returned unopposed.[6] Hawke's task was to restore the Corporation's confidence in the Admiralty and administration, in order that the latter might reassert political control.[7] His affable personality, his connections with the town[8] and his ability to manipulate such patronage as he had on behalf of his constituents made a difficult task slightly easier. The Corporation was strongly criticised for electing Hawke as Member in return, it was inferred, for the prize-money he was bringing to the town, together with advantages accruing from the trade with Newfoundland.[9] The money Hawke's victories brought the town was irrelevant to his election, though after the battle of Belle Isle (1747) it enhanced his popularity. The involvement of the Corporation with the Newfoundland or North American trade is much less clear, but there are clues that Missing, Rickman and Carter had interests in those areas.[10] Certainly the government was determined both during and after the war to curtail French influence in North America and encouraged policies of settlement and gradual expansion.[11] In June 1748 the Duke of Richmond went to London, partly for

---

[1] Bayly was admitted a Burgess on 27 Nov. 1732 (no. 10). Trail & Steer, pp. 1–2, give an outline of his career.

[2] B.L. Add. MS. 32709, f. 283: letter from Richmond to Newcastle, 30 Nov. 1746.

[3] W.Suss.R.O. Goodwood MS. 104, f. 299: letter from Newcastle to Richmond, 4 Dec. 1746. Newcastle cannot be taken seriously on this question. Sir Charles Wager had been responsible for Brady's appointment many years before, and the outcome of Bedford's intervention shows that nothing had changed in this respect. Furthermore Honywood and Richmond were old friends. At Dettingen Honywood had obligingly loaned the Duke a horse so that he could view the battle. He was a frequent visitor to Goodwood and took a prominent part in the activities of the Charlton Hunt. In 1747 Honywood was old, tired and eager for the retirement he could ill afford (B.L. Add. MS. 32714, f. 298: letter from Honywood to Newcastle, 2 Mar. 1747/8). Honywood was Governor of Portsmouth 1740–52.

[4] B.L. Add. MS. 32710, ff. 404, 419: letters from Richmond to Newcastle, [April 1747?], 7 April 1747.

[5] N.M.M. ADM/F/9 (30 Mar. 1747) refers to Cuthbert as 'the most proper Person to succeed Dr Brady'. P.C.R.O. S2/26 (30 Nov. 1747) describes Dr George Cuthbert as 'Physician to the Garrison & the Hospital at Forton'.

[6] Sedgwick, ii, p. 117; East, p. 360.

[7] This was not such an easy task. Bedford's successor Sandwich was abroad for much of 1749 attending the peace conference at the Hague. Richmond was in Paris as special ambassador and died on 2 Aug. 1750. In 1751 there was a further change of personnel in the government when Anson succeeded Sandwich at the Admiralty.

[8] The ceremony of swearing Hawke in as an Alderman was conducted on 13 Oct. 1749 at his house 'within the said Borough', the only instance of such practice during these years (no. 155).

[9] *Geese*, pp. 5–6, and the contemporary illustration, which is particularly instructive (see Appendix II and end papers).

[10] Missing's constituency, Poole, 'had a long and close connection with the Newfoundland and North American trade' and his fellow-Member there, Joseph Gulston, imported timber from New Hampshire some of which was used for masts in Portsmouth Dockyard; train oil, England's only direct import from Newfoundland at this time, was sold to the Admiralty by Rickman and his partners, and both Carter and Rickman had dealings with William Jolliffe, a merchant of Poole (Sedgwick, i, pp. 90, 235–6; ii, p. 260; N.M.M. POR/F/6, 7, 8, passim; R. G. Lounsbury, *The British fishery at Newfoundland 1634–1763* (1934), pp. 310–37).

[11] W. S. MacNutt, *The Atlantic Provinces: the emergence of colonial society 1712–1857* (1965), pp. 1–75 passim.

the purpose of discussing Nova Scotian business;[1] the following year the Governor of Newfoundland petitioned the Crown that Nova Scotia might be 'Peopled and Settled',[2] while the ubiquitous William Rickman sounded out the Duke of Richmond on the government's intentions:

> I am informed that a Contract for supplying with Provisions the new Intended Settlement at Nova Scotia is now on the tapis.[3]

Rickman inevitably hoped that a contract might come his way with Richmond's assistance.

Despite this concern with North America the majority of Corporation and town alike were more committed to the permanent interests that linked them to the Admiralty and the Board of Ordnance. Hawke's action in October 1748, on the receipt of a petition from the Mayor and Aldermen of Portsmouth that all monies then due to seamen should be paid out at Portsmouth rather than in London, showed a more realistic concern for the town's interests, particularly for those who had purchased seamen's tickets at a discount and might otherwise have difficulty in profitably disposing of them:

> by which (*i.e. payment in London*) the Inhabitants of this Town, who have purchased Tickets or otherwise credited Seamen, will be put to great Inconveniences and Expense in getting their Money beside the great detriment it will be to the Trade of this Town and of Gosport, by preventing a very large Sum of Money from circulating in them, therefore I would represent it to their Lordships of the Admiralty & use my Interest that the Ships which are paid off here, may be thoroughly recalled, before the Books shall be sent away from this Port. As I am circumscribed with regard to this Corporation I could not avoid giving attention to a Case wherein their Interest seems to be so much concerned.[4]

The following year he again petitioned the Admiralty, this time on behalf of 'Mr Rickman', who had asked him

> to use my interest with their Lordships for one Thomas Hill Serjeant Gunner of the 'Penzance' and a relation of his (*i.e. Rickman's*) . . . to succede the late gunner of the 'Royal William'.[5]

Hawke was made an Alderman in 1749, the first creation since 1744, and the first Member of Parliament to hold that office since Wager had been honoured in 1726. It was suggested that the creation of no fewer than sixty-three Burgesses at John Carter's house on 27 October 1750[6] was a direct protest against this overt display of outside influence but the evidence by no means confirms this thesis.[7] The fact that no Aldermen voted against the creation is surely significant – although it is interesting that Atkins and Stanyford took no part in the meeting in view of their opposition to further creations in September 1751.[8] True, some of those elected had obvious grudges against the Admiralty, not merely members of the Missing and Carter families, as one would expect,

---

[1] W.Suss.R.O. Goodwood MS. 104, f. 316: letter from Newcastle to Richmond, 28 June 1748.

[2] B.L. Add. MS. 32718, f. 179: letter from R. Philipps to Newcastle, 29 Apr. 1749.

[3] W.Suss.R.O. Goodwood MS. 112, f. 326: letter from Rickman to Richmond, 6 Apr. 1749.

[4] Hawke MSS. Out-Letters (2): Hawke to Clevland, 23 Oct. 1748. Contemporary comment on the purchase of seamen's tickets is made by Wilkins, p. 8 (see Appendix I).

[5] Hawke MSS. Out-Letters (2): Hawke to Corbett, 8 July 1749.

[6] No. 164.

[7] The sole contemporary source is the anonymous pamphlet, *The geese in disgrace* (see Appendix II), which was obviously written by someone with a close knowledge of the Corporation and its discontents. The universal dislike of Stanyford is mentioned, and the reluctance of Mounsher and Linzee to give their approval to what was taking place. An unknown outsider, '*A saucy Hern*' (perhaps John Vining Heron), urges the Corporation to make him a Burgess, in return for which he will lead them in their struggle for greater independence from the Admiralty. The idea of a Carter-inspired revolt finds its most vociferous exponent in Bonham-Carter, pp. 13–18.

[8] P.C.R.O. CE1/14, p. 93: 10 Sept. 1751.

but lesser men such as John Bayly, son of the unlucky doctor, Thomas Appleford and John Compton, who had forfeited their contracts at the Dockyard.[1] But if the measure was wholly designed as an anti-Admiralty move, why nominate Hawke's children, the young Duke of Richmond, or four members of the Mounsher family? Again, why was Varlo's nomination as a Burgess not included with the sixty-three, when the event took place the same day and also in Carter's house?[2] Lastly, there is the way these 'rebel' Burgesses were sworn in, if the term 'rebel' may be legitimately applied to them. If the issue really was so serious, why were only three Burgesses sworn in at Carter's house on 27 October[3] and another twenty-one at the Guildhall,[4] why did the next swearing-in of six Burgesses, nearly all local men, not occur until 8 November,[5] and what happened to the rest of the gargantuan creation?[6] Indeed the episode may be almost viewed in the opposite sense, as a clumsy move designed by the Admiralty to stifle further conflict between opponents and supporters of the existing order by last-minute concessions from above – transforming the 'revolt' into a prize-giving day.[7] In August 1751 John Clevland, Secretary of the Admiralty, wrote privately to Hawke informing him that Pelham, chief minister, and Anson, now First Lord of the Admiralty, were interested in the possibility of Hawke becoming Mayor of Portsmouth. Hawke accordingly sounded out Rickman, clearly regarded by the ministry as the leading figure in the Corporation, only to find that he had already pledged his support in favour of John Leeke. In Hawke's opinion all Rickman's party required was some small inducement to bring it to support the wishes of the Admiralty in the town.[8] Though ready and willing to act as intermediary in any negotiations he evinced no keenness to become Mayor himself. On 10 September 1751 the election of a further twenty Burgesses led to an open rift among the Aldermen and 'Alderman Stanyford, Alderman Atkins and Alderman Chandler attended at this Election, but refused to join or concurr in it',[9] the first two being of distinct Ordnance sympathies. Towards the close of that month, Leeke was elected Mayor, and thereafter relations between the Corporation and the Admiralty improved.[10] Despite their differences and despite areas of potential conflict, in the last analysis each was dependent upon the other, as John Missing tersely informed Sandwich in 1781:

> in all our Disputes we have never lost Sight of that Connection which so long subsisted to mutual advantage between the Board at which your Lordship presides and the Corporation; but there is a Point beyond which the Support from private Pockets must fail, and meer Despair will then drive Men to accept of any offered Assistance, and to run into any wild Extreams rather than submit to Force.[11]

---

[1] N.M.M. POR/F/8: 14 Dec. 1746, 5 Sept. 1749. John Carter's contract for cordage was also discontinued (N.M.M. POR/F/8: 14 Oct. 1748).

[2] No. 165.

[3] No. 166.

[4] No. 167.

[5] No. 168.

[6] John Heron was not sworn in until 11 Jan. 1774. Twenty-one of the Burgesses created in 1750 were removed by writ of mandamus in 1775; of these many had been minors in 1750, such as Hawke's and Carter's sons and Lord George Lennox.

[7] Hawke's ostensible concern with Newfoundland, noted in the contemporary illustration of *The geese in disgrace* (see end papers), was clearly designed to reconcile the powerful groups on the bench represented by Missing and Rickman.

[8] Mackay, p. 109. It is interesting to note that Rickman's family was well represented on the Corporation as a result of the 1750 crisis. Whatever his immediate rewards were, his son William benefited, becoming a Second Lieutenant in the Marines by 1756, while another relative, Thomas, was Postmaster of Portsmouth in 1759 (P.C.R.O. S2/26: 15 Mar. 1756, 12 Mar. 1759).

[9] P.C.R.O. CE1/14, p. 93: 10 Sept. 1751.

[10] Two admirals, Hawke and Townshend, were re-elected unopposed at the general election of 1754.

[11] Sandwich MS. 105/3/99 (formerly box 271/3): 19 Nov. 1781.

## 5  The manuscript

For centuries it has been customary for English corporate towns to keep a record of the ruling power's everyday business, but for Portsmouth the earliest extant record of this sort dates only from 1731–51.[1] The Book of Original Entries edited here is item CE6/1 in the Portsmouth City Record Office. It is a volume of six gatherings containing 93 paper leaves,[2] which measure 320 × 200 mm. and are watermarked with the arms of Amsterdam and countermark 'IV'.[3] The pages are numbered from 1 to 183 by the original writers, the last three pages, including the two-page index, being unnumbered. Nine pages are blank apart from the numbers.[4] The volume has been rebound, in parchment over boards, but on the front cover the original parchment has been retained. This is stamped with a double-lined border and with two royal ciphers of the crown surmounting the initials 'GR'; between them is written the original title, 'Originall Entrys of Orders, Towne Leases Burgesses ⌐etc.⌐ (? *faded*) 1731 – ⌐to 1751⌐ (*added in a different hand*)'. A pencilled note on the original front paste-down has been replaced inside the new front cover.[5] The back cover is completely new, as is the spine, which carries two modern double ties; the original spine, which has not been retained, bore the faded number 'II', suggesting that there was an earlier Book of Original Entries, now lost.[6] The volume has been in the Corporation's care throughout its life, and a report to the Borough Council in 1836 included it in a list of Corporation muniments.[7] That no mention was made of its predecessor shows that this had already disappeared.

### METHOD OF COMPOSITION

The Corporation that emerges from the pages of the text was one that relied heavily on its rights and privileges, especially its power to create Burgesses. At the same time, however, it was a body whose economic solvency left much to be desired. Had the Corporation been richer it would, no doubt, not have had to wait until Thomas Lewis gave the town £100 in 1735 before it could pay to John Arnold's widow a debt of £25. 6s. incurred when he was acting as Chamberlain in 1710.[8] The record revealed is of the minutiae of its routine business rather than the mainstream of national events. In the whole text there is only one direct mention of national developments, on 28 March 1751 when the Corporation ordered its pew to be 'hung with black Cloth ... on the melancholy Occasion of the Death of his late Royal Highness the Prince of Wales'.[9] The latent tensions and conflicts that existed between some of the Aldermen emerge in only a partial fashion, and have to be amplified and set in perspective by material drawn from other

---

1 Among earlier municipal records of this sort are those of York, with memorandum and house books, and minutes dating from 1372, and Plymouth and Penzance with minute books dating from 1561 and 1617 respectively.

2 The collation is as follows: 1¹² (pp. 1–24), 2²⁰ (18–20 cancelled; pp. 25–58), 3¹⁸ (1 cancelled; pp. 59–92), 4¹⁶ (pp. 93–124), 5²⁰ (1, 2 cancelled; pp. 125–60), 6¹⁴ (1 cancelled; pp. 161–[186]).

3 Similar to W. A. Churchill, *Watermarks in paper in Holland, England, France, etc.* (1935), no. 48 (dating from 1720); E. Heawood, *Watermarks mainly of the 17th and 18th centuries* (Monumenta Chartae Papyraceae I; 1950), no. 420 (1724–6); cf. *Turnpike Minute Book*, p. xxviiin.

4 Pp. 34, 36, 38, 62, 68, 181, 182, 183, [186].

5 See no. 1n.

6 Both the present editors saw the number on the original spine, while as additional evidence the third surviving Book of Original Entries, for 1801–33 (P.C.R.O. CE6/3), is numbered '4' on the spine.

7 P.C.R.O. CCR1, p. 6. The report was of a committee appointed to 'receive from the Cofferers an Account of the Muniments, Archives, etc., now in their Custody'.

8 No. 31.

9 No. 170.

sources. The leading example of objection to a Corporation appointment was Thomas Stanyford's disapproval of Chute and Pescod as Recorders, motivated more by frustration of personal ambition and aspirations than by marked political divergence.[1]

The Book of Original Entries must be read in conjunction with four contemporary sources: the Elections and Sessions Books, the Register of Grants, the Chamberlain's Vouchers and the Mayor's Election Papers.[2] It would be a mistake to see the book as a comprehensive record of the day-to-day orders of the Corporation at this period, much less to regard it as a minute book in the fullest sense of the word. The major themes that emerge from its pages are the election of Burgesses and Aldermen and the transacting of the Corporation's financial business. The dates of elections exactly correspond in both the Book of Original Entries and the Elections and Sessions Books.[3] Nevertheless, the elections of no fewer than eight Burgesses in these years, including such major figures as Lord Lymington, Sir Charles Wills and Lord Vere,[4] do not appear in the Book of Original Entries; they are entered, however, in the Mayor's Election Papers as peremptory Burgesses chosen by the Mayor, one of his prerogatives.

Entries for a considerable number of town leases are to be found in both the Book of Original Entries and the Register of Grants, and the parallel entry in the second source is often up to a month later in date,[5] suggesting a straightforward transfer of information to the latter. But other financial orders, some of considerable import, appear solely in the Chamberlain's Vouchers. Such matters as the major repairs to the Town Gaol carried out during William Rickman's mayoralty are passed over in silence in the present record, as are the payments totalling £265 to William Binstead 'towards building a new Town Hall'.[6]

In the period 1731–51 the Corporation met infrequently, on average seven times a year. There are some long gaps in the record given by the Book of Original Entries, such as from 26 February to 18 September 1733; this explains the inadequacy of the text as a source for Corporation orders. It explains too why additional information occurs in the Elections and Sessions Book, a volume that was in constant use, since whether or not the Mayor and Aldermen met as a body it was needed by the Mayor or his Deputy to record the election of Burgesses and the election or replacement of minor Corporation officials throughout the mayoral year. It is thus that it gives the additional material about rebuilding the Town Hall.[7] Likewise, further financial business, not necessarily unimportant, is to be found among the Chamberlain's Vouchers. The occasional reversal or other incorrect ordering of entries in the Book of Original Entries suggests that at times information was transferred there by the Town Clerk from the Elections and Sessions Book and the Mayor's Election Papers. This is not unlikely at a period when the Town Hall was being rebuilt (1738–9) and the Corporation was meeting at God's House, by courtesy of the town Governor, or even at the King's Arms. It may also be significant that on eight other occasions during the period meetings were held in Aldermen's or other private residences,[8] rather than at the Town Hall where the Corporation's record books would be readily to hand.

---

[1] Nos 98, 119.
[2] P.C.R.O. CE1/13, 14; CF20/1; CF2/1, 2; CE3/15–19.
[3] A concordance of these two sources is printed in Appendix VIII.
[4] The other five were Richard Andrews, James Brudenell, Cuthbert Brady, William Hervey and James Rickman; see Appendix V.
[5] E.g. no. 161, 25 Sept. 1750, is dated 23 Oct. 1750 in the Register of Grants (P.C.R.O. CF20/1, f. 196).
[6] P.C.R.O. CF2/2 (21 June 1739); CF3/2, nos 21, 23 (21 July and 9 Aug. 1743).
[7] See no. 59n.
[8] Nos 3, 10, 12, 66, 164–166, 169.

The keeping of the book was the responsibility of the Town Clerk, and thus the bulk of the volume is in the hands of George Huish senior and junior, who occupied the post during the years it spans. Sometimes George Huish senior signed the pages,[1] sometimes he did not.[2] Sometimes the two men worked together, the younger compiling a page and his father signing it.[3] Yet again the elder man wrote out a page, his son added a note and then passed it back to his father for signature.[4] Again the younger man compiled the page, his father adding a note.[5] The younger man also corrected his father's entries,[6] and he also amended his father's portion of the index, which was compiled as the entries were made. On two occasions clerks wrote out pages to be signed by the elder Huish, the Town Clerk amending the entry of the second of these.[7]

Transfer of office to the son on 12 September 1746 is marked by a specific entry and by the younger Huish signing himself as Town Clerk for the first time,[8] having previously signed as Deputy on several occasions.[9] The demise of the elder is indicated by his son simply signing himself as George Huish, not George Huish junior, in January 1746/7.[10] A fifth hand appears on three occasions, and though it cannot be positively identified it is safe to assume that it is that of a clerk, given the specific task of compiling these pages.[11] A sixth hand appears once, to make a minor correction.[12]

The hands are indicated throughout the text as follows:

Hand i: George Huish senior.

Hand ii: George Huish junior.

Hands iii, iv, v, vi: unidentified clerks.

### THE COMPILERS

From 1727 until 1782 the office of Town Clerk was occupied by two men, father and son, George Huish senior and junior. An inhabitant of Portsmouth for fifty years or more, the elder Huish was described in 1747 as having

> a Family consisting of a wife and several children and servants and was during the time aforesaid the Lawfull owner occupier or possessor of several messuages or Tenements Gardens and Outhouses thereunto belonging situate in the Town and parish of Portsmouth of a very considerable value.[13]

In 1715, along with many other important town personages, he served in the newly raised Company of Foot,[14] no doubt finding this a far cry from his legal calling. The only indication of the extent of his practice comes in 1736, when he was known to have been acting as an attorney of Common Pleas at Westminster.[15] As an attorney he not only

---

[1] E.g. nos 1, 3, 13. At first (to no. 11) the elder Huish used an abbreviated Latin form of 'Town Clerk' in signing.

[2] E.g. nos 5, 8, 9.

[3] E.g. nos 67, 104–109.

[4] E.g. no. 110.

[5] E.g. nos 64, 120.

[6] E.g. nos 30, 55.

[7] Nos 17, 36.

[8] Nos 129, 130.

[9] E.g. nos 48, 70, 100–102.

[10] No. 134.

[11] Nos 147, 159, 161.

[12] No. 159.

[13] Hants.R.O. C/10/A/456: Consistory Court allegation for Huish, 20 Nov. 1747.

[14] P.C.R.O. S2/20: 25 Sept. 1715.

[15] No. 39.

had recourse to the law but was himself the subject of at least one lawsuit. In August 1716 he complained to the Portsmouth Justices that his apprentice Thomas Money 'hath absented himselfe from this deponents service without his Leave, And that the Last night . . . was drunk'. To add to the problem, Money used vile language towards Huish and his family on several occasions and generally made such a disturbance in his house 'that his Family cannot Live all quiett'.[1] Thirty years later he again complained to the Justices, this time about two shipmasters who had ill-treated him. They had shaken their fists at him and threatened him with a cane 'shaking it over him, and using Abundance of menacing Language'.[2] The years in between these two appeals saw Huish in an entirely different light, however. In November 1713 Thomas Hanway left £1634. 14s. worth of South Sea stock to his wife and family, appointing as executors John Leeke, a Portsmouth goldsmith, and others. When Leeke tried to act on his own initiative, Hanway's widow obtained a Chancery decree in April 1720 ordering Leeke to dispose of the stock. It was at this point that Huish and Thomas Blackley approached Leeke with a view to purchasing part of the stock 'offering Five Thousand Pounds, for Five Hundred Pounds Capital Stock'. Trouble arose over a letter of attorney, drawn in a blank form by Leeke, who argued that his business interests called him away to Derbyshire. The two sides of the case were confused, for while Leeke maintained that Blackley had filled in the blank letter and Huish had witnessed it, they maintained that Leeke had induced Blackley to fill the letter and moreover was 'a Person very much concerned in Interest'. The sums involved were of no mean proportion and by 1725 were in excess of £6000, and the case was subsequently heard before the bar of the House of Lords, in May 1728.[3]

In contrast to his father the younger Huish was much more staid, though this did not prevent him from taking the family name to great heights. In 1746 he served as Town Clerk, Clerk of the Peace and Coroner, and was still occupying the last of these posts in 1760.[4] For all of them he had been trained under the skilful eye of his father, who not only left him all his law books but had him working with him as Deputy Town Clerk from September 1737 onwards.[5] His political stance was one of relative independence and when he died in 1788 he was described in glowing terms as having been late Town Clerk of Portsmouth, 'factor to the East India Company at that port, a master-extraordinary in chancery, and consul for Holland'.[6] With relatives in both the Navy and the legal profession,[7] the Huishes were obviously powerful figures in Portsmouth, although neither ever achieved the status of Alderman.

---

[1] P.C.R.O. S3/66: complaint to Borough Sessions, 21 Aug. 1716.
[2] P.C.R.O. S3/125: complaint to Borough Sessions, 19 Jan. 1746/7.
[3] Printed statements of the appellants' case and the respondents' case for Blackley and Huish v. Leeke and Hanway, both in 1724 and in 1728 (copies are in the Cope Collection, Southampton University Library, and photocopies are in P.C.L.); the final judgment is recorded in *Journals of the House of Lords*, xxiii, p. 271.
[4] P.C.R.O. S2/25 (25 Oct. 1746); S2/26 (22 Oct. 1760).
[5] No. 48.
[6] Obituary in *Gent. Mag.*, lviii (1788), p. 1129. He was also agent of the Dutch East India Company (C. & E. 58/1).
[7] Henry Huish, brother of George Huish junior, was a naval officer, while John Huish, a cousin, practised law in Gosport.

# Notes on editing

1 In principle the text is an exact copy of the manuscript, reproducing its spelling, punctuation and use of capital letters. Letters or words that are illegible or lost from the manuscript are supplied in square brackets. Other editorial additions are in italics.

2 Abbreviated names of persons and places have not been expanded.

3 Nearly all other abbreviations have been expanded except those that are still in current use. All letters supplied are in italics except in expanding the following forms (with capital initial or final *s* if on the manuscript) which occur very frequently:

| | | | |
|---|---|---|---|
| -m- | *line above word* | majestie | ma$^{\text{tie}}$ |
| -cion | $\overline{\text{-con}}$ | mayor | may$^{\text{r}}$ |
| administrator | adm$^{\text{r}}$ | pre- | p$^{\text{r}}$- |
| aforesaid | aforesd, afores$^{\text{d}}$ | said | s$^{\text{d}}$ |
| clerk | cl', $\overline{\text{clk}}$ | shipwright | shipw$^{\text{t}}$ |
| junior | jun$^{\text{r}}$ | | |

4 Catchwords, giving at the foot of one page the first words of the next, are omitted.

5 Punctuation marks are omitted (i) below superscript letters, and (ii) in a series of stops or dashes, where only the first is reproduced.

6 The hand is noted at the beginning of each entry and at each subsequent change of hand. Unless otherwise stated any added, inserted or cancelled words are in the same hand as the surrounding text. The hands are listed and, where possible, the writers identified on p. lx.

7 The signatures at the end of each entry have been printed in double column; this is not necessarily their arrangement in the manuscript, but their order is the presumed order of signing, reading first the right column then the left. The order of signing is, however, often open to question.

8 It is often doubtful whether a writer intended a capital or small initial letter, a final flourish or separate dash.

# Book of Original Entries 1731-1751

Portsmouth City Record Office, CE6/1

**1**

**5 October 1731**

*p. 1*[1]

*Hand i.* Burrough of Portesmouth S*essio*ns

Wee the Mayor and Aldermen of the Said Burrough whose hands are hereunto Sett, takeing into Consideracion the Decay of the Business of the Towne Serjants, And that as the Subsistance of Samuell Beven the Younger Serjant[2] is att present cheifley owing to the Sallery he Receives from this Corporacion

Wee doe hereby therefore agree that the Said Samuell Beven shall be paid the Sume of Five pounds out of the Chamberlaines Roll att Michaelmas next, as an Augmentation to his Sallery for the present yeare only, and noe Longer, without a further Agreement from the Mayor and Major parte of the Aldermen of the Said Burrough for the time being, Wittnes our hands the 5th of October Anno D*o*mini 1731 –

*Signed by:*

| | |
|---|---|
| Jn⁰ White Mayor. | Sam: Brady |
| John Vining | Jn⁰ Arnold |
| L: Barton | Rob*t* Newnham |
| Hen: Stanyford | |

Geo Huish C*l*ericus Com*munis*[3] –

**2**

**11 December 1731**

*p. 2*

*Hand ii.* Know all men by these presents That I Sir Charles Wager Knight one of the Aldermen of the Burrough of Portsmouth in the County of South'ton have Surrendered resigned yeilded and given up and by these presents do Surrender resigne yeild and give up into the Hands of the Mayor Aldermen and Burgesses of the said Burrough my said Office or Place of Alderman of the said Burrough,[4] And I do hereby desire that this my Surrender and Resignation may be accepted by them and Inrolled among the Records of the said Burrough In Witnes whereof I have hereunto sett my Hand and Seale the Eleventh day of December Anno D*o*mini 1731.

Cha: Wager. ⌐*Locus Sigilli*¬[5]

Sealed and delivered in the presence of, being first Interlined

Rob*t* Turvin

W*m* Wyatt.

Wee the Mayor and Aldermen of the within Burrough whose Hands are hereunto sett, Do hereby accept of the within written Surrender and Resignation of the within named S*r* Charles Wager of his Office or Place of Alderman of the said Burrough, And do order that the same be inrolled among the Records of the said

---

[1] Inside the front cover is a note in pencil in a hand that does not occur elsewhere in the manuscript: '5 July 1737 Ordered that Counterparts of Town Leases & admissions of Aldermen & Burgesses be brought by the Town Clerk to the Town Chest within three months' (see no. 46 and East, p. 269).

[2] Beven had been elected Sergeant-at-Mace and Water Bailiff in Sept. 1727 (P.C.R.O. CE1/13, p. 178).

[3] In the extreme bottom left corner of the page is a monogram 'WB(?)'.

[4] Wager had first been elected an Alderman in 1726 (East, p. 330).

[5] Encircled.

Burrough Wittnes our Hands the Eleventh day of December Anno Domini 1731.

| | |
|---|---|
| Jnᵒ White Mayor. | Hen: Stanyford. |
| John Vining | Sam: Brady |
| Henry Belfeild. | Jnᵒ Arnold. |
| L: Barton | Robᵗ Newnham |

*Hand i.* A true Coppy of the Originall Engrossed on Treble 6ᵈ Stampt paper, and Examined by (*signed by*) Geo Huish *Clericus Communis* –

**3**

**13 December 1731**

*p. 3*

*Hand ii.* 13ᵗʰ December 1731. Burrough of Portesmouth. S*ession*s

Being then present att the House of Doctor Samuell Brady within the said Burrough pursuant to Summons.

John White Esqʳ Mayor

John Vining Gent' –
Henry Belfeild Gent'
Lewis Barton Gent'
Henry Stanyford Esqʳ          } Aldermen
Samuell Brady M:D:
John Arnold Gent' –
Robert Newnham Gent'

Att which time and place the Honᵇˡᵉ Sʳ Charles Wager Knᵗ Admirall of the Blew Squadron of his Majesties Fleet and one of the Com*missione*rs for executeing the Office of Lord High Admirall of Great Britaine ⌈&c⌉¹ and ⌈alsoe⌉² one of the Burgesses of the said Burrough was by the said Mayor and Aldermen Nominated and Elected an Alderman of the said Burrough, And itt was then Ordered by the said Mayor and Aldermen that George Huish Gent' Town Clerk of the said Burrough should administer to the said Sʳ Charles Wager the Oaths of Allegiance & Supremacy the Abjuration Oath and the Test³ which was accordingly done, and all the said Oaths were taken & subscribed and the said Test repeated & subscribed by the said Sʳ Charles Wager, And itt was then further ordered by the said Mayor & Aldermen that the said Sʳ Charles Wager should be sworne an Alderman of the said Burrough and he was by the said Town Clerk sworne accordingly before the said Mayor & Aldermen In Testimony whereof they have hereunto sett their hands the day & yeare abovesaid –

*Signed by:*

| | |
|---|---|
| Jnᵒ White Mayor | Robᵗ Newnham |
| John Vining | L: Barton |
| Henry Belfeild | Hen: Stanyford |
| Jnᵒ Arnold. | Sam: Brady |

*Hand i.* per (*signed by*) Geo Huish *Clericum Communem* –

**4**

**13 December 1731**

*p. 4*

*Hand ii.* 13.ᵗʰ December 1731. Burrough of Portesmouth. S*ession*s

Wee the Mayor and Major part of the Aldermen of the said Burrough whose Hands are hereunto Subscribed have nominated and Elected Edmund Hooke Esqʳ Comander of his Majesties Ship the Canterbury⁴ to be a Burgess of the said Burrough and the said Captⁿ Hook was then imediately sworn before us Witnes our Hands the day and yeare above written –

---

¹ Inserted.
² Inserted.
³ Under Statutes 3 James I, c.4; 25 Cha. II, c.2; 30 Cha. II, st. 2, c.1.
⁴ The Canterbury was a fourth-rate vessel built in 1693 and broken up in 1770 (T. D. Manning and C. F. Walker, *British warship names* (1959), p. 128).

*Signed by:*

| | |
|---|---|
| Jn⁰ White Mayor. | Sam: Brady |
| John Vining | Jn⁰ Arnold. |
| L: Barton | Robᵗ Newnham |
| Hen: Stanyford | Cha: Wager |

*Hand i.* Iuratus *per (signed by)* Geo Huish Com*munem* Clericum –

**5**
**18 December 1731**

*p. 5*
*Hand ii.* Burrough of Portesmouth. S*essions*

Whereas John Arnold Gent' one of the Aldermen of the said Burrough whilst he acted as Mayor[1] and Clerk of the Markett of the same Burrough did by Vertue of his said Office seize severall Quantitys of Bread from severall of the Bakers within the said Burrough, For which Actions were brought against him by Freeman Sheath[2] and John Dawes, and the said Mʳ Arnold hath been obligded to pay for Costs and Damages in the said Actions the Sume of Eighty pounds, as by a Bill of Particulars for the same appears Now for the repaying of the said Sume of Eighty pounds to the said Mʳ Arnold Wee whose Hands are hereunto sett being the Mayor and Major part of the Aldermen of the said Burrough do hereby Consent and agree that an Assignment of the Rent ⌐of Ten pounds *per* Annum¬[3] to become due to this Corporation on their Lease to Thomas Smith[4] and others of the Dung and Soile within the Town of Portesmouth shall be made over under the Common Seale of the said Burrough to Doctor George Stepney in Trust for the said Mʳ Arnold his Executors Administrators and Assignes for the Terme of Eight years from Michaellmas last past for reimbursing the said Mʳ Arnold the said Sume of Eighty pounds Witnes our Hands the Eighteenth day of December 1731.

*Signed by:*

| | |
|---|---|
| Jn⁰ White Mayor | L: Barton |
| John Vining | Hen: Stanyford |
| W. Smith | Robᵗ Newnham |
| Henry Belfeild | |

**6**
**26 February 1731/2**

*p. 6*
*Hand ii.* 26ᵗʰ February 1731. Burrough of Portesmouth. S*essions*

Att an Assembly in the Councell Chamber of the Guildhall of the said Burrough being then present pursuant to Summons.

John White Esqʳ Mayor

John Vining Gent'–
Henry Belfeild Gent'–
Lewis Barton Gent'–
Henry Stanyford Esqʳ– ⎫
Thomas Missing Esqʳ– ⎬ Aldermen
Samuell Brady M.D.– ⎭
Robert Newnham Gent'–

Att which Time and Place John Mounsher Esqʳ one of the Burgesses of the said Burrough was by the above named Mayor and Aldermen nominated & Elected an Alderman of the said Burrough, And the said John Mounsher did then & there take and subscribe the Oaths of Allegiance Supremacy and Abjuration, and did repeat and subscribe the Test against Transubstantiation, and was then sworne an Alderman of the said Burrough before the above named Mayor and Aldermen In Testimony whereof they have hereunto sett their Hands the day and yeare above written –

---

[1] For the year 1729–30.
[2] A Constable of the Borough 1716 (P.C.R.O. S3/67); mortgaged property in the High Street to John Vining Nov. 1726 (Hants. R.O. 1 M.49/20); voted Whig 1734 (*Poll for Hants.*, 1734, p. 132).
[3] Inserted.
[4] In 1742 Smith was £1.13*s*.4*d*. in arrears (P.C.R.O. CF1/8).

*Signed by:*

| | |
|---|---|
| Jn⁰ White Mayor | Hen: Stanyford |
| John Vining | Thoˢ Missing |
| Henry Belfeild | Sam: Brady |
| L: Barton | Robᵗ Newnham |

*Hand i.* Iuratus per (*signed by*) Geo Huish Clericum Communem –

**7**

**18 September 1732**

*p. 7*

*Hand ii.* Burrough of Portesmouth. Sessions

Wee whose Hands are hereunto set being the Mayor and Major Part of the Aldermen of the said Burrough this day assembled at the Guildhall of the said Burrough do hereby nominate elect and choose Mʳ Edward Burford of Portesmouth to be a Burgess of the said Burrough, he being this day nominated by the said Mayor to be his Peremptory Burgess Witnes our Hands the Eighteenth day of September 1732.

*Signed by:*

| | |
|---|---|
| Jn⁰ White Mayor | Sam: Brady |
| Henry Belfeild | Robᵗ Newnham |
| L: Barton | John Mounsher |
| Hen: Stanyford | |

*Hand i.* Die & Anno Supradictis predictus Edwardus Burford Iuratus fuit Coram Supradictis Majore & Aldermannis per (*signed by*) Geo Huish Clericum Communem –

**8**

**18 September 1732**

*p. 8*

*Hand ii.* Burrough of Portesmouth. Sessions

Whereas on the Fifth day of October last past an Order was made by the Mayor and Major Part of the Aldermen of the said Burrough for paying the Sume of Five Pounds out of the Chamberlains Roll to Samuell Beven one of the Serjeants at Mace of the said Burrough as an Augmentation of his Sallery at Michaellmas next ensueing in Consideracion of the Decay of his Business, And the same Reason still continueing Wee whose Hands are hereunto set being the Mayor and Major Part of the Aldermen of the said Burrough do hereby agree that there shall be yearly paid to the said Samuell Beven from and after the said Michaellmas the Sume of Five Pounds out of the Chamberlains Roll as an Encrease of his Sallery, untill such Time as the Mayor and Major Part of the Aldermen of the said Burrough for the time being shall think it necessary to revoake this present Order Witnes our Hands the Eighteenth day of September Anno Domini 1732 –

*Signed by:*

| | |
|---|---|
| Jn⁰ White Mayor | Sam: Brady |
| Henry Belfeild | Robᵗ Newnham |
| L: Barton | John Mounsher |
| Hen: Stanyford | |

**9**

**18 September 1732**

*p. 9*

*Hand ii.* Burrough of Portesmouth. Sessions

Wee whose Hands are hereunto set being the Mayor and Major Part of the Aldermen of the said Burrough this day assembled in the Town Hall there do hereby nominate and appoint Henry Stanyford Esqʳ, Samuell Brady Doctor of Physick, Lewis Barton Gent' and John Mounsher Esqʳ Aldermen of the said Burrough or any Two of them to audit settle and adjust such of the Accounts of the Chamberlains of the said Burrough that have not yet been passed & allowed, and whatsoever they or any Two of them shall do in Pursuance of this Order we do hereby promise to rattify and confirme Witnes our Hands the Eighteenth day of September Anno Domini 1732.

*Signed by:*

| | |
|---|---|
| Jn⁰ White Mayor. | Sam: Brady |
| Henry Belfeild | Robᵗ Newnham |
| L: Barton | John Mounsher |
| Hen: Stanyford | |

**27 November 1732**   *Hand ii.* Burrough of Portesmouth. Se*ssion*s

    Wee the Mayor and Major Part of the Aldermen of the said Burrough being this day assembled at the House of the said Mayor within the said Burrough do hereby Nominate Elect and choose the severall Persons whose Names are under mencioned to be Burgesses of the said Burrough, that is to say.[1]

  1 Burrington Goldsworthy Esq[r]
  2 Pusey Brooke Esq[r]
  3 James Cockburne Esq[r]
  4 Robert Eddowes Esq[r]
  5 Isaac Townshend Esq[r]
  6 Thomas Bowerbank Gent'
  7 George Bayly, Doctor of Physick.
  8 Robert Turvin Gent'
  9 M[r] William Mathis Junior of Berry
10 M[r] John Poole
11 M[r] John Baxter
12 M[r] Joseph Gardner
13 M[r] John Munday
14 M[r] John Hunt
15 M[r] Robert Godwin
16 M[r] Richard Roy Sen*ior*
17 M[r] Thomas Missing
18 M[r] William Binsteed
19 M[r] Edward Clinch
20 M[r] John Shephard Son of Sam[ll]
21 M[r] William Robinson.
22 M[r] William Pike
23 M[r] John Carter
24 M[r] John Mounsher ⎫
25 M[r] James Mounsher ⎬ Sons of John Mounsher Esq[r] Mayor
26 M[r] John White ⌐(dead)¬[2] ⎫
27 M[r] William White  ⎬ Sons of John White Gent'
28 M[r] Charles Brady Son of Doctor Brady.
29 M[r] Edward Barton Junior
30 M[r] Henry Huish Son of M[r] George Huish.

Witnes our Hands the Twenty Seventh day of November Anno D*omini* 1732.[3]
*Signed by :*

| John Mounsher Mayor | Jn[o] White. |
| L: Barton | Sam: Brady |
| Hen: Stanyford | Rob[t] Newnham |
| Tho[s] Missing | |

     Geo Huish Cl*ericus* Com*munis* –

**22 March 1732/3**   *Hand ii.* 22[d] March 1732 Burrough of Portesmouth. Se*ssion*s

    At an Assembly in the Councell Chamber of the Guildhall of the said Burrough being then present pursuant to Summons.

John Mounsher Esq[r] Mayor

John Vining Gent'– ⎫
Henry Belfeild Gent'– ⎪
Lewis Barton Gent'– ⎪
Henry Stanyford Esq[r]– ⎬ Aldermen
Thomas Missing Esq[r]– ⎪
John White Gent'– ⎪
Samuell Brady M: D, &– ⎪
Robert Newnham Gent' ⎭

---

[1] There is a tick after each entry except 3, 26 and 28.
[2] Added.
[3] Goldsworthy, Brooke, Eddowes, Bowerbank, Turvin, Baxter, Gardner, Hunt, Goodwin, Binsteed, Clinch, Shephard, Robinson and Pike were sworn Burgesses the same day (P.C.R.O. CE1/13, p. 221).

Cornelious Colliss Gent' one of the Burgesses of the said Burrough was by the above named Mayor and Aldermen, (Except M^r Vining and M^r Belfeild) nominated and elected an Alderman of the said Burrough, And the said Cornelious Colliss did then and there take and subscribe the Oaths of Allegiance Supremacy and Abjuration, and did repeat and subscribe the Test against Transubstantiation, and was then sworn an ⌐Alderman⌐[1] of the said Burrough before the said M^r Mayor M^r Barton M^r Stanyford, M^r Missing M^r White D^r Brady and M^r Newnham (being the Major part of the Aldermen of the said Burrough so assembled) In Testimony whereof they have hereunto set their Hands the day and year above written[2] –

*Signed by:*

| | |
|---|---|
| John Mounsher Mayor | Jn° White. |
| L: Barton | Sam: Brady |
| Hen: Stanyford | Rob^t Newnham |
| Tho^s Missing | |

*Hand i. Iuratus per Geo Huish Clericum Communem*

**12**

**18 June 1733**

*p. 12*

*Hand ii.* Burrough of Portesmouth.

We the Mayor and Major Part of the Aldermen of the said Burrough whose Hands are hereunto set being this day assembled at the House called the Kings Arms[3] within the said Burrough do hereby nominate elect and choose the severall persons whose Names are under mentioned to be Burgesses of the said Burrough, that is to say.

1 S^r Thomas Franckland Baronett
2 Thomas Winnington Esq^r
3 George Trenchard Esq^r
4 Thomas Spence Esq^r
5 Thomas Revell Esq^r
6 William Thompson Esq^r &
7 Thomas Corbett Esq^r

Witnes our Hands the Eighteenth day of June One Thousand Seven Hundred & Thirty Three[4]

*Signed by:*

| | |
|---|---|
| John Mounsher Mayor | Jn° White. |
| John Vining | Sam: Brady |
| Henry Belfeild | Rob^t Newnham |
| L: Barton | Cha: Wager |
| Hen: Stanyford | Cornelius Colliss |
| Tho^s Missing | |
| Geo Huish Towne Clerk – | |

**13**

**8 August 1733**

*p. 13*

*Hand i.* 8^th August 1733 Burrough of Portesmouth

Att an Assembly in the Guild Hall of the Said Burrough being then present pursuant to Summons

John Mounsher Esq^r Mayor
John Vining gent'–
Henry Belfeild gent'.
Lewis Barton gent'–
Henry Stanyford Esq^r          } Aldermen.
John White gent'.
Sam: Brady d^r of phisick
Robert Newnham gent'
Cornelious Colliss gent'.

---

[1] MS. 'Aldermen'.
[2] P.C.R.O. CE1/13, p. 222, adds in the margin: 'M^r Colliss elected and sworn an Alderman in D^r Smiths Room'.
[3] The King's Arms formerly stood in St Thomas's Street (A. N. Y. Howell, *Notes on the topography of Portsmouth* (1913), p. 119).
[4] P.C.R.O. CE1/13, p. 223, adds: 'And the said Seven Persons were then imediately duely sworn Burgesses of the said Burrough before the said Mayor and Aldermen by (*signed by*) Geo Huish Town Clerke'.

William Rickman gent' one of the Burgeses of the Said Burrough was by the above named Mayor and Aldermen unanimously nominated and Elected an Alderman of the Said Burrough, And the Said William Rickman did then and there Imediatly take and Subscribe the Oaths of Allegiance Supremacy and Abjuration and did repeate and Subscribe the Test against Transubstantiacion, and was then and there Sworn an Alderman of the Said Burrough, Before the Said Mayor and Aldermen[1] –

*Signed by:*

| | |
|---|---|
| John Mounsher Mayor | Jnᵒ White. |
| John Vining | Sam: Brady |
| Henry Belfcild | Robᵗ Newnham |
| L. Barton | Cornelius Colliss |
| Hen: Stanyford | |
| Geo Huish Towne Clerk – | |

**14**

**28 August 1733**

p. 14

*Hand i.* Burrough of Portesmouth

Wee the Mayor and Major parte of the Aldermen of the Said Burrough whose hands are hereunto Sett being this day assembled att the Guild Hall of the Said Burrough doe hereby nominate Elect and Choose the Honᵇˡᵉ Charles Stewart Esqʳ Rear Admirall of the White Squadron to be a Burgesse of the Said Burrough Wittnes our hands the Twenty Eighth day of August 1733.

*Signed by:*

| | |
|---|---|
| John Mounsher Mayor | Sam: Brady |
| Henry Belfeild | Robᵗ Newnham |
| Hen: Stanyford | Cornelius Colliss |
| Jnᵒ White. | William Rickman |

The same day the said Rear Admirall Stewart was Sworne a Burgesse of the Said Burrough before the above named Mayor and Aldermen by (*signed by*) Geo Huish Towne Clerk.

**15**

**17 September 1733**

p. 15

*Hand ii.* Burrough of Portesmouth.

We the Mayor and Major part of the Aldermen of the said Burrough whose Hands are hereunto set being this day assembled at the Guildhall of the said Burrough do hereby nominate elect & choose the Honᵇˡᵉ Lord Harry Paulet one of the[2] Commiss*ione*rs for executing the Office of Lord High Admirall of Great Britain and Anthony Chute of the Vine Esqʳ to be Burgesses of the said Burrough, Witnes our Hands the Seventeenth day of September 1733 –

John Shepherd Esqʳ was also nominated and elected a Burgess of the said Burrough at the same time & place by us

*Signed by:*

| | |
|---|---|
| John Mounsher Mayor | Sam: Brady |
| L. Barton | Robᵗ Newnham |
| Hen: Stanyford | Cornelius Colliss |
| Jnᵒ White. | William Rickman |

And the said Lord Harry Paulet Anthony Chute Esqʳ and John Shepherd Esqʳ were then severally sworn Burgesses of the said Burrough before the above named Mayor & Aldermen by (*signed by*) Geo Huish Town Clerk.

**16**

**30 November 1733[3]**

p. 16

*Hand i.* Burrough of Portesmouth

Whereas there is now due from this Corporacion to Severall persons the Sume of One hundred pounds and upwards Wee the Mayor and Major parte of the Aldermen of the Said Burrough whose hands are hereunto Sett, Doe hereby Consent and agree

---

[1] P.C.R.O. CE1/13, p. 223, adds in the margin: 'Mʳ Rickman elected & sworn an Alderman in Mʳ Missings Room'.
[2] 'Lords' struck out.
[3] Printed in East, p. 267.

that the Sume of One hundred pounds shall be forthwith taken up and Borrowed of Philip Varlo of Portsm° aforesaid Grocer towards the Discharge of Such Debts, and for the Securety of the Repayment thereof with Legall Interest for the Same, a Bond under the ⌐Comon⌐1 Seale of this Corporacion Shall be given to the Said Phillip Varlo for the Said Sume Wittnes our hands the Thirtieth day of November 1733 –

*Signed by :*
      Sam: Brady Mayor          Rob$^t$ Newnham
      L. Barton                John Mounsher
      Hen: Stanyford        Cornelius Colliss
      Jn° White.

      Geo Huish Town Clerk.

**17**

**18 December 1733**

*p. 17*

*Hand iii.* Burrough of Portesmouth

    Wee whose hands are hereunto sett being the Mayor and Major part of the Aldermen of the said Burrough Do hereby Consent and agree that in Consideracion of the Summe of One and twenty Pounds to us in hand to be paid (for the use of this Corporation) by Henry Stanyford Esq$^r$ one of the Aldermen of the said Burrough,[2] to Grant a Lease under the Common Seal of the said Burrough to Samuell Wheeler of Portesmouth aforesaid House Carpenter In Trust for the said Henry Stanyford his Executors Administrators and assignes of All those Four Messuages or Tenements with the Yards backsides and Gardens thereunto belonging and adjoining Scituate lying and being in Kings Hall Green Within the Town of Portesmouth containing in Breadth from North to South Seventy foot of Assize and in Length from the East towards the West Seventy foot of Assize (being the same premisses formerly granted by this Corporacion to Joseph Standen) And also All that Encroachment or Land Encroached on the South side of the said Messuages containing in Length Seventy foot and in breadth ⌐Three foot & nine inches⌐3 or thereabouts whereon are now Standing the Porches and Pallasades of those Messuages or Tenements To hold the same for the Term of One thousand years from the Feast of S$^t$ Thomas the Apostle next ensuing the date hereof under the Rent of Eleven Shillings a year with all usual and necessary Clauses and Covenants to be contained in Such Lease Wittnes our hands the Eighteenth of December 1733[4]

*Signed by :*
      Sam: Brady Mayor        John Mounsher
      Henry Belfeild         Cornelius Colliss
      Jn° White.              William Rickman
      Rob$^t$ Newnham

      Geo Huish Town Clerk –

**18**

**8 January 1733/4**

*p. 18*

*Hand ii.* Burrough of Portesmouth.

    We the Mayor and Major Part of the Aldermen of the said Burrough whose Hands are hereunto set do hereby consent & agree to demise and grant by Lease under our Common Seal to Daniell Marsh of Portesmouth aforesaid Shipwright[5] in Consideration of Five Guineas to be paid by him for the Use of this Corporation All that their Piece of Land situate lyeing & being on the Point without the Point Gate of Portesmouth aforesaid in a Street there called Tower Street containing in Breadth at the South End thereof next the Land formerly of Richard Stone & now of the Widow Baker Fifty Four foot of Assize and in Breadth at the North End next the Land

---

1 Inserted.

2 On 24 Aug. 1734 the Chamberlain was ordered to settle the account between Stanyford and the Corporation (P.C.R.O. CE1/13, p. 233).

3 Inserted in space left blank; 'feet' struck out.

4 P.C.R.O. CF20/1, p. 185, dates this lease 20 Dec. 1733.

5 Paid rates on property on the west side of the Point (P.C.R.O. 81A/3/20/3, no. 4: 7 Aug. 1732); leased property in Tower Street 1733, 1755 (East, p. 547).

formerly of John Pope & now of the Heirs of Peter Levermore[1] Fifty Eight foot of Assize, in Length on the West Side towards the Sea Seventeen foot and at the East End next the said Street Seventeen foot And also All Houses Edifices Buildings Lights Ways Enteries Easments Profits Advantages & Appurtenances whatsoever thereunto belonging or apperteining And also All that piece of Beach Land adjoining to the West End of the said other piece of Land, which said piece of Beach Land contains in Front next the Harbour Seventeen foot in Breadth at the South End Sixteen foot & at the North End Thirteen foot as the same is now fenced in & parted off from the rest of the Beach there To hold for One Thousand Years from Michaelmas last at the yearly Rent of Four Shillings & Two pence with the usuall Covenants Witness our Hands the Eighth day of January 1733.[2]

*Signed by:*

| | |
|---|---|
| Sam: Brady Mayor | Rob^t Newnham |
| L. Barton | William Rickman |
| Hen: Stanyford | Cornelius Colliss |
| John Mounsher | |

**19**

**27 February 1733/4**   *p. 19*

*Hand ii.* Burrough of Portesmouth.

Whereas M^r John Bissell as Administrator of the Goods and Chattles of his late Father Charles Bissell Gentl' deceased, left unadministred by M^r Joseph Bissell also deceased, hath a Demand on this Corporation of a Debt of Forty One Pounds & Eleven Shillings, out of which there is due to them for Arrears of Town Rent and Capon Money Sixteen Pounds and Eleven Shillings[3] Now We whose Hands are hereunto set being the Mayor & Major Part of the Aldermen of the said Burrough do hereby consent and agree that M^r Hugh Grove the Chamberlain of the said Burrough shall forthwith pay to the said John Bissell the said Sum of Forty One Pounds & Eleven Shillings, out of which the said Hugh Grove is to deduct the said Sixteen pounds & Eleven Shillings for Arrears, And We do further agree that on the said John Bissells executing a Generall Release to this Corporation We will cause our Common Seal to be affixt to a General Release to the said John Bissell Witness our Hands the Twenty Seventh day of February 1733.

*Signed by:*

| | |
|---|---|
| Sam: Brady Mayor | Rob^t Newnham |
| John Vining | John Mounsher |
| L. Barton | Cornelius Colliss |
| Jn^o White. | William Rickman |

**20**

**13 May 1734**   *p. 20*

*Hand ii.* Burrough of Portesmouth.

We the Mayor and Major part of the Aldermen of the said Burrough whose Hands are hereunto set do hereby nominate elect & choose the Right Hon^ble Charles Earl of Tankerville ⌐Knight of the most noble Order of the Thistle⌐[4] to be a Burgess of the said Burrough, Witness our Hands the Thirteenth day of May 1734.

*Signed by:*

| | |
|---|---|
| Sam: Brady Mayor | Jn^o White. |
| John Vining | John Mounsher |
| Hen: Stanyford | Cornelius Colliss |
| Rob^t Newnham | William Rickman |

And his Lordship was immediately admitted a Burgess of the said Burrough upon his Honour by the above named Mayor and Aldermen – (*signed by*) Geo Huish Towne Clerke

---

[1] Served as agent at Portsmouth for the Commissioners of Sick and Hurt Seamen 1714 (*Cal.T.B. 1714*, p. 50); leased property in Broad Street Sept. 1719 (East, p. 542).

[2] P.C.R.O. CF20/1, p. 185, dates this lease 15 Jan. 1733/4.

[3] Bissell's heirs are recorded as being in debt to the Corporation in respect of 'the Porch & Pales incroach'd in the High Street' for the sum of 6*d.* (P.C.R.O. CF1/8). This may well have been the same piece of property, described as 'porch and Pales late Luns' for which Bissell was charged 6*d.* rent in the late 1690's (P.C.R.O. CF5/6).

[4] Inserted.

**21**

**27 May 1734**

*Hand ii.* Burrough of Portesmouth.

We the Mayor and Major Part of the Aldermen of the said Burrough whose Hands are hereunto set do hereby agree (as far as in us lyes or that we lawfully may) to grant a Lease under the Common Seal of this Corporation to Benjamin Smith o Portesmouth aforesaid Brewer[1] his Executors Administrators and Assignes for the Term of One Thousand Years and under the yearly Rent of Two Shillings & Six pence of All that Piece of Wast Ground situate & being near Kingwell Pound[2] within the Liberties of the said Burrough containing in Length from East to West on the North Side next M$^r$ Ridges Garden Wall Eighty Eight foot and on the South Side next the Land of Kilbury Garrett[3] Seventy Eight foot, in Breadth at the West End next the said Pound Forty Three Foot and a half, and at the East End next other Wast Land of this Corporation Twenty One foot, Out of which said Lease is to be Excepted the Watercourse that runs from the said Garden Wall of the said M$^r$ Ridge by the Corner of the said Pound, which Watercourse is at all times hereafter to be continued open in the manner it now is, and not to be obstructed or shut up, Witness our Hands the Twenty Seventh day of May 1734.

*Signed by:*

|  |  |
|---|---|
| Sam: Brady Mayor | John Mounsher |
| Hen: Stanyford | Cornelius Colliss |
| Jn$^o$ White. | William Rickman |
| Rob$^t$ Newnham |  |
| Geo Huish Town Clerk. |  |

**22**

**1 July 1734**[4]

*Hand i.* Burrough of Portesmouth

Wee the Mayor and Major parte of the Aldermen of the Said Burrough whose hands are hereunto Sett Doe hereby Consent and agree to demise and grant by Lease in writeing under the Common Seale of this Corporacion to the R$^t$ Hon$^{ble}$ Arthur Onslow, Richard Haddock John Fuller and Robert Byng Esq$^{rs}$ Four of the principall Officers and Comm*issione*rs of his Majesties Navy and their Successors (In Trust for his Majestie his heires and Successors)[5] All that peice or parcell of Land next the Harbour of Portesmouth and Scituate betweene the Wall of his Majesties Dock yard on the North, and the Gun Wharfe wall on the South containing in Length Seaven hundred Twenty Eight feet or thereabouts, and fronting Eastward to the High way Leading from the Towne of Portesmouth to the said Dock yard, and in Depth as farr as Low Water marke,[6] Out of which Grant is to ⌐be⌐[7] Excepted Two Leases made of parts of the Said Land, that is to say one to Robert Heart for Fifty ⌐one⌐[8] yeares from Lady day 1728 att the yearley Rent of Twenty Shillings, and the other to Henry Morlen[9] for Forty Eight yeares from Lady day 1731 att the Rent of Forty Shillings a yeare To hold the premisses hereby intended to be demised from the Feast of the Anunciacion of the Blessed Virgin Mary Last past for the terme of One Thousand yeares, att the yearley Rent of Twenty pounds payable att the said Feast free and cleer of all deduccions and payments whatsoev*er* And wee doe further agree to assigne over the Rents Reserved on the Said Two Leases, to the Said Comm*issione*rs (in Trust as aforesaid) for the Remainder of the Severall terms therein yett to come,

---

[1] Admitted as a Burgess 16 Sept. 1710 (East, p. 375); voted Whig 1734 (*Poll for Hants.*, *1734*, p. 133).

[2] Kingswell Pound formerly stood opposite the south end of Spring Street (A. N. Y. Howell, *Notes on the topography of Portsmouth* (1913), p. 46).

[3] Paid rates on property on the east side of the Point (P.C.R.O. 81A/3/20/3, no. 4: 7 Aug. 1732); voted Whig 1734 (*Poll for Hants.*, *1734*, p. 128).

[4] Printed in East, pp. 267–8; John Fuller is there wrongly named John Salter.

[5] MS. omits closing bracket.

[6] This piece of land was known as the Strand, and negotiations about it were carried out by Commissioner Hughes between 21 Nov. 1733 and 20 Oct. 1734 (N.M.M. POR/F/5, passim).

[7] Inserted.

[8] Inserted.

[9] P.C.R.O. CF20/1, p. 187, records only one of these leases, that to Robert Heart. The counterpart of the lease, dated 1 July 1734, recites a lease of 5 May 1727 and refers to the lessee as Robert Hart of Portsea, house-carpenter (P.C.R.O. DD2/1). Correspondence about Morlen's role in the matter is contained in N.M.M. POR/F/5 (the letter of 30 Dec. 1733 from Commissioner Hughes to the Navy Board is of particular interest); Morlen had been dismissed as shipwright in the Yard and had developed a personal grudge against Hughes.

And that att the Executeing the Said Grant the Said Comm*issione*rs Shall pay to the said Mayor for a Fyne as usuall in Such Cases the Sum of Twenty pounds, and alsoe all the charges and Expences of the said Grant, and the Assignement of the Said Two Leases and the Counter parts thereof, Wittnes our hands the first of July in the yeare 1734 –

*Signed by:*

Sam: Brady Mayor
Henry Belfeild
L. Barton
Hen: Stanyford
Robt Newnham
Cornelius Colliss
William Rickman

Geo Huish Town Clerk.

**23** *p. 23*

**9 July 1734** *Hand ii.* Burrough of Portesmouth.

We the Mayor and Major part of the Aldermen of the said Burrough whose Hands are hereunto set do hereby consent & agree to demise and grant by Lease under the Common Seal of this Corporation to Thomas Light the Younger of Portesmouth aforesaid Blacksmith his Executors Administrators & Assignes All that piece or parcell of Beach Ground situate & being on the Point without the Point Gate of Portesmouth aforesaid between the Land formerly granted to Robert Threlkild and now Mr Henry Belfields on the North, and the Custom House Watch House on the South, which said piece of Beach Ground hereby intended to be granted contains in the Front from North to South Fifty Seven foot & Six inches and to the West next the Harbour Sixty Eight foot and in Depth on the North & South Sides Thirty ⌜Three⌝[1] foot as the same is now markt & staked out To hold from Michaellmas next for One Thousand Years at the yearly Rent of Thirty Shillings payable at Lady day & Michaellmas, with all necessary Clauses & Covenants usually contained in such Leases Witness our Hands the Ninth day of July 1734.

*Signed by:*

Sam: Brady Mayor
Henry Belfeild
Hen: Stanyford
Robt Newnham
John Mounsher
Cornelius Colliss
William Rickman

Geo Huish Town Clerk.

**24** *p. 24*

**16 July 1734** *Hand ii.* Burrough of Portesmouth.

We the Mayor and Major Part of the Aldermen of the said Burrough whose Hands are hereunto set do hereby nominate elect and choose the Honble Sir William Thompson one of the Barons of his Majestys Court of Exchequer, to be a Burgess of the said Burrough Witness our Hands the Sixteenth day of July 1734.

*Signed by:*

Sam: Brady Mayor
John Vining
Henry Belfeild
L. Barton
Hen: Stanyford
Robt Newnham
Cornelius Colliss

*Hand i.* And the Said Baron was Immediatly Sworne ⌜a Burgess⌝[2] before the above Mayor and Aldermen, by (*signed by*) Geo Huish Town Clerk

**25** *p. 25*

**12 September 1734** *Hand ii.* Burrough of Portesmouth.

We the Mayor and Major Part of the Aldermen of the said Burrough whose Hands are hereunto set do hereby nominate elect and choose the Honble Nicholas Haddock Esqr Rear Admirall of the Blew Squadron of his Majesties Navy, to be a Burgess of the said Burrough, Witness our Hands the Twelfth day of September 1734.

---

[1] Inserted.

[2] Inserted (hand ii).

Signed by:

    Sam: Brady Mayor                        Rob$^t$ Newnham
    Henry Belfeild                          John Mounsher
    L. Barton                             Cornelius Colliss
    Hen: Stanyford

    *Hand i.* He was Sworne the 30$^{th}$ of September 1734 vide the Eleccion Booke folio. 238.[1] *Signed by* Geo Huish Town Clerk

**26**                 *p. 26*

**12 September 1734**    *Hand ii.* Burrough of Portesmouth

    We the Mayor and Major Part of the Aldermen of the said Burrough whose Hands are hereunto set do hereby agree to demise and lett to James Littlefield of Portesmouth aforesaid Carter by Lease under our Common Seal All the Wharfage Cranage and Petty Customs of this Corporation for the Term of ⌐Three⌐[2] Years from the Feast of S$^t$ Michaell the Archangell next ensueing the date hereof at the Yearly Rent of Forty Pounds and Ten Shillings & Two fat Capons and under the same Covenants Provisoes and Agreements as are mencioned in the Lease by which the said James Littlefield now holds the premisses from this Corporation,[3] which last mencioned Lease will expire on the said Feast of S$^t$ Michaell the Archangell next, And we do further agree that the said James Littlefield shall procure a sufficient person to be bound for the Performance of the Covenants in the said Lease so intended to be granted him which on the part & Behalf of the Lessee therein named ought to be done & performed Witness our Hands the Twelfth day of September 1734 –

    Signed by:

    Sam: Brady Mayor                        Rob$^t$ Newnham
    Henry Belfeild                          John Mounsher
    L. Barton                             Cornelius Colliss
    Hen: Stanyford

**27**                 *p. 27*

**12 September 1734**[4]    *Hand i.* Burrough of Portesmouth

    Wee the Mayor and Major parte of the Aldermen of the Said Burrough whose hands are hereunto Sett doe hereby agree that the Sume of One hundred pounds lately given by the R$^t$ Hon$^{ble}$ Sir Charles Wager for the use of this Corporacion, Shall be forthwith paid by the Chamberlain of the Said Burrough towards the Discharge of a Bond under the Common Seale of this Burrough for the Sume of One hundred pounds with one yeares ⌐Interest⌐[5] for the Same made to Philip Varlo the[6] Younger of Portesmouth aforesaid Grocer, Wittnes our hands the 12$^{th}$ of September 1734.

    Signed by:

    Sam: Brady Mayor                        Rob$^t$ Newnham
    Henry Belfeild                          John Mounsher
    L. Barton                             Cornelius Colliss
    Hen: Stanyford

---

[1] I.e. P.C.R.O. CE1/13, p. 238.

[2] Inserted (hand i) in space left blank.

[3] P.C.R.O. CF20/1, p. 188, dates this lease 28 Oct. 1734; it shows that in addition the Mayor and Aldermen approved 'all lawfull means used by the Lessee for recovering the Rates & to produce any of the Records for asserting their Right for better recovering the dues in any Courts & not to release any Actions brought in their names for any of the dues by Lessee without his Consent, Proviso that no Burgess shall pay any Petty Custom or Wharfage nor but Three pence per Tun Cranage for any Goods, & another Proviso that nothing therein contained shall debar Mayor &c from receiving to their own Use Sixteen pounds per Annum payable by the Commissioners of the Victualling for Wharfage Cranage & Petty Custom'.

[4] Printed in East, p. 268.

[5] Inserted.

[6] 'Ju(?)' struck out.

12

**28**

**14 January 1734/5**

*Hand iii.* Burrough of Portesmouth

We the Mayor & Major part of the Aldermen of the said Burrough whose[1] hands are hereunto Sett Doe hereby consent & agree (in consideracion of a Surrender of a former Lease made of the premisses herein after mencioned in the Mayoralty of Thos Blakley Esqr[2] to Richd Clapham & Thos Gattrell[3]) to Demise & Grant by Lease under the Seale of this Corporacion to Wm Knibloe of Portesmouth Chyrurgeon ⌐or some other person⌐[4] In Trust for Henry Belfeild Gent' one of the Aldermen of this Burrough All yt piece of Beach Ground Scituate lyeing & being next the Sea on the Poynt without the Poynt Gate of Portesmo aforesaid containeing on the East parte thereof Sixty Six foot & Six inches, on the West parte thereof Twenty foot, On the North parte thereof Fifty four foot Six inches & on the South parte Twenty Seven foot And All yt Messuage or Tenement & Buildings thereupon Erected formerly in the possession of Walter Wilmoth deceased To hold from Michaelmas last past for One Thousand years at the yearly rent of Ten Shillings with the Clauses & Covenants usually contained in such Leases Witnesse our hands the Fourteenth day of January 1734 –

*Signed by:*

|                              |                      |
|------------------------------|----------------------|
| Hen: Stanyford Mayor         | Robt Newnham         |
| John Vining                  | John Mounsher        |
| L. Barton                    | Cornelius Colliss    |
| Sam: Brady                   |                      |
| Geo Huish Town Clerk.        |                      |

**29**

**8 April 1735**

*Hand ii.* 8th Aprill 1735 Burrough of Portesmouth

At an Assembly in the Councell Chamber in the Guildhall of the said Burrough being then present pursuant to Summons,

Henry Stanyford Esqr Mayor

John Vining Gent'– ⎫
Henry Belfeild Gent'– ⎪
Lewis Barton Gent'– ⎪
John White Gent'– ⎪
Samuell Brady M.D– ⎬ Aldermen
Robert Newnham Gent' ⎪
John Mounsher Esqr– ⎪
Cornelius Colliss Gent'– ⎪
William Rickman Gent'– ⎭

Mr Daniell Smith & Mr Michaell Atkins Two of the Burgesses of the said Burrough were by the above named Mayor and Aldermen unanimously nominated & elected Aldermen of the said Burrough, the first in the Room of Sir John Suffeild Knt lately deceased, and the Latter in the Room of the Rt Honble Sir Charles Wager Knt (who hath lately resigned that Office)[5] And the said Daniell Smith & Michaell Atkins did then & there immediately take and subscribe the Oaths of Allegiance Supremacy & Abjuration and did repeat & subscribe the Test against Transubstantiation, and were then and there severally sworn Aldermen of the said Burrough before the said Mayor & Aldermen, In witness whereof the said Mayor & Aldermen have hereunto set their Hands the day & year above written

*Signed by:*

|                              |                      |
|------------------------------|----------------------|
| Hen: Stanyford Mayor         | Sam: Brady           |
| John Vining                  | Robt Newnham         |
| Henry Belfeild               | John Mounsher        |
| L. Barton                    | Cornelius Colliss    |
| Jno White.                   | William Rickman      |
| Geo Huish Town Clerk         |                      |

---

1 'names' struck out.
2 1719–20 (East, p. 317). The lease in question, dated 30 Sept. 1719, is in P.C.R.O. CF20/1, p. 177. Blackley was admitted as a Burgess in 1705, made an Alderman in 1710 and re-elected in 1716 (East, pp. 373, 330).
3 Sergeant-at-Mace 1717–27 (P.C.R.O. CE1/13, pp. 89, 178: 29 Sept. 1717, 29 Sept. 1727).
4 Inserted. P.C.R.O. CF20/1, p. 177, names the 'some other person' as Robert Cook.
5 P.C.R.O. CE1/13, p. 240, dates Wager's resignation 3 Apr. 1735.

**30**

**28 May 1735**

*p. 30*

*Hand i.* Burrough of Portesmouth

Wee the Mayor and Major parte of the Aldermen of the said Burrough whose hands are hereunto Sett Doe hereby Nominate elect and Choose the Hon^ble Richard Haddock Esq^r Comptroller of his Majesties Navy to be a Burgesse of the Said Burrough Wittnes our hands the 28^th of May 1735.

*Signed by:*

| | |
|---|---|
| Hen: Stanyford Mayor | John Mounsher |
| Henry Belfeild | Cornelius Colliss |
| Jn^o White. | Dan: Smith |
| Sam: Brady | Michael Atkins |
| Rob^t Newnham | |

The Said[1] Richard Haddock ⌐Esq^r¬[2] was Imediatly Sworne a Burgesse before the above Mayor and Aldermen By (*signed by*) Geo Huish Town Clerk.

**31**

**30 June 1735[3]**

*p. 31*

*Hand i.* Burrough of Portesmouth

Wee the Mayor and Major parte of the Aldermen of the Said Burrough whose hands are hereunto Sett, Doe hereby agree that the Sume of One hundred pounds lately given by Thomas Lewes Esq^r to be disposed off by us the Said Mayor and the Major parte of the said Aldermen, shall be forthwith paid into the hands of M^r Hugh Grove the present Chamberlaine for dischargeing the Severall Sumes following that is to Say

| | |
|---|---|
| To Sam^ll Sheppard for what Remains due to him for repairing the Common Sewer on the parade – | 17: 17[4]: 4 |
| To the Administrators of Thomas Crameden' for worke done by him for the Corporacion – | 4: 16[5]: 9 |
| To M^r Alderman Vining for the Ballance of[6] his Account – | 10: 8 :10 |
| To M^rs Arnold' for money due to her late Husband | 25: 6 : 0 |
| | 58: 8 :11 |

And that the Residue of the Said One hundred pounds Shall Remaine in the Said Chamberlaines hands to be paid as wee the Mayor & Major parte of the Aldermen of the Said Burrough Shall direct Wittnes our hands the 30^th of June in the yeare 1735.

*Signed by:*

| | |
|---|---|
| Hen: Stanyford Mayor | John Mounsher |
| Henry Belfeild | Cornelius Colliss |
| L. Barton | Dan: Smith |
| Jn^o White. | Michael Atkins |
| Rob^t Newnham | |

**32**

**2 August 1735**

*p. 32*

*Hand i.* 2^d August 1735. Burrough of Portesmouth

Att an Assembly in the Councell Chamber in the Guild Hall of the Said Burrough, being then present pursuant to Sumons.

John White Esq^r Mayor

| | |
|---|---|
| Henry Belfeild gent' | |
| Lewis Barton gent' | |
| Sam: Brady M:D. | |
| Rob^t Newnham gent' | Aldermen. |
| Cornelious Collis gent' | |
| Dan^ll Smith gent' | |
| Mich^ll Attkins gent' | |

---

[1] 'S^r' struck out.
[2] Inserted (hand ii).
[3] Printed in East, pp. 268–9.
[4] Tick above figure.
[5] Tick above figure.
[6] 'the' struck out.

Thomas Stanyford Esq[r] one of the Burgesses of the Said Burrough was by the above named Mayor and Aldermen (Except M[r] Belfeild whoe gave his voate for M[r] James Deacon) nominated and Elected an Alderman of the Said Burrough in the Roome of Henry Stanyford Esq[r] deceased, And the Said Thomas Stanyford did then and there Immediately take & subscribe the Oaths of Allegiance Supremacy & Abjuration, and did alsoe repeate & Subscribe the Test against Transubstantiacion, and was then Sworne an Alderman of the Said Burrough[1] before the Said Mayor & Aldermen (Except the Said M[r] Belfeild, whoe first Left the Assembly) In Witnes whereof the Said Mayor, and the Aldermen whoe voted for the Said Tho: Stanyford (being the Major parte of the Aldermen of the Said Burrough) have hereunto Sett their hands the day and yeare above written

*Signed by:*

Jn[o] White Mayor             Cornelius Colliss
L. Barton                         Dan: Smith
Sam: Brady                       Michael Atkins
Rob[t] Newnham
Geo Huish Town Clerk –

**33**

**2 September 1735**

*p. 33*

*Hand i.* 2[d] September 1735 Burrough of Portesmouth

Wee whose hands are hereunto Sett being the Mayor and Major parte of the Aldermen of the Said Burrough ⌐in Councell assembled⌐[2] Doe hereby Nominate elect and Choose M[r] Thomas Blanckley Junior and M[r] James Peers to be Burgesses of the Said Burrough Wittnes our hands the day and yeare above written –

*Signed by:*

Jn[o] White Mayor             Cornelius Colliss
L. Barton                         Dan: Smith
Sam: Brady                       Michael Atkins
Rob[t] Newnham               Thomas Stanyford
John Mounsher

The Said M[r] ⌐James⌐[3] Peers was Immediatly Sworne before the above Mayor and Aldermen by (*signed by*) Geo Huish Town Clerk.

**34**

**28 October 1735**

*p. 34 blank; p. 35*

*Hand ii.* Burrough of Portesmouth.

We the Mayor and Major Part of the Aldermen of the said Burrough whose Hands are hereunto set do hereby consent and agree to demise and grant by Lease under our Common Seal to James Pafoot of Portsea Joyner All that Piece or Parcell of Land containing Forty foot square being part of the Wast Lands belonging to this Corporation & situate lyeing & being on a Place called the Common without the Mill Gate & within the Liberties of the said Burrough, bounded with Ten foot & a half ⌐of Land⌐[4] being part of the same Lands ⌐next⌐[5] the Cage[6] there on the South fronting towards the Gun Wharf Wall on the West, to other parts of the same Lands on the North & East parts, as the Same is now marked & staked out To hold from Michaelmas last past for One Thousand years at the yearly Rent of Forty Shillings payable half yearly with the usuall Covenants contained in such Leases, Witness our Hands the Twenty Eighth day of October 1735.

*Signed by:*

Cornelius Colliss Mayor       Rob[t] Newnham
Henry Belfeild                    John Mounsher
L. Barton                          William Rickman
Jn[o] White.                      Dan: Smith
Sam: Brady                        Michael Atkins
Geo Huish Town Clerk –

---

[1] P.C.R.O. CE1/13, p. 242, adds in the margin: 'Sworn an Alderman in his Father's Room'.
[2] Inserted.
[3] Inserted; 'Thomas' struck out.
[4] Inserted.
[5] Inserted; 'on' struck out.
[6] Bodies of executed criminals were hung in the Cage as a deterrent to would-be wrong-doers.

*Hand i.* I doe hereby disclaime all Right to the above Lease, & doe Refuse to accept the Same (*signed by*) James Pafoot Wittnes (*signed by*) Tho^s Huish[1]

**35**

**7 June 1736**

*p. 36 blank; p. 37*

*Hand ii.* Burrough of Portesmouth.

We whose Hands are hereunto set being the Mayor & Major Part of the Aldermen of the said Burrough in Councell assembled do hereby nominate elect and choose the most Noble John Duke of Montague the Right Hon^ble George Earl of Cardigan and the Right Hon^ble John Baron of Delaware, the Hon^ble Hollis S^t John Esq^r, Charles Stanhope Esq^r and Edward Young Esq^r to be Burgesses of the said Burrough, Witness our Hands the Seventh day of June 1736.

*Signed by:*

| | |
|---|---|
| Cornelius Colliss Mayor | John Mounsher |
| Jn^o White. | Dan: Smith |
| Sam: Brady | Michael Atkins |
| Rob^t Newnham | |

His Grace John Duke of Montague, the R^t Hon^ble George Earl of Cardigan & the R^t Hon^ble John Baron of Delawar were severally admitted Burgesses on their Honours; and the above named Hollis S^t John Charles Stanhope & Edward Young ⌐Esq^rs¬[2] were severally sworn Burgesses on the day & year above written at the Guildhall of the said Burrough before the above Mayor & Aldermen –

At the same Time and Place & in the Presence of the said Mayor & Aldermen M^r John Carter was sworn a Burgess pursuant to his Election on the 27^th of November 1732 by (*signed by*) Geo Huish Town Clerk –

**36**

**22 June 1736**

*p. 38 blank; p. 39*

*Hand iv.* Burrough of Portesmouth

We the Mayor and Major part of the Aldermen of the said Burrough whose Hands are hereunto Sett do hereby consent & agree to demise and grant by Lease under our Common Seal to John Bowes of Portesmouth aforesaid D^r of Physick[3] All that Incroachment or Lands incroached and adjoining to the Six severall Messuages or Tenements of him the said John situate lyeing and being in the Parish of Portsea within the Liberties of the said Burrough faceing against the Harbour of Portesmouth aforesaid (on part whereof are placed Cellar Windows and Steps) containing in Length from North to South Ninety Nine foot & Eight Inches and in Breadth Three foot and Four Inches To hold from Lady Day last past for One Thousand years at the Yearly Rent of ⌐Nine Shillings¬[4] payable half yearly with the Clauses and Covenants usually contained in such Leases Witness our Hands the Twenty Second day of June 1736.

*Signed by:*

| | |
|---|---|
| Cornelius Colliss Mayor | John Mounsher |
| Jn^o White. | Dan: Smith |
| Sam: Brady | Michael Atkins |
| Rob^t Newnham | Thomas Stanyford |

*Hand i.* Entered by (*signed by*) Geo Huish Town Clerk.

**37**

**21 July 1736[5]**

*p. 40*

*Hand i.* Burrough of Portesmouth

Whereas Thomas Lewis Esq^r hath lately made a present to the Mayor and Aldermen of this Burrough of the Sume of One hundred pounds to be disposed

---

[1] A grant of attorney to Thomas Huish is in P.C.R.O. CF20/1, p. 163 (29 Sept. 1736). He was buried 22 Jan. 1743/4 (P.C.R.O. 22A/2/1/1/5).

[2] Inserted.

[3] Elected a Burgess 14 Sept. 1751 (East, p. 383); described in 1775 as 'An old Physician, a Dissenter and therefore attached to Mr Carter' (Sandwich MS. 380: list of Portsmouth voters). The counterpart of the lease, dated 18 June 1736, refers to Bowes as 'doctor of physick to the Corporation' (P.C.R.O. CD10/43/4).

[4] Inserted (hand i) in space left blank.

[5] Printed in East, p. 269.

off as the Said Mayor and Aldermen or the greater parte of them Shall thinke fitt to direct, Wee the Mayor and Major parte of the Aldermen of the Said Burrough whose hands are hereunto Sett, Doe hereby Consent direct and agree That the Said One hundred pounds, Shall be putt into the Towne Chest in the Guild Hall of the Said Burrough, there to Remaine till the Same Shall be otherwise disposed off by the Mayor and greater parte of the Aldermen of the Said Burrough, for the time being, Wittnes our hands the Twenty first day of July 1736 –

*Signed by:*

| | |
|---|---|
| Cornelius Colliss Mayor | Rob^t Newnham |
| John Vining | John Mounsher |
| Henry Belfeild | Dan: Smith |
| L. Barton | Michael Atkins |
| Jn^o White. | Thomas Stanyford |
| Sam: Brady | |

*Hand i.* Entered by (*signed by*) Geo Huish Town Clerk.

**38**

**3 August 1736**

*p. 41*

*Hand ii.* Burrough of Portesmouth

We the Mayor & Major Part of the Aldermen of the said Burrough whose Hands are hereunto set do hereby consent & agree to demise & grant by Lease under our Common Seal to Robert Grigg of Portsmouth aforesaid Grocer[1] or some other person In Trust for William Binsteed of the same House Carpenter one of the Burgesses of the said Burrough his Executors Administrators & Assigns All that Incroachment or Piece of Ground incroached before a Messuage or Tenement of the said William Binsteed which he is now erecting and building in Penny Street within the said Burrough, which said Piece of Ground contains in Length Twenty Three foot and in Breadth Three Foot and whereon the said William Binsteed may erect put and place Cellar Windows Steps Posts Rails & Pales but no other Edifice or Building whatsoever To hold from Lady day last past for One Thousand years under the yearly Rent of One Shilling & Six pence payable half yearly with the Clauses & Covenants usually contained in such Leases, Witness our Hands the Third day of August 1736.

*Signed by:*

| | |
|---|---|
| Cornelius Colliss Mayor | John Mounsher |
| John Vining | William Rickman |
| Henry Belfeild | Dan: Smith |
| L. Barton | Michael Atkins |
| Rob^t Newnham | Thomas Stanyford[2] |

*Hand i.* Entered by (*signed by*) Geo Huish Town Clerk.

**39**

**3 August 1736**

*p. 42*

*Hand ii.* Burrough of Portesmouth.

Whereas at his Majesties Court Leet held in & for the said Burrough & the Liberties thereof by Adjournment on the Twenty Second day of June last past before Cornelius Colliss Esq^r Mayor & the Aldermen of the said Burrough the following Persons being Inhabitants within the said Burrough and Liberties were presented & amerced by the Leet Jury at the said Court as follows, viz^t

| | s | d |
|---|---|---|
| Philip Sugar for exposing to Sale within the said Burrough a pretended Six penny Loaf ⌐of Bread¬[3] Three Ounces too light & a pretended Three penny Loaf Two Ounces too light – | 6 : | 8 |
| William Wathell for a Three penny Loaf Two Ounces too light – | 6 : | 8 |
| Edward Sharp for a Three penny Loaf One Ounce & a half too light – | 6 : | 8 |
| Edward Wareham for the Like – | 6 : | 8 |
| William Jeffery for a Three penny Loaf Six Ounces too light – | 6 : | 8 |

---

[1] Contributed to the organ fund at St Thomas's Church 1718 (Everitt, 'Church notes', ii, p. 135); paid rates on property in High Street (P.C.R.O. 81A/3/20/3, no. 4: 7 Aug. 1732); voted Tory 1734 (*Poll for Hants.*, *1734*, p. 128).

[2] 'M' struck out before the signature.

[3] Inserted.

Peter Adams for the Same Three Ounces too light –                                    6 : 8
John Knight for the Same Eight Ounces too light –                                    6 : 8

And Whereas the said Mayor hath sent to demand the said severall Fines of the said severall persons which they have refused to pay Now We whose Hands are hereunto set being the Mayor & Major part of the Aldermen of the said Burrough do hereby consent & agree that in Case any Action or Actions Bills Suits or Plaints shall be brought comenced or prosecuted by the said severall persons or any of them against the said Mayor the Serjeants at Mace of the said Burrough or any other person for or touching the levying collecting or receiving the said Fines or any of them That then the Costs & Expences in defending such Action or Actions Bills Suits or Plaints shall be born & paid out of the Rent Roll (commonly called the Chamberlains Roll) or other the Revenues & Income of this Corporation, Witness our Hands the 3ᵈ day of August 1736[1]

*Signed by:*

| | |
|---|---|
| Cornelius Colliss Mayor | Robᵗ Newnham |
| John Vining | John Mounsher |
| Henry Belfeild | Dan: Smith |
| L. Barton | Michael Atkins |
| Sam: Brady | Thomas Stanyford |

*Hand i.* Entered by (*signed by*) Geo Huish Town Clerk.

**40**

**3 August 1736**

*p. 43*

*Hand ii.* Burrough of Portesmouth

Whereas the Town Hall of this Burrough is now become so old & ruinous that there is an absolute Necessity of pulling down & rebuilding the Same, We the Mayor & Major Part of the Aldermen of the said Burrough whose Hands are hereunto set do agree to the following Resolutions.

1. That the Town Hall to be new erected shall be built on the same Land or Ground where the old one now stands according to such Draught Methods & Dimentions as We or the Major Part of the Aldermen (of which the Mayor for the time being to be one) shall agree.

2. That in Case Money sufficient shall not be raised by Subscription or Gift for the[2] building the said New Town Hall such ⌐Deficiency¬[3] shall be borrowed on Interest under the Common Seal of this Corporation,
Witness our Hands the Third day of August 1736.

*Signed by:*

| | |
|---|---|
| Cornelius Colliss Mayor | John Mounsher |
| John Vining | Dan: Smith |
| Henry Belfeild | Michael Atkins |
| L. Barton | Thomas Stanyford |
| Robᵗ Newnham | |

*Hand i.* Entered by (*signed by*) Geo Huish Town Clerk.

---

¹ P.C.R.O. CF20/1, p. 162, dated 17 Aug. 1736, names additional persons to be proceeded against:

Mr Joshua Taylor of London for the Arrears of several years Town Rent and Capon Money due for a Messuage on the Point within the said Burrough called the London late Oades's 15s per Annum and 2 Capons.

The Heirs of Mr John Mellish for the Tenement and Ground part of Chappell Close late the Magazine, 1s: 8d' per Annum.

For the Porch incroached in Penny Street late Freemans sometime Mounshers now built upon 4ᵈ' per Annum.

For the Cellar Window Porch and Pales there incroached since the premisses new built, 5s per Annum.

For a piece of Ground in St Nicholas's Street late Websters formerly Mullins's 6d' per Annum.

Mathew Phripp for part of the Incroachment on the Point at the North End of the House formerly called the Unicorn to the House late Nevills 9s: 6d' per Annum.

For a piece of Ground incroached into the Camber formerly Daniell Grovers and whereon is now built a Storehouse 1 li': 10s: od' per annum.

George Huish, as Attorney of Common Pleas, was ordered to bring actions against all these individuals. Mellish's heirs and several others on the list had relapsed into debt by 1740 (P.C.R.O. CF1/8).

² 'new' struck out.

³ MS. 'Defiency'.

**41**

**4 August 1736**

p. 44

*Hand i.* Burrough of Portesmouth

Wee whose hands are hereunto Sett being the Mayor & Major parte of the Aldermen of the Said Burrough Doe hereby Consent and agree That itt Shall be Left to the Care and Mannagement of M^r Daniell Smith and M^r Michaell Attkins (Two of the Aldermen of the Said Burrough) to Cause a proper plan, to be drawn, and an Estimate made for the Building a new Town Hall here, And when Such plan is drawn, and Estimate made, and Liked off by the Mayor and Major parte of the Aldermen of the Said Burrough, to waite on Thomas Lewis Esq^r and Admirall Cavendish our Representatives in Parliament for their Approbacion thereof Wittnes our hands the 4^th of August 1736.

*Signed by:*

| | |
|---|---|
| Cornelius Colliss Mayor | Rob^t Newnham |
| John Vining | John Mounsher |
| Henry Belfeild | Dan: Smith |
| L. Barton | Michael Atkins |
| Jn^o White. | Thomas Stanyford |
| Sam: Brady | |

Entered by (*signed by*) Geo Huish Town Clerk –

**42**

**16 August 1736**

p. 45

*Hand i.* Burrough of Portesmouth

Att an Assembly att the Towne Hall of the Said Burrough the Sixteenth day of August in the yeare 1736 ⌐Being then present⌐¹ the undermencioned Mayor and Aldermen of the Said Burrough M^r George Stanyford Son of Henry Stanyford Esq^r deceased, and Thomas Missing Esq^r Son of Thomas Missing Esq^r dec*eased* were Sworne Burgesses of the Said Burrough pursuant to their Eleccion on the Tenth day of Aprill One Thousand Seaven hundred and Twenty Eight, In witnes whereof the Said Mayor & Aldermen have hereunto Sett their hands.

*Signed by:*

| | |
|---|---|
| Cornelius Colliss Mayor | John Mounsher |
| Henry Belfeild | William Rickman |
| L. Barton | Dan: Smith |
| Jn^o White. | Thomas Stanyford |
| Rob^t Newnham | |

Entered by (*signed by*) Geo Huish Town Clerk

**43**

**21 September 1736**

p. 46

*Hand ii.* Burrough of Portesmouth.

At an Assembly at the Guildhall of the said Burrough the 21^st of September 1736. Present.

M^r Mayor
M^r Barton –
M^r White –
D^r Brady –
M^r Newnham – ⎫
M^r Mounsher – ⎬ Aldermen –
M^r Rickman – ⎭
M^r Atkins –
M^r Stanyford –

Leave was given by the said Mayor & Aldermen to William Rout² to erect a Sign Post before his Dwelling House called the Man in the Moon on the Parade in Portesmouth aforesaid and to continue the Same during their Pleasure, he paying yearly One Shilling to the Chamberlains Roll, to commence from the Feast of S^t Michaell the Archangell next ensuing. *Signed by* Geo Huish Town Clerk –

---

¹ Inserted; 'Before' struck out.
² Possibly the William Rout dismissed as Customs boatman at Portsmouth 1744 (*Cal. T.B. & P. 1742–5*, p. 654).

**44**
**1 June 1737**

*p. 47*

*Hand i.* Burrough of Portesmouth

Wee whose hands are hereunto Sett being the Deputy Mayor and Major parte of the Aldermen[1] of the Said Burrough, Doe hereby Nominate elect and Choose the R^t Hon^ble James Reynolds Esq^r Lord Cheife Baron of his Majesties Court of Exchequer to be a Burgess of the Said Burrough Wittnes our hands the first of June 1737.

*Signed by:*

| | |
|---|---|
| Cornelius Colliss D*eputy* Mayor | John Mounsher |
| Jn^o White. | Michael Atkins |
| Sam: Brady | Thomas Stanyford |
| Rob^t Newnham | |

The above Lord Cheife Baron was Immediatly Sworne Before the above named Deputy Mayor & Aldermen by (*signed by*) Geo Huish Town Clerk –

**45**
**[June or July 1737 ?]**

*p. 48*

*Hand ii.* Burrough of Portesmouth

Whereas the Town Hall of this Burrough is now become so old and ruinous that there is an absolute Necessity of pulling down and rebuilding the Same Now We the Mayor and Major Part of the Aldermen of the said Burrough whose hands are hereunto set do agree to the following Resolutions

1 That the Town Hall to be new erected shall be built according to the Dimensions Form and Method of the Draughts or Plans and Elevations made by M^r Thomas Bowerbank in that Place of the High Street of the said Burrough as is described and mentioned in the said Draughts or Plans and Elevations, to which We have subscribed our severall Names.

**46**
**5 July 1737**

*p. 49*

*Hand ii.* Burrough of Portesmouth

At the Guildhall of the said Burrough the Fifth day of July 1737 being present the undermentioned Mayor & Aldermen It was then and there ordered by them that for the Future all Counterparts of Town Leases and Admissions of Aldermen and Burgesses[2] shall be brought by the Town Clerk of the said Burrough into the Town Chest within Three Months next after the executing such Counterparts and the Admissions of such Aldermen and Burgesses, there to be kept among the Records of the said Burrough, Witnes their Hands.

*Signed by:*

| | |
|---|---|
| William Rickman Maijor | John Mounsher |
| John Vining | Cornelius Colliss |
| Jn^o White. | Michael Atkins |
| Sam: Brady | Thomas Stanyford |
| Rob^t Newnham | |

**47**
**16 August 1737**

*p. 50*

*Hand i.* Burrough of Portesmouth

Att an Assembly att the Towne Hall of the Said Burrough the 16. of August 1737 being then present the undermencioned Mayor and Aldermen M^r Thomas Barton who was duely nominated & Elected a Burgess of the Said Burrough on the 27. of December 1726, & M^r Henry Huish whoe was duely nominated and Elected a Burgess of the Said Burrough on the 27. of November 1732 were Sevrally Sworne Burgesses pursuant to their Severall Eleccions In witnes whereof the Said Mayor & Aldermen have hereunto Sett their hands.

*Signed by:*

| | |
|---|---|
| William Rickman Maijor | Rob^t Newnham |
| John Vining | John Mounsher |
| Henry Belfeild | Cornelius Colliss |
| L. Barton | Michael Atkins |
| Sam: Brady | Thomas Stanyford |
| Geo Huish Town Clerk – | |

---

[1] 'of the Aldermen', repeated, struck out.
[2] There is a cross in the left margin; cf. no. 1n.

**48**

**14 September 1737**

*Hand ii.* Burrough of Portesmouth.

We whose Hands[1] are hereunto set being the Mayor and Major Part of the Aldermen of the said Burrough do hereby nominate elect & choose the Right Reverend Father in God Benjamin Lord Bishop of Winchester to be a Burgess of the said Burrough, Witness our Hands the Fourteenth day of September 1737.

*Signed by:*

| | |
|---|---|
| William Rickman Maijor | John Mounsher |
| John Vining | Cornelius Colliss |
| L. Barton | Michael Atkins |
| Sam: Brady | Thomas Stanyford |
| Rob$^t$ Newnham | |

The above named Lord Bishop was immediately admitted a Burgess on his Honour in the Presence of the above Mayor & Aldermen at the House of Doctor Bliss within the said Burrough. by (*signed by*) Geo Huish Junior Dep*uty* Town Clerk

**49**

**4 October 1737**

*Hand i.* Burrough of Portesmouth

Wee the Mayor and Major parte of the Aldermen of the Said Burrough whose hands are hereunto Sett doe hereby agree to demise and Lett to James Littlefeild of Portesmouth aforesaid Carter by Lease under our Common Seale All the Wharfage Cranage and Petty Customes of this Corporacion for the Terme of ⌐One yeare¬[2] from the Feast of Saint Michaell Tharchangell ⌐Last past before¬[3] the date hereof att the yearley Rent of ⌐Forty pounds & Ten Shillings¬[4] and Two fatt Capons, and under the Same Covenants Provisoes and Agreements as are mencioned in the Lease by which the Said James Littlefeild now holds the premisses from us, which Lease ⌐did¬[5] Expire on the Said Feast of Saint Michaell Tharchangell wittnes our hands the 4$^{th}$ of October 1737.

*Signed by:*

| | |
|---|---|
| Michael Atkins Mayor | Rob$^t$ Newnham |
| John Vining | John Mounsher |
| L. Barton | William Rickman |
| Jn$^o$ White. | Thomas Stanyford |
| Sam: Brady | |

**50**

**22 February 1737/8**

*Hand i.* Burrough of Portesmouth

Whereas M$^r$ Hugh Grove Chamberlain of the Said Burrough hath this day passed his Account before us, and paid the Ballance thereof being One hundred and Thirty Six pounds into our hands, which wee doe hereby agree Shall be putt into the Towne Chest there to Remaine untill the Same Shall be otherwise disposed off by the Mayor and Major parte of the Aldermen of the Said Burrough for the time being. Dated the 22$^d$ of February 1737 –

*Signed by:*

| | |
|---|---|
| Michael Atkins Mayor | John Mounsher |
| John Vining | Cornelius Colliss |
| L. Barton | William Rickman |
| Sam: Brady | Thomas Stanyford |
| Rob$^t$ Newnham | |

**51**

**14 March 1737/8**[6]

*Hand ii.* Burrough of Portesmouth.

Whereas Admiral Stewart one of the present Representatives in Parliament for the said Burrough hath lately caused to be delivered into the Hands of the Mayor of the said Burrough the Sum of Two Hundred Pounds in Bank Notes for the Use

---

[1] 'and' struck out.

[2] Inserted in space left blank.

[3] Inserted; 'next ensueing' struck out.

[4] Inserted in space left blank.

[5] Inserted; 'will' struck out.

[6] Printed in East, p. 269.

of this Corporation We whose Hands are hereunto set do hereby consent & agree that the said Bank Notes (being Two in Number & each of the Value of One Hundred Pounds) shall be put into the Town Chest there to remain untill the Same shall be otherwise disposed of by the Mayor & Major Part of the Aldermen of the said Burrough for the time being, Witness our Hands the Fourteenth of March 1737.

*Signed by:*

| | |
|---|---|
| Michael Atkins Mayor | John Mounsher |
| John Vining | Cornelius Colliss |
| L. Barton | Thomas Stanyford |
| Sam: Brady | |

**52**

**30 March 1738**

*p. 55*

*Hand ii.* Burrough of Portesmouth

Whereas on the Twenty Eighth day of this instant March a Jury[1] was duely impannelled sworn & charged by the Coroner of the said Burrough & the Liberties thereof to enquire & present how & in what manner Thomas Sharp late Carpenter of his Majesties Ship the Berwick then lyeing dead on board the said Ship in his Majesties Dock Yard within the said Liberties to his Death came, And Whereas the said Coroner and Jury were obstructed & hinder'd by the Officer who then commanded on board the said Ship Berwick in going on board her to take an Inquisition on View of the Body of the said Thomas Sharp contrary to the[2] antient Usage and Custom of the said Burrough We whose Hands are hereunto set being the Mayor & greater part of the Aldermen of the said Burrough do hereby consent & agree that the said Coroner do proceed in the most proper manner against the person or persons for so obstructing & hindering the said Coroner & Jury in the Execution of their respective Duties, in order to defend & maintain the Rights Privileges & Jurisdiction of this Corporation at the Expence of the Corporation Witness our Hands the Thirtieth day of March 1738.[3]

*Signed by:*

| | |
|---|---|
| Michael Atkins Mayor | Sam: Brady |
| John Vining | Rob[t] Newnham |
| Thomas Stanyford | John Mounsher |
| L. Barton | Cornelius Colliss |
| Jn⁰ White. | |

**53**

**25 July 1738**

*p. 56*

*Hand i.* 25. July 1738 Burrough of Portesmouth

M[r] Thomas Blanckley the younger whoe was on the Second of September 1735 duely nominated and Elected a Burgess of the Said Burrough was this day Sworn into that Office by the Mayor and Major parte of the Aldermen of the Said Burrough whose names are under written, Wittnes their hands.

*Signed by:*

| | |
|---|---|
| Michael Atkins Mayor | Rob[t] Newnham |
| L. Barton | Cornelius Colliss |
| Sam: Brady | Thomas Stanyford |

Entered by (*signed by*) Geo Huish Town Clerk –

---

[1] P.C.R.O. L1 lists the jury.

[2] 'Us' struck out.

[3] P.C.R.O. CE1/13, p. 261, gives the sequel to this entry:

10th June 1738. Thursday last the Judges of the Court of Kings Bench, Westminster upon the Motion of Mr Strange Solicitor General, on the behalf of George Huish Gentleman Coroner of the Borough of Portsmouth, granted as Information against Captain Solgard, of the Berwick Man of War, for refusing the said Coroner to come on board the said Ship, when in Portesmouth Harbour, to take an Inquest on Thomas Sharp the Carpenter of the said Ship, who had hanged himself in his Cabbin, the Captain that it was within the Jurisdiction of the High Court of Admiralty. But it appeared that the Corps was afterwards interred privately without any Coroners Inquest sitting on the Body, and after hearing the Civillans and several Councel, the Court were of Opinion that it was a concurrent Jurisdiction, as the Ship was not upon the High Seas.

**54**

**25 July 1738**

*p. 57*

*Hand i.* Burrough of Portesmouth

Att an Assembly held att the Guild Hall of the Said Burrough the Twenty Fifth day of July 1738 being then present the Mayor and Major parte of the Aldermen of the Said Burrough whose names are hereunto Sett, itt was then and there ordered That the Sume of Forty pounds be paid out of the money now in the Towne Chest to George Huish Gent' Coroner of the Said Burrough towards the Carrying on a prosecucion in his Majesties Court of Kings Bench against Peter Solgard Esq$^r$ Comander of his Majesties Ship the Berwick for the obstructing and hindering the Said Coroner in the Execucion of his Said Office,[1] Wittnes their hands –

*Signed by:*

| | |
|---|---|
| Michael Atkins Mayor | Rob$^t$ Newnham |
| John Vining | Cornelius Colliss |
| L. Barton | William Rickman |
| Jn$^o$ White. | Thomas Stanyford |

**55**

**8 August 1738**

*p. 58*

*Hand i.* Burrough of Portesmouth

Att an Assembly held att the Guild Hall of the Said Burrough the Eighth day of August 1738 ⌐by¬[2] the Mayor and Aldermen of the Said Burrough whose hands are hereunto Sett, itt was then and there unanimously agreed That Thomas Stanyford Esq$^r$ one of the Aldermen of the said Burrough, Shall the first oppertunity he hath make Application to the Keeper of the Records in the Tower of London, in order to Search for Such[3] Charters or Evidences as any ways Relate to, or belong to the Said Burrough, and to take out Copys or Transcripts of Such of them, as he Shall thinke necessary, The Charges and Expenses of which Shall be paid out of the Towne Chest.[4] Wittnes their hands –

*Signed by:*

| | |
|---|---|
| Michael Atkins Mayor | Rob$^t$ Newnham |
| John Vining | Cornelius Colliss |
| L. Barton | William Rickman |
| Sam: Brady | |

**56**

**12 September 1738**

*p. 59*

*Hand i.* 12. September 1738. Burrough of Portesmouth

Then agreed by the undernamed Mayor & Aldermen of the Said Burrough whose hands are hereunto Sett to demise by Lease under the Common Seale of the Said Burrough to William Du Gard of Portesmouth aforesaid gent'[5] (in Consideracion of a Lease by him Surrendred into the hands of the Mayor Aldermen & Burgesses of the Said Burrough of parte of the Incroachment hereinafter mencioned to Edmund Ward dec*eased*) of All that Incroachment or Lands incroached to the now dwelling house of the Said William Du Gard Scituate on the South Side of the High Street in Portesmouth aforesaid containing in Length ⌐Twenty Four foot¬[6] and in breadth att each end ⌐Four foot & Two inches¬[7] upon parte whereof is already erected a Sellar Window in Length Six foot and in breadth Four foot, and a building of Fifteene foot in Length and Two foot Four inches broad adjoining to the Said dwelling house, And the Said Additionall Encroachment is only for the erecting pales before the Front of the Said house, and for noe other building or Ediffice whatsoever To

---

[1] The case is cited in *F.R.M.C.C.*, ii, pp. 809–10. Solgard was captain of the Royal Oak in 1732 (P.R.O. Adm.110/11, p. 74); voted Whig 1734, when he was described as of Alverstoke (*Poll for Hants.*, *1734*, p. 113); died 24 Oct. 1739 (*Gent. Mag.*, ix (1739), p. 106). The Berwick was a third-rate vessel, built in 1679 and broken up in 1742 (T. D. Manning and C. F. Walker, *British warship names* (1959), p. 105).

[2] Inserted (hand ii); 'Before' struck out.

[3] 'Records' struck out.

[4] The Chamberlain was authorised to pay Stanyford £2. 8s. for expenses incurred in visiting the Tower (P.C.R.O. CF2/2, no. 1: 20 Feb. 1738/9).

[5] Paid rates on property in Portsmouth (P.C.R.O. 81A/3/20/3, no. 4: 7 Aug. 1732); voted Tory 1734 (*Poll for Hants.*, *1734*, p. 129); served as a Portsmouth and Sheet Turnpike Commissioner under the 1742 Act (*Turnpike Minute Book*, p. 177); died 1742 or 1743 (ibid., pp. 121, 126).

[6] Inserted in space left blank.

[7] Inserted in space left blank; altered from 'Four foot & one halfe'.

have and to hold the Said Incroachment with the Building and Sellar window thereon erected unto the Said William Du Gard his Executors Administrators and assignes from the Twenty ninth day of this instant September for the Terme of One Thousand yeares, att and under the yearley Rent of Three Shillings, with a Clause of Reentry and Covenants as usuall In Witnes whereof the Said Mayor & Aldermen have hereunto Sett their hands the day and yeare above written[1] –

*Signed by:*

| | |
|---|---|
| Michael Atkins Mayor | John Mounsher |
| John Vining | Cornelius Colliss |
| Sam: Brady | Thomas Stanyford |
| Rob[t] Newnham | |

**57**

**29 September 1738**  *p. 60*

*Hand i.* Burrough of Portesmouth

The Mayor and Major parte of the Aldermen of the Said Burrough whose hands are hereunto Sett, Doe hereby Nominate elect and Choose M[r] ⌐William⌐[2] Attkins the[3] Son of Michaell Attkins Esq[r] the present Mayor, to be a Burgess of the Said Burrough (as the *p*eremtory Burgess of him the Said Mayor) Wittnes their hands the Twenty ninth day of September 1738 –

*Signed by:*

| | |
|---|---|
| Michael Atkins Mayor | John Mounsher |
| John Vining | Cornelius Colliss |
| L. Barton | William Rickman |
| Sam: Brady | Thomas Stanyford |
| Geo Huish *Town* Clerk | |

**58**

**29 September 1738**  *p. 61*[4]

*Hand i.* Burrough of Portesmouth.

Wee the Mayor & Major parte of the Aldermen of the Said Burrough whose hands are hereunto Sett ⌐do⌐[5] hereby agree to demise and Lett to William Mathews of Portesmouth aforesaid Labourer[6] by Lease under our Comon Seale All the Wharfage Cranage and Petty Customs of this Corporacion for the Terme of Three yeares from the date hereof att the yearley Rent of Forty pounds and Ten Shillings to be paid att Two equall halfe yearly payments and Two fatt Capons, and under the Same Covenants provisoes and Agreements as are mencioned in the Lease made to James Littlefeild which this day Expires[7] And that the Said William Mathews Shall procure William Pope of Portesmouth aforesaid Carter to become Bound in a Bond for the performance of the Covenants in Such Lease to be granted to the Said William Mathews on his parte to be paid and performed Wittnes our hands the 29. of September 1738.[8]

*Signed by:*

| | |
|---|---|
| John Vining Mayor | Cornelius Colliss |
| L. Barton | William Rickman |
| Sam: Brady | Michael Atkins |
| John Mounsher | Thomas Stanyford |

I doe hereby agree to accept of a Lease according to the above Agreement, and to Execute a Counterparte thereof, and to procure the above named W[m] Pope to become bound with me for performance of Covenants in the Said Lease. the marke of + W[m] Mathews Wittnes (*signed by*) Geo Huish

---

[1] P.C.R.O. CF20/1, p. 191, dates this lease 19 Sept. 1738. In 1747, although a new lease had been granted to Du Gard's heirs, the rent of 3*s.* was outstanding (P.C.R.O. CF1/8).

[2] Written over 'Michaell' erased.

[3] 'younger(?)' struck out.

[4] For a reproduction of this page see fig. 4.

[5] MS 'to'.

[6] Also described as husbandman (no. 87); paid rates on property in Crown Street (P.C.R.O. 81A/3/20/20, no. 16: 28 Apr. 1750).

[7] See no. 49.

[8] P.C.R.O. CF20/1, p. 191, dates this lease 3 Oct. 1738.

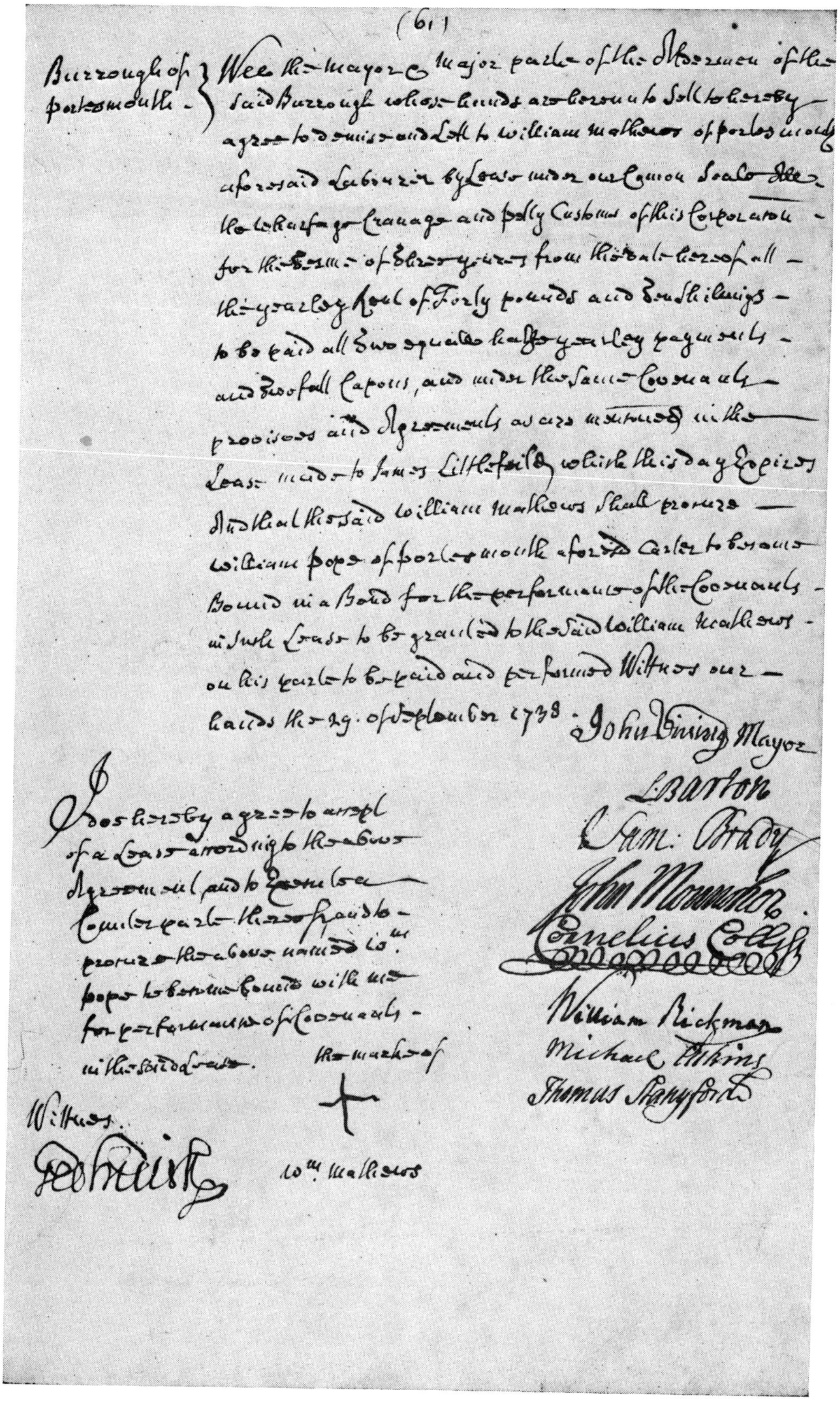

(61)

Burrough of Portsmouth }  Wee the Mayor & Major parte of the Aldermen of the
said Burrough whose names are hereunto sett doe hereby
agree to demise and lett to William Mathews of Portsmouth
aforesaid Labourer by Lease under our Common Seale all
the Wharfage Cranage and petty Customs of this Corporation
for the terme of three yeares from the date hereof all
the yearely Rent of Forty pounds and Ten shillings
to be paid att two equall halfe yearly payments
and two fatt Capons, and under the same Covenants
provisoes and Agreements as are mentioned in the
Lease made to James Littlefield which this day Expires
And that the said William Mathews shall procure
William Pope of Portsmouth aforesaid Carter to become
Bound in a Bond for the performance of the Covenants
in such Lease to be granted to the said William Mathews
on his parte to be paid and performed Witnes our
hands the 29 of September 1738 - John Vivian Mayor

L Barton
Sam: Brady
John Mounsher
Cornelius Colliss
William Rickman
Michael Atkins
Thomas Sharysford

I doe hereby agree to accept
of a Lease according to the above
Agreement and to ........
Counterpart thereof and to
procure the above named Wm
Pope to become Bound with me
for performance of Covenants
in the said Lease.    the marke of

                              ✝

Witnes.                    Wm Mathews

*Fig 4*  MEETING OF 29 SEPTEMBER 1738 (no. 58). CE6/1, p. 61

25

**59**

**4 January 1738/9**

*p. 62 blank; p. 63*

*Hand ii.* Burrough of Portesmouth.

Whereas on the Third day of August which was in the Year 1736 an Order was made & signed by the then Mayor & Major Part of the Aldermen of the said Burrough relating to the building of a new Town Hall, whereby they did agree that the said Town Hall so to be erected should be built on the same Land or Ground where the old one now stands according to such Draught Methods & Dimentions as they or the Major part of them (of which the Mayor for the time being to be one) should agree, And that ⌐in⌐¹ Case Money sufficient should not be raised by Subscription or Gift for the building the said new Town Hall such Deficiency should be borrowed on Interest under the Common Seal of the Corporation Now We the Mayor & Major part of the Aldermen of the said Burrough whose Hands are hereunto set do hereby confirm the said Order & the severall Resolutions therein contained Provided the Sum so to be borrowed doth not exceed the Sum of Seven Hundred Pounds, any Thing in the said recited Order² contained to the Contrary notwithstanding Witness our Hands the Fourth day of January 1738.³

*Signed by:*

| | |
|---|---|
| John Vining Mayor | John Mounsher |
| L. Barton | Cornelius Colliss |
| Jnᵒ White. | William Rickman |
| Sam: Brady | Thomas Stanyford |

**60**

**16 January 1738/9**

*p. 64*

*Hand i.* Burrough of Portesmouth

Wee the Mayor & Major parte of the Aldermen of the said Burrough whose hands are hereunto Sett, Doe hereby agree that the Chamberlain of the Said Burrough Shall from Michaelmas Last past pay to the Turnkey of this Garrison one Guinea every Three months in Consideracion of his keeping open the Key and Poynt Gates beyond the usuall time⁴ Wittnes our hands the 16. of January 1738.

*Signed by:*

| | |
|---|---|
| John Vining Mayor | Cornelius Colliss |
| L. Barton | Michael Atkins |
| John Mounsher | Thomas Stanyford |

**61**

**26 June 1739⁵**

*Hand i.* 26. June 1739 Burrough of Portesmouth

Orderd by Mʳ Mayor, Mʳ White, Dʳ Brady, Mʳ Mounsher, Mʳ Colliss & Mʳ Attkins that in Consideracion the Turnkey of this Garrison doe keep open the Key Gate & Mill Gate to Eleven of the Clock in the Summer and Ten in the Winter, and the Poynt Gate till Eleven of the Clock in the Evening all the yeare, the Chamberlaine Shall pay him a Guinea a Quarter, but not otherwise.⁶ *Signed by* G Huish T*own* Clerk.

---

¹ Inserted.

² 'to the' struck out.

³ The Chamberlain was ordered to pay George Huish £1. 16s. 6d. 'being the halfe of the Expences for drawing and Engrossing the Articles for erecting a new Towne Hall here' (P.C.R.O. CF2/2, no. 2: 6 Mar. 1738/9). P.C.R.O. CE1/13, p. 266, adds this to the subject under the date 22 Feb. 1738/9: 'This Day the old Guildhall of Portesmouth which had been standing about Two Hundred Years as supposed, was begun to be pulled down in order to the building of a new one in the same Place, and all the Courts were adjourn'd to the Great Hall at Godshouse commonly called the Governours House' till the same is finished.' And also, under the date 14 Mar. 1738/9: 'This Day the first Stone of the Foundation of the new Town Hall was laid in the Presence of the Mayor & severall of the Aldermen, and afterwards between the Plinth and the first Rustick at the North East Corner of the Building was put a Copper Plate with the following Letters & Figures cut thereon viz: Inᵒ VINING. MAYOR. 1739.' For the financial hazards attached to having a guildhall rebuilt cf. R. Howell, *Newcastle upon Tyne and the puritan revolution* (1967), pp. 296–7.

⁴ A similar practice prevailed at Berwick-upon-Tweed until the early nineteenth century 'to the great annoyance not only of the inhabitants within the gates but also of those in the suburbs' (Webb, ii, p. 506n, quoting J. Fuller, *The history of Berwick upon Tweed* (1799), p. 582).

⁵ Printed in East, p. 270.

⁶ P.C.R.O. CF1/8 records payments of this sum.

26

**62**

**19 May 1739**

*Hand ii.* Burrough of Portesmouth

Whereas by a Confirmation of an Order (dated the Third day of August 1736) signed by the Mayor & Major Part of the Aldermen of the said Burrough & dated the Fourth day of January last it was[1] agreed that a Sum of Money should be raised ⌐or borrowed at Interest under the Common Seal of this Corporation⌐[2] for building a new Town Hall within the said Burrough, provided the said Sum did not exceed[3] Seven Hundred Pounds Now We whose Hands are hereunto set being the Mayor & Major Part of the Aldermen of the said Burrough do hereby agree that the Sum of Seven Hundred Pounds shall be forthwith borrowed of Paul Green of Fareham in the County of South'ton Malster,[4] For Security of which he shall have Two Bonds, each for the Sum of Three Hundred & Fifty Pounds, under the Common Seal of this Corporation payable with Interest for the Same at the Rate of Four Pounds in the Hundred by the Year ⌐which Interest shall be paid yearly by the Chamberlain of the said Burrough as the Same shall become due⌐[5] Witness our Hands the Nineteenth day of May 1739.

*Signed by:*

| | |
|---|---|
| John Vining Mayor | Sam: Brady |
| L. Barton | John Mounsher |
| Jn⁰ White. | Cornelius Colliss |

**63**

**29 May 1739**

*Hand i.* 29. May 1739. Burrough of Portesmouth

Mr John Mounsher Son of John Mounsher Esqʳ late Mayor whoe was Nominated and Elected a Burgess of the Said Burrough on the Twenty Seaventh of November 1732 was this day Sworne a Burgess pursuant to the Said Eleccion in the presence of the Mayor and Major parte of the Aldermen of the Said Burrough, whose hands are hereunto Sett –

*Signed by:*

| | |
|---|---|
| John Vining Mayor | John Mounsher |
| L. Barton | Cornelius Colliss |
| Sam: Brady | Michael Atkins[6] |
| Jn⁰ White. | |

Wittnes. *Signed by* Geo Huish

**64**

**19 July 1739**

*Hand ii.* Burrough of Portesmouth

We whose Hands are hereunto set being the Mayor & Major Part of the Aldermen of the said Burrough do hereby nominate elect & choose the Honᵇˡᵉ Edward Vernon Esqʳ Vice Admiral of the Blue Squadron of his Majesties Fleet to be a Burgess of the said Burrough Witness our Hands the Nineteenth day of July 1739.[7]

*Signed by:*

| | |
|---|---|
| John Vining Mayor | Cornelius Colliss |
| Jn⁰ White. | Michael Atkins |
| Sam: Brady | Thomas Stanyford |
| John Mounsher | |

*Hand i.* The Oath of a Burgess was Immediatly adminstred to the above named Admirall Vernon in the presence of the above Mayor and Aldermen By *(signed by)* Geo Huish Town Clerk.

---

[1] 'provided &' struck out.
[2] Inserted.
[3] 'the sum of' struck out.
[4] 'in(?)' struck out.
[5] Inserted.
[6] Followed by 'Jo', apparently the beginning of a second signature of John Mounsher.
[7] The Corporation feast to celebrate Vernon's election cost £14. 17s. 7d. (P.C.R.O. CF2/2, no. 12: 21 Feb. 1740/1). Vernon returned the compliment by presenting the Corporation with 'The Flag of Don Blas De Lesso the Spanish Admiral' (P.C.R.O. CE3/17: inventory of plate, etc., 29 Sept. 1742).

**65**

**25 July 1739**

p. 68 blank; p. 69

*Hand i.* 25. July 1739. Burrough of Portesmouth

His Royall Highness William Duke of Cumberland was Elected ⌐and admitted⌐[1] a Burgess of the Said Burrough by the Mayor and Aldermen whose hands are hereunto Sett

*Signed by:*

| | |
|---|---|
| John Vining Mayor | Cornelius Colliss |
| Jnº White. | Michael Atkins |
| Sam: Brady | Thomas Stanyford |
| John Mounsher | |

His Royall Highness was by the above Mayor and Aldermen ordered to be Enrolled as a Burgess among the Records of the Said Burrough By (*signed by*) Geo Huish Town Clerk[2] –

**66**

**22 August 1739**

p. 70

*Hand ii.* Burrough of Portesmouth.

We whose Hands[3] are hereunto set ⌐being⌐[4] the Mayor & Major Part of the Aldermen of the said Burrough do hereby nominate elect & choose the Right Honourable Philip Lord Hardwicke ⌐Baron of Hardwicke in the County of Glocester,⌐[5] Lord High Chancellor of Great Britain, to be a Burgess of the said Burrough, Witness our Hands the Twenty Second day of August 1739

*Signed by:*

| | |
|---|---|
| John Vining Mayor | Cornelius Colliss |
| Jnº White. | Michael Atkins |
| Sam: Brady | Thomas Stanyford |
| John Mounsher | |

His Lordship was admitted a Burgess on his Honour at the Kings Arms Inn[6] within the said Burrough in the Presence of the above Mayor & Aldermen (Except Mr White), and the Exemplification of his Lordships Freedom (on a double Five Shilling Stamp) was presented to him by (*signed by*) Geo Huish Town Clerk.[7]

**67**

**29 September 1739**

p. 71

*Hand ii.* Burrough of Portesmouth. 29ᵗʰ September 1739 at ⌐the Guildhall⌐[8] being present

John Vining Esqʳ Mayor
John White Gent' Mayor Elect
Samˡˡ Brady M: D:
John Mounsher Esqʳ – ⎫
Cornelius Colliss Gent' ⎬ Aldermen
Michˡˡ Atkins Gent' – ⎪
Thoˢ Stanyford Esqʳ – ⎭

Mr Edward Barton Junior was sworn a Burgess of the said Burrough pursuant to his Election on the Twenty Seventh day of November 1732. by (*signed by*) Geo Huish Town Clerk.

---

[1] Inserted.

[2] P.C.R.O. CE1/13, p. 267, adds: 'The Exemplification of his Royal Highness's Freedom (on a double Five Shilling Stamp) was sent to Sir Charles Wager to present to him, his Royal Highness's Stay here being too short for the Mayor to present it to him himself'.

[3] '& S' struck out.

[4] Inserted.

[5] Inserted.

[6] See no. 12n.

[7] P.C.R.O. CE1/13, p. 267, adds 'Yᵉ same 22ᵈ August 1739'. The Hon. Joseph Yorke, Hardwicke's son, attended the ceremony and gave his sister an account of it in a letter dated 31 Aug. 1739; the Yorkes stayed at Dr Brady's house and during their visit found time to walk the fortifications, view the Dockyard and inspect the Royal Academy (P. C. Yorke, *The life and correspondence of Philip Yorke, Earl of Hardwicke, Lord High Chancellor of Great Britain* (3v., 1913), i, p. 226).

[8] Inserted; 'Godshouse' struck out. P.C.R.O. CE1/13, p. 271, notes that the election of the Mayor and other officers on 17 Sept. 1739 had taken place in the new Guildhall and that on 18 Sept. 'the Sessions of the Peace and Court of Record were for the first Time held therein'.

**68**

**11 September 1739**  *Hand i.* Burrough of Portesmouth

                          *p. 72*

Wee the Mayor and Major parte of the Aldermen of the Said Burrough whose hands are hereunto Sett Doe hereby agree, that there Shall be paid to M^r William Binsteed the Sume of Ten pounds and Ten Shillings for the Additionall Stoco worke, in the Ceiling of the New Towne Hall over and above what is mencioned to be paid him in the Articles of Agreement made between him and us, Wittnes our hands the 11^th of September 1739.[1]

*Signed by:*

| | |
|---|---|
| John Vining Mayor | John Mounsher |
| L. Barton | Cornelius Colliss |
| Jn⁰ White. | Thomas Stanyford |
| Sam: Brady | |

**69**

**29 September 1739**  *Hand ii.* Borough of Portesmouth.[2]

                          *p. 73*

We whose Hands are hereunto set being the Mayor & Major Part of the Aldermen of the said Borough do hereby elect & choose M^r Benjamin Heron the Grandson of John Vining Esq^r the present Mayor to be a Burgess of the said Burrough, the said Benjamin Heron being nominated by the said Mayor to be his Peremptory Burgess, Witness our Hands the 29^th day of September 1739.

*Signed by:*

| | |
|---|---|
| John Vining Mayor | Cornelius Colliss |
| Jn⁰ White. | Michael Atkins |
| Sam: Brady | Thomas Stanyford |
| John Mounsher | |
| Geo Huish Town Clerk. | |

**70**

**11 December 1739**  *Hand ii.* Burrough of Portesmouth

                          *p. 74*

At the Guildhall of the said Burrough the Eleventh day of December 1739 Present

John White Esq^r Mayor

| | |
|---|---|
| John Vining Esq^r – | |
| Lewis Barton Esq^r – | |
| Sam. Brady M.D. – | |
| John Mounsher Esq^r – | } Aldermen |
| Cornelius Colliss Gent' – | |
| Tho^s Stanyford Esq^r – | |

M^r Matteate Brady Son of the said Doctor Samuell Brady was sworn a Burgess of the said Burrough pursuant to his Election on the Tenth day of Aprill 1728. by (*signed by*) Geo Huish Junior Deputy Town Clerk

**71**

**20 December 1739**  *Hand ii.* Burrough of Portesmouth

                          *p. 75*

We whose Hands are hereunto set being the Mayor & Major Part of the Aldermen of the said Burrough do hereby order & direct that there shall be paid to M^r John Turner[3] the Sum of Thirty Guineas out of the Money in the Town Chest, as a Gratuity for his Care & Trouble in surveying & directing the Work of the New Town Hall, Witness our Hands the 20^th of December 1739.

*Signed by:*

| | |
|---|---|
| Jn⁰ White Mayor | Sam: Brady |
| John Vining | John Mounsher |
| L. Barton | Cornelius Colliss |

---

[1] Binsteed was paid £265 on 19 May 1739 (P.C.R.O. CF2/2, no. 3) and £52.0s.6d. between Nov. 1739 and Oct. 1744 (P.C.R.O. CF1/8).

[2] '29th September 1739 at the Guildhall present John Vining Esq^r Mayor John White Gent' ' struck out.

[3] Described as master house-carpenter of His Majesty's Dockyard 1730 (P.C.R.O. S2/24); voted Whig 1734 (*Poll for Hants.*, *1734*, p. 130).

**72**

**4 March 1739/40**

*p. 76*

*Hand i.* Burrough of Portesmouth

    *Hand ii.* We whose Hands are hereunto set being the Mayor & Major Part of the Aldermen of the said Burrough do hereby empower[1] & authorize M^r John Turner of Portsmouth aforesaid to contract & agree for Six whole Vases & Two half Ones to be set over the Pilasters of the Portico of the New Town Hall, And We agree that the Expence of the said Vases with the Charge of setting them up shall be paid out of the Money belonging to this Corporation, Witness our Hands the Fourth of March 1739.[2]

*Signed by:*

| | |
|---|---|
| Jn^o White Mayor | Sam: Brady |
| John Vining | John Mounsher |
| L. Barton | Cornelius Colliss |

**73**

**11 March 1739/40**

*p. 77*

*Hand i.* Burrough of Portesmouth

    Wee the Mayor & Major parte of the Aldermen of the Said Burrough whose hands are hereunto Sett Considering the Long illness of Samuell Beven one of our Serjants att Mace, which hath hindred him from makeing any profitt or advantage of his Office, Doe in Consideracion thereof think fitt to allow the Said Samuell Beven Four Guineas out of the Chamberlains Roll, and doe hereby order and direct M^r Hugh Grove the Chamberlaine to pay the Same accordingly Wittnes our hands the Eleventh day of March 1739 –

*Signed by:*

| | |
|---|---|
| Jn^o White Mayor | Cornelius Colliss |
| John Vining | Michael Atkins |
| L. Barton | Thomas Stanyford |

**74**

**5 August 1740**

*p. 78*

*Hand ii.* Burrough of Portesmouth –

    We whose Hands are hereunto set being the Mayor & Major Part of the Aldermen of the said Burrough do hereby nominate elect & choose Francis Gashry Esq^r & M^r Henry Shales to be Burgesses of the said Burrough, Witness our Hands the Fifth day of August 1740.

*Signed by:*

| | |
|---|---|
| Jn^o White Mayor | Cornelius Colliss |
| John Vining | William Rickman |
| Sam: Brady | Michael Atkins |
| John Mounsher | Thomas Stanyford |

    The said M^r Henry Shales was immediately sworn a Burgess before the above Mayor & M^r Vining D^r Brady M^r Rickman M^r Atkins & M^r Stanyford by (*signed by*) Geo Huish Town Clerk.

**75**

**21 August 1740**[3]

*p. 79*

*Hand ii.* Burrough of Portesmouth

    Whereas Charles Stewart Esq^r hath lately by M^r Neale his Secretary[4] paid into the Hands of John White Esq^r Mayor the Sum of One Hundred Pounds as a Present to this Corporation Now We the Mayor & Major Part of the Aldermen of the said Burrough whose Hands are hereunto set do hereby order & direct that the said One Hundred Pounds shall be paid in Discharge of the Debts of this Corporation, that is

---

[1] 'to contract' struck out.

[2] P.C.R.O. CF1/8 records this additional payment on 26 Mar. 1740.

[3] Printed in East, p. 270.

[4] Thomas Neale combined the posts of secretary to Adm. Stewart and purser to the Lion (N.M.M. POR/F/5: letter from Commissioner Hughes to the Admiralty Board, 2 Mar. 1732/3).

to say Fifty Pounds part thereof to D<sup>r</sup> Samuell Brady in part of the Principal Sum of Three[1] Hundred & Fifty Pounds due on a Bond from this Corporation to M<sup>r</sup> Paul Green in Trust for the said D<sup>r</sup> Brady dated the 30<sup>th</sup> day of June 1739,[2] and the remaining Fifty Pounds to M<sup>r</sup> Cornelius Colliss in part of the Principal Sum of Three Hundred & Fifty Pounds due on another Bond from this Corporation to the said Paul Green in Trust for the said M<sup>r</sup> Colliss dated the 11<sup>th</sup> day of September 1739, Witness our Hands the Twenty First day of August 1740 –

*Signed by:*

| | |
|---|---|
| Jn<sup>o</sup> White Mayor. | Cornelius Colliss |
| Sam: Brady | Michael Atkins |
| John Mounsher | Thomas Stanyford |

**76**

**15 September 1740**   *Hand ii.* Burrough of Portesmouth.

We whose Hands are hereunto set being the Mayor & Major Part of the Aldermen of the said Burrough do hereby nominate elect & choose the Hon<sup>ble</sup> Sir Chaloner Ogle Kn<sup>t</sup> Rear Admiral of the Blue Squadron of his Majesties Fleet, to be a Burgess of the said Burrough Witness our Hands the Fifteenth day of September 1740 –

*p. 80*

*Signed by:*

| | |
|---|---|
| Jn<sup>o</sup> White Mayor | Cornelius Colliss |
| John Vining | Michael Atkins |
| L. Barton | Thomas Stanyford |
| Sam: Brady | |

The above named Sir Chaloner Ogle was immediately sworn a Burgess before the above Mayor & Aldermen by (*signed by*) Geo Huish Town Clerk –

**77**

**29 September 1740**   *Hand ii.* Burrough of Portesmouth.

We the Mayor & Major Part of the Aldermen of the said Burrough whose Hands are hereunto set do hereby nominate elect & choose William Ballard the Younger, Gent', to be a Burgess of the said Burrough, (he being nominated by the said Mayor to be his Peremptory Burgess) Witness our Hands the 29<sup>th</sup> of September 1740 –

*p. 81*

*Signed by:*

| | |
|---|---|
| Jn<sup>o</sup> White Mayor | William Rickman |
| L. Barton | Michael Atkins |
| Sam: Brady | Thomas Stanyford |
| Cornelius Colliss | |

The said William Ballard was immediately sworn a Burgess in the Presence of the said Mayor & Aldermen by (*signed by*) Geo Huish Town Clerke –

**78**

**11 October 1740**   *Hand i.* Burrough of Portsmouth

Wee whose hands are hereunto Sett being the Mayor and Major parte of the Aldermen of the Said Burrough doe hereby Nominate elect and Choose John Philipson Esq<sup>r</sup> one of the Commissioners of his Majesties Navy to be a Burgess of the Said Burrough, Wittnes our hands the 11<sup>th</sup> of October 1740 –

*p. 82*

*Signed by:*

| | |
|---|---|
| Sam: Brady Mayor | Cornelius Colliss |
| John Vining | Michael Atkins |
| L. Barton | Thomas Stanyford |
| John Mounsher | |

The Said Commissioner Philipson was Immediatly Sworne a Burgess in the presence of the above Mayor & Aldermen M<sup>r</sup> Attkins only Excepted By (*signed by*) Geo Huish Town Clerke.

---

[1] 'Pounds' struck out.
[2] Following Brady's death the Chamberlain was ordered to pay his widow the £150 due on this bond; with interest the total was £156. 15*s*. (P.C.R.O. CF2/2, no. 29: 25 Dec. 1740).

**79**

**22 October 1740**

p. 83

*Hand i.* Burrough of Portesmouth

Wee whose hands are hereunto Sett being the Mayor and Major parte of the Aldermen of the Said Burrough Doe hereby Nominate elect and Choose the Hon^ble Lieu^t Generall Phillip Honywood ⌐Governour⌐[1] of his Majesties Garrison of Portesmouth to be a Burgess of the Said Burrough Wittnes our hands the 22^d of October 1740 –

*Signed by:*

| | |
|---|---|
| Sam: Brady Mayor | John Mounsher |
| John Vining | Cornelius Colliss |
| L. Barton | Michael Atkins |

The Said Lieu^t Generall Honywood was Immediatly Sworne a Burgess in the presence of the above Mayor and Aldermen By (*signed by*) Geo Huish Town Clerk –

**80**

**7 April 1741**

p. 84

*Hand i.* 7^th Aprill 1741. Burrough of Portesmouth

Then agreed by the under named Mayor, and Major parte of the Aldermen of the Said Burrough, whose hands are hereunto Sett to demise by Lease in writeing under their Common Seale to Gregory Carlos of Portesmouth aforesaid Surgeon[2] All that Encroachment or Land Encroached to the now dwelling house of the Said Gregory Carlos Scituate on the South Side of the High Streete in Portesmouth aforesaid containing in Length Five foot and Ten Inches, and in breadth att each end Four foot whereon is to be erected and placed a ⌐Flat⌐[3] Sellar Window, and noe other Ediffice or building whatsoever To hold to the Said Gregory Carlos his Executors Administrators and assignes from the Twenty Fifth day of March Last past for the Terme of One Thousand yeares, att and under the yearley Rent of Three Shillings and Six pence allways on the Feast of the Annunciacion of the Blessed Virgin Mary, with a Clause of Reentry and all other usuall Covenants, In Witnes whereof the Said Mayor and Aldermen have hereunto Sett their hands the day and yeare first above written[4]–

*Signed by:*

| | |
|---|---|
| Sam: Brady Mayor | John Mounsher |
| John Vining | Cornelius Colliss |
| L. Barton | Michael Atkins |
| Jn^o White. | |

**81**

**4 May 1741**

p. 85

*Hand ii.* Burrough of Portesmouth.

We the Mayor & Major Part of the Aldermen of the said Burrough whose Hands are hereunto set do hereby nominate elect & choose the Hon^ble Martin Bladen Esq^r one of the Commissioners for Trade & Plantations to be a Burgess of the said Burrough, Witness our Hands the Fourth day of May 1741.

*Signed by:*

| | |
|---|---|
| Sam: Brady Mayor | John Mounsher |
| John Vining | Cornelius Colliss |
| L. Barton | Michael Atkins |
| Jn^o White. | |

*Hand i.* ⌐The said Martin Bladen Esq^r⌐[5] was Immediatly Sworne before the Said Mayor & Aldermen by (*signed by*) Geo Huish Town Clerk[6] –

---

[1] Inserted; 'Governor' struck out.

[2] A testimonial for Carlos, dated 26 Aug. 1735, states that he was educated under Robert Heart, another Portsmouth physician and surgeon (A. J. Willis, *Laymen's licences in the diocese of Winchester 1675–1834* (*A Hampshire Miscellany*, pt 3; 1964), p. 94); he was admitted as a Burgess 15 Sept. 1751, described as 'Surgeon, Haslar Hospital' (East, p. 383).

[3] Inserted.

[4] P.C.R.O. CF20/1, p. 192, dates this lease 17 Apr. 1741 and states that the rent was 'payable at Michaelmas and Lady day by equal portions'.

[5] Inserted (hand ii); 'And' struck out.

[6] P.C.R.O. CE1/14, pp. 8–9, dates his swearing in 6 May 1741, when he was also elected Member of Parliament for Portsmouth. In the contested election the votes cast were Adm. Cavendish 60, Bladen 54, Adm. Vernon 9; Vernon's supporters, who all gave their second votes to Cavendish, were John Monday, John Hunt, Geo. Huish junior, Jos. Taylor, John Vining-Reade, Tho. Maidlow, Hugh Grove, Wil. Du Gard and Cha. Reade (P.C.R.O. PE2/5C).

**82**

**1 September 1741**

*p. 86*

*Hand ii.* Burrough of Portesmouth.

At the Guildhall of the said Burrough the First day of September 1741. Present
Samuell Brady M.D. Mayor

Lewis Barton Esq^r –
John Mounsher Esq^r –
Cornelius Colliss Gent' – ⎫ Aldermen
Michaell Atkins Gent' ⎬
Thomas Stanyford Esq^r – ⎭

M^r William Atkins, who on the Twenty Ninth day of September ⌐1738⌐¹ was elected the Peremptory Burgess of the said Alderman Atkins ⌐his Father (then Mayor)⌐² was duly sworn a Burgess of the said Burrough by (*signed by*) Geo Huish Town Clerk –

**83**

**23 September 1741**

*p. 87*

*Hand ii.* Burrough of Portesmouth.

We the Mayor & Major Part of the Aldermen of the said Burrough whose Hands are hereunto set do hereby agree to demise & let to Robert Longcroft of Portesmouth aforesaid Merchant³ by Lease under our Common Seal All the Wharfage Cranage & Petty Customs of this Corporation for the Term of Eleven Years from Michaelmas next ensuing the Date hereof at the yearly Rent of Ninety Six Pounds to be paid at Two equal half yearly ⌐Payments⌐⁴ and Two fat Capons, & under the same Covenants Provisoes & Agreements as are mentioned in the Lease made to William Mathews which expires at the said Michaelmas, Provided the said Robert Longcroft doth procure William Bartlett of Portesmouth aforesaid Brazier⁵ to become bound in a Bond with the said Robert Longcroft for the Performance of the Covenants in such Lease to be granted to the said Robert on his part to be paid done & performed Witness our Hands the Twenty Third day of September 1741.

*Signed by :*

Sam: Brady Mayor            John Mounsher
John Vining                 Cornelius Colliss
L. Barton                   Michael Atkins
Jn^o White                  Thomas Stanyford

I do hereby agree to accept of a Lease according to the above Agreement & to execute a Counterpart thereof, & also to procure the above named William Bartlett to become bound with me in a Bond ⌐in the Penalty of Five Hundred Pounds⌐⁶ for the Performance of the Covenants in the said Lease (*signed by*) Rob^t Longcroft Witness (*signed by*) Geo Huish

**84**

**29 September 1741**

*p. 88*

*Hand ii.* Burrough of Portesmouth.

We whose Hands are hereunto set being the Mayor & Major Part of the Aldermen of the said Burrough do hereby⁷ elect & choose ⌐M^r Philip Brady Son of Doctor Brady (the present Mayor)⌐⁸ to be a Burgess of the said Burrough (he being named by the said Mayor to be his Peremptory Burgess) Witness our Hands the Twenty Ninth day of September 1741 –

*Signed by :*

Sam: Brady Mayor            Cornelius Colliss
L. Barton                   Thomas Stanyford
John Vining                 Jn^o White.
John Mounsher               Michael Atkins

M^r Philip Brady died & was not sworn

---

¹ Inserted; 'last past' struck out.
² Inserted.
³ Godson of Alderman John Vining (P.R.O. Prob.11/909, f. 225); paid rates on property in Portsmouth (P.C.R.O. 81A/3/20/15, no. 1: 16 May 1743); served as a Portsmouth and Sheet Turnpike Commissioner 1743–7 (*Turnpike Minute Book*, pp. 125, 143).
⁴ Inserted; 'Rents' struck out.
⁵ Contractor for brass and foundry work at Portsmouth and Plymouth yards (N.M.M. POR/F/5, 6, 7, *passim*); had extensive property interests in Portsmouth (P.C.R.O. 81A/3/20/20, no. 16: 28 Apr. 1750); voted Whig 1734 (*Poll for Hants.*, *1734*, p. 131).
⁶ Inserted.
⁷ 'nominate' struck out.
⁸ Inserted, partly in space left blank.

**85**

**13 October 1741**

*p. 89*

*Hand ii.* Burrough of Portesmouth.

We the Mayor & Major Part of the Aldermen of the said Burrough whose Hands are hereunto set do hereby order consent & agree that there shall be forthwith erected & put Iron Rails on each Side of the Portico at the Town Hall of the said Burrough, and that a Carpet for the Table, & Cushions for the Mayor & Aldermen to sit on in the said Hall shall be provided, And that the Expence of such Iron Rails Carpet & Cushions shall be paid by the Chamberlain of the said Burrough out of the Arrears of Town Rent now in his Hands, or hereafter to be collected by him,[1] Witness our Hands the Thirteenth day of October 1741.

*Signed by:*

| | |
|---|---|
| L. Barton Mayor | Cornelius Colliss |
| John Vining | Michael Atkins |
| Sam: Brady | Thomas Stanyford |
| John Mounsher | |

**86**

**3 December 1741**

*p. 90*

*Hand i.* Burrough of Portesmouth

Wee the Mayor and Major parte of the Aldermen of the Said Burrough whose hands are hereunto Sett doe hereby Nominate elect and Choose ⌐the Hon^ble⌐[2] Richard Lestock Esq^r Commodore of a Squardon bound for the Mediterranean to be a Burgess of the Said Burrough Wittnes our hands the ⌐Third⌐[3] day of December 1741 –

*Signed by:*

| | |
|---|---|
| L. Barton Mayor | John Mounsher |
| John Vining | Cornelius Colliss |
| Jn^o White. | William Rickman |
| Sam: Brady | |

*Hand ii.* The said Richard Lestock Esq^r was immediately sworn a Burgess of the said Burrough in the Guildhall of the said Burrough in the Presence of the above Mayor & Aldermen by (*signed by*) Geo Huish Junior Dep*uty* Town Clerk.

**87**

**11 January 1741/2**

*p. 91*

*Hand ii.* Burrough of Portesmouth.

Whereas on the Twenty Third day of September last past Samuell Brady Doctor of Physick the then Mayor & the Major Part of the Aldermen of the said Burrough did agree to demise & let to Robert Longcroft of Portesmouth aforesaid Merchant by Lease under their Common Seal All the Wharfage Cranage & Petty Customs of the said Corporation for the Term of Eleven Years from Michaelmas next ensuing the Date of the said Agreement at the yearly Rent of Ninety Six Pounds payable half yearly & Two fat Capons, and under the same Covenants Provisoes & Agreem*ents* as are mentioned in the Lease made to William Mathews which expired at the said Michaelmas, Provided the said Robert Longcroft did procure William Bartlett of Portesmouth aforesaid Brazier to become bound in a Bond with him for the Performance of the Covenants in such Lease to be granted to the said Robert on his part to be paid done & performed; And Whereas the said Robert Longcroft did agree to accept of such Lease & to execute a Counterpart thereof & also to procure the said William Bartlett to become bound with him in a Bond of the Penalty of Five Hundred Pounds for the Performance of the Covenants in the said Lease And whereas the said Robert Longcroft hath by his Letter of the 28^th of December last to the Mayor & Aldermen of the said Burrough intimating its not being convenient for him to hold the said Lease resigned & surrender'd up his Right & Title to the said Lease which he desires they'll be pleased to accept on Condition the Same be granted to William Mathews of Portsmouth aforesaid Husbandman for the Term

---

[1] James Brown was paid £17. 7s. 2d. for iron rails and other ironwork, John Dear, 'Upholsterer', £5. 8s. for cushions and curtains, and Edward Barton £12. 8s. 2d. 'For green Broad Cloth for a table Cloth & Cushions for the Town Hall' (P.C.R.O. CF2/2, nos 14, 15, 17: 18 Nov. 1741–9 Feb. 1741/2).

[2] Inserted (hand ii).

[3] Inserted (hand ii) in space left blank.

of Seven Years from Michaelmas last at the Rent of Seventy Pounds *Per Annum* & Two fat Capons, the said William Mathews keeping the Premises in good Repair & so leaving them at the End of the Term & procuring James Whitehead of Portsmouth aforesaid Merch*a*nt to be bound with him in a Bond of the Penalty of Five Hundred Pounds for the Performance of the Covenants in such Lease Now We whose Hands are hereunto set being the Mayor & Major Part of the Aldermen of the said Burrough considering (*p. 92*) with ourselves that the said Wharfage Cranage & Petty Customs were let to the said Robert Longcroft at too high a Rent & for considerably more than they will produce clear of all Expences do therefore at the Request of the said Robert Longcroft hereby agree to accept of such his Resignation & Surrender of his Right & Title to the said Lease agreed to be let him Provided a new Lease be granted to the said William Mathews at the Rent & on the Terms & Conditions mentioned in the said Letter & not otherwise, Witness our Hands the Eleventh day of January 1741 –

*Signed by:*

| | |
|---|---|
| L. Barton Mayor | Cornelius Colliss |
| Jn⁰ White. | Michael Atkins |
| Sam: Brady | Thomas Stanyford |
| John Mounsher | |

**88**

**12 January 1741/2**  *p. 93*

*Hand ii.* Burrough of Portesmouth.

We the Mayor & Major Part of the Aldermen of the said Burrough whose Hands are hereunto set do hereby agree to demise & let to William Mathews of Portsmouth aforesaid Husbandman by Lease under our Common Seal All the Wharfage Cranage & Petty Customs of this Corporation for the Term of Seven Years from Michaelmas last past at the yearly Rent of Seventy Pounds to be paid at Two equal half yearly Payments, & Two fat Capons, & under the same Covenants Provisoes & Agreements as are mentioned in a former Lease made to the said William Mathews which expired at the said Michaelmas; The said William Mathews keeping the Premises in good Repair & so leaving them at the End of the Term & procuring James Whitehead of Portsmouth aforesaid Merch*a*nt to become bound in a Bond of the Penalty of Five Hundred Pounds with him the said William Mathews for the Performance of the Covenants in such Lease to be granted to the said William on his Part to be paid done & performed, Witness our Hands the Twelfth day of January 1741 –

*Signed by:*

| | |
|---|---|
| L. Barton Mayor | Cornelius Colliss |
| Jn⁰ White. | Michael Atkins |
| Sam: Brady | Thomas Stanyford |
| John Mounsher | |

I do hereby agree to accept of a Lease according to the above Agreem*en*t & to execute a Counterpart thereof, & also to procure the above named James Whitehead to become bound with me in a Bond of the Penalty of Five Hundred Pounds for the Performance of the Covenants in the said Lease Witness my Hand The Mark of + William Mathews. Witness (*signed by*) Rob*t* Longcroft

**89**

**16 February 1741/2**  *p. 94*

*Hand i.* 16. February 1741 Burrough of Portesmouth

Then Agreed by the under named Mayor and Aldermen of the Said Burrough whose hands are hereunto Sett to demise by Lease under the Common Seale of the Said Burrough to Charles Morgan of Portsmouth aforesaid Gent'[1] All that their peice of Beach Ground containing in ⌐Depth⌐[2] from East to West Thirty Foote and in breadth from North to South Thirty Six foot scituate Lyeing and being on the

---

[1] Described, Aug. 1741, as 'one of the Capital Burgesses of the Borough of Yarmouth Isle of Wight' (P.C.R.O. S2/25). Possibly the Charles Morgan described as 'Surveyor of the Customhouse for the Excise and Salt' (P.C.R.O. S2/21: 6 Oct. 1719); in April 1720 Mr Morgan and several tidesmen brought into port two hoys (see p. xxivn) 'for Hovering on the coast' (C.U.L. C(H) Papers 44/20/4).

[2] Inserted; 'Breadth' struck out.

D

Poynt without the Poynt Gate of Portesmouth aforesaid, whereon is now Erected a Watch house and Boate house for the use of his Majesties Customes att Portesmouth aforesaid (But noe dwelling house or open Shop for the Exposeing of Goods wares or Merchandizes therein Shall att any time hereafter be erected on the Said peice of Beach Ground or any parte thereof) To hold for the Terme of One and Twenty yeares from the Feast of Saint Michaell the Arch Angell Last past before the date hereof att the yearley Rent of Five pounds payable halfe yearly, And under the Same Covenants Restriccions and Agreements as are mencioned in a former Lease of the Premisses granted to the said Charles Morgan, which is Lately Expired In witnes whereof the Said Mayor and Aldermen have hereunto Sett their hands the day and yeare above written – [1]

*Signed by:*

| | |
|---|---|
| L. Barton Mayor | Cornelius Colliss |
| Jn⁰ White. | Michael Atkins |
| Sam: Brady | Thomas Stanyford |
| John Mounsher | William Rickman |

**90**
**10 April 1742**

*p. 95*

*Hand i.* Burrough of Portesmouth

Wee the Mayor and Major parte of the Aldermen of the Said Burrough whose hands are hereunto Sett Doe hereby Nominate Elect and Choose the Honble Thomas Mathews Esqr Vice Admirall of the Red Squadron of his Majesties Fleete, to be a Burgess of the Said Burrough, Wittnes our hands the Tenth day of Aprill 1742. [2]

*Signed by:*

| | |
|---|---|
| L. Barton Mayor | John Mounsher |
| John Vining | Cornelius Colliss |
| Sam: Brady | Michael Atkins |

**91**
**13 April 1742**

*p. 96*

*Hand i.* 13. Aprill 1742. Burrough of Portesmouth

Then Agreed by the Mayor and Aldermen of the Said Burrough whose hands are hereunto Sett to demise by Lease under their Comon Seale to Richard New of Gosport in the County of South'ton Esqr [3] ( in Trust for Richard Lestock of Portesmouth aforesaid Esqr) All that Incroachment or Land incroached att the Front of the new Erected Messuage or Tenement of the Said Richard Lestock Situate on the North Side of the High Streete in Portesmouth aforesaid Containing in Length Sixteene foot and in breadth att Each end Four foot whereon is to be Erected pales or pallisadoes, and noe other Building or Ediffice whatsoever To hold to the Said Richard New his Executors Administrators and assignes (in Trust as aforesaid) from the Feast of the Anunciacion of the Blessed Virgin Mary Last past before the date hereof for the Terme of One Thousand Yeares att the yearley Rent of Five Shillings with a Clause of Reentry and Covenants as usuall, In witnes whereof the Said Mayor & Aldermen (being the Major parte of them) have hereunto Sett their hands and Seales the day and Yeare above written [4] –

*Signed by:*

| | |
|---|---|
| L. Barton Mayor | Cornelius Colliss |
| John Vining | John Mounsher |
| Sam: Brady | Michael Atkins |
| Jn⁰ White. | |

**92**
**6 August 1742**

*p. 97*

*Hand i.* 6. August 1742. Burrough of Portesmouth

His Royall Highness Fredrick Prince of Wales was Elected and admitted a Burgess of the Said Burrough by the Mayor and Aldermen whose hands are hereunto Sett, and by them ordered to be Enrolled as a Burgess among the Records of the said Burrough

---

[1] P.C.R.O. CF20/1, p. 193, dates this lease 28 Aug. 1742.
[2] East, p. 381, dates this election 6 Apr. 1742.
[3] Contributed to the organ fund at St Thomas's Church 1718 (Everitt, 'Church notes', ii, p. 135); voted Whig 1734 (*Poll for Hants.*, *1734*, p. 114).
[4] P.C.R.O. CF20/1, p. 193, dates this lease 4 May 1742.

Signed by:

| | |
|---|---|
| L. Barton Mayor | Cornelius Colliss |
| Sam: Brady | William Rickman |
| John Mounsher | Michael Atkins |

**93**

**28 September 1742**  *Hand i.* Burrough of Portesmouth

Wee the Mayor and Major parte of the Aldermen of the Said Burrough whose hands are hereunto Sett Doe hereby Nominate Elect and Choose the Hon^ble ⌐James ⌐¹ Stewart Esq^r Rear Admirall of the Blew Squadron of his Majesties Fleete to be a Burgess of the Said Burrough, Wittnes our hands the 28^th of September 1742.

Signed by:

| | |
|---|---|
| L. Barton Mayor | Cornelius Colliss |
| Jn^o White. | William Rickman |
| Sam: Brady | Michael Atkins |
| John Mounsher | Thomas Stanyford |

The above named Admirall Stewart was Immediatly Sworn a Burgess before the above Mayor and Aldermen By (signed by) Geo Huish Town Clerk.

p. 98

**94**

**28 September 1742**  *Hand i.* Burrough of Portesmouth

Wee the Mayor and Major parte of the Aldermen of the Said Burrough whose hands are hereunto Sett doe hereby Nominate Elect and Choose² Peirson Lock ⌐Esq^r ⌐³ Master Shipwright of his Majesties Dockyard att Portesmouth to be a Burgess of the Said Burrough, Wittnes our hands the 28^th of September 1742.

Signed by:

| | |
|---|---|
| L. Barton Mayor | Cornelius Colliss |
| Jn^o White. | William Rickman |
| Sam: Brady | Michael Atkins |
| John Mounsher | Thomas Stanyford |

The above named M^r Lock was Immediatly Sworne a Burgess before the above Mayor and Aldermen By (signed by) Geo Huish Town Clerk –

p. 99

**95**

**29 September 1742**  *Hand i.* Burrough of Portesmouth

Wee the Mayor and Major parte of the Aldermen of the Said Burrough whose hands are hereunto Sett Doe hereby Nominate Elect and Choose Edward Strode Esq^r to be a Burgess of the Said Burrough (he being Nominated by the Said Mayor to be his Peremptory Burgesse) Wittnes our hands the Twenty Ninth of September 1742 –

Signed by:

| | |
|---|---|
| L. Barton Mayor | Cornelius Colliss |
| John Vining | William Rickman |
| Jn^o White. | Michael Atkins |
| Sam: Brady | Thomas Stanyford |
| John Mounsher | |

The above named Edward Strode Esq^r was Immediatly Sworne a Burgess before the above Mayor & Aldermen By (signed by) Geo Huish Town Clerk –

p. 100

**96**

**18 December 1742**  *Hand ii.* Borough of Portesmouth

We whose Hands are hereunto set being the Mayor & Major Part of the Aldermen of the said Borough do hereby nominate elect & choose the Hon^ble Sir Charles Hardy Kn^t one of the Rear Admirals of the Blue Squadron of his Majesty's Fleet to be a Burgess of the said Borough, Witness our Hands the Eighteenth day of December 1742.

p. 101

---

¹ Inserted in space left blank.
² 'M^r' struck out.
³ Inserted.

*Signed by:*

| | |
|---|---|
| William Rickman Maijor | John Mounsher |
| L. Barton | Cornelius Colliss |
| Jn° White. | Michael Atkins |
| Sam: Brady | Thomas Stanyford |

*Hand i.* The above named S^r Cha: Hardy was Immediatly Sworne a Burgess before the above Mayor & Aldermen By (*signed by*) Geo Huish Town Clerk.

**97**

**12 April 1743**

*p. 102*

*Hand ii.* Borough of Portesmouth

At the Guildhall of the said Borough the 12^th day of Aprill 1743. Present

William Rickman Esq^r Mayor
Lewis Barton Esq^r –
Samuell Brady M.D. –
John Mounsher Esq^r –      } Aldermen
Cornelius Colliss Gent' –
Michaell Atkins Gent' –

M^r Samuell Brady the Younger was sworn a Burgess of the said Borough before the above Mayor & Aldermen pursuant to his Election on the 10^th of Aprill 1728. by Geo Huish Junior Dep*uty* Town Clerk.

**98**

**20 September 1743**

*p. 103*

*Hand ii.* Borough of Portesmouth

At[1] the Guildhall of the said Borough the Twentieth day of September 1743 being then present pursuant to Summons

William Rickman Esq^r Mayor
Lewis Barton Esq^r –
John White Gent' –
Samuel Brady M.D.
John Mounsher Esq^r      } Aldermen
Cornelius Colliss Gent'
Michaell Atkins Gent'
Thomas Stanyford Esq^r

The Hon^ble Francis Chute Esq^r one of his Majesties Councell learned in the Law was proposed by M^r Alderman White to be Recorder of the said Borough in the Room & Place of James Crosse Esq^r lately deceased, but M^r Alderman Stanyford offering himself as a Candidate for the said Recordership[2] the Question was severally put to the said Aldermen, and Five of them, that is to say the said William Rickman Esq^r Mayor Lewis Barton John White Samuell Brady & Cornelius Colliss voted for the said[3] Francis Chute Esq^r to be Recorder, and Three of them that is to say the said John Mounsher Michaell Atkins & Thomas Stanyford voted for the said M^r Stanyford to be Recorder, Whereupon the said Francis Chute Esq^r having the Majority of Votes was declared duly elected; And he is hereby nominated (*p. 104*) elected & chosen by us whose Hands are hereunto set (being the Mayor & Major Part of the Aldermen of the said Borough) to be Recorder of the said Borough in the Room & Place of the said James Crosse, Witness our Hands

*Signed by:*

| | |
|---|---|
| William Rickman Maijor | Sam: Brady |
| L. Barton | Cornelius Colliss |
| Jn° White | |

Witness (*signed by*) Geo Huish Junior Deputy Town Clerk

---

[1] 'We the Mayor & Major Part of the Aldermen of the said Borough' struck out before 'At'.

[2] On 2 Apr. 1733 Stanyford was described as Deputy Recorder, and he may have been carrying out the Recorder's duties during the two years after Crosse's death (P.C.R.O. L1). He subsequently refused to vote for Chute's successor, William Pescod (no. 119).

[3] 'Mr' struck out.

**5 October 1744**  *Hand i.* Fryday 5th October 1744 Burrough of Portesmouth
Att an Assembly att the Guild Hall then and there being present

| | | |
|---|---|---|
| Thomas Stanyford Esqr Mayor | Cornelius Collis gent' | |
| Lewis Barton Esqr | Edwd Linzee gent' | |
| Sam: Brady M:D. | ⎰Aldermen⌐2⌐1 John Carter gent' | ⎬ Aldermen |
| John Mounsher Esqr | ⌐1⌐2 Samll Chandler gent' | |

Francis Chute Esqr (who on the Twentieth day of September 1743 was duely elected Recorder of the Said Burrough) did take and Subscribe the Oathes of Allegiance[3] Supremacy ⌐and Abjuration⌐4 and Repeate and Subscribe the Test against Transubstantiation and was then Sworne Recorder and a Justice of the peace of the Said Burrough By (*signed by*) Geo Huish Town Clerk –

*p. 105*

**29 September 1743**  *Hand ii.* Borough of Portesmouth
We whose Hands are hereunto set being the Mayor & Major Part of the Aldermen of the said Borough do hereby elect & choose John Burrard Esqr to be a Burgess of the said Borough (he being nominated by me the said Mayor to be my Peremptory Burgess) Witness our Hands the Twenty Ninth day of September 1743.

*Signed by:*

| | |
|---|---|
| William Rickman Maijor | Cornelius Colliss |
| L. Barton | Michael Atkins |
| Sam: Brady | Thomas Stanyford |

Geo Huish Junior Dep*uty* Town Clerk.

*p. 106*

**28 December 1743**  *Hand ii.* Borough of Portesmouth
We whose Hands are hereunto set being the Mayor & Major Part of the Aldermen of the said Borough do hereby nominate elect & choose the Honble Thomas Davers Esqr one of the Rear Admirals of the Red Squadron of his Majesties Navy to be a Burgess of the said Borough Witness our Hands the 28th day of December 1743 –

*Signed by:*

| | |
|---|---|
| Michael Atkins Mayor | John Mounsher |
| L. Barton | Cornelius Colliss |
| Sam: Brady | Thomas Stanyford |

The above named Admiral Davers was immediately sworn a Burgess in the Presence of the above Mayor & Aldermen by (*signed by*) Geo Huish Junior Dep*uty* Town Clerk

*p. 107*

**7 February 1743/4**  *Hand ii.* Borough of Portesmouth
We whose Hands are hereunto set being the Mayor & Major Part of the Aldermen of the said Borough do hereby nominate elect & choose the Honble William Martin Esqr Rear Admiral of the Blue Squadron of his Majestys Fleet to be a Burgess of the said Borough Witness our Hands the Seventh day of February 1743.

*Signed by:*

| | |
|---|---|
| Michael Atkins Mayor | John Mounsher |
| L. Barton | Cornelius Colliss |
| Sam: Brady | |

The above named Admiral Martin was immediately Sworn a Burgess in the Presence of the above Mayor & Aldermen by (*signed by*) Geo Huish Junior Dep*uty* Town Clerk

---

[1] Added.
[2] Added.
[3] 'and' struck out.
[4] Inserted.

| 103 | *p. 108* |
|---|---|
| **21 August 1744** | *Hand i.* 21. August 1744. Burrough of Portesmouth |

This day M^r James Mounsher Son of John Mounsher Esq^r whoe on the Twenty Seaventh day of November 1732 was nominated and Elected a Burgess of the Said Burrough was[1] Sworne a Burgess of the Same Burrough in the presence of us the Mayor and Aldermen hereto Subscribeing.

⌐M^r James Mounsher Sworn a Burgess.¬[2]

*Signed by:*

| Michael Atkins Mayor | John Mounsher |
|---|---|
| L. Barton | Cornelius Colliss |
| Sam: Brady | |
| Geo Huish Town Clerk. | |

| 104 | *p. 109* |
|---|---|
| **11 September 1744** | *Hand ii.* Borough of Portesmouth |

We whose Hands are hereunto set being the Mayor & Major Part of the Aldermen of the said Borough do hereby nominate elect & choose the Right Hon^ble Daniell Earl of Winchelsea & Nottingham to be a Burgess of the said Borough, Witness our Hands the Eleventh day of September 1744.

*Signed by:*

| Michael Atkins Mayor – | John Mounsher |
|---|---|
| L. Barton | Cornelius Colliss |
| Jn^o White. | Thomas Stanyford |
| Sam: Brady | William Rickman |
| Geo Huish Town Clerk. | |

| 105 | *p. 110* |
|---|---|
| **13 September 1744** | *Hand ii.* 13^th September 1744 Borough of Portesmouth |

At an Assembly in the Council Chamber in the Guildhall of the said Borough being then present pursuant to Summons

Michaell Atkins Esq^r Mayor

Lewis Barton Esq^r –
John White Gent' –
Samuell Brady M.D.
John Mounsher Esq^r – ⎫
Cornelius Colliss Gent' – ⎬ Aldermen
William Rickman Esq^r – ⎭
Thomas Stanyford Esq^r –

James Deacon Gent' Edward Linzee Gent' Samuell Chandler Gent' & John Carter Gent' Four of the Burgesses of the said Borough were by the above named Mayor & Aldermen unanimously nominated elected & chosen Aldermen of the said Borough And the said James Deacon Edward Linzee Samuell Chandler & John Carter did then & there immediately take & subscribe the Oaths of Allegiance Supremacy & Abjuration and did repeat & subscribe the Test against Transubstantiation, and were then & there severally sworn Aldermen of the said Borough before the said Mayor & Aldermen In Witness whereof the said Mayor & Aldermen have hereunto set their Hands the day & year above written –

*Signed by:*

| Michael Atkins Mayor | John Mounsher |
|---|---|
| L. Barton | Cornelius Colliss |
| Jn^o White. | William Rickman |
| Sam: Brady | Thomas Stanyford |
| Geo Huish Town Clerk | |

---

[1] 'this day' struck out.
[2] Added in left margin.

**106**

**13 September 1744**

*p. 111*

*Hand ii.* Borough of Portesmouth

We whose Hands are hereunto set being the Mayor & Major Part of the Aldermen of the said Borough do hereby nominate elect & choose the Hon^ble Henry Medley Esq^r Rear Admiral of the White Squadron of His Majestys Navy to be a Burgess of the said Borough, Witness our Hands the Thirteenth day of September 1744.

*Signed by:*

| | |
|---|---|
| Michael Atkins Mayor | John Mounsher |
| L. Barton | Cornelius Colliss |
| Jn^o White. | William Rickman |
| Sam: Brady | Thomas Stanyford |
| Geo Huish Town Clerk. | |

**107**

**17 September 1744**

*p. 112*

*Hand ii.* Borough of Portesmouth

At the Guildhall of the said Borough the 17^th of September 1744 present

Michaell Atkins Esq^r Mayor

Lewis Barton Esq^r –
Samuell Brady M.D. –
Cornelius Colliss Gent' –
William Rickman Esq^r –         } Aldermen
James Deacon Gent' –
Samuell Chandler Gent'
John Carter Gent' –

John Burrard Esq^r the Peremptory Burgess of William Rickman Esq^r late Mayor was duly sworn a Burgess before the above Mayor & Aldermen by (*signed by*) Geo Huish Town Clerk.

**108**

**17 September 1744**

*p. 113*

*Hand ii.* Borough of Portesmouth

At the Guildhall of the said Borough the 17^th of September 1744 present

Michaell Atkins Esq^r Mayor

Lewis Barton Esq^r –
John White Gent' –
Samuell Brady M.D. –
⌐John Mounsher Esq^r –⌐1
Cornelius Colliss Gent'
William Rickman Esq^r –         } Aldermen
Thomas Stanyford Esq^r –
James Deacon Gent' –
Edward Linzee Gent' –
Samuell Chandler Gent'
John Carter Gent' –

The Hon^ble Henry Medley Esq^r Rear Admiral of the White Squadron of His Majesties Fleet was duly sworn a Burgess of the said Borough before the above Mayor & Aldermen pursuant to his Election on the Thirteenth day of this instant September by (*signed by*) Geo Huish Town Clerk.

**109**

**29 September 1744**

*p. 114*

*Hand ii.* Borough of Portesmouth

We whose Hands are hereunto set being the Mayor & Major Part of the Aldermen of the said Borough do hereby elect & choose M^r John Eddowes Son of Robert Eddowes Esq^r to be a Burgess of the said Borough (he being nominated by me the said Mayor to be my Peremptory Burgess) Witness our Hands the Twenty Ninth day of September 1744.

---

[1] Inserted.

*Signed by:*

Michael Atkins Mayor          Thomas Stanyford
L. Barton                              Edw^d Linzee
Sam: Brady                          John Carter
Cornelius Colliss

The above named M^r John Eddowes was duly sworn a Burgess before the above Mayor & Aldermen by (*signed by*) Geo Huish Town Clerk

**110**
**5 October 1744**

*p. 115*

*Hand i.* Burrough of Portesmouth

We whose hands are hereunto Sett being the Mayor and Major parte of the Aldermen of the Said Burrough Doe hereby Elect and Choose Francis Chute Esq^r (Recorder of the Said Burrough) to be one of the Burgesses of the Same Burrough, Wittnes our hands the Fifth day of October 1744.

*Signed by:*

Thomas Stanyford Mayor          Cornelius Colliss
L. Barton                                    Edw^d Linzee
Sam: Brady                                John Carter
John Mounsher                          Sam: Chandler.

*Hand ii.* The above named Francis Chute Esq^r was duly sworn a Burgess before the above Mayor & Aldermen by (*signed by*) Geo Huish Town Clerk.

**111**
**11 October 1744**

*p. 116*

*Hand ii.* Borough of Portesmouth

At an Assembly of us the Mayor & Aldermen of the said Borough whose Hands are hereunto set, at the Guild Hall there this Eleventh day of October 1744 We do order & direct as followeth

1. That M^r George Huish Town Clerk of the said Borough do forthwith send to M^r John Bissell, the Person that owns the House wherein M^rs Peers lives in S^t Thomas's Street, the Heirs of Amos Bowyer, the Heirs of Thomas Hancock,[1] the Heirs of D^r William Smith, William Elson Esq^r[2] & the Commissioners for Victualling his Majesties Navy, to demand of them the Arrears of Quit Rent & Capon Money due from each of them to this Corporation, and on their Refusal to pay the Same to bring Actions or take such other legal Course as the said George Huish shall be advised to.[3]

2. That the said George Huish shall forthwith send to M^r William Bartlett & to any other person or persons he shall be directed by us for all such Arrears as are due from them for Wharfage Cranage & Petty Customs[4] to this Corporation, and on their refusing to pay, to commence Actions or take any other legal Course for Recovery of the Same.

3. That some proper Method shall be forthwith taken for the regulating the several Markets within this Borough, And We do hereby undertake & promise to indemnify any of our Officers or other Persons who shall legally act therein under the Direction of the Mayor of the said Borough for the Time being,[5] Witness our Hands the day & year above written

*Signed by:*

Thomas Stanyford Mayor          Michael Atkins
L. Barton                                    Ja^s Deacon
Sam: Brady                                Edw^d Linzee
John Mounsher                          Sam: Chandler.
Cornelius Colliss                      John Carter
William Rickman

---

[1] Alderman 1679; Mayor 1681, 1688 (East, pp. 329, 316).

[2] Possibly the William Elson admitted as a Burgess 29 Sept. 1719 (East, p. 377).

[3] Bowyer's heirs still owed 1s. 6d. in 1745 and again in 1747; Hancock's heirs owed 4s. in 1745 and were again in debt in 1746; Smith's heirs owed 1s. in 1745 and, after defaulting again in 1746, 10s. in 1747; the Commissioners of Victualling owed 15s. 2d. in 1743 and 15s. in 1744 (P.C.R.O. CF1/8).

[4] 'due' struck out.

[5] On 27 Apr. 1745 the Chamberlain was ordered to pay Abraham Stallard, the Town Crier, £17. 4s., the cost of his defence in a suit brought against him in the King's Bench 'by one Howard and his wife for a thing done in the Execucion of his Office' (P.C.R.O. CF2/2, no. 26).

**112**

**18 April 1745**

*Hand ii.* Borough of Portesmouth

Whereas that Part of the Road or Highway which leads from the Key Gate to the Victualling Office Key within the said Borough is very much out of Repair & is presented by the Grand Jury in his Majesties General Sessions of the Peace held this Day in & for the said Borough as a common Nusance & dangerous to his Majesties Subjects Now We the Mayor & Major Part of the Aldermen of the said Borough do hereby order & direct the Chamberlain of the said Borough forthwith at the Expence of this Corporation to cause such Part of the said Road or Highway to be repaired & amended as belongs to this Corporation, Witness our Hands the Eighteenth day of Aprill 1745.[1]

*Signed by:*

| | |
|---|---|
| Thomas Stanyford Mayor | Cornelius Colliss |
| L. Barton | Sam: Chandler. |
| Jno White. | John Carter |
| Sam: Brady | |

**113**

**13 August 1745**

*Hand ii.* Borough of Portesmouth

We the Mayor & Major Part of the Aldermen of the said Borough whose Hands are hereunto set do hereby consent & agree to demise & grant by Lease under our Common Seal to William Norris of Portsmouth aforesaid Sawyer All that Incroachment or Land incroached to the Messuage or Tenement of the said William Norris situate on the North Side of the High Street in Portsmouth aforesaid over against the Butchers Shambles there containing in Length Four foot and in Breadth at each End Four foot whereon is to be erected & placed a flat Cellar Window and no other Edifice or Building whatsoever To hold to the said William Norris his Executors Administrators & Assigns from the Twenty Fifth day of March last past for the Term of One Thousand Years, at & under the yearly Rent of Three Shillings & Six Pence, payable always on the Feast of the Annuntiation of the Blessed Virgin Mary, with a Clause for Reentry & all other usual Covenants Witness our Hands the Thirteenth day of August 1745.[2]

*Signed by:*

| | |
|---|---|
| Cornelius Colliss Deputy Mayor | Jas Deacon |
| L. Barton | Edwd Linzee |
| Sam: Brady | Sam: Chandler. |
| John Mounsher | John Carter |

**114**

**3 September 1745**

*Hand ii.* Borough of Portesmouth

We the Mayor & Major Part of the Aldermen of the said Borough whose Hands are hereunto set do hereby consent & agree to demise & grant by Lease under our Common Seal to Charles Childe of Gosport in the County of South'ton Merchant[3] All that Incroachment or Land incroached to the Messuage or Tenement of the said Charles Childe called the Blue Anchor situate on the West Side of the High Street on the Point without the Point Gates of Portsmouth aforesaid containing in the Front from North to South Fifteen Foot & Six Inches & in Depth from East to West Four Foot & Two Inches, whereon the new erected Front of the said Messuage now stands To hold to the said Charles Childe his Executors Administrators & Assigns from Lady day last past for One Thousand Years, under the yearly Rent of Two Shillings & Six Pence, payable ⌐half⌐[4] yearly, with the Clauses & Covenants usually contained in such Leases Witness our Hands the 3d day of September 1745.[5]

---

[1] On 27 Sept. 1745 the Chamberlain was ordered to pay £1. 0s. 3d. to William Mathews for twenty-seven loads of gravel carried on 17 and 18 May 'from Mr Allin to Mend the Road by the Key' (P.C.R.O. CF2/1).

[2] P.C.R.O. CF20/1, p. 193, dates this lease 28 Aug. 1745.

[3] Voted Tory 1734 (*Poll for Hants.*, *1734*, p. 114).

[4] Inserted.

[5] P.C.R.O. CF20/1, p. 194, dates this lease 1 Oct. 1745.

D*

*Signed by:*

| | |
|---|---|
| Thomas Stanyford Mayor | Michael Atkins |
| Cornelius Colliss | Edw^d Linzee |
| L. Barton | Sam: Chandler. |
| Sam: Brady | John Carter |

**115**

**29 September 1745**

*p. 120*

*Hand ii.* Borough of Portesmouth

We whose Hands[1] are hereunto set being the Mayor & Major Part of the Aldermen of the said Borough do hereby elect & choose Sir John Miller Baronet to be a Burgess of the said Borough (he being nominated by me the said Mayor to be my Peremptory Burgess) Witness our Hands the 29th day of September 1745 –

*Signed by:*

| | |
|---|---|
| Thomas Stanyford Mayor | Michael Atkins |
| Edw^d Linzee Mayor elect | Sam: Chandler. |
| L. Barton | John Carter |
| Sam: Brady | |
| Geo Huish Town Clerk. | |

**116**

**8 October 1745**

*p. 121*

*Hand ii.* Borough of Portesmouth

We the Mayor & Major Part of the Aldermen of the said Borough whose Hands[2] are hereunto set do hereby consent & agree to demise & grant by Lease under our Common Seal to Andrew Mounsher of Portsmouth aforesaid Sailmaker[3] All that Piece of Beach Ground situate lying & being at the lower End of the Poynt without the Point Gate of Portsmouth aforesaid & adjoining to the Messuage or Tenem*ent* late of Henry Belfeild Gent' dec*eas*ed on the West, to the Engine House on the South & facing the Road or Highway on the East & North, which said Piece of Beach Ground hereby intended to be granted contains in Length from East to West Ten foot of Assize & in Breadth from North to South Nine foot of Assize as the same is now marked & staked out To hold to the said Andrew Mounsher his Executors Administrators & Assigns from Lady day last past for One Thousand Years under the yearly Rent of Five Shillings payable half yearly, with the Clauses & Covenants usually contained in such Leases, Witness our Hands the Eighth day of October 1745.

*Signed by:*

| | |
|---|---|
| Edw^d Linzee Mayor | Michael Atkins |
| L. Barton | Thomas Stanyford |
| Sam: Brady | Sam: Chandler. |
| Cornelius Colliss | John Carter |

**117**

**17 October 1745**

*p. 122*

*Hand ii.* Borough of Portesmouth

At the Guildhall of the said Borough the 17^th of October 1745 Present

Edw^d Linzee Esq^r Mayor

Lewis Barton Esq^r –  
Samuel Brady M.D –  
William Rickman Esq^r –  
Mich^ll Atkins Gent' –  } Aldermen
Tho^s Stanyford Esq^r –  
Samuel Chandler Gent' –  
John Carter Gent' –  

Sir John Miller Bar^t the Peremptory Burgess of the said Thomas Stanyford Esq^r (late Mayor) was duly sworn a Burgess of the said Borough pursuant to his Nomination & Election on the Twenty Ninth day of September last by (*signed by*) Geo Huish Town Clerk.

---

[1] '& Seals' struck out.
[2] '&' struck out.
[3] 'of' struck out.

**118**
**17 December 1745**

p. 123

*Hand ii.* Borough of Portesmouth

We[1] whose Hands[2] are hereunto set being the Mayor & Major Part of the Aldermen of the said Borough and this day assembled in Council do hereby nominate elect & choose William Pescod Esq<sup>r</sup> of the City of Winchester Barrister at Law[3] to be Recorder of the said Borough in the Room & Place of Francis Chute Esq<sup>r</sup> lately deceased, Witness our Hands the Seventeenth day of December 1745.

*Signed by:*

| | |
|---|---|
| Edw<sup>d</sup> Linzee Mayor | William Rickman |
| L: Barton | Sam: Chandler. |
| Sam: Brady – | John Carter |
| Cornelius Colliss | |
| Geo Huish Town Clerk. | |

**119**
**28 December 1745**

p. 124

*Hand ii.* Borough of Portesmouth

At the Guild Hall of the said Borough the Twenty Eighth day of December 1745 being then present pursuant to Summons

Edward Linzee Esq<sup>r</sup> Mayor

Lewis Barton Esq<sup>r</sup> –
John White Gent' –
Samuel Brady M.D. –
John Mounsher Esq<sup>r</sup>
Cornelius Colliss Gent'         } Aldermen
William Rickman Esq<sup>r</sup>
Michael Atkins Gent'
Thomas Stanyford Esq<sup>r</sup>
Samuel Chandler Gent'
John Carter Gent' –

William Pescod Esq<sup>r</sup> of the City of Winchester Barrister at Law was proposed by M<sup>r</sup> Mayor & M<sup>r</sup> Rickman to be Recorder of the said Borough, and the said Mayor & Aldermen (except the said M<sup>r</sup> Stanyford who refused to give his Vote) voted ⌈for⌉[4] the said William Pescod to be Recorder; And the said William Pescod is hereby nominated elected & chosen by us whose Hands are hereunto set (being the Mayor & Major Part of the Aldermen of the said Borough) to be Recorder of the said ⌈Borough⌉[5] Witness our Hands –

*Signed by:*

| | |
|---|---|
| Edw<sup>d</sup> Linzee Mayor | Cornelius Colliss |
| L. Barton | William Rickman |
| Jn<sup>o</sup> White. | Michael Atkins |
| Sam: Brady | Sam: Chandler. |
| John Mounsher | John Carter |
| Geo Huish Town Clerk – | |

**120**
**28 January 1745/6**

p. 125

*Hand ii.* Borough of Portesmouth

We the Mayor & Major Part of the Aldermen of the said Borough whose Hands are hereunto set do hereby nominate elect & choose the Hon<sup>ble</sup> William Rowley Esq<sup>r</sup> one of the Vice Admirals of the White Squadron of his Majestys Fleet to be a Burgess of the said Borough, Witness our Hands the Twenty Eighth day of January 1745.

*Signed by:*

| | |
|---|---|
| Edw<sup>d</sup> Linzee Mayor | Cornelius Colliss |
| Jn<sup>o</sup> White. | Ja<sup>s</sup> Deacon |
| Sam: Brady | John Carter |
| John Mounsher | |
| Geo Huish Town Clerk | |

---

[1] 'the' struck out; 'At the Guild' struck out before 'We'.
[2] '& Seals' struck out.
[3] P.C.R.O. CE1/14, p. 48, refers to Pescod as 'Counsellor Pescod'.
[4] Added.
[5] Inserted.

*Hand i.* The above named Admirall was ⌐Immediately⌐[1] Sworn a Burgesse before the above Mayor & Aldermen By (*signed by*) Geo Huish Town Clerk.

**121**
**28 February 1745/6**   *p. 126*
*Hand ii.* Borough of Portesmouth

We whose Hands are hereunto set being the Mayor & Major Part of the Aldermen of the said Borough do hereby nominate elect & choose Thomas Gore Esqʳ Commissary General of the Musters and Chief Muster Master of all his Majestys Forces in Great Britain, to be a Burgess of the said Borough, Witness our Hands the Twenty Eighth day of February 1745.
*Signed by:*

| | |
|---|---|
| Edwᵈ Linzee Mayor | Thomas Stanyford |
| Jnᵒ White. | Jaˢ Deacon |
| Sam: Brady | Sam Chandler |
| John Mounsher | John Carter |
| Cornelius Colliss | |

Geo Huish Junior Dep*uty* Town Clerk

The above named Thomas Gore Esqʳ was immediately sworn a Burgess of the said Borough in the Presence of the above Mayor & Aldermen by (*signed by*) Geo Huish Junior Dep*uty* Town Clerk

**122**
**28 February 1745/6**   *p. 127*
*Hand ii.* Borough of Portesmouth

We the Mayor & Major Part of the Aldermen of the said Borough whose Hands are hereunto set do hereby nominate elect & choose the most Noble John Duke of Bedford to be a Burgess of the said Borough Witness our Hands the Twenty Eighth day of February 1745.
*Signed by:*

| | |
|---|---|
| Edwᵈ Linzee Mayor | Thomas Stanyford |
| Jnᵒ White. | Jaˢ Deacon |
| Sam: Brady | Sam Chandler |
| John Mounsher | John Carter |
| Cornelius Colliss | |

Geo Huish Junior Dep*uty* Town Clerk

**123**
**15 April 1746**   *p. 128*
*Hand ii.* 15ᵗʰ April 1746 Borough of Portesmouth

At an Assembly at the Guild Hall of the said Borough Present

Edward Linzee Esqʳ Mayor

Lewis Barton Esqʳ –
John White Gent' –
Samuel Brady M.D. –
Cornelius Colliss Gent' –   } Aldermen
Samuel Chandler Gent'
John Carter Gent' –

William Pescod Esqʳ who on the Twenty Eighth day of December last was duly elected Recorder of the said Borough did take & subscribe the Oaths of Allegiance Supremacy & Abjuration, and repeat & subscribe the Test against Transubstantiation, and was then sworn Recorder & a Justice of the Peace of the said Borough by (*signed by*) Geo Huish Junior Dep*uty* Town Clerk

**124**
**15 April 1746**   *p. 129*
*Hand ii.* Borough of Portesmouth

We whose Hands are hereunto set being the Mayor & Major Part of the Aldermen of the said Borough do hereby nominate elect & choose William Pescod Esqʳ Recorder of the said Borough to be a Burgess of the same Borough, Witness our Hands the 15ᵗʰ day of April 1746.

---

[1] Altered from 'Immediatly'.

*Signed by:*

Edw<sup>d</sup> Linzee Mayor      Cornelius Colliss
L. Barton                          Sam: Chandler.
Jn<sup>o</sup> White.                         John Carter
Sam: Brady

Geo Huish Junior Dep*uty* Town Clerk

The above named William Pescod Esq<sup>r</sup> was duly sworn a Burgess of the said Borough in the Presence of the above Mayor & Aldermen by (*signed by*) Geo Huish Junior Dep*uty* Town Clerk.

**125**

**24 June 1746**

*p. 130*

*Hand ii.* Borough of Portesmouth

We the Mayor & Major Part of the Aldermen of the said Borough whose Hands are hereunto set do hereby consent & agree to demise & grant by Lease under our Common Seal to Adam Strong of Portsmouth aforesaid Cordwainer All that Incroachment or ⌈Ground⌉[1] incroached to the ⌈Front of the⌉[2] Messuage or Tenement of the said Adam Strong situate on the West Side of the High Street on the Point without the Point Gates of Portsmouth aforesaid whereon the said Adam hath erected & placed ⌈or is at Liberty to erect & place⌉[3] Two Bulks containing in Length under each Window Six Foot & in Depth Two Foot & Four Inches ⌈but no other Edifice or Building whatsoever⌉[4] To hold to the said Adam Strong his Executors Administrators & Assigns from Lady Day last past for the Term of One Thousand Years under the yearly Rent of ⌈Five Shillings⌉[5] payable half yearly, with the usual Clauses & Covenants in such Leases, Witness our Hands the Twenty Fourth day of June 1746.

*Signed by:*

Edw<sup>d</sup> Linzee Mayor      Ja<sup>s</sup> Deacon
L. Barton                          Sam: Chandler.
Sam: Brady                        John Carter
Michael Atkins

**126**

**29 July 1746**

*p. 131*

*Hand ii.* Borough of Portesmouth

We the Mayor & Major Part of the Aldermen of the said Borough whose Hands are hereunto set do hereby consent & agree to demise & grant by Lease under our Common Seal to John Vining Heron of Portsmouth aforesaid[6] Mercer All that Incroachment or Ground incroached to the Messuage or Tenement of the said John Vining Heron situate on the North Side of the High Street in Portsmouth aforesaid & nigh the Parade there containing in Length Four Feet & in Breadth at each End Two Feet, & adjoining to the House of M<sup>r</sup> John Leeke, which said Incroachment is intended to fix & place a Writing Desk therein for keeping the Shop Books & Books of Accompt of the said John Vining Heron & is not to be applied to any other Use, & no other Edifice or Building whatsoever is to be erected on the said Ground To hold to the said John Vining Heron his Executors Administrators & Assigns from Lady day last past for the Term of One Thousand Years under the yearly Rent of Three Shillings payable half yearly, with the Clauses & Covenants usually contained in such Leases, Witness our Hands the Twenty Ninth day of July 1746 –

*Signed by:*

Edw<sup>d</sup> Linzee Mayor      Thomas Stanyford
Sam: Brady                        Sam: Chandler.
Michael Atkins

---

[1] Inserted; 'Land' struck out.
[2] Inserted.
[3] Inserted.
[4] Inserted.
[5] Inserted (hand i) in space left blank.
[6] 'Gro' struck out.

**11 August 1746**

*Hand i.* Burrough of Portesmouth

Whereas by an Order dated the Nineteenth day of May 1739, under the hands of the then Mayor, and Major part of the Aldermen of the Said Burrough, Itt was agreed that the Sume of Seaven hundred pounds Should be forthwith borrowed of Paul Green of Fareham in the County of South'ton Maulster, For Securety of which he was to have Two Bonds each for the Sume of Three hundred and Fifty pounds under the Common Seale of this Corporacion, payable with Interest att the Rate of Four pounds in the hundered by the yeare, And whereas pursuant to Such Order the Said Mayor and Aldermen did borrow and take up of the Said Paul Green the Sume of Three hundred and Fifty Pounds (part of the Said Seaven hundred pounds) and for Repayment thereof did by their Bond or Obligacion under their Common Seale bearing date the Eleventh day of September 1739 become bound to the Said Paul Green in the penalty of Seaven hundred pounds Condicioned for the payment of Three hundred and Fifty pounds with Interest for the Same att the Rate of Four pounds in the hundred by the yeare, att a certaine day therein mencioned, and now Since past' which Said Three hundred and Fifty pounds was by a writeing under the hand and Seale of the Said Paul Green declared to be the proper money of Cornelius Collis, then of Portesmouth aforesaid Gent' (lately dec*eased*) And that his name was therein only used in Trust for the Said Cornelius Collis his Executors Administrators and assignes And whereas on the Twenty First day of August 1740 the Sume of Fifty pounds in parte of the principall money due on the Said Bond, was paid to the Said Cornelius Collis, and there (*p. 133*) now Remains due thereon the Sume of Three hundred pounds principall money, and noe more, all Interest for which is paid to the day of the date hereof And whereas the Said Cornelius Collis by his Last will and Testament in writeing did Nominate and appoint M^r John Carter and M^r Richard Strugnell his Executors whoe have Called in the Said Sume of Three hundred pounds Now wee the Mayor and Major parte of the Aldermen of the Said Burrough whose hands are hereunto Sett Doe hereby Consent and agree that the Said Sume of Three hundred pounds Shall be borrowed and taken up of any person who is willing to advance the Same, And that wee will give a Bond under the Common Seale of this Corporacion for Repaym*ent* thereof with Interest for the Same att the Rate of Four pounds and Ten Shillings in the hundred by the yeare, Wittnes our hands the Eleventh day of August 1746 –

*Signed by:*

| | |
|---|---|
| Edw^d Linzee Mayor | John Mounsher |
| L. Barton | Michael Atkins |
| Jn^o White. | Sam: Chandler. |
| Sam: Brady | John Carter |

**14 August 1746**

*Hand i.* Burrough of Portesmouth

Wee whose hands are hereunto Sett being the Mayor and Major parte of the Aldermen of the Said Burrough assembled in Councell att the Towne Hall there Doe hereby Nominate Elect and Choose the Hon^ble George Anson Esq^r Vice Admirall of the Blew Squadron of his Majesties Fleet to be a Burgess of the Said Burrough Wittnes our hands the 14^th of August 1746 –

*Signed by:*

| | |
|---|---|
| Edw^d Linzee Mayor | John Mounsher |
| L. Barton | Michael Atkins |
| Jn^o White | Sam: Chandler. |
| Sam: Brady | John Carter |

The Said Vice Admirall Anson was Immediatly Sworne a Burgess before the above Mayor & Aldermen By (*signed by*) Geo Huish Town Clerk.

**12 September 1746**

*Hand ii.* Borough of Portesmouth

12^th day of September 1746 at the House of James Deacon Gent' within the said Borough Being present pursuant to Summons

Edward Linzee Esq<sup>r</sup> Mayor
John White Gent' –
Samuel Brady M.D –
John Mounsher Esq<sup>r</sup> –
Michael Atkins Gent' –        } Aldermen
Thomas Stanyford Esq<sup>r</sup> –
James Deacon Gent' –
Samuel Chandler Gent'
John Carter Gent' –

Memorandum that this present day the above Mayor & Aldermen being assembled in Council George Huish Gent' did surrender into the Hands of the said Mayor & Aldermen the Office of Common Clerk or Town Clerk and Clerk of the Peace of the said Borough, which is now accepted by the said Mayor & Aldermen; And George Huish the Younger Gent' is by the unanimous Consent of the said Mayor & Aldermen nominated elected & chosen Common Clerk or Town Clerk of the said Borough

And the said George Huish the Younger doth now here take ⌜& subscribe⌝[1] the Oaths of Allegiance[2] Supremacy & Abjuration and doth repeat & subscribe the Test, and is now sworn Common Clerk or Town Clerk and Clerk of the Peace of the said Borough

Ordered that the said George Huish the Younger do cause the said Surrender and this present (*p. 136*) Writing to be enrolled among the Records of the said Borough
*Signed by:*

| | |
|---|---|
| Edw<sup>d</sup> Linzee Mayor | Michael Atkins |
| Jn<sup>o</sup> White. | Thomas Stanyford |
| L. Barton | Ja<sup>s</sup> Deacon |
| Sam: Brady | Sam: Chandler. |
| John Mounsher | John Carter |

**130**
**12 September 1746**

*p. 137*

*Hand ii.* Borough of Portesmouth
Memorandum it is this day agreed by us whose Hands are hereunto set being the Mayor & Major Part of the Aldermen of the said Borough that from the Thirtieth day of June last past the Bond made from this Corporation to M<sup>r</sup> Paul Green dated the 30<sup>th</sup> of June 1739 on which there is now due the Principal Sum of Three Hundred Pounds shall carry Interest for the Same after the Rate of Four Pounds[3] & Ten Shillings in the Hundred by the Year; and the Chamberlain of the said Borough is hereby directed to pay such Interest on the said Bond; Witness our Hands the 12<sup>th</sup> day of September 1746.
*Signed by:*

| | |
|---|---|
| Edw<sup>d</sup> Linzee Mayor | Michael Atkins |
| L. Barton | Thomas Stanyford |
| Jn<sup>o</sup> White. | Ja<sup>s</sup> Deacon |
| Sam: Brady | Sam: Chandler |
| John Mounsher | John Carter |
| Geo Huish Junior Town Clerk | |

**131**
**15 September 1746**

*p. 138*

*Hand ii.* Borough of Portesmouth
At the Guild Hall of the said Borough the 15<sup>th</sup> day of September 1746 Present

Edward Linzee Esq<sup>r</sup> Mayor
Lewis Barton Esq<sup>r</sup> –
John White Gent' –
Michael Atkins Gent'        } Aldermen
Thomas Stanyford Esq<sup>r</sup>
Samuel Chandler Gent'
John Carter Gent' –

---

[1] Inserted.
[2] '&' struck out.
[3] 'in the Hundred by the Year' struck out.

Benjamin Heron Gent'[1] the Peremptory Burgess of John Vining Esq^r ⌐(deceased)⌐[2] late Mayor was duly sworn ⌐a Burgess⌐[3] of the said Borough before the above Mayor & Aldermen by (*signed by*) Geo Huish Junior Town Clerk

**132**
**29 September 1746**

*p. 139*
*Hand ii.* Borough of Portesmouth
We the Mayor & Major Part of the Aldermen of the said Borough whose Hands are hereunto set do hereby elect & choose John Amherst Esq^r (Son in Law of the present Mayor) to be a Burgess of the said Borough, he being nominated by the said Mayor to be my Peremptory Burgess, Witness our Hands the Twenty Ninth day of September 1746 –
*Signed by:*

| | |
|---|---|
| Edw^d Linzee Mayor | Michael Atkins |
| Sam: Chandler. Mayor Elect. | Thomas Stanyford |
| L. Barton | John Carter |
| Sam: Brady | |

Geo Huish Junior Town Clerk

**133**
**25 December 1746**

*p. 140*
*Hand ii.* Borough of Portesmouth
We whose Hands are hereunto set being the Mayor & Major Part of the Aldermen of the said Borough assembled in Council do hereby nominate elect & choose the Hon^ble Peter Warren Esq^r Rear Admiral of the Blue Squadron of his Majesties Fleet to be a Burgess of the said Borough, Witness our Hands the 25^th day of December 1746 –
*Signed by:*

| | |
|---|---|
| Sam: Chandler. Mayor | Thomas Stanyford |
| Jn^o White. | Edw^d Linzee |
| Sam: Brady | John Carter |
| John Mounsher | |

The above named Rear Admiral Warren was immediately sworn a Burgess before the above Mayor & Aldermen by (*signed by*) Geo Huish Junior Town Clerk.

**134**
**9 January 1746/7**

*p. 141*
*Hand ii.* Borough of Portesmouth
We whose Hands are hereunto set being the Mayor & Major Part of the Aldermen of the said Borough assembled in Council do hereby nominate elect & choose the Hon^ble John Byng Esq^r Rear Admiral of the Blue Squadron of his Majesties Fleet to be a Burgess of the said Borough, Witness our Hands the 9^th day of January 1746 –
*Signed by:*

| | |
|---|---|
| Sam: Chandler. Mayor | L. Barton |
| Jn^o White. | Thomas Stanyford |
| Sam: Brady | Edw^d Linzee |
| John Mounsher | John Carter |

The said Rear Admiral Byng was immediately sworn a Burgess in the Presence of the above Mayor & Aldermen by (*signed by*) Geo Huish Town Clerk

**135**
**21 March 1746/7**

*p. 142*
*Hand ii.* 21^st March 1746 Borough of Portesmouth
Present at the Council Chamber in the Guild Hall of the said Borough
Samuel Chandler Esq^r Mayor
Lewis Barton Esq^r –
John Mounsher Esq^r
Michael Atkins Gent'           } Aldermen
Thomas Stanyford Esq^r
Edward Linzee Gent'

---

¹ P.C.R.O. CE1/14, p. 53, refers to Heron as 'Lieut^t Benj^n Heron'.
² Inserted.
³ Inserted.

Toll Esqʳ Pl*aintiff* & Piggott & others De*fendan*ts

The Mayor & Aldermen of the said Borough being subpoena'd to bring before the Justices appointed to hold the Assizes at Winchester in & for the County of South'ton on Tuesday the 24ᵗʰ day of this instant March the Charter granted by[1] King Charles ⌐the First⌐[2] to this Corporation in order to be produced & given in Evidence in a Cause to be tried at the said Assizes, It is ordered by the Mayor & Aldermen now present that the said Charter be taken out of the Town Chest & delivered into the Custody of the said Mayor in order to be produced at the said Assizes ⌐at the Trial of the said Cause⌐[3] and after it has been so produced it is to be safely brought back & put into the said Chest again –

*Signed by:*

| | |
|---|---|
| Sam: Chandler. Mayor | Michael Atkins |
| L. Barton | Thomas Stanyford |
| John Mounsher | Edwᵈ Linzee |
| Geo Huish Town Clerk | |

**136**
**14 May 1747**

*p. 143*

*Hand ii.* Borough of Portesmouth

We whose Hands[4] are hereunto set being the Mayor & Major Part of the Aldermen of the said Borough do hereby nominate elect & choose the Right Honᵇˡᵉ James Earl of Kildare & Baron Ophaly in the Kingdom of Ireland, and Viscount Leinster of Taplow in the Kingdom of England to be a Burgess of the said Borough, Witness our Hands the Fourteenth day of May 1747.

*Signed by:*

| | |
|---|---|
| Sam: Chandler. Mayor | Michael Atkins |
| L. Barton | Edwᵈ Linzee |
| John Mounsher | John Carter |
| Geo Huish Town Clerk | |

The above named Earl was immediately[5] admitted a Burgess of the said Borough on his Honour in the Presence of the above Mayor & Aldermen by (*signed by*) Geo Huish Town Clerk

**137**
**16 June 1747**

*p. 144*

*Hand ii.* Borough of Portesmouth

We whose Hands are hereunto set being the Mayor & Major Part of the Aldermen of the said Borough do hereby order & direct the Chamberlain of the said Borough to purchase & buy the Statutes at large for the Use of this Corporation,[6] the Expence of which shall be defrayed out of the Money now in his Hands belonging to this Corporation Witness our Hands the 16ᵗʰ June 1747

*Signed by:*

| | |
|---|---|
| Sam: Chandler. Mayor | John Carter |
| L. Barton | Edwᵈ Linzee |
| John Mounsher | Michael Atkins |
| Geo Huish Town Clerk | |

**138**
**1 July 1747**

*p. 145*

*Hand ii.* Borough of Portesmouth

At the Guild Hall of the said Borough the 1ˢᵗ day of July 1747 Present

Samuel Chandler Esqʳ Mayor

Lewis Barton Esqʳ ⎫
William Rickman Esqʳ ⎪
Michael Atkins Gent' ⎬ Aldermen
Edward Linzee Gent' ⎪
John Carter Gent' – ⎭

---

[1] 'this Co' struck out.
[2] Inserted.
[3] Inserted.
[4] '& Seals' struck out.
[5] 'sworn a' struck out.
[6] On 7 Oct. 1750 £9. 18s. was paid to James Wilkinson 'for the Statutes at Large in Seven Volumes' (P.C.R.O. CF1/5, f. 17).

Thomas[1] White Gent' Son of John White Gent' ⌐deceased⌐[2] late one of the Aldermen of this Borough was duly sworn a Burgess of the said Borough pursuant to his Election on the 10th day of April 1728, before the above Mayor & Aldermen by (*signed by*) Geo Huish Town Clerk

**139**
**3 July 1747[3]**

p. 146

*Hand ii.* Borough of Portsmouth

Whereas Binsteed Jeffery House Carpenter and William Ward an Upholder have in open Defiance & contrary to the repeated Orders of the Mayor of this Borough signifyed to them by the Serjeant at Mace built a Stall or Standing ⌐in the Fair or Free Mart⌐[4] against the Town Hall of the said Borough whereby one of the Arches is darkened & the Passage of the Street so much obstructed that the said Standing is a common Nusance, and they having been required to remove the said Standing have obstinately & contemptuously refused to do the Same, and the said William Ward in particular hath greatly insulted & abused the said Mayor Now We whose Hands are hereunto set being the Mayor & Major Part of the Aldermen of the said Borough do hereby order & direct the Serjeants at Mace of the said Borough & each of them immediately to give Notice to the said Binsteed Jeffery & William Ward or one of them to pull down & remove the said Standing forthwith, & on their ⌐or either of their⌐[5] neglecting or refusing to comply therewith the said Serjeants are hereby authorized & directed to pull down & remove the Same Witness our Hands the 3d day of July 1747.

*Signed by:*

Sam: Chandler. Mayor        John Mounsher
L. Barton                            Michael Atkins

**140**
**29 September 1747**

p. 147

*Hand ii.* Borough of Portsmouth

We whose Hands are hereunto set being the Mayor & Major Part of the Aldermen of the said Borough do hereby elect & choose Samuel Chandler Gent' the Younger (Son of Samuel Chandler Esqr the present Mayor) to be a Burgess of the said Borough, he being nominated by me the said Mayor to be my Peremptory Burgess, Witness our Hands the 29th day of September 1747.

*Signed by:*

Sam: Chandler. Mayor        Michael Atkins
John Carter Mayor Elect      Thomas Stanyford
John Mounsher                   Edwd Linzee

The said Mr Chandler the Younger was immediately sworn a Burgess of the said Borough in the Presence of the above Mayor & Aldermen by (*signed by*) Geo Huish Town Clerk

**141**
**13 November 1747**

p. 148

*Hand ii.* Borough of Portsmouth

We whose Hands are hereunto set being the Mayor & Major Part of the Aldermen of the said Borough assembled in Council do hereby nominate elect & choose the Honble Edward Legge Esqr to be a Burgess of the said Borough, Witness our Hands the 13th November 1747 –

*Signed by:*

John Carter Mayor            Jas Deacon
John Mounsher                 Sam: Chandler
William Rickman               Edwd Linzee
Michael Atkins
Geo Huish Town Clerk

---

[1] 'John' struck out before 'Thomas'.
[2] Inserted.
[3] The entire entry is struck out.
[4] Inserted.
[5] Inserted.

**142**

**21 December 1747**     *p. 149*[1]

*Hand ii.* Borough of Portesmouth

We whose Hands are hereunto set being the Mayor & Major Part of the Aldermen of the said Borough do hereby nominate elect & choose[2] Sir Edward Hawke Knight of the most Honourable Order of the Bath to be a Burgess of the said Borough, Witness our Hands the Twenty First day of December 1747

*Signed by:*

| | |
|---|---|
| John Carter Mayor | Thomas Stanyford |
| L. Barton | Edw^d Linzee |
| John Mounsher | Sam: Chandler. |
| Geo Huish Town Clerk | |

**143**

**28 December 1747**     *Hand ii.* Borough of Portesmouth

At the Guild Hall of the said Borough the 28^th of December 1747, Present

John Carter Esq^r Mayor

Lewis Barton Esq^r –
John Mounsher Esq^r –
Michael Atkins Gent' –          } Aldermen
Thomas Stanyford Esq^r –
Samuel Chandler Gent'

The Hon^ble Sir Edward Hawke Kn^t of the Bath was duly sworn a Burgess of the said Borough pursuant to the above Election by (*signed by*) Geo Huish Town Clerk

**144**

**22 March 1747/8**     *p. 150*

*Hand ii.* Borough of Portesmouth

We whose Hands are hereunto set being the Mayor & Major Part of the Aldermen of the said Borough do hereby consent & agree to demise & grant by Lease under our Common Seal to James Robinson of Portsea in the said Borough Husbandman[3] All that long Slip or Piece of[4] Ground being Part of the Wast Lands belonging to this Corporation situate lying & being near the Green Post & within the Liberties of the said Borough & on the West Side of the Road or Highway leading from the Land Port Gate of Portsmouth aforesaid to Cosham, containing in Length from North to South One Hundred & Eighty Yards & in Breadth from East to West ⌐at the South End thereof Seventeen Yards & at the North End⌐[5] Eight Yards be it more or less, as the Same is now marked & staked out, and bounded as followeth that is to say, with Lands of      [6] Cobden &      [7] Brouncker[8] on the West & with the said Highway on the North East & South parts thereof, Out of which said Demise & Grant is to be always excepted & reserved a Way of Ten Feet wide leading from the said Highway into the said Lands of the said Cobden & Brouncker To hold to the said James Robinson his Executors Administrators & Assigns from Lady Day next ensuing for the Term of One Thousand Years under the yearly Rent of Thirteen Shillings & Four Pence payable half yearly, with the Clauses & Covenants usually contained in such Leases, Witness our Hands the Twenty Second day of March 1747.[9]

*Signed by:*

| | |
|---|---|
| John Carter Mayor | Sam: Chandler. |
| L. Barton | Ja^s Deacon |
| John Mounsher | Edw^d Linzee |

---

[1] For a reproduction of this page see fig. 1.
[2] 'the Hon^ble' struck out.
[3] Robinson took a lease of the Green Post for 1000 years in May 1748 (East, p. 557).
[4] 'Wast' struck out.
[5] Inserted.
[6] Space left blank.
[7] Space left blank.
[8] In 1725 Dr Samuel Brady paid rates on 'Brunkerds' in Kingston and Buckland (P.C.R.O. 81A/3/21/1); he was also in possession two years later (East, p. 721).
[9] P.C.R.O. CF20/1, p. 195, dates this lease 3 May 1748.

**145**

**9 August 1748**

*p. 151*

*Hand ii.* Borough of Portesmouth

We the Mayor & Major Part of the Aldermen of the said Borough whose Hands are hereunto set do hereby agree to demise & let to William Hodgkin of Portsmouth aforesaid Carter by Lease under our Common Seal All the Wharfage Cranage & Petty Customs of this Corporation[1] for the Term of Three Years from Michaelmas next ensuing at the yearly Rent of Seventy Pounds to be paid at Two equal half Yearly Payments, & two fat Capons, & under the same Covenants Provisoes & Agreements as are mentioned in the Lease by which William Mathews now holds the Same which will expire at the said Michaelmas; The said William Hodgkin keeping the Premises in good Repair & so leaving them at the End of the Term, & procuring James Whitehead of Portsmouth aforesaid Merchant to become bound in a Bond of the Penalty of Five Hundred Pounds with him the said William Hodgkin for the Performance of the Covenants in such Lease to be granted to the said William on his Part to be Paid done & performed, Witness our Hands the 9th day of August 1748.[2]

*Signed by:*

| | |
|---|---|
| John Carter Mayor | Michael Atkins |
| L. Barton | Sam: Chandler |
| John Mounsher | Edwd Linzee |

I do hereby agree to accept of a Lease according to the above Agreement & to execute a Counterpart thereof, and also to procure the above named James Whitehead to become bound with me in a Bond of the Penalty of Five Hundred Pounds for the Performance of the Covenants in the said Lease, Witness my Hand. *Signed by* William Hodgkin Witness (*signed by*) James Martin

**146**

**29 September 1748**

*p. 152*

*Hand ii.* Borough of Portesmouth

We whose Hands are hereunto set being the Mayor & Major Part of the Aldermen of the said Borough do hereby elect & choose Mr John Rickman the Younger to be a Burgess of the said Borough (he being nominated by me the said Mayor to be my Peremptory Burgess) Witness our Hands the 29th of September 1748.

*Signed by:*

| | |
|---|---|
| John Carter Mayor | Thomas Stanyford |
| William Rickman Mayor Elect | Edwd Linzee |
| John Mounsher | Sam: Chandler. |

The said Mr Rickman the Younger was immediately sworn a Burgess of the said Borough in the Presence of the above Mayor & Aldermen by (*signed by*) Geo Huish Town Clerk

**147**

**12 June 1749**

*p. 153*

*Hand v.* Know all Men by these Presents that the Mayor Aldermen and Burgesses of the Borough of Portsmouth in the County of South'ton, have made nominated constituted and appointed and by these presents Do make nominate constitute and appoint Thomas Imber Notary Publick one of the Procurators General of the Consistory Court of the Right Reverend Father in God Benjamin by divine Permission Lord Bishop of Winchester their lawfull Proctor to all Intents and Purposes whatsoever for them and in their Names to cite or cause to be cited into the said Court and for that purpose to issue out a Citation against John Goven of the Parish of Portsmouth aforesaid to answer them the said Mayor Aldermen and Burgesses in a certain Cause of Perturbation of Seat, and to give in and exhibit a Libell for them against the said John Goven in the said Cause, and farther to expedite and do all and singular such Acts Matters and things as may or shall be needfull and necessary to be done for and on the behalf of the Mayor Aldermen

---

[1] On 4 Aug. 1747 2s. 6d. was paid 'for printing an[d] Advertising for Letting the Wharfage' (P.C.R.O. CF1/5, f. 1).

[2] P.C.R.O. CF20/1, p. 195, dates this lease 1 Oct. 1748.

and Burgesses aforesaid in the premisses And whatsoever their said Proctor shall lawfully do or cause to be done in or touching the Premisses, they do promise to ratify and confirm In Witness Whereof the said Mayor Aldermen and Burgesses of the Borough of Portsmouth aforesaid have hereunto affixed their Common Seal the Twelfth day of June in the Twenty Third Year of the Reign of our Sovereign Lord George the Second by the Grace of God of Great Britain France and Ireland King Defender of the Faith and so forth And in the Year of our Lord One Thousand Seven Hundred and Forty Nine.[1]

*Hand ii.* Examined with the Original by me (*signed by*) Geo Huish Town Clerk

**148**

**2 August 1749**

*p. 154*

*Hand ii.* Borough of Portesmouth

We whose Hands are hereunto set being the Mayor and Major Part of the Aldermen of the said Borough do hereby nominate elect & choose the Right Hon^ble John Earl of Sandwich to be a Burgess of the said Borough, Witness our Hands the 2^d day of August 1749.

*Signed by:*

| William Rickman Maijor | Edw^d Linzee |
| John Mounsher | Sam: Chandler. |
| Michael Atkins | John Carter |

His Lordship was immediately admitted a Burgess on his Honour in the Presence of the above Mayor & Aldermen by (*signed by*) Geo Huish Town Clerk

**149**

**2 August 1749**

*p. 155*

*Hand ii.* Borough of Portesmouth

We whose Hands are hereunto set being the Mayor & Major Part of the Aldermen of the said Borough do hereby nominate elect & choose the Right Hon^ble William Viscount Barrington, and the Hon^ble Thomas Villiers Esq^r, to be Burgesses of the said Borough, Witness our Hands the 2^d of August 1749.

*Signed by:*

| William Rickman Maijor | Edw^d Linzee |
| John Mounsher | Sam: Chandler. |
| Michael Atkins | John Carter |

His Lordship was immediately admitted a Burgess on his Honour, and the above named M^r Villiers was immediately sworn a Burgess, in the Presence of the above Mayor & Aldermen by (*signed by*) Geo Huish Town Clerk

**150**

**4 August 1749**

*p. 156*

*Hand ii.* Borough of Portesmouth

We whose Hands are hereunto subscribed being the ⌐Deputy⌐[2] Mayor & Major Part of the Aldermen of the said Borough do hereby nominate elect & choose Savage Mostyn Esq^r Comptroller of his Majesties Navy & John Clevland Esq^r Secretary of the Admiralty to be Burgesses of the said Borough, Witness our Hands the 4^th of August 1749.

*Signed by:*

| Edw^d Linzee Dep*uty* Mayor | Sam: Chandler. |
| John Mounsher | John Carter |
| Michael Atkins | |
| Geo Huish Town Clerk | |

**151**

**5 August 1749**

*Hand ii.* 5^th August 1749

The above named Savage Mostyn Esq^r & John Clevland Esq^r were severally sworn Burgesses of the said Borough in the Presence of the above Deputy Mayor & Aldermen by (*signed by*) Geo Huish Town Clerk

---

[1] East, pp. 739–43, gives an account of this case; the papers of the case in the Consistory Court are Hants.R.O. C/10/A/642.
[2] Inserted.

**152**
**19 September 1749**[1] *p. 157*

*Hand ii.* Borough of Portesmouth

We whose Hands are hereunto set being the Mayor & Major Part of the Aldermen of the said Borough do hereby order & direct the Chamberlain of the said Borough to cause a Well to be digged & a Pump to be placed[2] in the Street before the Goal of the said Borough for the better supplying the said Goal with Water, and what Expence he shall be at for making the said Well & setting in the said Pump he is to place to the Account of this Corporation, Witness our Hands the 19th September 1749.

*Signed by:*

| | |
|---|---|
| William Rickman Maijor | Thomas Stanyford |
| Edwd Linzee | Michael Atkins |
| John Carter | John Mounsher |
| Sam: Chandler. | |

**153**
**27 September 1749** *p. 158*

*Hand ii.* 27th day of September 1749 Borough of Portesmouth

At an Assembly in the Council Chamber in the Guild Hall of the said Borough, being then present pursuant to Summons

William Rickman Esqr Mayor

Lewis Barton Esqr –
John Mounsher Esqr –
Michael Atkins Esqr –
Thomas Stanyford Esqr – ⎫ Aldermen
Edward Linzee Gent' ⎬
Samuel Chandler Gent' ⎭
John Carter Esqr –

The Honble Sir Edward Hawke Knt of the Bath, Thomas Missing Esqr, John Leeke Gent' & Thomas White Gent' Four of the Burgesses of the said Borough were by the above named Mayor & Aldermen unanimously nominated elected & chosen Aldermen of the said Borough; And the said Thomas Missing John Leeke & Thomas White did then & there immediately take & subscribe the Oaths of Allegiance Supremacy & Abjuration and did repeat & subscribe the Test against Transubstantiation, and were then & there severally sworn Aldermen of the said Borough before the said Mayor & Aldermen In witness whereof the said Mayor and Aldermen have hereunto set their Hands the day & year above written –

*Signed by:*

| | |
|---|---|
| William Rickman Maijor | Thomas Stanyford |
| L. Barton | Edwd Linzee |
| John Mounsher | Sam: Chandler. |
| Michael Atkins | John Carter |
| Geo Huish Town Clerk | |

**154**
**29 September 1749** *p. 159*

*Hand ii.* Borough of Portesmouth

We whose Hands are hereunto set being the Mayor & Major Part of the Aldermen of the said Borough do hereby elect & choose Mr John Gawler to be a Burgess of the said Borough (he being nominated by me the said Mayor to be my Peremptory Burgess) Witness our Hands the 29th of September 1749.

*Signed by:*

| | |
|---|---|
| William Rickman Maijor | John Carter |
| Thomas Stanyford Mayor elect | Thomas Missing |
| John Mounsher | Jno Leeke |
| Edwd Linzee | Thos White. |
| Sam: Chandler. | |

The said Mr John Gawler was immediately sworn a Burgess of the said Borough in the Presence of the above Mayor & Aldermen by *(signed by)* Geo Huish Town Clerk

---

[1] Printed in East, p. 270.
[2] 'b' struck out.

**155**

**13 October 1749**

*Hand ii.* 13<sup>th</sup> October 1749 Borough of Portesmouth
At the House of Sir Edward Hawke within the said Borough, present

Thomas Stanyford Esq<sup>r</sup> Mayor

John Mounsher Esq<sup>r</sup> –
Michael Atkins Esq<sup>r</sup> –
Edward Linzee Gent' –
Samuel Chandler Gent' – } Aldermen
John Carter Esq<sup>r</sup> –
John Leeke Gent' –
Thomas White Gent' –

The Hon<sup>ble</sup> Sir Edward Hawke Kn<sup>t</sup> of the Bath, who on the Twenty Seventh day of September last was nominated elected & chosen an Alderman of the said Borough, did take & subscribe the Oaths of Allegiance Supremacy & Abjuration, and did repeat & subscribe the Test against Transubstantiation, and was duly sworn an Alderman of the said Borough before the said Mayor by (*signed by*) Geo Huish Town Clerk

**156**

**14 November 1749**

*p. 161*

*Hand ii.* Borough of Portesmouth
We whose Hands are hereunto set being the Mayor & Major Part of the Aldermen of the said Borough do hereby consent & agree to demise & grant by Lease under our Common Seal to Thomas Earley of Portsmouth aforesaid Victualler[1] All that Incroachment or Land incroached to the Messuage or Tenement of the said Thomas Earley called the Duke of Cumberlands Head situate on the South Side of the High Street & nigh the Old Magazine in Portsmouth aforesaid containing in Length at the Front thereof Twenty Four Feet & Two Inches, in Breadth on the East Side Two Feet & Three Inches & on the West Side One Foot & Eleven Inches, whereon the new erected Front of the said Messuage now stands To hold to the said Thomas Earley his Executors Administrators & Assigns from Lady Day last past for the Term of One Thousand Years under the yearly Rent of ⌐Five Shillings⌐[2] payable half yearly ⌐& one Capon yearly⌐[3] with the Clauses & Covenants usually contained in such Leases Witness our Hands the Fourteenth day of November 1749.

*Signed by:*

Sam: Chandler. D*eputy* Mayor        Michael Atkins
John Mounsher                        Jn<sup>o</sup> Leeke
Edw<sup>d</sup> Linzee                       Tho<sup>s</sup> White.
John Carter

**157**

**28 November 1749**

*p. 162*

*Hand ii.* Borough of Portesmouth
We whose Hands are hereunto set being the Mayor & Major Part of the Aldermen of the said Borough do hereby consent & agree to demise & grant by Lease under our Common Seal to William Legg of Portsmouth aforesaid Distiller[4] All that Piece of Beach Ground situate lying & being at the lower End of the Point without the Point Gate of Portsmouth aforesaid & adjoining to the Messuage or Tenement late of Henry Belfield Gent' dec*eased* now belonging to the said William Legg ⌐on the West⌐[5] & a Stable lately built by Andrew Mounsher on the South, and facing to the Road or Highway on the East & North, which said Piece of Beach Ground hereby intended to be granted contains on the North Side next the Sea or Harbour of Portsmouth Eight Feet & Six Inches, on the West Side next the said William Leggs House Eight Feet & Eight Inches, on the South Side next the said Andrew Mounshers Stable Ten Feet & Three Inches, & on the East Side next the said Road or Highway

---

[1] Paid rates on property in High Street (P.R.C.O. 81A/3/20/20, no. 16: 28 Apr. 1750).
[2] Inserted in space left blank.
[3] Inserted.
[4] Paid rates on property on the Point (P.C.R.O. 81A/3/20/20, no. 16: 28 Apr. 1750).
[5] Inserted.

Eight Feet & Four Inches or thereabout, as the Same is now marked & staked out, To hold to the said William Legg his Executors Administrators & Assigns from Michaelmas last past for the Term of One Thousand Years under the yearly Rent of Thirteen Shillings & Four Pence payable half yearly, with the Clauses & Covenants usually contained in such Leases, Witness our Hands the 28th Day of November 1749. [1]

*Signed by:*

Sam: Chandler *Deputy* Mayor       Michael Atkins
John Mounsher      Jno Leeke
Edwd Linzee      Thos White.
John Carter

**158**

**5 January 1749/50** [2]      *p. 163*

*Hand ii.* Borough of Portsmouth

We whose Hands are hereunto set being the Mayor & Major Part of the Aldermen of the said Borough this day assembled in Council at the Guild Hall of the same Borough do hereby consent & agree to the following Resolutions,

1. That[3] Mr John Shepherd the Chamberlain of the said Borough shall forthwith cause a new Pound to be erected & made at the Expence of this Corporation at Kingwell or[4] in such other convenient Place within the Liberties of the said Borough as we shall pitch upon

2. That the ⌐Common⌐[5] Seal of this Borough shall be affixed to the Syndickship[6] for commencing a Suit in the Spiritual Court at Winchester against John Goven of Portsmouth for Perturbation of a Seat in the Parish Church there

3. That the Town Clerk of this Borough do forthwith purchase the Statutes at large for the Use & at the Expence of this Corporation in the best Manner he possibly can

4. That Actions at Law shall be brought & prosecuted, or Distresses according to antient Custom made on all & every such Persons & Person as shall refuse to pay the several Sums of Money due & payable to this Corporation for Anchorage Groundage & Bushellage of all Ships & Vessells & their Goods within the Harbour of Portsmouth. Witness our Hands the Fifth day of January 1749.

*Signed by:*

Thomas Stanyford Mayor      John Carter
Michael Atkins      Jno Leeke
John Mounsher      Thos White.
Edwd Linzee

**159**

**5 January 1749/50**      *p. 164*

*Hand v.* Whereas a certain Cause of Perturbation of Seat is intended to be instituted in the Consistory Court of the Right Reverend Father in God Benjamin by Divine permission Lord Bishop of Winchester on the Behalf of the Mayor Aldermen and Burgesses of the Borough of Portsmouth in the County of Southampton against John Goven of the Parish of Portsmouth in the said County of Southampton and Diocess of Winchester.

Now Know all men by these Presents That We the Mayor Aldermen and Burgesses of the Borough of Portsmouth aforesaid by virtue of ⌐our⌐[7] Common Seal affixed hereto for divers good Causes and Considerations us thereunto moving have and by these presents Do nominate constitute and appoint Edward Hooker of Martyr Worthy in the County aforesaid Esquire to be our true and lawfull Syndick[8] for us and on our behalf as the Mayor Aldermen and Burgesses of the

---

[1] P.C.R.O. CF20/1, p. 196, dates this lease 16 Jan. 1749/50.
[2] Printed in East, pp. 270–1.
[3] 'a new Pound' struck out.
[4] 'at' struck out.
[5] MS. 'Commõn'.
[6] A document appointing a syndic (a usage not recorded in *The Oxford English dictionary* (13v., 1933), under syndic).
[7] Inserted (hand vi); 'their' struck out.
[8] 'One deputed to represent, and transact the affairs of, a corporation' (*The Oxford English dictionary* (13v., 1933), syndic sb 2).

said Borough of Portsmouth to procure and obtain a Citation or Decree to issue under the Seal of the said Consistory Court of Winchester against the said John Goven to appear on a certain day time and place to be therein named then and there to answer to us the Mayor Aldermen and Burgesses of the Borough of Portsmouth aforesaid acting by the said Edward Hooker our Syndick in a Cause of Perturbation of Seat and to give a Libell therein and to expedite and do all and singular such other Acts Matters and Things as may or shall be ⌈needfull⌉[1] and necessary to be done for and on the behalf of us the Mayor Aldermen and Burgesses aforesaid in the said Cause untill a Definitive Sentence or Final Decree shall be had made and given thereto And We do hereby promise to allow for firm and valid all and whatsoever our said Syndick shall lawfully do or cause to be done in the (*p. 165*) premisses by Virtue of these presents In Witness whereof we the said Mayor Aldermen and Burgesses of the Borough of Portsmouth aforesaid have hereunto put our Common Seal this Fifth Day of January in the Year of our Lord One Thousand Seven Hundred and Forty Nine.

*Hand ii.* Examined with the Original by me (*signed by*) Geo Huish Town Clerk

**160**

**20 March 1749/50**[2]     *Hand ii.* Borough of Portesmouth

Whereas on our making the Earl of Sandwich, the Lord Viscount Barrington, the Hon^ble Thomas Villiers Esq^r, Savage Mostyn Esq^r & John Clevland Esq^r Burgesses of the said Borough in the Month of August last We gave Directions that neither the Town Clerk, nor Serjeants at Mace, or Cryer of this Borough should demand or receive any Fees from them, but that we would make those Officers Satisfaction for such Fees, Now we whose Hands are hereunto set being the Mayor & Major Part of the Aldermen of the said Borough do hereby order & direct the Chamberlain of the said Borough to pay to the Town Clerk Five Guineas, to the Two Serjeants at Mace between them Two Pounds Twelve Shillings & Six Pence, & to the Common Beadle or Cryer One Pound & Five Shillings as a Gratuity or Present from this Corporation on the making those Burgesses. Witness our Hands the 20^th March 1749.

*Signed by:*

| | |
|---|---|
| Sam: Chandler. *Deputy* Mayor | Jn^o Leeke |
| John Mounsher | Tho^s White. |
| Michael Atkins | Edw^d Linzee |
| John Carter | |

**161**

**25 September 1750**     *p. 166*

*Hand v.* Borough of Portsmouth

We whose Hands are hereunto set being the Mayor and Major Part of the Aldermen of the said Borough do hereby consent and agree to demise and grant by Lease under our Common Seal to John Compton and John Merac of Portsmouth aforesaid Ropemakers All that Piece of Ground being Part of the Wast Lands belonging to this Corporation situate lying and being on the Common within the Liberties of the said Borough ⌈and⌉[3] on the South Side of the Ropewalk now belonging to them the said John Compton and John Merac And formerly M^r Richard Brambles[4] and bounded by the Mill Pond, which said Piece of Ground contains in Length from the Tenements now or late Arnolds to the Mill Dam ⌈Six Hundred and Sixty⌉[5] Feet of Assize or thereabout, And also All that small Slip of Ground on the North or Outside of the said Ropewalk containing in Length Four Hundred and ⌈Ninety Six⌉[6] Feet of Assize and in Breadth Three Feet of Assize and commencing at the End of the small Tar House now belonging to the said Ropewalk; Which Ropewalk now ranges down to the Pales or Fence of the Dwelling house of Joshua Woodman on the East and contains in Length from the East End of the Westmost Ropehouse

---

[1] MS. 'needfall'.

[2] Printed in East, p. 271.

[3] Inserted.

[4] Took 1000-year leases on a rope-house and ground on the north side of Mill Pond 10 Jan. 1680/1 and 10 Jan. 1681/2 (East, p. 480).

[5] Inserted in space left blank.

[6] Possibly inserted in space left blank.

of the said John Compton and John Merac to the said Pales or Fence of the said Joshua Woodmans Dwelling house Eleven Hundred and ⌐Thirty Eight¬[1] Feet of Assize or thereabout, and the said Pales or Fence are at all times hereafter to be the Boundary or utmost Length of the said Ropewalk; and the said John Compton and John Merac in Consideration of granting this present Lease are to surrender and yield up to the Corporation all their Right to the Soil and Ground which they claim from the said Woodmans Pales or Fence down to the Fence which formerly belonged to the House of John Hattam on the East and was Part of the said Ropewalk To hold to the said John Compton and John Merac their Executors Administrators and Assigns from Michaelmas next ensuing for the Term of ⌐Nine Hundred & Thirty One¬[2] Years under the yearly Rent of Six Shillings and Eight Pence payable half yearly, with the Clauses and Covenants usually contained in such Leases Witness our hands the Twenty Fifth day of September 1750.[3]

*Signed by:*

| | |
|---|---|
| Thomas Stanyford Mayor | Sam Chandler. |
| John Mounsher | Edw<sup>d</sup> Linzee |
| Tho<sup>s</sup> Missing | Jn<sup>o</sup> Leeke |
| John Carter | Tho<sup>s</sup> White. |

**162**

**29 September 1750**

p. 167

*Hand ii.* Borough of Portesmouth

We whose Hands are hereunto set being the Major & Mayor Part of the Aldermen of the said Borough do hereby elect & choose M<sup>r</sup> Stanyford Blanckley to be a Burgess of the said Borough (he being nominated by me the said Mayor to be my Peremptory Burgess) Witness our Hands the 29<sup>th</sup> day of September 1750 –

*Signed by:*

| | |
|---|---|
| Thomas Stanyford Mayor | Sam Chandler. |
| Tho<sup>s</sup> Missing Mayor Elect | John Carter |
| John Mounsher | Jn<sup>o</sup> Leeke |
| Edw<sup>d</sup> Linzee | Tho<sup>s</sup> White. |

The said M<sup>r</sup> Stanyford Blanckley was immediately sworn a Burgess of the said Borough in the Presence of the above Mayor & Aldermen by (*signed by*) Geo Huish Town Clerk

**163**

**2 October 1750[4]**

p. 168

*Hand ii.* Borough of Portesmouth

We whose Hands are hereunto set being the Mayor & Major Part of the Aldermen of the said Borough do hereby order & direct M<sup>r</sup> John Shepherd the Chamberlain of the said Borough to cause the Pump & Well near the Fish Market in the High Street of the said Borough to be forthwith repaired & put into good Order at the Expence of this Corporation, Witness our Hands the 2<sup>d</sup> day of October 1750[5]

*Signed by:*

| | |
|---|---|
| Thomas Missing Mayor | Jn<sup>o</sup> Leeke |
| Edw<sup>d</sup> Linzee | Michael Atkins |
| Sam: Chandler. | Tho<sup>s</sup> White. |
| John Carter | John Mounsher |

**164**

**27 October 1750**

p. 169

*Hand ii.* Borough of Portesmouth

We whose Hands are hereunto set being the Mayor & Major Part of the Aldermen[6] of the said Borough do hereby nominate elect & choose the Sixty Three following Persons to be Burgesses of the said Borough, viz<sup>t</sup> [7]

---

[1] Possibly inserted in space left blank.
[2] Inserted (hand ii); 'One Thousand' struck out.
[3] P.C.R.O. CF20/1, p. 196, dates this lease 23 Oct. 1750.
[4] Printed in East, p. 271.
[5] On 3 Oct. 1750 5*s.* was paid to 'W<sup>m</sup> Atkins for Repairing a pump' (P.C.R.O. CF1/5, f. 17).
[6] 'do' struck out.
[7] There is a tick after each entry except 1, 2, 8–10, 13, 20 and 37–63.

| | |
|---|---|
| 1 | Francis Whithed Esq^r |
| 2 | Richard Champneys Esq^r |
| 3 | William Green Esq^r |
| 4 | The Rev^d M^r Henry Taylor |
| 5 | M^r Samuel Leeke |
| 6 | M^r John Vining Heron |
| 7 | M^r Mathew Metcalfe |
| 8 | M^r Michael Francklin of Poole |
| 9 | M^r James Royston of London |
| 10 | M^r Richard Boyfield of London |
| 11 | M^r James Bucknall |
| 12 | M^r Thomas Eyer |
| 13 | M^r James Kirkpatrick of Newport |
| 14 | M^r John Rickman of Yarmouth |
| 15 | M^r John Bissell |
| 16 | M^r Henry Friend |
| 17 | M^r John Merac |
| 18 | M^r John Compton |
| 19 | M^r James Wilkinson |
| 20 | M^r Thomas Appleford |
| 21 | M^r Joseph Collins |
| 22 | M^r Robert Orr |
| 23 | M^r John Missing |
| 24 | M^r James Stares of ⌐Crofton¬¹ |
| 25 | M^r James Stares Junior of Newland |
| 26 | M^r John Hewett of Crofton |
| 27 | M^r Thomas White of Crabthorn |
| 28 | M^r Henry Lys |
| 29 | M^r Richard Laugharne |
| 30 | M^r George Clarke |
| 31 | M^r John Lowe |
| 32 | M^r Samuel Spicer |
| 33 | M^r Timothy Pike |
| 34 | M^r Thomas Monday |
| 35 | M^r Jonathan Shepherd |
| 36² | M^r Andrew Mounsher |
| 37 | The most Noble Charles Duke of Richmond &c |
| 38 | Lord George Lenox |
| 39 | ⌐M^r¬³ Thomas Missing Son of Thomas Missing Esq^r Mayor. |
| 40 | M^r Thomas Mounsher Son of Alderman Mounsher. |
| 41 | M^r Eyles Mounsher |
| 42 | M^r John Mounsher |
| 43 | M^r Thomas Jones – |
| 44 | M^r Thomas Rickman |
| 45 | M^r William Rickman |
| 46 | M^r John Rickman – |
| 47 | M^r Elias Benjamin De La Fontaine of London |
| 48 | M^r Edward Linzee |
| 49 | M^r Robert Linzee |
| 50 | M^r Samuel Hood Grandson of Alderman Linzee |
| 51 | M^r George Walton Son of M^r John Walton Head Master of the Royal Academy |
| 52 | M^r John Carter – |
| 53 | M^r William Carter |
| 54 | M^r Daniel Carter |

41–43 } Grandsons of Alderman Mounsher

44–46 } Sons of Alderman Rickman

48–49 } Sons of Alderman Linzee

52–54 } Sons of Alderman Carter

¹ Inserted; 'Titchfield' struck out.
² Two lines are drawn below this figure.
³ Inserted.

55    M^r John Bayly Son of Doctor George Bayly of Chichester.
56    Martin[1] Bladen Hawke Esq^r ⎫
57    M^r Edward Hawke –        ⎬    Sons of Sir Edward Hawke Kn^t of the Bath
⌐58⌐[2] M^r William Hawke –     ⎬      & Alderman
⌐59⌐[3] M^r Chaloner[4] Hawke –   ⎭
⌐60⌐[5] M^r John Heron Grandson of Alderman Leeke
⌐61⌐[6] M^r Charles White Brother of Alderman White
⌐62⌐[7] M^r William Deacon Son of the late Alderman Deacon
⌐63⌐[8] M^r Richard Jones[9] Grandson of Alderman Mounsher

Witness our Hands (at the House of John Carter Esq^r within the said Borough, where we are now assembled) the Twenty Seventh day of October in the Year of our Lord 1750

*Signed by:*

| | |
|---|---|
| Thomas Missing Mayor | Sam Chandler. |
| John Mounsher | John Carter |
| William Rickman | Jn^o Leeke |
| Edw^d Linzee | Tho^s White. |
| Geo Huish Town Clerk | |

**165**

**27 October 1750**

*Hand ii.* Borough of Portesmouth

     We whose Hands are hereunto set being the Mayor & Major Part of the Aldermen of the said Borough this day assembled at the House of John Carter Esq^r within the said Borough, do hereby nominate elect & choose M^r Philip Varlo Son in Law of Alderman Atkins to be a Burgess of the said Borough, Witness our Hands the 27^th of October 1750

*Signed by:*

| | |
|---|---|
| Thomas Missing Mayor | Sam: Chandler. |
| John Mounsher | John Carter |
| William Rickman | Jn^o Leeke |
| Michael Atkins | Tho^s White. |
| Edw^d Linzee | |
| Geo Huish Town Clerk | |

**166**

**27 October 1750**

*Hand ii.* 27^th October 1750 Borough of Portesmouth
     Present at the House of John Carter Esq^r within the said Borough

Thomas Missing Esq^r Mayor
John Mounsher Esq^r –       ⎫
William Rickman Esq^r      ⎬
Edward Linzee Gent' –     ⎬
Samuel Chandler Gent'    ⎬    Aldermen
John Carter Esq^r –        ⎬
John Leeke Gent' –       ⎬
Thomas White Gent' –    ⎭

1. The Reverend M^r Henry Taylor, M^r John Rickman Sen*ior* & M^r Thomas
2. Monday were severally sworn Burgesses of the said Borough pursuant to their
3. Election this day by (*signed by*) Geo Huish Town Clerk

---

[1] 'M^r' struck out before 'Martin'.
[2] Altered from '57'.
[3] Altered from '58'.
[4] 'O' struck out.
[5] Added; '59' struck out.
[6] Altered from '60'.
[7] Altered from '61'.
[8] Altered from '62'.
[9] 'M', half-written, struck out.

**167**

**27 October 1750**

*p. 173*

*Hand ii.* Borough of Portesmouth

At the Guild Hall of the said Borough the 27<sup>th</sup> of October 1750 Present

Thomas Missing Esq<sup>r</sup> Mayor

John Mounsher Esq<sup>r</sup>
William Rickman Esq<sup>r</sup>
Edward Linzcc Gent'
Samuel Chandler Gent' } Aldermen
John Carter Esq<sup>r</sup> –
John Leeke Gent' –
Thomas White Gent' –

1. M<sup>r</sup> Samuel Leeke
2. M<sup>r</sup> John Vining Heron –
3. M<sup>r</sup> Mathew Metcalfe
4. M<sup>r</sup> James Bucknall –
5. M<sup>r</sup> Thomas Eyer –
6. M<sup>r</sup> John Bissell –
7. M<sup>r</sup> Philip Varlo –
8. M<sup>r</sup> Henry Friend –
9. M<sup>r</sup> John Merac –
10. M<sup>r</sup> John Compton –
11. M<sup>r</sup> James Wilkinson –
12. M<sup>r</sup> Robert Orr –
13. M<sup>r</sup> John Missing –
14. M<sup>r</sup> Thomas White –
15. M<sup>r</sup> Henry Lys –
16. M<sup>r</sup> Richard Laugharne
17. M<sup>r</sup> John Lowe –
18. M<sup>r</sup> Samuel Spicer –
19. M<sup>r</sup> Timothy Pike –
20. M<sup>r</sup> Jonathan Shepherd, &
21. M<sup>r</sup> Andrew Mounsher –

were severally sworn Burgesses of the said Borough pursuant to their Election this day by (*signed by*) Geo Huish Town Clerk

**168**

**8 November 1750**

*p. 174*

*Hand ii.* Borough of Portesmouth

At the Guild Hall of the said Borough the 8<sup>th</sup> day of November 1750 Present

Thomas Missing Esq<sup>r</sup> Mayor
John Mounsher Esq<sup>r</sup> –
William Rickman Esq<sup>r</sup> –
Samuel Chandler Gent' } Aldermen
John Carter Esq<sup>r</sup> –
John Leeke Gent' –
Thomas White Gent' –

1. William Green Esq<sup>r</sup> –
2. M<sup>r</sup> Joseph Collins –
3. M<sup>r</sup> James Stares Sen*ior* –
4. M<sup>r</sup> James Stares Junior –
5. M<sup>r</sup> John Hewett, & –
6. M<sup>r</sup> George Clarke –

were severally sworn Burgesses of the said Borough pursuant to their Election on the 27<sup>th</sup> of October last by (*signed by*) Geo Huish Town Clerk

**169**

**28 March 1751**

*p. 175*

*Hand ii.* Borough of Portesmouth

At the House of John Carter Esq<sup>r</sup> within the said Borough the 28<sup>th</sup> March 1751.

Present

Thomas Missing Esq<sup>r</sup> Mayor
John Mounsher Esq<sup>r</sup> –
William Rickman Esq<sup>r</sup> –
Edward Linzee Gent' –
Samuel Chandler Gent' — Aldermen
John Carter Esq<sup>r</sup> –
John Leeke Gent' –

John Amherst Esq<sup>r</sup> Son in Law and the Peremptory Burgess of the said Alderman Linzee (late Mayor) was duly sworn a Burgess of the said Borough before the above Mayor & Aldermen by (*signed by*) Geo Huish Town Clerk

**170**

**28 March 1751**[1]

*p. 176*

*Hand ii*. Borough of Portesmouth

We the Mayor & Major Part of the Aldermen of the said Borough whose Hands are hereunto set do hereby order & direct M<sup>r</sup> John Shepherd the Chamberlain of the said Borough to cause our Seat or Pew in the Parish Church here to be forthwith hung with black Cloth at the Expence of this Corporation, on the melancholy Occasion of the Death of his late Royal Highness the Prince of Wales, Witness our Hands the 28<sup>th</sup> of March 1751.

*Signed by:*

| | |
|---|---|
| Thomas Missing Mayor | Sam Chandler |
| John Mounsher | John Carter |
| William Rickman | Jn<sup>o</sup> Leeke |
| Edw<sup>d</sup> Linzee | |

**171**

**[19 November 1751]**[2]

*p. 177*

*Hand ii*. Borough of Portesmouth

We whose Hands are hereunto set being the Mayor & Major Part of the Aldermen of the said Borough do hereby consent & agree to grant by Feoffment under our Common Seal to ⌐Henry Friend Grocer¬,[3] Francis Benson Shipwright, ⌐John Missing Gent'¬,[4] Thomas Gill Shipwright, William Maine Shipwright, Richard Poate Shipwright, John Newnum Shipwright, William Daniel House Carpen*ter*, Richard Burch Shipwright, William Fleet Shipwright, William Grossmith Tallow Chandler, James Russell Gent', Joseph Lee Shipwright, Joseph Nicholls Shipwright, John White Shipwright, Richard Coles Shipwright, John Loney Shipwright, William Waugh Shipwright, John Randall Shipwright, William Johnson Shipwright & James Bowden Grocer all of the Parish of Portsea within the Liberties of the said Borough[5] All that Piece or Parcel of Wast Ground as the Same is now marked & staked out for erecting & building a Chapel of Ease to the Parish Church of Portsea aforesaid containing from East to West Sixty Six Feet & from North to South Sixty Six Feet situate lying & being on the Common near the Cage there in the said Parish of Portsea & within the Liberties of the said Borough To hold to the said ⌐Henry Friend¬[6] Francis Benson ⌐John Missing¬[7] Tho<sup>s</sup> Gill W<sup>m</sup> Maine Rich<sup>d</sup> Poate John Newnum W<sup>m</sup> Daniel Rich<sup>d</sup> Burch W<sup>m</sup> Fleet Will<sup>m</sup> Grossmith James Russell Joseph Lee Jos<sup>ph</sup> Nicholls John White Rich<sup>d</sup> Coles John Loney W<sup>m</sup> Waugh John Randall Will<sup>m</sup> Johnson & James Bowden their Heirs & Assigns forever, In Trust ⌐& upon Condition¬[8] that they the said Lessees or the Survivors or Survivor of them or the Heirs of such Survivor do within Three Years next ensuing the Date of such

---

[1] Printed in East, p. 272.
[2] P.C.R.O. CE6/2, pp. 21–2, the final version of the lease, supplies the date.
[3] Underlined.
[4] Underlined.
[5] Of these names the following occur in the 1730's: Richard Poate junior paid rates on property in Prince George Street, voted Whig in 1734; William Fleet paid rates in Hanover Row, voted Whig; Richard Coles voted Whig; John Loney paid rates in 'Chapple Row', voted Whig; William Waugh paid rates in Bishop Street, voted Tory (P.C.R.O. 81A/3/21/1, passim; *Poll for Hants.*, *1734*, pp. 136, 138, 139).
[6] Underlined.
[7] Underlined.
[8] Inserted.

Grant erect & build or cause to be erected & built in & upon the said Piece of Wast Ground a Chapel Sixty Six Feet Square from Outside to Outside for the Use & Benefit of all & every the Inhabitants of the said Parish of Portsea, and do within Twelve ⌐Kalendar⌐[1] Months next after the Same shall be so erected & built cause & procure the said Chapel to be by proper Ecclesiastical Authority consecrated or appropriated to divine Service in such Manner as the Bishop of the Diocess for the time being shall think proper. Witness our Hands the

**172**
**[19 November**
**1751][2]**

*p. 178*

*Hand ii.* Borough of Portesmouth

We whose Hands are hereunto set being the Mayor & Major Part of the Aldermen of the said Borough do hereby consent & agree to demise & grant by Lease under our Common Seal to ⌐Henry Friend Grocer⌐,[3] Francis Benson Shipwright, ⌐John Missing Gent'⌐,[4] Thomas Gill Shipwright, William Maine Shipwright, Richard Poate Shipwright, John Newnum Shipwright, William Daniel House Carpenter, Richard Burch Shipwright, William Fleet Shipwright, William Grossmith Tallow Chandler, James Russell Gent', Joseph Lee Shipwright, Joseph Nicholls Shipwright, John White Shipwright, Richard Coles Shipwright, John Loney Shipwright, William Waugh Shipwright, John Randall Shipwright, William Johnson Shipwright, & James Bowden Grocer all of the Parish of Portsea within the Liberties of the said Borough All that Piece or Parcel of Wast Ground adjoining to & on the West Side of a Piece or Parcel of Wast Ground ⌐Sixty Six Feet square⌐[5] now marked & staked out ⌐which We the said Mayor & Aldermen have this day consented & agreed to grant to them⌐[6] for erecting & building a Chapel of Ease to the Parish Church of Portsea aforesaid situate lying & being on the Common near the Cage there in the said Parish of Portsea & within the Liberties of the said Borough, containing in Length from North to South Ninety Eight Feet & in Breadth Twenty Feet, And also All that Piece or Parcel of Wast Ground adjoining to & on the North Side of the said Piece of Ground whereon the said Chapel is intended to be built containing in Length Sixty Six Feet & in Breadth Sixteen Feet, And also All that Piece or Parcel of Wast Ground adjoining to & on the East Part of the said Piece of Ground whereon the said Chapel is intended to be built containing in Length ⌐Eighty Two Feet⌐[7] & in Breadth Fifty Four Feet, And Also All that Piece or Parcel of Wast Ground adjoining to & on the South Side of the said Piece of Ground whereon the said Chapel is intended to be built containing in Length One Hundred & Twenty Feet & at the West End thereof Sixteen Feet in Breadth & containing Sixteen Feet in Breadth from the West End thereof for ⌐Sixty Six Feet⌐[8] of the Length & then beveling or narrowing to ⌐Two⌐[9] Feet at the East End thereof, with free Liberty to enclose the Same with Posts Rails & Palisadoes or with Brick or Stone Walls To hold unto the said ⌐Henry Friend⌐[10] Francis Benson ⌐John Missing⌐[11] Thos Gill Willm Maine Richd Poate John Newnum Willm Daniel Richd Burch Wm Fleet Willm Grossmith James Russell Joseph Lee Josph Nicholls John White Richd Coles John Loney Willm Waugh John Randall Willm Johnson & James Bowden their Executors Administrators & Assigns from the Date hereof for One Thousand Years under the yearly Rent of a Pepper Corn payable at Lady Day, with a Proviso that if the Rent shall be behind or unpaid at the Time limited for (*p. 179*) Payment thereof, Or if the Lessees or the Survivors or Survivor of them or the Executors or Administrators of such Survivor shall at any Time during the Term demised bury or interr or cause or permit to be buried or interr'd any dead Corps in or upon the said Pieces or Parcels of Wast Ground intended to be demised or the said Piece or Parcel of Ground so granted for building a Chapel or in or upon any or either of them, then & in either of such Cases the Corporation

---

[1] Inserted.
[2] P.C.R.O. CE6/2, pp. 23–6, the final version of the lease, supplies the date.
[3] Underlined.
[4] Underlined.
[5] Inserted, with 'GH' added in the left margin.
[6] Inserted, with 'GH' added in the left margin; altered from 'which the said Mayor & Aldermen . . .'
[7] Underlined, with '90' added in the left margin.
[8] Underlined, with '80' added in the left margin; altered from 'Sixty Four Feet', with 'GH' added in the left margin.
[9] Underlined, with '8' added in the left margin.
[10] Underlined.
[11] Underlined.

may reenter into & upon the said several Pieces or Parcels of Wast Ground intended to be demised & repossess them as formerly. Witness our Hands the

**173**
**[25 June 1751]**[1]

*p. 180*

*Hand ii.* Borough of Portesmouth

We whose Hands are hereunto set being the Mayor & Major Part of the Aldermen of the said Borough do hereby consent & agree to demise & grant by Lease under our Common Seal to        [2] All that Piece or Parcel of Wast Ground adjoining to & on the East Side of the Dwelling House & Yard of Thoˢ Eyer House Carpen*te*r on the Common in the said parish of Portsea & within the Liberties of the said Borough containing in Length from North to South One Hundred & Twenty Feet or thereabout & ⌐in⌐[3] Breadth from East to West Sixty Feet or thereabout as the same is now marked & staked out To hold to the said        [4] their Executors Administrators & Assigns from Lady Day last past for the Term of        [5] Years, under the yearly Rent of        [6] payable half yearly, with the Clauses & Covenants usually contained in such Leases, Witness our Hands the

**174**
**Index**

*pp. 181–3 blank; p. [184]*[7]

*Hand i.* A Table of the Orders &c' in this Booke.
*Left column*

---

[1] P.C.R.O. CE6/2, pp. 5–6, the final version of the lease, supplies the date.
[2] Five lines left blank.
[3] Inserted; 'from' struck out.
[4] Three lines left blank.
[5] Space left blank.
[6] Space left blank.
[7] For a reproduction of this page see fig. 5.

| | page | | page |
|---|---|---|---|
| Order for the Adorning of Bevis Gallery | 1 | Order for mr Stanyford to search for Chartrs | 58 |
| Sr Cha: Wagers Resignation of his Aldermanship | 2 | Lease to mr Dugard | 59 |
| his Resolution | 3 | mr Atkins a Burgesse | 60 |
| Capt Rooke a Burgess | 4 | Lease of the Wharfage to Wm Mathews 61 · 87 | 91 · 93 |
| Agreemt for paying mr Clento 80 | 5 | Order to pay the Ourickey | 64 |
| mr Momber elected an Alderman | 6 | Roy Bevis oll a Burgess | 67 |
| Edward Burford a Burgess | 7 | Mr John Monckton Jun a Burgess | 66 |
| Continuance of the Adorning of Bevis Gallery | 8 | Duke of Cumberland a Burgess | 69 |
| Order for passing Chamberlains Accompts | 9 | Lord Chancellor Hardwick a Burgess | 70 |
| Election of severall Burgesses | 10 | Mr Edw: Byron Juer a Burgess | 71 |
| | | Benjamin Bacon a Burgess | 74 |
| mr Collis an Alderman | 11 | Mr Maffey Blery a Burgess | 74 |
| Sr Thomas Frankland & others Burgesses | 12 | mr Henry Hales a Burgess | 78 |
| | | Order for paying Byron 4 Guineas | 77 |
| mr Kirkman an Alderman | 13 | Sr Challoner Ogle a Burgess | 80 |
| Dom: Stewart a Burgess | 14 | Order for the Disposall of Edw: Stewart's 100 | 79 |
| Lord Harry Powlett & others Burgesses | 15 | Burgesses 81 · 82 · 83 · 85 · 86 · 88 · 90 · 95 · 97 | 98 · 99 |
| order to Borrow 100 on the Common Seale | 16 | Lease to Gregory Carlos | 84 |
| Lease of severall houses in Town for the Stanyford | 17 | Order for the works ꝑ for the Town hall | 89 |
| Lease to Dan: Marsh | 18 | Lease of the Custom House to the house | 94 |
| order to pay John Bishop a debt from ye Corporation | 19 | Lease to mr Kirk: Nevis (in Trust) | 96 |
| Earl of Sandwich a Burgess | 20 | 101 |
| Lease to Dan: Smith | 21 | Burgesses 100 · 102 · 105 · 106 · 107 · 108 · 109 | 111 |
| Lease of the Land between the Dock and ye Gun wherefore the Commd of the Navy | 22 | Mr Cleate Recorder | 103 |
| Baron Thompson a Burgess | 24 | Mr Bacon, Mr Luzzo, Mr Claudon | 110 |
| Dom: Haddock a Burgess | 25 | Mr Carter Alderman | |
| Lease to Thomas Light | 23 | Burgesses 112 · 113 · 114 · 115 · 120 · 122 · 125 | 126 |
| Lease of the Wharfage to Littlefield | 26 | Order abt Quit Rents, Wharfage & Markt | 116 |
| Order to pay Sr Cha: Wagers 100 | 27 | Order to mend the Road on the Town Key | 117 |
| Lease to Wm Knible (in Trust) | 28 | Lease to Wm Norris | 118 |
| mr Smith & mr Atkins Alderman | 29 | Lease to Cha: Childs | 119 |
| Comptroller Haddock a Burgess | 30 | Lease to Andrew Monckton | 121 |
| order for disposing the Levies 100 | 31 | 52. Wm Pennod Esq Recorder 120 · 123 | 124 |
| Councillor Stanyford an Alderman | 32 | Burgesses 127 · 129 · 134 · 138 · 139 · 140 · 141 · 143 | 145 |
| mr Blankley & mr Peers Burgesses | 33 | Lease to Adam Strong | 130 |
| Duke of Montague & others Burgesses | 37 | Do to John Vining Horon | 131 |
| Lease to mr Bowis | 39 | Agreemt for borrowing £300 | 132 |
| Lease to Robert Grigg (in Trust) | 41 | 40. Mr Huish's Surrender of his Town | |
| order to prosecute &c on the rds of the rd | 42 | Clerkship Vaz: Mr Huish Jun elected | 135 |
| orders about Building a New Townhall 43 · 44 · 63 · 65 | 72 · 75 | 56. Order abt Interest Money | 137 |
| order to Erect a new post | 46 | Order for carrying the Charter to the Assizes | 142 |
| mr Stanyford & mr Missing Burgesses | 45 | Do to buy the Statutes at large | 144 |
| order for bringing in Town Leases | 49 | Burgesses 147 · 148 · 149 · 152 · 154 · 155 · 156 · 159 | |
| mr Hen: Huish sworn a Burgess & mr Tho: Barton | 50 | Lease to James Robinson | 150 |
| Lord Ellis & George Reynolds a Burgess | 47 | Do to Wm Hodgkin of the Wharfage | 151 |
| Bishop of London a Burgess | 51 | Authority for removing a Suit in the Spirit Court | 153 |
| order for putting Chamberlains Accompts into ye Chest | 53 | Order for digging a Wch for ye use of the Goal | 157 |
| Do for paying the Cronr 40 to carry on | 55 | Sr Edw: Hawke, mr Missing, mr Leeke & mr | 156 |
| a prosecutn against Capt Solande | 57 | White Alderman 160 | |
| Order for putting Edw: Howard 20s into the Chest | 54 | Lease to Tho: Earley | 161 |
| | | Do to Wm Legg | 162 |
| | | Order for making a new Pound, saving for sensle | 163 |

Fig 5   PART OF ORIGINAL INDEX (no. 174). CE6/1, p. [184]

---

[1] Added (hand ii).
[2] Inserted (hand ii).
[3] Added (hand ii).
[4] Inserted (hand ii).
[5] Inserted (hand ii).
[6] Inserted (hand ii).
[7] Inserted (hand ii).
[8] Inserted (hand ii).
[9] Inserted (hand ii).
[10] Inserted (hand ii).
[11] Inserted (hand ii).
[12] Inserted (hand ii).
[13] Inserted (hand ii).
[14] Inserted (hand ii).

*p.* [*185*]
*Left column*

---

¹ Added.
² Added.
³ 'Burgesses' struck out before 'Lease'.

# Appendix I

R. Wilkins, *The borough* (1748)

*p. [i]*

THE / BOROUGH: / Being a Faithful, tho' Humorous, / DESCRIPTION, / Of ONE of the / STRONGEST GARRISONS, / AND / SEA-PORT TOWNS, / IN / *GREAT-BRITAIN:* / With an ACCOUNT of the / Temper and Commerce of the / *INHABITANTS:* / Left by a *Native* of the Place, who was lost in / the Victory *Man of War:* / And now published for the *Benefit* of the Gentlemen of the / Navy, and the *Entertainment* of the rest of Mankind. / By *ROBERT WILKINS.* / *LONDON:* / Printed for M. Payne, at the *White Hart,* in *Pater-* / *Noster-Row.* M.DCC.XLVIII. / (Price SIX-PENCE.)

*p. [ii] blank, p. iii*

To the Right Honourable GEORGE, Lord *ANSON*, Baron of *SOBERTON*, &c.

*My Lord,*

The following little Tract, formed upon your Lordship's Manor of *Soberton*, was left with me by a very particular Friend, before he went to Sea, in the late Victory Man of War; and being an Orphan, does with all Humility, crave your Lordship's favourable Notice. It contains some Observations that may be of Use to (*p. iv*) the Gentlemen of the Navy, in particular, and others who visit a Town of so great Resort, on their necessary Vocations, or to gratify a laudable Curiosity.

With what Transport must every *Briton* behold the floating Trophies of your Lordship's happy Success? And how must that Transport encrease, when he sees and reflects upon the suddenly animating Influence of so noble a Precedent? Your Lordship, and Sir *Peter Warren*, gloriously restored the almost decayed Honour of the *British* Flag; and Sir *Edward Hawke*, well deserves the Honour he has obtained, in bravely following so gallant an Example. Surely, my Lord, this is (*p. v*) a Theme I might be excused to dwell upon, but as you posess other Virtues, besides Valour and Conduct, and, like a true Heroe, love rather to do great Actions, than to hear them published, I shall forbear the Attempt; and only say, I do not doubt, but your Lordship, and the other great Examples, will inspire the whole Navy of *England*, with such Ardour, as shall convince our Enemies, that his most excellent Majesty King George has Maritime Plenipotentiaries enough, willing and able to treat with them in such a Language, as shall bring them to Reason. This is what may well be expected and hoped for, as (*p. vi*) your Lordship can both direct and execute, whatever may concern the Glory of the *British* Navy, and in that, the Honour of the Nation.

Permit me then, my Lord, to hope your Pardon for this public Address; and to have the Honour to subscribe myself,

*May it please your Lordship, Your Lordship's most Obedient, and most Humble Servant,* Robert Wilkins.

*p. vii*

PREFACE TO THE READER.

*HAVING observed, that no kind of Writing so naturally induces us to read, as that which contains an Account of different Sorts of People, Customs, and Manners; because there we find something new and uncommon, that pleases and informs us: I have presumed, in the following Sheets, to give you a full and true, tho' short History of my Native Town. And could I answer as well for my Mother, as I think I can for my Father, I might venture also to affirm my Legitimacy, and give my Narrative the Air of being Authentic, by subscribing my Name to this Address: but having some Suspicion on that Side, I leave it to your Candour to determine for me and my Performance, and shall make no further Apology for the Omission. I have still the Satisfaction to believe, that I came into the World pretty much like my Neighbours here, and retain a good deal of the Spirit and Complexion of the Place: I differ indeed in this, that I am willing to look a little beyond myself, (p. viii) and do something that may tend to the Advantage of Persons I never saw, and have no sort of Expectations from, but this single One, that such a rare Instance of Benevolence, will recommend this disjointed Piece to their favourable Perusal.*

*I shall only add, by way of Caution, that I hope no Chronologists will take it into their wise Heads, to contend about fixing the Time when these Sheets were composed; because such Disputes generally tend to inflame the Passions, without giving any Light to the Understanding. All that I can declare about is, that the greater Part is a transcript from some loose Papers, left by a Great Uncle on my Fathers Side, a very merry old Batchelor; with which I have taken the Liberty to blend an Observation or two of my own, but without any Distinction, but what arises from those very Facts themselves, which have taken Place since his death: upon the whole, though, I may pretty roundly affirm, that it is but* little *applicable to the* present Stock, *my* most worthy Cotemporaries *of this Place, whom I exceedingly reverence and esteem for their* ex-traordinary Capacities and Virtues.

*p. 1*

THE Borough of Boroughs, &c.

THE Town I am about to dissect, is situated in a small Island, close to the Sea; and is not only a Garrison, but a very considerable Sea-Port, from whence it takes it's Name; having the Advantage of one of the finest Harbors in the known World, wherein are constantly seen Forty or Fifty Men of War, with Room for as many more, which may go in or out every Tide.

The Town, consisting of about Six Hundred Houses, is enclosed within a Stone-Wall, several Feet thick and deep; and upon that, a very thick Mud-Wall, as high, or rather higher, than the Tops of the Houses; so that the Inhabitants are constantly buried in Smoak: But as the greatest Part of them are Natives of the Place, and upon that Account inured to it, they seldom mention it as an Inconvenience. They are badly supplied with Water, having none but what partakes of a saline Quality; and even this so very scarce, that were it not for Showers of Rain, which is most industriously catched by every Body, the People could not possibly subsist. As it is, if their Constitutions were not of a very peculiar Make, they would long before now have attempted a Remedy for so great an Evil; but when such a Thing is proposed, they wisely answer, that their Fathers and Grandfathers contented themselves with what Water the Town afforded, and why should they irreverently quit the Road of their Pro-(*p. 2*)genitors? Not considering, what Danger they are in of a Conflagration, should a Fire happen in the Town, especially at Low-Tide; and yet, by the Force of such sagacious Reasoning, they are contented to pay, one House with another, Forty Shillings *per Annum*, for so wretched a Supply of this Commodity.

You will naturally expect some substantial Reason should be given for this extreme Supineness, in a People, who (if you will take their own Words for it) are, without Exception, as wise and politic, as any of his Majesty's good Subjects. Indeed none can be assigned, but a low, sordid Spirit, arising from the Circumstances they have been constantly brought up in; for you must know, the Traders here, whose Origin I cannot boast of, subsist themselves and Families, by dealing one amongst another; by which, and the exorbitant Advantages they make of all Strangers that resort thither, they commonly get a pretty handsome Livelihood.—And yet the Generality of these Dealers, are so modest, as to rank themselves *above* common Tradesmen; but for no other Reason, that I could ever learn, than the very large, but *secret* Traffick they constantly carry on with the Shipping; which is so very notorious, that tho' we have a Custom-House here, I am credibly informed, the whole Income for Imports and Exports, rarely pays the Officer's Salaries: having, therefore, no Men of Property among us, it is but small Wonder, that no sort of Improvements have ever been thought of; and truly (two Persons excepted, who were *infamous* for their Gains, by the Methods aforesaid) I could never hear of any properly qualified for Members of Parliament; which doubtless is the true Reason, why our Representatives are always sent us from a-loft. A *rich Burgher* is one, who has met with so much Success in the (*p. 3*) World, as to be able to purchase the House he lives in; and if, by a further Improvement of his Stock, he is afterwards in a Condition to buy a Publick-House, (which is always both Tavern and Ale-House) and supply it with his own Merchandise, we then esteem him *a very great Man*. I fancy this State of ours is to be envied; for as we constantly rate the Value of Persons and Things, meerly, by the closer, or more distant Relation they stand in to our own Interest; and most of us very well knowing that our Fathers began the World with *Forty Shillings*, and gave us their Children *suitable* Educations; we are not liable to be imposed upon by the Riches, Honour, or Understanding of Strangers, whom we respect, no further than as we get by them; preferring a Cobler, by whom we profit Five Shillings, to a Prince in any other View. Upon such sort of Principles, we maintain ourselves like a little Republic; being most harmoniously united in one common Disposition, to make every Advantage we can, without troubling ourselves with the nice Distinctions of Honour and Justice, and I know not what hard Names, which we, nor our Fore-fathers ever understood.

It sometimes falls out, that we have but few, or no Ships in our Port, and scarce any Strangers in Town to view the Fortifications; in that Case, we live penuriously upon the last Profits, except the Time, which (during this Vacation) we take up in settling Accounts with one another; for then, if they turn out well, we entertain ourselves handsomely, and live for a little while, in some kind of Neighbourly Society: but at no Time else; for he who entertains his Neighbours out of due Season, is shrewdly suspected of having some clandestine Design; and is always looked upon, as a Person dangerous to the Corporation. It being a settled (*p. 4*) Maxim with us, that the Man who shews any Appearances of Hospitality, must have some very bad Scheme in his Pate, or else is going the High-Road to Poverty, a Sin we have in the utmost Abhorrence. This Maxim, however strange, is founded upon each Individual's private Experience; who is conscious, that he never bestows any Thing upon others, without having a sinister View to his own Advantage. In short, the very Essence of our Corporation is *Interest*: for the Mayor, who is our chief Magistrate, has a Profit accruing from every Thing we eat or drink; and presiding (like any little *Abridgement* of Law and Equity) in our supreme Court of Judicature, makes great Advantages from a skilful Management of the *Scale*—for all Fines are his own.

As I have mentioned his Worship, our Mayor, and the Corporation, it may be expected I should give some Account of the Manner, and Form of his Election, and of the worthy Members, that compose that venerable Body.

The Mayors used to be annually chosen by a Majority of Votes, of the Aldermen and Burgesses together; but of later Years, it is generally settled by the Aldermen alone, previous to the Day of Election. There should be Twelve of this Denomination, (the Mayor included, who has two Votes) but for Reasons of State, it has for some Time been looked upon as a Thing quite needless, to fill up the Vacancies of Aldermen who were dead, or had lost their Senses, that the Management of the Town might be thereby vested in fewer Voices, which is judged a very prudent Method, as it certainly balances the Votes on the right Side. There was once a Scheme on foot, for the Magistrates to succeed in turn, but that was thought to be attended with some Hazard, as the Majority might (*p. 5*) chance to warp on the wrong Side: tho' I rather believe it was dropped, upon Account of the next Election; the Benefit of which, to the returning Officer, is known to be Five Times the Advantage of being Mayor.

This Right Worshipful Body, till within these few Years, would have been puzzled to produce one Man among them, that could both write and read in a tolerable Manner; but having introduced some of the learned in the Law among them, they are really greatly improved; and I believe more than half have given over setting their Mark. And it is to be hoped, with the Assistance of the aforesaid Gentlemen, they will be enabled, in Time, to make a further Progress in what has been so happily begun; if they don't chance to fall into the same ⌐Dilemma⌐[1] with the Sheep in the Fable, who chose the Wolves for their Keepers: how literally the whole may be applied, both to one and the other, I leave other People to determine.

I think I have said all that is necessary, of those we call the chief People of the Town, exclusive of the Gentlemen of the Garrison, whom we never rank among us. But, like a true Burgher, I think of the principal Thing last, and have omitted to give an Account of our Religion—which, as it chiefly consists in outside Shew, may be done, by just enumerating the Places of Publick Worship. The only Church in the Town, is large and handsome; we have besides, a Meeting-House built by Subscription, which may well vie with the House of God; and a Chapel for the Use of the Garrison.

Our Church is very much crouded on a Sabbath-Day, and a Stranger would be

---

[1] Original 'Dilemna'.

apt to imagine, at his first Entrance, that he was surrounded, by a very opulent and polite Set of People, as well by the (*p. 6*) Elegance of their Dress, as Behaviour; for he would certainly stand the whole Service out, without being disturbed by any Civilities offered him.

If his Devotion led him to the Meeting House, he would think by the profound Silence which reigned there, and the strict Attention paid the Preacher, that the Congregation were assembled, with no other Intent but to serve the Lord.—However, if he was to stay any Time among us, I fancy he would be convinced that he was too precipitate in his conclusion.

The Chapel, which is large, and extremely well situated, seems to be designed for those who frequent such Places, with no other View, but to offer the Sacrifice of Praise and Thanksgiving; and I believe it is never made use of, but by such devout Worshippers; for there is room at *all times*, for a whole Regiment of Soldiers.

Now if my sagacious Reader can discern by this, what our Religion really is, I will readily confess it is more than I was ever able to do, who have lived here from my Birth.

The next Thing I shall take notice of, is the Town-Hall. This Edifice has been lately rebuilt, at the Expence of the Corporation; but not without Hopes of being one Day reimbursed, by the large Contributions of our present, and future Members of Parliament: It is supported by Stone Arches; the superstructure Brick; containing one (it ought to be spacious) Room, and a Council-Chamber; but both ill contrived and excessive small. The Outside (for which in all Things we have, by much, the greatest Regard) is indeed noble and uniform; one End being ornamented by a handsome Portico, and the other by a *Venetian* Window. Indeed the whole Building may be well compared to the Members of the Borough, in their Scarlet and Furs; a (*p. 7*) pompous External, but very small, dirty and irregular within.

Having said enough of the *civil* Constituents of this Town, and the Public Edifices, that at different Times enclose them; I shall now consider a little particularly, the *mercantile* Part; of which I have already made some Mention.

Our People assume the Character of *Merchants*, because of the Purchases that are commonly made of all Goods (on Board every Vessel that comes into Port) that are damaged by Distress of Weather, or other Accidents; which they carefully land, and carry generally to the Tops of Houses, leaded for that Purpose. Some are placed in large upper Rooms; and after being well dried and sorted, the greatest Part is dispersed among their Dealers in the Inland Country; who, to save the Charge of Land-Carriage from *London*, traffick with us with great Satisfaction, imagining that upon an Average, they have these Commodities much cheaper. What does not go off this Way, we retail in our own Shops, at *Twenty per Cent.* more than the same Goods are sold for, in every trading City, or Town in *Great-Britain*: and lest any accidental Customer, with more than common Optics, should penetrate into this *Mystery of Righteousness*; we have always Samples of the best Goods exposed in our Shops—while the grand Affair lies safe in our Warehouses.

But the Ships afford us a still more enlarged (and, as it is secret and illegal, a better relished) Source of Wealth; namely, the prime Commodities, the produce of Sailors Ventures, Perquisites of the Cargoe, and so forth; which, tho' we procure them very cheap, we never fail to sell at the same Price as others do, who not understanding the World, pay Custom, *&c.* particularly Tea, Cof-(*p. 8*)fee, Chocolate; Wines of all Sorts; spirituous Liquors; Silks, and many other Things, both for Use and Ornament. The Wines and Spirits we procure thus, we never fail adulterating for our Shops, but always reserve a Quantity neat and intire for our own Tables. Thus we support ourselves in full, and most luxurious Plenty: We I mean, who deem ourselves, substantial, honest Dealers; while our Gains are constantly laid out in buying up Sailors Tickets, whom we make pay thirty or forty per Cent. Discount, besides oblige them to take Parcels of our heavy Wares, by way of Acknowledgment for the Favour we shew them.

The poor People among us, are chiefly supported by their Labour in the Dock-Yard, a Place I shall take Notice of hereafter. These Men are much eased in their House-keeping, by the Beef and Pork they procure from the Ships, and the Firing they constantly bring home with them once a Day from the Yard. But even *their* best Gains arise from the secret Trade of the more honourable Sort, which yet would scarcely be so beneficial to them, if it was possible to do without their Assistance.

Add to this, the great Number of Beeves and Hogs that are killed here for victualling the Navy, makes offal a very plentiful and cheap Commodity. So that one Thing with another, the *Poor* are but a slight Burthen to this industrious Borough.

As I don't consider the Officers of the Navy, and other Residents of the like Kind, as genuine Townsmen; I shall give no further Account of them, than as we get by them, which will be best included in a short Description of our *Female Merchants,* and their Method of Traffick. A distinguished Body I assure you! who do almost as much for the Advantage of the Community, and with as great Success, as the Men themselves.

*p. 9*

But perhaps I already stand condemned in my Reader's Opinion, as a rude and unpolished Writer, for omitting to mention our fair Ladies sooner. I can only say, in my Excuse, that I am an old Bachelor, and seldom care to think of them, but when I can't avoid it. And since I have unfortunately stumbled on the uncouth Subject, and being sensible too, that my Age will not let me please them, nor my Poverty profit them; I shall without any kind of Ceremony give them their just Character, which perhaps I am better able to do, than a younger or a richer Man: hoping (so much regard for the Sex have I still alive within me) that the rising Generation may profit by the Examples of the maturer Part, and learn betimes to abhor the Practices, which have made their Mothers, Aunts and Grandmothers, infamous.

The Ladies of this Place, and the Parts adjacent, are very numerous, and most of them accounted handsome; and if my poor weak Eyes enable me to judge aright, I think in any small Town, I never saw prettier Women: their Complexions are fine; their Shapes very good—at a certain Age; and their Clothes, what no one could expect from People of such small Beginnings, who was unacquainted with the great Art and Industry they use to equip themselves so gaily,—I wish I could add genteely.

The young Sea-Officers, in particular, who continually frequent this Place in great Numbers, are the natural and lawful Prey of these Female Cormorants. With them they labour, by all the Arts in their Power, to cultivate the most intimate Acquaintance: and as Gentlemen of this Order are not over shy, it is no difficult Thing for a pretty designing Woman to make her Advantage; for as they profess this to be their grand View, they are not over scrupulous as to the Methods of securing it, be-(*p. 10*)ing very liberal of their Company and their Charms, be what will their Station, either Wives or single Women.

After a course of Gallantries abroad, the next Step is the alluring these free, open-hearted Sparks (who would pursue their Pleasures even in a Lion's Den) to their own Houses; where they regale them with the greatest Freedom and Profuseness—that is, with the Produce of their own former Favours: for these notable Housewives seldom return from on Board empty-handed; to say nothing of what is sent after them by the Ship's Boats.—Velvets, Silks, &c. for the young Ladies to dispose of among their Friends, who for selling two Pieces, have one for themselves, at least, some acceptable Present for their Trouble. And this sort of Commerce is esteemed so honourable and so beneficial among us, that even the grave Matrons engage in it; who, for the Sake of a Commission now and then, connive at all the Excesses of their Daughters. The Women who have no Habitations of their own, can but barter meer Dalliance for their Apparel; but they do it so effectually, and withal so openly and professedly, that there are some here who will undertake to tell you, from whom every visible Ornament about them is derived, nay, and from what particular RATE too: and I have heard some expert young Fellows aver, that they could pick out any young Woman of this Town, from among Forty strange ones, in the Dark, only by touching her Lips: my own *Nephew, a Man of about Fifty, and a Sailor, confirms this from his own Experience. When I reflect on these Things, I thank Heaven that I have never been in a Condition to have Children of my own: for what Man of any Feeling could bear, as my Neighbours do, to have

---

*This was my Father's elder Brother.

*p. 11*

their Wives and Daughters grappled by every young Fellow, for a paltry Present, to make them appear better than they ought.

This insatiable Thirst of Gain, which (like Hell and the Grave can never be satisfied) is not confined to *single* young Fellows, as the Objects of Prey; but even married Men are industriously entrapped, to the Destruction of the Harmony and Welfare of many a hopeful Family. All is Fish that comes to Net; the Young or Old, Married or Unmarried, Handsome or Ugly, Drunk or Sober, all are alike received, provided they pay well. Nor do I find in this noble Traffick there is any Difference maintained between the *married* and *single* Women—except, that the latter have larger Conveniences of Trade. Nor do the single Women seem to envy this Situation, since they think they can enjoy all they esteem valuable without Husbands; publickly professing, they will marry *any Body*—or *no Body*, but—for Interest. These Lasses, intoxicated by their unbounded Pleasures, do not imagine they shall ever grow old; never once dream that the Time will come, when all they can do or suffer, won't procure them any more Civilities: the severest Instances of this Kind have no manner of Power over them. Nay, the Married ones seem equally infatuated; who, in Opposition to Examples, attended with the most shocking Circumstances, resolutely pursue the same Path; and, tho' their very Dealers have confessed and betrayed them, will turn to the next Comer, and traffick away.

Thus much, indeed, I am bound in Justice to say in their Excuse, that this Conduct is in a good Measure owing to the mercenary Tempers of their Husbands; who will not see any Thing amiss, while they gain by it either in their Shops or at their Tables; never betraying the least Symptoms of Un-(*p. 12*)easiness, but when the Chaps fail in their Presents. To such excess has this proceeded, that it is no uncommon Thing among us, contentedly to hear the infallible Tokens of other Mens Civilities to our Wives, visibly pointed out in the Childrens Faces that feed at our Tables; and there is sufficient Reason to presume that we have very good Men among us, who became Husbands with no other View, but to increase the Number of their saleable Commodities; for they do every thing, but openly prostitute their Wives, for a valuable Consideration. But if it happens that the poor Woman should have the Sex's Failing, and be civil to a Man she likes, who pays only in Returns of meer Love; she can never expect any Sort of civil Usage at Home, till she has found some other, who by his Generosity and Profuseness, enables her to compound—for the loss of her Honour.

Thus we see, how the Tempers and Constitutions of People are, by Degrees, adapted to the State of Life they are engaged in; and how Custom and long Habitude, makes all Thing not only easy but delightful. For my own Part, I can't help concluding, but that were we to inure ourselves, Step by Step, to what is generally agreed to be virtuous and good, we might, in Time, make great Advances towards Perfection, and with much less Difficulty than we retreat to it's contrary. But I will leave it to wiser Heads than mine to determine this Point: for while so many Nations of Men, differ so widely in their Opinions of Right and Wrong; and what is deemed laudable in one Place, is diametrically opposite in another; I despair of ever knowing one Universal Rule, either for *Actions* or *Opinions*: and as long as Men have the Liberty of *thinking* for themselves, I am strongly inclined to believe they will take that of *acting* for themselves. (*p. 13*) Many and bold Attempts, indeed, have been made to circumscribe *both*; but I could never find they had any very useful Effects, except at particular Times and Places. This Female-Subject, as it always does, has made me more grave than suits with my natural Temper.

I think I have said enough of the *inbred* Inhabitants of this Town, their Methods of Trade, their Religion and Morals, and the industrious and communicative Tempers of the Female Part. I shall now consider the Officers of the Government, both Civil and Military; and so proceed with the Fortifications, and other curious Particulars, in their Order.

The First in Profit, tho' not Dignity of Office, (for this is our Rule of Estimation) is the President of the Customs; who with the several Employments annexed makes it, *communibus Annis*, a good Thousand Pounds. The Gentleman who fills this Station, is sometimes the younger Son of a good Family, who being thrust into the World very early, is, to rid his Honour, the eldest Brother, of an Incumbrance, advanced by Degrees to Posts of considerable Profit. But it is much to be lamented, that he does not always bring with him a Gentleman's Education; or at least, that he has not been used to the Conversation of those, who enjoy that advantage: he would not then have recourse to the Authority and Power of his Office, to support his Credit as a Man of

Sense; which he never fails to do, when he happens in the Company of Men of more Understanding, but less Fortune than himself.

The next is our Primier Minister for his Majesty's Fleet.—A Post of nobody knows what Profit!—Now, if any Gentleman in this Office, should happen to have two or three Sons, and out of Deference to his great Merit, they are placed under (*p. 14*) him, with handsome Salaries, and the Addition of a pretty Sine-cure, or so; a Pursery for Example, tho' ⌐neither⌐1 of them ever did or ever would go to Sea,—I ask, Would not this be thought a remarkable Piece of Œconomy in the Disposal of the Public Money. I only put the Question, *en passant*, because I remember about thirty Years ago, an Instance of such Frugality in a Neighbouring Seaport-Town.

These two Commission-Men, (who are the only ones of Note in the Civil ⌐Employ-ment⌐2) are Persons of great Power here, and inseparable in their Company and Interest; affecting very little Familiarity with any but their own Species, except at Election-Times.

The Military Gentlemen also keep themselves a distinct People, and never care to herd with us Townsfolk: but this is easily accounted for, as they are generally well bred Men, who cannot bear Rusticity, and brutal Ill-Manners. We endeavour tho' to be as remiss as they in cultivating a Correspondence; not because they shew that Contempt for us we perhaps deserve, but for their professing to know us too well, to be over-reached by us; for their extreme Parsimony and Unwillingness to increase our Stock. Soldiers make their Fortunes with Danger and Difficulty, and spend them with Caution; especially the graver Sort, of which ours chiefly consist.

We have also a Physician or two among us, one of which, by his interfering with Concerns, that do not properly belong to him, may be called an *Officer*, tho' whether civil or military, I am at a Loss to determine; but by the Sword he wears sometimes, and a certain blustering Air he puts on, I am inclined to range him with the military Band; especially as he acquires very considerable Profits (*p. 15*) by that body. This Gentleman is so great a Favourite with some People, that all our Placemen and their Dependants must encourage him or be frowned upon. But notwithstanding these Advantages, there is another, who has no Power to recommend him but his Know-ledge and Skill in his Profession, nor any Influence but what his humane and polite Behaviour gives him, who may well vie for true Merit with any Man in the whole County.

As we have no Right of approving or disapproving our Parson, but passively take such as the neighbouring College is pleased to send us; we are seldom troubled with Master Vicar's Residence, but take up with his Curate; who to do him Justice, by his great Qualifications has gained our Hearts, as well as our Subscriptions. Many he wins by the Force of his Eloquence, who do not understand it; more by his sound and useful Doctrine, who do not practise it; and all by his sociable Temper and chearful-Conversation, over a Pipe and a Bottle.

Before I wholly take my Leave of the Town, I must make Mention of our Assembly, which was originally constituted by a late venerable leading Member of the Corpor-ation, in Charity to three old Maids, who kept House together; which this Gentleman enlarged in Order to make a convenient Dancing-Room, and by his Family's Interest, and the Influence of so good a Motive, procured a very handsome Subscription Quarterly, at Two Shillings and Six-pence. For a considerable Time, this Rendesvous of Pleasure, continued frequented by the grave as well as gay of both Sexes, and was conducted with great Decency; till at length the young Ones made it not quite so convenient for the Matronly Ladies to come there; and some Sea-Gentlemen joining vigorously with them carried the Point: so that it is now of a very different Nature, (*p. 16*) tho' more polite; for the Candles are changed into Wax, and the Method of chusing Partners, accommodated in an approved Manner: and that the Gallants may not want good Partners, they pay Subscriptions for some of them, and rather than stand still, a Gentleman may dance with a Wench, who the Morning before, sold him a Pair of Gloves; and, by the Alteration of a little false Hair before, and cropping and curling behind, not know the Semstress's Shop-Maid, from my young Lady of good Family and great Fortune.

I have now done with all Persons and Things *within* our Gates; and shall proceed

---

1 Original 'neither'.
2 Original 'Emyloyment'.

towards our Dock-Yard; but in my Way must just step into the Gun-Wharf, which manifestly shews under whose Nomination the Officers there are appointed. Every thing is noble, neat and regular; and so well disposed, as to be ready, at the least Warning, on all Emergencies; indeed, it must be seen, in order to form a competent Judgment of it's Use and Exactness, and therefore, I shall not attempt a more particular Description.

About five Hundred Paces from hence, you enter the Dock-Yard; which, for it's Conveniencies, is scarcely to be parallell'd. The Officers here are generally sent by the Government; and are such as by their Services at Sea have very well merited the pleasant, comfortable Subsistence, they enjoy for Life; which is never disturbed, but when a Favourite creeps in, who always distinguishes himself, by his haughty and supercilious Deportment. Most of these Gentlemen, by their constant Attendance on, and Application to their several Duties, very justly acquire the Advantages they make; and I doubt not, but the Government are highly satisfied, as well with their Integrity as Ability; or otherwise (*p. 17*) we should not hear so much of their prudent Conduct in the Management of publick Affairs.

One great Instance of the Usefulness of this ⌐Establishment⌐[1], is the *Academy Royal*, which will remain a lasting Monument of the Projector's great Design. This Academy was intended for the Education and Nursery of Noblemen, and Gentlemens Sons, in the Art of Navigation, and for a constant Supply of able Officers, to serve on Board his Majesty's Ships of War. The Edifice cost the Nation originally, *Eight Thousand Pounds.*—And the Mathematical Instruments of all Sorts, and other Implements, *One Thousand* more. The Salaries of all the different Masters amount to *Five Hundred Pounds per Annum*, besides an additional Allowance to every Officer in the Yard, for his Attendance to instruct the Pupils in the several Branches of the Art.— So that there is but a Rent Charge on the Nation, of *One Thousand Pounds a Year*—for training up our Youth, in a Science the most Beneficial to this Island! and the Education of them is entrusted to so able a Preceptor, that there is little Room to doubt, but many excellent Men will receive the finishing Part of their Education in this noble Seminary.—How much is it to be wished, that some one was established, for the training up young Gentlemen for the *Land* Service also.

As I hope my Reader has done going to School, I shall do my best to conduct him safe back towards Town, and give him a cursory View of it's Fortifications, Magazines, and other Curiosities of the like Nature. But before we entirely leave this Place, I must beg you to observe, that this Yard, and all the Stores it contains, to the Value of *One Million* and a *Half*, together with the *Gun-Wharf*, are guarded only by the Fortifications we are now going to see.

*p. 18*

The Town is very strong towards the Sea, which doubtless is designed principally, to guard, not only the Ships that ride at Anchor yonder, but those that are moored in the Harbour. That old Castle you see on the *South* Side, contains a very strong Battery of Guns; under which, every Ship that comes in or out of this Port, is obliged to pass very near. In times of Danger, there is, or should be, a Governor, and a competent Number of Soldiers; but for many Years past, it has been kept by an old Serjeant and three or four Men, who sell Cakes and Ale. As for Powder and Ball, our long profound Tranquility has superseded all Occasion for such dangerous Implements.

On the opposite Side of this narrow Water, is another Fort, with a Row of large Cannon, and a House and Barracks strongly guarded by an old *Irish* Gunner, and four or five Invalids—but no such Thing as Ammunition (except Bread, Cheese, Small Beer, and Gin) has appeared there for many Years; the chief Use it is put to, is to accommodate the Ladies, who come there for the Benefit of the fresh Sea Breezes, or as a Place of retirement to recover a broken Constitution.

The Rest of the Fortifications, they say, will be very regular and strong, when they are finished; but when that will be, other People must inform you. No one here can pretend to calculate the Time, any more, than they can assign a Reason, why we have had no Ammunition in the Town to defend it in Case of a Surprize: we presume

---

[1] Original 'Es-stablishment', the hyphen being at the end of a line.

indeed, it was because there have been such vast Sums of secret Service Money so well disposed of, that our Enemies, either abroad or at Home, will certainly give us timely notice, to furnish the Garrison with every Thing necessary: and tho' it has been frequent with us to have Fifty Men of War laid up in our Har-(*p. 19*)bour, and their Stores in the Dock Yard, we place so great a Dependance upon the Vigilance of our Superiors aloft, that we take no Notice of the Deficiency, notwithstanding some of us have very good Salaries for that very Purpose.

I have now finished, in the most concise Manner I could, this Description of our famous Town; and before my Reader proceeds to pass Judgment upon it, let me desire him to attend to the following Story of two honest Tars I was acquainted with in my Youth.—They were in a Room together, where some Boards lay higher by two Feet than the Floor: one of them walking on the highest Board, the other says, *Bob*, I have followed you through all the Shoe-Makers Shops you have used these three Years, and cursed them all for not making my Shoes *like* yours—but never found out the Reason they were not so, till this Minute—why d—m it, I see the Fault is in *my Foot*.

If, therefore, any peculiar Oddity appears in my Performance; I beg it may be considered, that I am just in the Case with the Shoemaker, who could not make a *neat* SHOE, to fit a particular *misshapen* FOOT.

*FINIS*

*p.* [*20*] *contains advertisements of the publisher, M. Payne.*

# Appendix II

*The geese in disgrace* (1751) and associated texts

*The geese in disgrace* and an illustrative engraving, 'The Gothamites in council', were both published early in 1751; the events they refer to are related above, pp. lvi–lvii and nos 164, 166–168. A full description of the engraving, with references to contemporary notices of both publications, is in *Catalogue of prints and drawings in the British Museum: Division 1. Political and personal satires* (11v., 1870–1954), iii, pt 2, pp. 803–5. The engraving is reproduced on the end papers of the present volume; printed below are:

1 The original text of *The geese in disgrace*. The superior numbers and the numeration of lines are not in the original text but are printed here as references to the annotations in (2) and (3).

2 Contemporary annotations added in manuscript to a copy of *The geese in disgrace* which is in vol. LXIII of the bound pamphlets in the Cope Collection, Southampton University Library. The manuscript numbers showing their position in the text have been printed with (1) above. A note by Sir Frederic Madden (1801–73) on the title-page of this copy of the poem reads 'This copy formerly belonged to George Huish, ⌐Coroner¬ (*altered from* Town Clerk) of Portsmouth'; the annotations are not, however, in the hand of George Huish (d. 1788).

3 Printed *Annotations on The geese in disgrace* by 'Martinus Scriblerus' published in 1751, earlier than 'The Gothamites in council' which contains a reference to it. After line 125 the author has misnumbered his references to the lines of the original text; the correct references have been added here.

## 1 The original text, 1751

*p.* [1]
THE / Geese in Disgrace, / A / TALE. / Humbly inscribed to the / CORPORATION / OF / P—ts—th. / ornament / *PORTSMOUTH:* / Printed by *W. Horton*, for J. WILKINSON, / near the *Point Gates*, / MDCCLI.

*p.* [2] *blank; p. 3*
THE Geese in Disgrace, A TALE.

IN Days of yore, when Brutes (content
With Nature's Laws and Government)
Knew no Ambition, Envy, Strife,
Or any Bane of social Life,
Each had his Pleasure, each his Joy,
Each bore some Title, or Employ,
Each knew his Duty, Rank and Place,
The Fox "My Lord, the Wolf "Your Grace,
The Ass, "Your Honour, and the Goose
" Good Mr. Alderman! What News?                                            *10*
No modern Government of State
Was half so happy, half so great;
Their Laws (a Barrier to Distress)
Were nicely fram'd for Happiness;

*p. 4*
Their Regulations were design'd
To make all Creatures of one Mind,
And whilst the *Golden Age*¹ prevail'd
This happy Issue never fail'd:
What Pitty 'tis such wholesome Laws,
Have fall'n a Prey to *Saturn*'s Claws!                                      *20*

79

That Envy, Malice, Discord, Hate,
Should now preside in ev'ry State!
What sordid Avarice we find
Possess the Helm of ev'ry Mind!
Ambition, the prevailing Lust,
Like Sheep, *All* pressing to be first.
The Consequence is plain and clear,
As by Example may appear.

   A little Colony of *Geese*,
Who long had peckt their Corn in Peace,       *30*
Were Strangers to *Domestick* Jars,
Nor fear'd th' Effects of foreign Wars;
For this, both Art and Nature join'd,
High Walls secur'd their *Pen* behind,
A spacious *Ditch* close to their *Door*
Prevented all Attacks before;
No Fox or Stote disturb'd their Ease,
They eat, they drink, do what they please,
*p. 5*
Dispute, commend, or disapprove,
Yet all was Harmony and Love.       *40*

   THESE *Geese* became incorporate,
Whether by *Charter*[2] out of Date
Or Grant more modern,[2] 'tis all one,
And not so needful to be shewn.
Let it suffice, " That three and ten
Were dub'd " The Mayor[2] and Aldermen,
" That Custom,[3] or their Charter[3] sent
" Two Members up to Parliament;
But as that House would not admit
Of *Geese* to be[4] return'd and sit,       *50*
Well judging that such shallow Pates
Were ne'er intended for Debates,
They wisely paid the Compliment[5]
Of chosing those the *Eagle* sent.

   THIS *Eagle* was their Lord supreme
His Eye was sharp, his Talons keen,
His Power extensive, and his Word
Pass'd for a Law with ev'ry *Bird*;
'Twas his Decree; The little *Hawke*
(Ordain'd for *Drubbing*[6] more than Talk)       *60*
Was very fit to represent
This cackling Flock in Parliament;[7]
*p. 6*
None disobey'd their Sovereign's Word,
" We'll chose, whoe'er you please, my Lord;
" Our Wills and Int'rests are the same;
" We must approve the Bird you name.[8]

   WHILST Matters stood in this Condition,
Peace was the Offspring of Submission;
Their Happiness was quite compleat,
Their Granarys were still replete,[9]       *70*
With Vetches, Barley, Oats and Wheat.

   BUT mark Ambition's dire Effect![10]
The Goose that climbs can ne'er expect
His Legs or Neck will be so sound
As if he waddled on the Ground.

ONE of the *Aldermen*, 'tis true,
Had much of Meat and Honour too;
But to his Credit be it said,
He labour'd for his daily Bread;
He hew'd and chopt great *Oaken-Blocks*     *80*
To make the *Eagle*'s *Pop-Gun* Stocks;
But 'twas imagin'd that his Gains
At least, were equal to his Pains;
Be that as 'twill; 'twas plainly such
As caus'd his being envy'd much;

*p. 7*
Besides 'twas evident and clear
He shar'd too much the *Eagle*'s Ear,
And he might possibly suggest
Things not so true, or kind, at best.[11]

    FROM hence great Jealousies were bred,     *90*
Too soon the dire Contagion spread,
" Some saw no Reason why one *Brother*
" Should have the Preference of another;
" Some hinted that their daily Bread
" Should fairly be distributed;
But honestly to state the Case,
Each Goose was hankering for a Place.[12]

    THE Thing that first employ'd their Care
Was how to rout the *Carpenter*.
Two *Black-crown'd Geese* of middle-Age,     *100*
(By some call'd, *Cunning*; few thought *Sage*)
Who oft had smother'd Discontent,
And long on Mischief been intent,
Now found it opportune to try
The Force of Independency.
The Means that they propos'd were these
To make some *Goslins—Burgesses*.[13]

*p. 8*
    A Court was summon'd for that End
The Day was fixt, and all attend,
Except the *Carpenter*, and He     *110*
Knew nothing of this *Treachery*.

    THE Mayor advanc'd his *swarthy Face*,
And *only bow'd* with *Goose-like* Grace;
A Brother, who had learn'd to read,[14]
Became the Speaker in his Stead;
" My dearest Friends! with Joy I see
" Your Disposition to be free,
" How much I wish'd this happy Hour,
" How much detest the Eagle's Power,
" How long abhorr'd this servile State,     *120*
" I find is needless to relate.
" There's not a Look but plainly tells
" What Rancour in each Bosom dwells;
" This Day shall give us Liberty[15]
" And crush our vile Dependency;
" If you approve of my Intent,
" I dare believe you'll not repent.

    " *You Geese* that are dispos'd to eat
" Your Share of Corn, *Hold up your Feet!*

p. 9
THE Question put, such as were able 130
Hoisted their *Giblets* on the Table;
One *bald-pate*, lame, decrepit Bird
Neither his Legs or Pinions stir'd,
Not that he varied from the rest,
But Gout his Limbs had so possest
That tho' 'twas *Bliss divine* to eat,
He could not gather up his Meat.
This seem'd to be a Judgment sent
From Heav'n, by Way of Punishment 140
For all the Vices of a Life
Employ'd in propagating *Strife*.

Two others seem'd to hesitate[16]
And put their Feet up very late;
The Cause by ev'ry Goose was known
They both were *Servants* of the *Crown*;
The *One* collected *Herbs and Seeds*,
Let *Blood and clyster'd Invalids*;
The other circulated *News*,
And am'rous *Goslins Billet-doux*; 150
These Places yielding certain Pay,
Were thought too good to fool away.

THE *Tempter* smoaking their Distress,
With Art continu'd his Address.

p. 10
" My Friends, says he, dispel this Fear,
" Depend upon my constant Care,
" Whatever *Losses* may attend
" Your Struggles for this glorious End,
" If I don't faithfully supply,
" The Day I fail you, let me die !

By these Allurements both concurr'd, 160
Nor longer to the Scheme demurr'd.

The Goslins waiting at the Door,
Were now call'd in; about *Three Score*;
The major Part of these ne'er fled,[17]
Still bearing *Egg-shells* on the Head.

*A saucy Hern* brought up the Rear
(Stranger to Modesty or Fear)
His Fare was sumptuous ev'ry Day,
Poor silly *Gudgeons* were his Prey; 170
Sometimes a foolish *Trout* wou'd get
Within the Foldings of his Net.

SAYS he, " Your Worships so well know
" The Strength and Number of the Foe,
" It makes it needless to advise
" A Junction with your best Allies;
p. 11
" Such are the *Herns* of old Renown;
" We'll bring this *Eagle*'s Spirit down,
" Make me a *Burgess*, you shall see
" I'll teach the *Chap*—Humility.

82

’Tis such Impertinence as this                                    *180*
Which gains the Hearts of silly Geese.

" ’Twas very kind" They all confest
And swore him in among the rest.

*Their Folly* reach'd the *Eagle*'s Ears
And soon the *noble Bird* appears;

" What's to be done ? you stupid Crew ?
" Must I, your Sovereign, stoop to you ?
" Shall you compel me to prefer,
" The Goose you chose for Carpenter ?
" If e'er you had no Corn to eat,                                  *190*
" Or had been stinted in your Meat,
" Or not supply'd with best of Grain,
" There might be Reason to complain;
" But I have very often thought
" Your *Geeseships* better fed than taught;
" Perhaps you soon, too soon, may see
" The Fruits of Independency;
*p. 12*
" Henceforth let all your Clamours cease
" Be gone ! I hate such grumbling Geese.

On ev'ry Face Confusion sat,                                      *200*
Each dreading his impending Fate;
Their Folly they confess with Shame,[18]
And curse Ambition's very Name;[19]
" They hope his Lordship will forgive
" Or else what *mortal* Goose can live?[20]

But this Submission was in vain[21]
The Eagle heard them with Disdain,
" ’Tis my Command you quit the *Pen*,[22]
" And seek your Food in yonder *Fen*;
" There learn Obedience to your Lord,                             *210*
" If you design to be restor'd;
" Till then I solemnly ordain
" No Goose shall touch one single Grain.

Their *Sentence* publish'd, they retire
And spend their Time in *Dirt and Mire*;
No Joy by Day, by Night no Rest,
With Cold and pinching Want opprest,
They still lament that fatal Hour
In which they dar'd the *Eagle*'s Power.

The *Moral* of the Tale[23] is this;        ⎫                     *220*
(Design'd for Men as well as Geese)         ⎬
*Contentment is the greatest Bliss.*        ⎭

                    *F I N I S*


**2  Manuscript annotations, circa 1751**

*p. 4*
*line 17*   1   The Golden age was under the Reign of Saturn, which the Author of
this did not know, but very simply imagin'd Saturn to be the Devil mistaking his Name
Satan      We shall track him by his claw as we go on

*p. 5*
 *lines 42, 43, 46* 2 The Lawer
 *line 47* 3 Lawer again
 *lines 49, 50* 4 No Lawer for Geese may be return'd & Sit
 *line 53* 5 it was no Compliment when they were oblig'd to do as they were bid
 *line 60* 6 ordain'd smells of the Parson
 *lines 59, 61, 62* 7 an excellent reason the Hawke was very fitt to represent a cackling Flock because he was not a Cackler

*p. 6*
 *line 66* 8 Now the Compliment in line 54 is lost
 *line 70* 9 and so they are still
 *line 72* 10 N B : A dire Ambition in a Borough to choose their own Burgesses, & the subject much safer, who gives up his liberties than he that contends for them

*p. 7*
 *lines 88, 89* [11] if the Author does not know what he here Suggest 'tis rascally to hint it
 *lines 96, 97* 12 This is false The Author may call it poetical fiction if he pleases, but it has certainly the mark of Saturn's claw upon it See line 20 & Note
 *line 107* 13 They were Friends of the Government, and of [the] Administration & chosen by such as had been allways stanch to the present Royall Family

*p. 8*
 *line 114* 14 This hint is too low for either Parson or Lawer & probably hoisted in by one of the Captains
 *line 124* 15 Well said

*p. 9*
 *line 142* 16 Not true Saturns claw again See note 1

*p. 10*
 *line 164* 17 Fled is this English or Irish?

*p. 12*
 *line 202* 18 Saturns claw: See note 1 They know their power of electing Burgesses to be their Legal right, and that the depriving Boroughs of that priviledge is sapping y^e Constitution of their Country
 *line 203* 19 which is most Ambitious the asserting one's own rights or attempting to deprive other persons of theirs
 *line 205* 20 A Puff
 *line 206* 21 If this Submission means the giving up the right of election it was never made & if the geese continue true and honest whigs & Friends to their country never will be made
 *line 208* 22 Another Puff If the Author means that the Eagle has a right to make the geese quit the Town, it must be own'd he has just the Same, as he has to their elective power –
 The Author here makes his Eagle a Tyrant
 *line 220* 23 The moral of the Tale is this, That the Aldermen shou'd give up their rights & priviledges: That 'tis insolent in them to assert them & they shou'd be content to be despis'd as they us'd to be

## 3 Printed annotations, 1751

*p. [1]*
ANNOTATIONS / ON THE / GEESE in DISGRACE. / Very necessary for all who would com- / prehend the true Design of the / Author of that elaborately-abstruse / Performance. / By *Martinus Scriblerus.* / Scribendi rectè Sapere est & Principium & Fons. / Horat. / *PORTSMOUTH :* / Printed and sold by W. Horton. / M.DCC.LI.

*p. [2] blank; p. 3*
ANNOTATIONS ON THE GEESE in DISGRACE, *&c.*

I, MARTINUS SCRIBLERUS, do hereby declare to the inquisitive Reader, that nothing but a sincere Desire to set the Public right in their Notions, has ever tempted me, even in my younger Years, to commit my Thoughts to the Press; much less therefore am I in Danger, at my Decline of Life, to be infected with a Cacoethes, or Itch of Writing, unless some great Occasion calls: And such a One now offers itself; for travelling lately (as I am often wont) (*p. 4*) from Town to Town for my Amusement, I arrived in *Portsmouth* a few Days since; and finding the Place full of Commotion, the Streets filled with laced Coats and Cockades, and the Wearers of them carrying in their Looks a greater Air of Importance than ordinary, I began to fear that War and Tumult were again to take Place of Peace and Quietness, and that all my Hopes of ending my Days while *Britain* rejoiced in Plenty, and Tranquillity, were vanished into Air. While I walk'd along the Street musing on these Things, a Man following me close behind, cry'd aloud, "Stay Purser, I have got a Dozen of them for my Friends"; and then, clapping me on the Back,—"D—n me! here they are" says he, "The Dogs are well roasted, and I'll present you with one". On which turning myself about I perceived a little contemptible Figure, dress'd in the Uniform of a Lieutenant, with a Bundle of Pamphlets under his Arm, which he seemed to carry in Triumph: I gaz'd with Astonishment at such a Salutation from a Stranger, and he immediately excused himself by exclaiming, "G— Z—! Sir, I ask your Pardon; I was (*p. 5*) full of Zeal for the Cause of the A—y, and mistook you for Purser *B*—"; I told him I was surprized at the Countenances of all the Gentlemen of the Navy, and begg'd him to inform me, what fill'd them with such unusual Gladness; he reply'd "an *unanswerable Poem* was publish'd against the C—n, for having dar'd to become *independant*; and that I might hear more at the Crown Coffee-House, where all the Officers were assembled"; having said thus, the little Wretch shot away from me, and I saw no more of him. I soon after found out the Coffee-House, and, scarce getting Room for Entrance, for the Multitude of Officers, pass'd thro' them unobserv'd, and took my Stand near one of the Windows, where a most extra-ordinary Scene presented to my View. On all Sides of me was the Room throng'd with *naval Heroes,

---

*Naval Hero's, an ancient Word with a modern Signification; for altho those whom our Great Gransires foolishly deck'd with that Title, were Men who fought bravely to maintain their Country's Freedom, we in this politer Age, have wisely revers'd its original Import, and *naval Hero* in modern Writers, is only ascribed to those who love Slavery and detest Fight-(*p. 6*)ing at all: and in like Manner is the Meaning of the Words *great, brave,* &c. of late Years quite opposite to the ancient Interpretations of 'em: To prove this, see a Fragment lately publish'd, and consider who these Terms are there apply'd to.

---

each carrying in his Hand a Pamphlet, which some prais'd as they read, and others prais'd without reading. After some Time the Hubbub in a great Measure ceas'd, many departing, and leaving me less incumber'd with Objects, and more at Leasure to examine those that offer'd themselves to my View: when lo, one of their Chiefs approach'd pretty near me, and was soon surrounded by a Crowd of the lesser Fry. He harrangu'd them long on the Disobedience of the C—n to the L—ds, and concluded with wishing them under martial Discipline, to which all the Throng assented; and one among them, superior to the rest in Size, but not in Sense, with a Horse Laugh, exclaimed, "G— Z—! *they deserve all to be brought to the Gears*": At this the Haranguer smil'd and began to read, but, tho the Crew of Sycophants around him applauded as he went on, I soon grew weary (*p. 7*) of hearing the Ass utter Nonsense; for half the Words were pronounced wrong, nor did he understand the Meaning of the Stops, or the Cadence of the Verse: I then left the Room, pitying from my Soul, the poor Writer, whose Works were scandaliz'd by the Applause of such a Company of Blockheads; and passing by the Bookseller's, paid my six Pence for a Pamphlet, and went to the other Coffee-House to peruse it. In running it over, the following Observations occur'd to me, which I here present you with, by Way of Annotations on the Text; finding not only the martial Gentlemen, but those of the Town, have to a Man, misunderstood the Meaning of the Author.

As Truth is said by the Ancients to be hid in the Bottom of a Well, and to be drawn up with much Difficulty, so, Authors skill'd like mine in the Art of Sinking in Poetry, hide their Meaning so deep, that themselves are hardly able again to discover it; I therefore, being descended from a Race of Commentators, and having commented myself on many (*p. 8*) Books, in most Languages, undertake for the Ease of the Author (who otherwise might have remain'd eternally ignorant of his own original Design) and all Sorts and Degrees of Readers and Hearers, this Herculean Labor.

THE Poet very judiciously begins with an elaborate Introduction; shewing you, that being content with Nature's Laws and Government, will not make you discontented; and that while you are not ambitious, you shall not be fill'd with Ambition, &c. a great Truth! and very necessary to be known by all Degrees of Men.

*Each had his Pleasure*, &c. Line 5. Here are six Lines very needful to be weigh'd, if we would find out the true Intent of the Writer: He sets forth, that by Nature all Brutes knew their Pleasure, Business and Station, nor ever attempted to interfere with each other; but as all had some Titles, or Employments, they were satisfied with their own, nor sought to prejudice their Neighbours; and he concludes the Para-(*p. 9*)graph with declaring Matters to be alter'd in this Respect: Now, that the Sting of this Satire is not meant for *Portsmouth*, is pretty plain, for *my Lord, your Grace, your Honor*, bear very little Resemblance to the Titles used here, and the Alderman is only foisted in, the better to obscure the Author's true Aim: What he plainly means, is, that certain Persons, usually saluted by certain such Titles, as my Lord, your Grace, your Honor, at first indeed, acted according to the Duties of their Posts, and consequently enjoy'd the pleasing Satisfaction attendant on Righteousness; but that now they are fallen from this happy Condition.

Line 11 and 12. *No modern Government of State*
        *Was half so happy, half so great;*
These two Lines confirm the above Assertion, hinting plainly and boldly, at the very Thing by Name.

*Their Laws*, &c. Line 13. Would a Man writing in Favor of the Navy, have mentioned the Word Law? for can any one read it, and not think of J— W—les, and the C—t M—l? 'tis plain, very (*p. 10*) plain already, that the Author intends to *sneer* at those he pretends to *praise*; but the dull Rogues of O—rs (I suppose) will scarce be brought to credit their own Folly, in crying up the very Piece which condemns them.

*And whilst*, &c. Line 17. In these four Lines have we the Golden Age, resulting from wholsome Laws, falling a Prey to the Claws of *Saturn*: what can be hence inferr'd, but that *Saturn*, or Lead, (for I take his Fox and his Eagle, to bear the same Interpretation) presides so much in the Head of the Fox's Lordship, that, thro' meer Insensibility, he has kindled up this Discord, which might never have arisen, or, at least, had been happily terminated, had he exerted a little more of his wonted Policy; and not trusted too much to the Strength of his Compeers, the Wolf and the Ass, being doubtless sensible he had none of his own to confide in?

*What sordid Avarice*, &c. Line 23. Here our Author boldly declares himself; and do not the Gentle-(*p. 11*)men of the C—n wonder that they could once imagin him to be their Foe? the Helm is the Director of the whole Ship, and the B—d of A—y directs the whole N—y; now, as Poets may by a Figure express a Whole by a Part, so has our Author by the Regulator of a Part, express'd the Regulator of the whole; and, by a well-tim'd Exclamation, proclaim'd the Avarice of the Great.

Line 25. Here give me Leave to observe how much a right Understanding of a Book helps an Author to Fame; for were we to take that to be the Meaning of this Poet which appears to be so, were he a School-boy, he ought to be flogg'd for such an Afternoon's Exercise; but when we search the Matter to the Bottom, then his Merit shines abroad with brightest Lustre: so that had not I, *Martinus Scriblerus*, undertook to discover the Truth of Things, the silly Gudgeons of O—rs, swallowing the Bait, for what it appear'd to be, would have damn'd this excellent Piece, and defam'd the Writer: but tho I have hitherto profess'd myself an Admirer of the Author,

I must act the Part (*p. 12*) of an impartial Critic, and shew the Faults, as well as the Beauties, of the Poem: The Simile therefore used here I must pronounce to be bad, nor have the fourteen Lines following any Merit that I can descry, but rather many Blemishes, which I need not particularize, or trouble the Reader with, they being obvious, to the meanest Capacity.

Line 41. I should in my last Note have included all this Paragraph, had I not thought it necessary to put the Public in Mind of the Author's great Veneration for Law, which manifestly appears from his making Use of the Terms, as naturally as one of the Tribe; and can any Man imagin this done with an Intention to oblige the martial Men, whose Court the Law has stigmatiz'd with Folly, and reduced to Submission, sorely against their Wills.

Line 55. The Eagle is here describ'd to be in great Power, but not one Word do we hear of his Wisdom; and can we believe if the Author had not intended to ridicule his Eagle, that he would have let him pass a (*p. 13*) Decree for so *shallow-pated* a Reason? one would really be inclin'd to think that the Eagle had lost his first Form, and was turn'd *Goose*.

Line 67. These five Lines contain a good Irony, at which the Poet is skilful when he has a Mind to cloak his real Sentiments.

Line 72. These four Lines are worth more than all the Tale besides; notwithstanding which, as the Author's Hopes of Fame, depend only upon the Profundity of his sinking, the least sublimity in Thought or Expression, must be deem'd a Fault, by all true Admirers of the Bathos.

Line 80. Oak is Timber, and Elm is Timber; now by *poeticâ Licentiâ* one may be fairly put for the other, and oaken Blocks must be here understood Blocks of Elm.

Line 82. to the End of this Paragraph. Here is another Confirmation of the Author's good Wishes to (*p. 14*) the Freedom of the C—n, for the Friends of the Eagle are stung home with Satire, while on the opposite Side, many are taken no Notice of, and others prais'd, tho covertly.

Line 90. The whole Paragraph has in it—nothing worth remarking.

Line 100. Here is an Error of the Press, *few* for *most*, and then the Sense will run well enough, otherwise the Sentence is a Contradiction in Terms; for had not the black-crown'd Geese been *sage* (ay and in a great Degree too) they would have try'd for Independency before it became *opportune*, and so have blown their Scheme; or they would never have hit so exactly on the only right Means of carrying their Point.

Line 111. He has given the Side he favor'd a bad Epithet in this Place, and his calling 'em treacherous, I fancy he will deem himself somewhat too harsh, and consequently leave it out in the *next* Edition.

*p. 15*

Line 112. The Author has been much abus'd with Respect to this Line; certain Annotators having describ'd it as a low personal Reflection; when in Reality the Author design'd it as a high Compliment; Men who talk much and well in public before they are invested with Power, generally then forbear; and the Poet only meant to liken the Mayor in that Respect to a certain noble Lord whom we all know: The Term *Goose-like* must be here interpreted *Alderman-like*, so that the Writer only intended to say, the Mayor acted in this Circumstance as a Man invested with Power, and just as he ought. The Epithet *swarthy*, by no Means contradicts this Assertion, the Writer being under a Necessity of eking out the Line, by adding two Syllables; and if an Epithet must be had on Account of the Measure, I defy him to find a fitter.

Line 116. This whole Speech is a Confirmation of what I have all along declared; or can we imagin that he would put such Words into the Mouth of his (*p. 16*) Antagonist, as a noble *Briton* ought in the like Case to utter?

Line 125. We must allow this Paragraph to be full of Faults, notwithstanding it is a further Assurance to the Public, of what has been the principal Subject of these Annotations, *viz.* that the Writer is a Friend to Liberty.

Line 137 (*i.e. 142*). This Paragraph contains—nothing material.

Line 147 (*i.e. 152*). This Line evinces the Truth of my former Assertion concerning the Error of the Press; for no Man without Sagacity can be an effectual *Tempter, or continue his Address with Art,* nor is there any Evil in the Name of Tempter, for we may as well tempt others to Goodness, as the Contrary, and 'tis plain this is the Sense in which the Author wrote it.

Line 149 (*i.e. 154*). Here is another Speech, every Word of (*p. 17*) which the Heart of an honest Man must at once pronounce to be just.

Line 157 (*i.e. 162*). Here is a Mistake of Consequence made by the Poet, for I apprehend no Goslins could be sworn in 'till long after the Egg-shells had dropt from their Heads; but Authors professing the Art of Sinking in Poetry, by no Means think themselves oblig'd to stick to Truth.

Line 161 (*i.e. 166*). This playing on the Word is but low Wit; however, Gudgeons and Trouts plainly meaning S—a O—rs, it serves as a further Proof of my former Assertion, that the Author is no Friend to the A—y: And it amounts to Demonstration, that he is a Professor of the glorious Art, mention'd in the last Note.

Line 175 (*i.e. 180*). *Impertinence* and *silly*; harsh Words for Friends;—but when spoken ironically they never offend.

*p. 18*
Line 181 (*i.e. 186*). This Speech of the Eagle's is by much the worst Speech made, and smells so much of the Tyrant, that 'tis impossible the Author could intend it as a Praise.

Line 195 (*i.e. 200*). This and the five following Lines, even as strong as mathematical Evidence, prove, that the Poet has been writing ironically throughout the Piece, for the whole Nation knows *Portsmouth* has never yet submitted, tho flatter'd, promis'd, threaten'd and sooth'd, abus'd and sooth'd again; even I, a Stranger, am not unacquainted with this; so that it must have been the Height of Madness to attempt such an Imposition on the Public; besides, could he without a Sneer (Line 203 (*i.e. 208*).) have made the Eagle weak enough to command the Extirpation of the Geese, who will in the Nature of Things hold their Pen in Peace, spite of his Menaces, when the Power shall be flown out of this noble Bird's * Hands, and all his Wiles are insufficient to catch it again?

---

*A Morsel for the naval Critics, and tho this is the only one we thought proper to take Notice of, we have purposely left several others for them to chew upon.

*p. 19*
Line 209 (*i.e. 214*). The Author concludes his Tale in the same ironical Style which he has carry'd it on with, and even to the last ridicules the Eagle's unavailing Threats.

Line 215 (*i.e. 220*). The Moral can only be apply'd to their L—ps; for 'tis impossible he would be thought to say, 'tis better for Men to be contented Slaves, than by striving, to obtain Freedom: He certainly means, that those in Power had better be satisfied with that which they lawfully hold, than by grasping after more, like the Dog in the Fable, to lose the Substance for the Shadow.

And now I must address myself in a few Words of Advice to the Author: Tho thou art right Friend, in expressing thy Mind thus covertly, yet should'st thou take Care thou dost not thereby entirely secrete the Sense, lest the Public should (as the O—rs now do) interpret thy Words according to the Appearance, and thou be blam'd instead of applauded: Had not I (*p. 20*) arose to vindicate thee, how poor a Figure had'st thou cut among the Class of *deep* Writers ? And surely I have interpreted thy Meaning aright; for otherwise thou hast pen'd a Satire which has given no Body Offence; and that would be an indisputable Proof of thy having attain'd to the profoundest Skill in Sinking.

*Martinus Scriblerus.*

*F I N I S.*

# Appendix III

Table of Mayors and Justices of the Peace in Portsmouth 1730-1752

Under the terms of the governing Charter the Mayor, ex-Mayor and three Aldermen served as Justices of the Peace. The names are given in the order they are listed in the Election and Sessions Books (P.C.R.O. CE1/13, 14). Whether this indicates an order of precedence is not known. Normally they were sworn in soon after their election in September.

| Year | Mayor | Immediate Past Mayor | Other Justices |
|---|---|---|---|
| 1730-1 | Rob. Newnham | John Arnold | Henry Stanyford; Sam. Brady; Tho. Missing. |
| 1731-2 | John White | Rob. Newnham | Henry Stanyford; Sam. Brady; John Arnold (died); John Vining (replaced Arnold 22 Feb. 1731/2). |
| 1732-3 | John Mounsher | John White | Henry Stanyford; Sam. Brady; John Vining. |
| 1733-4 | Sam. Brady | John Mounsher | John Vining; Henry Stanyford; John White. |
| 1734-5 | Henry Stanyford (died 14 July 1735) John White | Sam. Brady | John Mounsher; John Vining; John White (sworn 1 Apr. 1735). |
| 1735-6 | Cornelius Colliss | John White | Lewis Barton; Sam. Brady; John Mounsher. |
| 1736-7 | Wil. Rickman | Cornelius Colliss | John White; Sam. Brady; Rob. Newnham. |
| 1737-8 | Mic. Atkins | Wil. Rickman | John Vining; Sam. Brady; John Mounsher. |
| 1738-9 | John Vining | Mic. Atkins | Sam. Brady; Rob. Newnham (died); Wil. Rickman; John Mounsher (replaced Newnham 24 Nov. 1738). |
| 1739-40 | John White | John Vining | Sam. Brady; Mic. Atkins; Wil. Rickman. |
| 1740-1 | Sam. Brady | John White | Lewis Barton; Wil. Rickman; Mic. Atkins. |
| 1741-2 | Lewis Barton | Sam. Brady | John White; Tho. Stanyford; Wil. Rickman. |
| 1742-3 | Wil. Rickman | Lewis Barton | Sam. Brady; Cornelius Colliss; Mic. Atkins. |
| 1743-4 | Mic. Atkins | Wil. Rickman | Lewis Barton; Sam. Brady; Tho. Stanyford. |
| 1744-5 | Tho. Stanyford | Mic. Atkins | Lewis Barton; Sam. Brady; Cornelius Colliss. |
| 1745-6 | Edw. Linzee | Tho. Stanyford | Sam. Brady; Mic. Atkins; John Carter. |
| 1746-7 | Sam. Chandler | Edw. Linzee | Sam. Brady (died); Mic. Atkins; John Carter; Lewis Barton (replaced Brady 7 Apr. 1747). |
| 1747-8 | John Carter | Sam. Chandler | Mic. Atkins; Edw. Linzee; Lewis Barton (sworn 24 Nov. 1747). |
| 1748-9 | Wil. Rickman | John Carter | Mic. Atkins; Edw. Linzee; Sam. Chandler. |
| 1749-50 | Tho. Stanyford | Wil. Rickman | Edw. Linzee; Sam. Chandler; John Carter. |
| 1750-1 | Tho. Missing | Tho. Stanyford | Edw. Linzee; Sam. Chandler; John Carter. |
| 1751-2 | John Leeke | Tho. Missing | Edw. Linzee; John Carter; Tho. White. |

# Appendix IV

Table of officers of Portsmouth Corporation 1730-1752

The names in each office are given in the order they are listed in the Election and Sessions Books (P.C.R.O. CE1/13, 14). Whether this indicates an order of precedence is not always clear.

| | | |
|---|---|---|
| **1**<br>**Recorder** | 1730–41<br>1741–3<br>1743–5<br>1745–52 | James Crosse<br>vacant<br>Fra. Chute<br>Wil. Pescod |
| **2**<br>**Town Clerk** | 1730–46<br>1746–52 | Geo. Huish (died 1747)<br>Geo. Huish (died 1788) |
| **3**<br>**Chamberlain** | 1730–1<br>1731–47<br>1747–52 | Dan. Smith<br>Hugh Grove<br>John Shepherd |
| **4**<br>**Sergeants-at-Mace and Town Water Bailiffs** | 1730–43 | Ric. Clapham (died); Sam. Beven; Ric. Storey (held office during Clapham's illness and Beven's absence 1737–8; replaced Clapham 23 Nov. 1742). |
| | 1743–4 | Sam. Beven; Ric. Storey (died); John Brand (replaced Storey 10 Jan. 1743–4). |
| | 1744–52 | Sam. Beven (sworn for 1751–2, 18 Oct. 1751); John Brand; Wil. Woodyer (held office during Beven's illness and Brand's absence 1747–8). |
| **5**<br>**Town Crier** | 1730–43<br>1743–52 | John Edwards<br>Abraham Stallard |
| **6**<br>**Searchers of Markets** | 1730–34<br>1734–8<br>1738–9<br>1739–42<br>1742–3<br>1743–52 | Dan. Grigg; James Lipscomb jun.<br>James Lipscomb jun.; Dan. Grigg.<br>Dan. Grigg; John Redman.<br>Dan. Grigg; Wil. Trattle.<br>Henry Grigg; Wil. Trattle.<br>Wil. Trattle; Henry Grigg. |
| **7**<br>**Searchers of Leather** | 1730–2<br>1732–3<br>1733–5<br>1735–7<br>1737–9<br>1739–44<br><br>1744–8<br>1748–52 | Geo. Roach; Jos. Carter.<br>James Roach; Geo. Roach.<br>Geo. Roach; James Roach.<br>James Roach; Geo. Roach.<br>Wil. Raggett jun.; Geo. Roach.<br>Wil. Raggett jun.; Jos. Carter (died); John Hugony (replaced Carter 10 Jan. 1743/4).<br>Wil. Raggett jun.; John Hugony.<br>Wil. Raggett; John Hugony. |
| **8**<br>**Constables** | 1730–1 | Peter Edmunds; Henry Edwards; John Prior; Edw. Bottom; Laramore Hugley; Wil. Snooke. |
| | 1731–2 | John Butler; John Poor; Henry Dernell; Rob. Browne; Tho. Light; Jos. Gilbert. |
| | 1732–3 | Henry Dernell; Geo. Barlow; John Bartlett; Henry Hallsey; Tho. Light; Jos. Carter. |
| | 1733–4 | Wil. Pafford; James Deacon; Ric. Attweek; Ric. Howlett; Wil. Wattle; John Webb. |

| | |
|---|---|
| 1734–5 | Henry Halsey; John Goodeve; John How; Moses Mullins; John Webb; Geo. House. |
| 1735–6 | Ben. Whiteing; Wil. Horsfill jun.; Phil. Sugar; Kempster Lipscomb; Tho. Light jun.; John Webb. |
| 1736–7 | John Deborah; John Hartman; Jos. Sturdy; Jos. Jarman; Ric. Long; Ric. Dee. |
| 1737–8 | John Deborah; John Hartman; Jos. Blose; Jos. Lunn; Ric. Long; Ric. Dee. |
| 1738–9 | James Littlefield; John Poor; Joshua Kipling; Tho. Tollery; Wil. Owen; John Fry; Henry Bird (sworn 17 Oct. 1738). |
| 1739–40 | John Hawkins; John Newman; Jos. Bridger; Tho. Bayly; Henry Bird; Cha. Loyd. |
| 1740–1 | Dan. Garrett; Wil. Rowlidge; James Clungeon; John Merac; Ric. Mellish; Jos. Miles. |
| 1741–2 | John Herring; Ric. Lipscomb; Jos. Seyton; Tho. Allen jun.; Tim. Lamb; John Martin. |
| 1742–3 | Geo. Godman; James Money: Wil. Hodgkin; Jacob Maynard; Adam Strong; Wil. Oades jun. |
| 1743–4 | Geo. Seymour; Rob. Lee (sworn 11 Oct. 1743); James Norris; Wil. Drayton; Wil. Owen; Jos. Trattle. |
| 1744–5 | Wil. Butler jun.; Ben. Sparkman; Tho. Bevis; John Hugony; Tho. Paffard; John Evarnden. |
| 1745–6 | Stanton Davies; Abraham Adams; Wil. Grigg; Wil. Smith; John Bolton; Fra. Dodford. |
| 1746–7 | Ric. Wilshire; Step. Humphreys; Abraham Adams; Peter Ireland; Jos. Drake; John Symon. |
| 1747–8 | Wil. Norris; Binsteed Jeffery; Tho. Whitear; Nic. Corbin; John Tucker; Dan. Tribe. |
| 1748–9 | Geo. Damerum; James Cheesman; Jos. Quick; Ben. Rider (sworn 18 Oct. 1748); Geo. Blagden; Cha. Collins. |
| 1749–50 | Rob. Field; John Patten; Rob. Swift; Ant. Huson; Jos. Dawes; Tho. Wattell. |
| 1750–1 | Ben. Whiteing (sworn 2 Oct. 1750); Wil. Winter; Rob. Rout; James Brown jun.; Peter Evenson; Step. Beale. |
| 1751–2 | John Boyes; Henry Crutch; Wil. Carter (moved from Portsmouth); Jos. Hain; Emanuel Gristock; John Sparshatt; Wil. Butler (replaced Carter 3 Dec. 1751). |

## 9 Constables of Kingston and Buckland

| | |
|---|---|
| 1730–1 | Henry Chitty; Dan. Baverstock; Wil. Crapon. |
| 1731–2 | James Hodgson; Tho. White; John Bond; Jos. Lowe (replaced Hodgson 21 Dec. 1731). |
| 1732–3 | Wil. Horwood; Tho. Stables; Wil. Gower. |
| 1733–4 | Tho. Gibbs; Fra. Furmidge; Ant. Moaze. |
| 1734–5 | Ric. Sparshott; John Gordon; Ant. Moaze. |
| 1735–6 | Ric. Trotten; Geo. Hamond; Wil. Ware. |
| 1736–7 | Edw. Benson ('excused'); John Wade jun.; Wil. Ware; Nic. Bettesworth (replaced Benson 5 Oct. 1736). |
| 1737–8 | Ric. Maine; Tho. Rogers; Wil. Ware. |
| 1738–9 | John Fry; Step. Fisher; Wil. Weare. |
| 1739–40 | Henry Vernell; David Mearus; Rob. Foster (sworn 2 Oct. 1739). |
| 1740–1 | Dan. Dear; James Bowden; Rob. Foster. |
| 1741–2 | Wil. Arnold; John Hellyer; Peter Grant (sworn 6 Oct. 1741). |
| 1742–3 | Jos. Frith; Wil. Ward; John Drayton. |
| 1743–4 | Dan. Howard; Wil. Wittell; John Drayton. |
| 1744–5 | Tho. White; Tho. Eyer; Wil. Williams; Sam. Lucas (replaced White 9 Oct. 1744). |
| 1745–6 | John Hibberd; John Knight; Rob. Mew (sworn 8 Oct. 1745); John Good (replaced Hibberd 15 Oct. 1745). |
| 1746–7 | John Thornton; Peter Gover; John Drayton; Dan. Newton. |
| 1747–8 | John Bussey; John Oakshott jun.; Tho. Bull (sworn 6 Oct. 1747). |

|  |  |  |
|---|---|---|
|  | 1748–9 | John Marvell; John Waldron; Edw. Englefield; Walt. Smith (replaced Marvell 4 Oct. 1748). |
|  | 1749–50 | John Young; Wil. Cox; Tho. Mallard; Tho. Preston. |
|  | 1750–1 | James Parsons; James Charles; Paul Wood; Wil. Cole. |
|  | 1751–2 | Geo. Godden; Tho. Rampton; Ric. Nunn; John Gale (sworn 18 Oct. 1751). |

**10**
**Measurer**

| 1730–3 | And. Mears |
|---|---|
| 1733–43 | James Goodeve (declared 'incapable'); Rob. Payne (replaced Goodeve 15 Mar. 1742/3). |
| 1743–52 | Rob. Payne |

**11**
**Town Hayward**

| 1730–5 | Roger Hyde (sworn for 1734–5, 8 Oct. 1734) |
|---|---|
| 1735–8 | Tho. Walter (sworn for 1735–6, 7 Oct. 1735; died); Roger Hyde (replaced Walter 22 Aug. 1738). |
| 1738–43 | Roger Hyde |
| 1743–5 | John Carter |
| 1745–8 | vacant |
| 1748–50 | Tho. Luke (sworn for 1748–9, 2 May 1749) |
| 1750–2 | Ric. Higgs |

**12**
**Auditors and Cofferers**

| 1730–1 | John Arnold; Henry Stanyford; Sam. Brady. |
|---|---|
| 1731–2 | Henry Stanyford; Sam. Brady; John Arnold (died); John Vining (replaced Arnold 22 Feb. 1731/2). |
| 1732–3 | John White; Henry Stanyford; Sam. Brady. |
| 1733–4 | John Vining; Henry Stanyford; John White. |
| 1734–5 | John Vining; John White; John Mounsher. |
| 1735–6 | Lewis Barton; Sam. Brady; John Mounsher. |
| 1736–7 | John White; Sam. Brady; Rob. Newnham. |
| 1737–8 | John Vining; Sam. Brady; John Mounsher. |
| 1738–9 | Sam. Brady; Rob. Newnham (died); Wil. Rickman; John Mounsher (replaced Newnham 24 Nov. 1738). |
| 1739–40 | John Vining; Sam. Brady; Wil. Rickman; Mic. Atkins. |
| 1740–1 | Lewis Barton; Wil. Rickman; Mic. Atkins. |
| 1741–2 | Sam. Brady; John White; Tho. Stanyford. |
| 1742–3 | Sam. Brady; Cornelius Colliss; Mic. Atkins. |
| 1743–4 | Lewis Barton; Sam. Brady; Tho. Stanyford. |
| 1744–5 | Lewis Barton; Sam. Brady; Cornelius Colliss. |
| 1745–7 | Sam. Brady (died); Mic. Atkins; John Carter; Lewis Barton (replaced Brady 7 Apr. 1747). |
| 1747–8 | Lewis Barton (sworn 24 Nov. 1747); Mic. Atkins; Edw. Linzee. |
| 1748–9 | Mic. Atkins; Edw. Linzee; Sam. Chandler. |
| 1749–51 | Edw. Linzee; Sam. Chandler; John Carter. |
| 1751–2 | Edw. Linzee; John Carter; Tho. White. |

# Appendix V

Biographical notes on Aldermen and Burgesses elected 1731-1751

The following information, if known and applicable, is given for each Alderman and Burgess admitted during the period covered by the Book of Original Entries printed here (i.e. between December 1731 and March 1751):

1 Name and title at time of admission. Local residents are indicated by an asterisk.

2 Dates of birth (or baptism) and death (or burial). In some cases dates of birth have been calculated from stated age at death or other information and thus may be subject to error.

3 Dates of admission and swearing in as Burgess and Alderman; honorary status is noted. Unless otherwise stated the swearing in took place on the day of admission.

4 Names of parents.

5 Name of wife and date of marriage.

6 Status, career or occupation. The attainment of titles and honours is not included. The dates given of promotion of rear-admirals, vice-admirals and admirals are normally of appointment to the Blue Squadron.

7 Offices, etc., held in the Portsmouth region or in Hampshire county administration. 'Turnpike' means the Portsmouth and Sheet Turnpike Trust.

8 Voting record in parliamentary elections or other information on political allegiance. This is omitted in the case of national figures.

9 Membership of the House of Commons, with constituencies and dates.

10 Religious sympathies. Known adherence to the Church of England is not mentioned, but office within a parish church is noted.

11 Relationship to other Aldermen and Burgesses.

References are given in the same order as the notes on each individual, but references to sources that have supplied more than one piece of information on a person are not repeated.

| | | | |
|---|---|---|---|
| ad. | = admitted | C.-in-C. | = Commander-in-Chief |
| Ald. | = Alderman | d. | = died |
| bapt. | = baptised | dau. | = daughter |
| bro. | = brother | hon. | = honorary |
| Bt | = Baronet | mar. | = married |
| bur. | = buried | sw. | = sworn |

**1
Amherst, John**

Bapt. 6 Jan. 1717/8; d. Feb. 1778. Ad. 29 Sept. 1746; sw. 28 Mar. 1751. Son of Jeffrey and Elizabeth, *née* Kerrill. Mar. Anne, eldest dau. of Edw. Linzee. Naval officer: Capt. 1744, Rear-Adm. 1764, Vice-Adm. 1770, Adm. 1778. Son-in-law of Ald. Edw. Linzee; his widow married Tho. Monday.

Linzee, ii, pp. 488, 494, 459, 489; nos 132, 169; East, p. 381; P.R.O. Adm.3/62.

**2
Andrews, Richard**

D. by 16 Sept. 1765. Ad. 29 Sept. 1736 (not in Book of Original Entries). Mar. Ann Warrington 10 Feb. 1737/8. Farmer at Havant, merchant. Turnpike Commissioner under 1726 and 1742 Acts. Voted Whig 1734.

P.C.R.O. CE1/14, p. 188; P.C.R.O. 169A/2/1/4; East, p. 380; C. & E. 58/146; *Turnpike Minute Book*, pp. 173, 177; *Poll for Hants., 1734*, p. 126.

**3**
**Anson, George,**
**1st Baron Anson**

Born 23 Apr. 1697; d. 6 June 1762. Ad. 14 Aug. 1746; hon. Second son of Wil. and Isabella, *née* Carrier. Mar. Elizabeth, dau. of Phil. Yorke, 1st Earl of Hardwicke, 25 Apr. 1748. Naval officer: entered Navy 1712, Post-Capt. 1724, Rear-Adm. 1744, Vice-Adm. 1746, C.-in-C. Channel Fleet 1746, 1758, Adm. 1748, Vice-Adm. of Great Britain 1749 to death, Adm. of Fleet 1761 to death; First Lord of Admiralty 1751–6, 1757 to death. M.P. for Hedon 1744–7. Son-in-law of Phil. Yorke, 1st Earl of Hardwicke.

*D.N.B.*; no. 128; East, p. 381; Murrell & East, p. 350; Sedgwick, i, p. 415; G.E.C., i. pp. 172–3.

**4**
**Appleford,**
**Thomas***

Bapt. 26 Apr. 1703; d. by 16 Sept. 1751. Ad. 27 Oct. 1750. Son of Humf. and Mary, *née* Cosens. Tallow-chandler, general dealer. Voted Tory 1734.

P.C.R.O. 100A/1/1/1/2; P.C.R.O. CE1/14, p. 97; no. 164; East, p. 382; N.M.M. POR/F/5; C. & E. 58/1; *Poll for Hants.*, *1734*, p. 117.

**5**
**Atkins, Michael***

Bapt. 18 Jan. 1690/1; d. 11 Jan. 1752. Ad. 27 Dec. 1726; Ald. 8 Apr. 1735. Son of Mic. and Elizabeth, *née* Darrell. Mar. Jane Bromley 8 Aug. 1717. Block maker, brewer; Clerk of Cheque, Portsmouth. Surveyor of Turnpike 1719 to death; serving as Turnpike Commissioner 1746. Churchwarden, St Thomas's, 1724. Father of Wil. Atkins; father-in-law of Ald. Phil. Varlo and Ald. Tho. White.

P.C.R.O. 22A/2/1/1/2; P.R.O. Prob.11/792, f.27; no. 29; East, pp. 378, 330; P.C.R.O. 22A/2/1/1/4; P.R.O. Adm.3/62; *Turnpike Minute Book*, pp. xxii, 156, 137; P.C.R.O. S2/23; B.L. Add.MS. 8153, f. 119; Everitt, 'Pedigrees', i, p. 23.

**6**
**Atkins, William**

Bapt. 7 Aug. 1719; d. by 21 Sept. 1772. Ad. 29 Sept. 1738; sw. 1 Sept. 1741. Son of Mic. and Jane, *née* Bromley. Mar. Ann Boulton 3 Oct. 1757. Timber merchant. Turnpike Commissioner 1747. Son of Ald. Mic. Atkins; bro.-in-law of Ald. Tho. White and Ald. Phil. Varlo.

P.C.R.O. 22A/2/1/1/4; P.C.R.O. CE1/14, p. 225; no. 57; East, p. 380; no. 82; P.C.R.O. 100A/1/1/1/5; N.M.M. POR/F/6; *Turnpike Minute Book*, p.143; Everitt, 'Pedigrees', i, p. 22.

**7**
**Ballard, William**

Bapt. 15 May 1715; bur. 11 May 1756. Ad. 29 Sept. 1740. Son of Wil. and Rachel, *née* Chandler. Mar. (1) Mary Arney 4 Sept. 1743; (2) Elizabeth —. Attorney, in partnership with Ald. John White. Leet juror 1743; Turnpike Commissioner 1747. Churchwarden, St Thomas's, 1729.

P.C.R.O. 22A/2/1/1/4, 5; no. 77; East, p. 381; *Hants. Allegns*, i, p. 37; P.C.R.O. 100A/1/1/1/3; Hants.R.O. A Wills 1756; Everitt, 'Misc. collns', ii, p. 29; P.C.R.O. L1; *Turnpike Minute Book*, p. 143; B.L. Add. MS. 8153, f. 119.

**8**
**Barton, Edward***

Born 1681; d. by 16 Sept. 1751(?). Ad. 27 Nov. 1732; sw. 29 Sept. 1739. Second son of Lewis and Miriam. Mar. Mary Butler 31 Jan. 1720/1. Draper, mercer. Turnpike Commissioner under 1742 Act. Presbyterian: trustee and subscriber, High Street Chapel, 1735. Nephew of Tho. Barton(?).

Everitt, 'Misc. collns', i, p. 138; ibid., ii, p.176; P.C.R.O. CE1/14, p. 97; no. 10; East, p. 380; no. 67; P.C.R.O. 100A/1/1/1/3; P.R.O. W.O.55/1988; *Turnpike Minute Book*, p. 177; P.C.R.O. 257A/1/9/3.

**9**
**Barton, Thomas**

Bur. 10 Dec. 1758. Ad. 27 Dec. 1726; sw. 16 Aug. 1737. Mar. Mary Hayles 27 Aug. 1749. Goldsmith: fined £2. 3s. 2d. for selling gold wares 'worse than standard' 1706. Voted Whig 1705. Presbyterian. Uncle of Edw. Barton(?).

P.C.R.O. 22A/2/1/1/6; no. 47; East, p. 379; P.C.R.O. 100A/1/1/1/5; P.R.O. W.O.55/1988; Goldsmiths' Company, London, Court Books, x, p. 318a; *Poll*, *1705*, p. 60; P.C.R.O. 257A/1/9/1.

**10**
**Baxter, John**

Born 1634 or 1635; d. 30 Sept. 1736. Ad. 27 Nov. 1732. Storekeeper, Gun Wharf, Portsmouth, from at least 1719 to 1735. Turnpike Commissioner under 1726 Act.

*Gent. Mag.*, vi (1736), p. 620; no. 10; East, p. 379; P.C.R.O. S2/21; B.L. Add. MS. 33283, f. 322; *Turnpike Minute Book*, p. 173.

**11**
**Bayly, George**

Born 1693; d. 1 Dec. 1771. Ad. 27 Nov. 1732. Mar. (1) Sarah, daughter of John Carter, 29 Jan. 1729/30; (2) Mary —. Physician. Freeman of Chichester 1719. Whig affiliations by inference. Bro.-in-law of John Carter (d.1794); father of John Bayly.

Trail & Steer, pp. 1–2; *Gent. Mag.*, xli (1771), p. 571; no. 10; East, p. 379 (ad. 6 Nov. 1732); P.C.R.O. 22A/2/1/1/5; W.Suss.R.O. C.C.A. C. 1, f. 296; B.L. Add. MS. 32709, f. 285.

**12**
**Bayly, John**

Born 17 Feb. 1735/6; d. 11 Nov. 1815. Ad. 27 Oct. 1750. Son of Geo. and Mary. Physician. Voted Whig 1779. Son of Geo. Bayly.

Trail & Steer, passim; no. 164; *Poll*, *1779*, p. 71; *A tribute to the memory of John Bayly, M.D.* (1816), passim.

**13**
**Beauclerk, Vere,**
**1st Baron Vere**

Born 14 July 1699; d. 2 Oct. 1781. Ad. 1750 (not in Book of Original Entries); hon. Third son of Cha., 1st Duke of St Albans, and Diana, dau. of Aubrey de Vere, 20th Earl of Oxford. Mar. Mary, dau. of Tho. Chambers, 13 Apr. 1736. Naval officer: entered Navy c. 1713, Capt. 1721, Rear-Adm. 1745, Vice-Adm. 1746, Adm. 1748; Extra Commissioner of Navy 1732; Lord of Admiralty 1738–42, 1744–9; Lord Lieutenant of Berkshire 1761–71. M.P. for New Windsor 1726–41, Plymouth 1741–50.

Sedgwick, i, p. 450; G.E.C., xii, pt ii, p. 256; Murrell & East, p. 351.

**14**
**Bennett, Charles,**
**2nd Earl of**
**Tankerville**

Bapt. 21 Dec. 1697; d. 14 Mar. 1753. Ad. 13 May 1734; hon. First son of Cha., 1st Earl of Tankerville, and Bridget, *née* Howe. Mar. Camilla, dau. of Edw. Colville, c. 1715. Army Capt. 1716; Lord of Bedchamber to Prince of Wales 1729–33; Master of Buckhounds 1733–7; Lord of Bedchamber 1737–8; Lord Lieutenant of Northumberland 1740 to death. Turnpike Commissioner under 1726 Act; Free Burgess of Newport, I.W., 1734; Freeman of Chichester 1727.

G.E.C., xii, pt i, pp. 633–4; *Gent. Mag.*, xxiii (1753), p. 148; no. 20; East, p. 380; Murrell & East, p. 349; *Turnpike Minute Book*, p. 173; N.B.A. Class 2, Admissions 1717–1833; W.Suss.R.O. C.C.A. C.1, f. 361.

**15**
**Binsteed, William***

D. 1745. Ad. 27 Nov. 1732. Mar. Mary Coleman 24 Oct. 1734. Carpenter, mason(?). Leet juror 1734, 1736, 1738. Voted Whig 1734. Churchwarden, St Thomas's, 1727; dissenting affiliations(?).

Hants.R.O. A Wills 1745; no. 10; East, p. 380; P.C.R.O. 83A/1/1/2; nos 38, 68; P.C.R.O. L1; *Poll for Hants, 1734*, p. 131; B.L. Add. MS. 8153, f. 119; P.C.R.O. 257A/1/9/3.

**16**
**Bissell, John***

Born 1699; d. 1758. Ad. 27 Oct. 1750. First son of Cha. and Mary, *née* Voake. Attorney. Turnpike Commissioner under 1742 Act. Voted Tory 1734. Churchwarden, St Thomas's, 1713. Son of Cha. Bissell.

Everitt, 'Pedigrees', i, p. 77; Hants.R.O. B Wills 1758; nos 164, 167; East, p. 382; *Turnpike Minute Book*, p. 177; *Poll for Hants., 1734*, p. 128; B.L. Add. MS. 8153, f. 119.

**17**
**Bladen, Martin**

Born 1680(?); d. 14 Feb. 1745/6. Ad. 4 May 1741. Third son of Nat. and Isabella, *née* Fairfax. Mar. (1) Mary Gibbs; (2) Frances Foche, widow, 1728. Army service in Low Countries and Spain; Controller of Mint 1714–28; Commissioner of Trade and Plantations 1717–46; First Commissioner, Antwerp Conference, 1732–42. M.P. for Stockbridge 1715–34, Maldon 1734–41, Portsmouth 1741–6. Uncle of Ald. Sir Edw. Hawke.

*D.N.B.*; Sedgwick, i, pp. 465–6; no. 81; East, p. 381.

**18**
**Blanckley,**
**Stanyford***

Bapt. 11 June 1718; d. by 15 Sept. 1766. Ad. 29 Sept. 1750. Son of Tho. and Anne. Naval officer at Gibraltar. Overseer of Poor, Portsmouth, 1750. Voted Tory 1734. Nephew(?) of Ald. Henry Stanyford; bro. of Tho. Blanckley.

P.C.R.O. 100A/1/1/1/3; P.C.R.O. CE1/14, p. 193; no. 162; East, p. 381; P.C.R.O. 22A/2/1/1/4; P.R.O. Adm.3/62; P.C.R.O. S3/132; *Poll for Hants., 1734*, p. 129.

**19**
**Blanckley,**
**Thomas***

D. 1747 or 1748. Ad. 2 Sept. 1735; sw. 25 July 1738. Son of Tho. and Anne. Clerk of Survey, Portsmouth Dockyard, 1718–37. Turnpike Commissioner under 1726 Act. Nephew(?) of Ald. Henry Stanyford; bro. of Stanyford Blanckley.

B.L. Add. MS. 15955, f. 159; B.L. Add. MS. 32714, ff. 42–3; P.C.R.O. S2/21; P.C.R.O. 67A/13: copy of Slight annotated by Sir Frederic Madden, p. 166; *Turnpike Minute Book*, p. 173; P.R.O. Prob. 11/673, f. 193; nos 33, 53; East, p. 380; P.C.R.O. 22A/2/1/1/4.

**20**
**Bowerbank,**
**Thomas***

Bur. 24 May 1768. Ad. 27 Nov. 1732. Mar. Cathrine Ridge 15 Feb. 1712/3. Overseer, Gun Wharf, Portsmouth, 1708; Clerk of Survey 1731–7; Barrack Master; contractor 1735.

P.C.R.O. 100A/1/1/1/7; no. 10; East, p. 379 (ad. 6 Nov. 1732); P.C.R.O. 100A/1/1/1/3; P.R.O. W.O.49/109, p. 8; P.C.R.O. S2/17, 24; P.R.O. W.O.55/1988.

**21**
**Boyfield, Richard**

D. by 17 Sept. 1770. Ad. 27 Oct. 1750.

P.C.R.O. CE1/14, p.214; no. 164; East, p. 382.

**22**
**Brady, Charles**

Bur. 13 Mar. 1760. Ad. 27 Nov. 1732. Son of Sam. and Anne, *née* Colby(?). Commander of Customs vessels, London 1736, Southampton 1743. Son of Ald. Sam. Brady; bro. of Cuthbert and Phil. Brady; half-bro. of Sam. and Matteate Brady.

No. 10; East, p. 380; P.R.O. Prob.11/753, f. 89; *Cal. T.B. & P. 1735–8*, p. 286; C. & E. 62/65.

**23**
**Brady, Cuthbert***

Ad. 16 Sept. 1734 (not in Book of Original Entries). Son of Sam. and Anne, *née* Colby(?). Minor(?). Son of Ald. Sam. Brady; bro. of Cha. and Phil. Brady; half-bro. of Sam. and Matteate Brady.

East, p. 380; P.R.O. Prob.11/753, f. 89.

**24**
**Brady, Matteate**

Bapt. 23 Dec. 1718; d. by 18 Sept. 1786. Ad. 10 Apr. 1728; sw. 11 Dec. 1739. Son of Sam. and Elizabeth, *née* Teate. Mar. Mrs Jane Mathews 3 May 1744. Naval officer: Lieut. on half pay 1775-7. Turnpike Commissioner under 1742 Act. Son of Ald. Sam. Brady; bro. of Sam. Brady; half-bro. of Cha., Cuthbert and Phil. Brady.

P.C.R.O. 22A/2/1/1/4; P.C.R.O. CE1/15, p. 83; no. 70; East, p. 379; P.R.O. Prob.11/753, f. 89; P.C.R.O. 83A/1/1/3; Sandwich MS. 380; *Rider's British Merlin for the year 1777* [1776], p. 153; *Turnpike Minute Book*, p. 177.

**25**
**Brady, Philip***

D. Sept. or Oct. 1741. Ad. 29 Sept. 1741; d. before being sworn in. Son of Sam. and Anne, *née* Colby(?). Son of Ald. Sam. Brady; bro. of Cha. and Cuthbert Brady; half-bro. of Sam. and Matteate Brady.

No. 84; East, p. 381; P.R.O. Prob.11/753, f. 89.

**26**
**Brady, Samuel**

Bapt. 28 Apr. 1720; bur. 4 Dec. 1769. Ad. 10 Apr. 1728; sw. 12 Apr. 1743. First son of Sam. and Elizabeth, *née* Teate. Mar. Rachel —. Son of Ald. Sam. Brady; bro. of Matteate Brady; half-bro. of Cha., Cuthbert and Phil. Brady.

P.C.R.O. 22A/2/1/1/4, 6; Everitt, 'Pedigrees', i, p. 103; Everitt, 'Misc. collns', ii, p. 371; no. 97; East, p. 379; P.C.R.O. 22A/2/1/1/7; P.R.O. Prob.11/753, f. 89.

**27**
**Brooke, Pusey***

D. by 19 Sept. 1768. Ad. 27 Nov. 1732. Collector of Customs, Portsmouth, 1726–46; Surveyor-General for Hampshire and Dorset, 1731–61; commissary for French prisoners, Portsmouth, 1739–48. Turnpike Commissioner under 1742 Act; Free Burgess of Yarmouth, I.W., 1733 (dismissed and re-admitted 1741).

P.C.R.O. CE1/14, p. 206; no. 10; East, p. 379 (adm. 6 Nov. 1732); P.C.R.O. S2/23; C. & E. 58/148; *Cal. T.B. & P. 1735-8*, p. 149; C. & E. 58/156, p. 107; *Turnpike Minute Book*, p. 177; B.L. Add. MS. 15955, f. 197; Y.T.T. Corporation Proceedings 1710–85, ff. 26, 49–51, 54.

**28**
**Brudenell, George, 4th Earl of Cardigan**

Born 26 July 1712; d. 23 May 1790. Ad. 7 June 1736; hon. First son of Geo., 3rd Earl of Cardigan, and Elizabeth, dau. of Tho. Bruce, 2nd Earl of Aylesbury. Mar. Mary, dau. of John Montagu, 2nd Duke of Montagu, 7 July 1730. Chief Justice in Eyre north of Trent 1742–52; Constable of Windsor Castle 1752 to death; Privy Councillor 1766; Governor of Prince of Wales and Prince Frederick 1776–80; Master of Horse 1780 to death. Nephew of Hon. James Brudenell; son-in-law of John Montagu, 2nd Duke of Montagu.

G.E.C., iii, pp. 14–15; no. 35; East, p. 380; Murrell & East, p. 349; Joan Wake, *The Brudenells of Deene* (1953), pp. 247–327.

**29**
**Brudenell, James**

Born 20 Apr. 1725; d. 24 Feb. 1811. Ad. 25 Dec. 1746 (not in Book of Original Entries). Second son of Geo., 3rd Earl of Cardigan, and Elizabeth, dau. of Tho. Bruce, 2nd Earl of Aylesbury. Mar. (1) Anne, dau. of Geo. Legge, Viscount Lewisham, 24 Nov. 1760; (2) Elizabeth, dau. of John Waldegrave, 3rd Earl Waldegrave, 18 Apr. 1791. Deputy Cofferer to the Household 1755–60; Master of Robes to Prince of Wales 1758–60, to King 1760–91; Keeper of Privy Purse to Prince of Wales 1758–60, to King 1760 to death; Constable of Windsor Castle 1791 to death. M.P. for Shaftesbury 1754–61, Hastings 1761–8, Great Bedwyn Mar.–Nov. 1768, Marlborough 1768–80.

G.E.C., iii, pp. 15–16; Namier & Brooke, ii, pp. 124–5; East, p. 381.

**30**
**Bucknall, James***

D. 21 Nov. 1771. Ad. 27 Oct. 1750. Mar.(1) Jane Podd 19 Sept. 1720; (2) Mary Bates 16 June 1737. Merchant, general dealer in used stores, agent of London merchants. Turnpike Commissioner under 1742 Act. Churchwarden, St Thomas's, 1740(?).

*Gent. Mag.*, xli (1771), p. 523; P.C.R.O. 22A/2/1/1/7; nos 164, 167; East, p. 382; P.C.R.O. 22A/2/1/1/4; P.C.R.O. 83A/1/1/2; B.L. Add. MS. 32726, f. 3; N.M.M. POR/F/8; C. & E. 58/143, pp. 154, 164; C. & E. 58/148; *Turnpike Minute Book*, pp. 177, 121; P.C.R.O. 22A/2/1/12/1.

**31**
**Burford, Edward***

D. by 19 Sept. 1743. Ad. 18 Sept. 1732. Mar. (1) Sarah Wattson 14 Feb. 1716/7; (2) Mary Sturt 2 June 1734(?). Carpenter of H.M.S. Ipswich 1734 to death. Presbyterian: trustee and subscriber, High Street Chapel, 1735. Widow was housekeeper, then (after 1769) second wife, of Ald. John Carter.

Hants.R.O. B Wills 1743; no. 7; East, p. 379 (ad. 29 Sept. 1732); P.C.R.O. 22A/2/1/1/4,5; N.M.M. POR/F/5; P.C.R.O. 257A/1/9/3; Bonham-Carter, pp. 8, 21.

**32**
**Burrard, John**

D. 1765. Ad. 29 Sept. 1743; sw. 17 Sept. 1744. Gentleman(?). Free Burgess of Lymington, Hants., 1727; Sheriff of Hampshire 1738–9.

*V.C.H. Hants.*, iv, p. 628; no. 100; East, p. 381; no. 107; St Barbe, p. 12; *Cal. T.B. & P. 1735–8*, p. 596; *Cal. T.B. & P. 1739–41*, p. 169.

**33**
**Byng, John**

Bapt. 29 Oct. 1704; executed at Portsmouth 14 Mar. 1757. Ad. 9 Jan. 1746/7; hon. Fourth son of Geo., 1st Viscount Torrington, and Margaret, *née* Master. Unmarried. Naval officer: entered Navy 1718, 2nd Lieut. 1724, Capt. 1727, Rear-Adm. 1745, Vice-Adm. 1747, C.-in-C. Mediterranean 1747, Adm. 1755. M.P. for Rochester 1751 to death.

*D.N.B.*; Sedgwick, i, p. 511; no. 134; East, p. 381; Murrell & East, p. 350.

**34**
**Carter, Daniel***

D. by May 1751. Ad. 27 Oct. 1750. Third son of John and Susanna, *née* Pike. Minor(?). Son of Ald. John Carter; bro. of John and Wil. Carter.

No. 164; East, p. 383.

**35**
**Carter, John***

Born 1715; d. 7 Feb. 1794. Ad. 27 Nov. 1732; sw. 7 June 1736; Ald. 13 Sept. 1744. Son of John and Mary, *née* White. Mar. (1) Susanna Pike 27 Oct. 1737; (2) Mary, widow of Edw. Burford, after 1769. Merchant. Free Burgess of Yarmouth, I.W., 1741; Turnpike Commissioner under 1742 Act; Justice of the Peace for Hampshire 1748; Mayor of Portsmouth 1754, 1759, 1762, 1765, 1767, 1779. Voted Whig 1734, 1779; described in 1775 as 'A man of fortune and director of the Opposition'. Presbyterian: trustee, High Street Chapel, 1735. Cousin of Ald. John White; son of John Carter; son-in-law of Wil. Pike; bro.-in-law of John Bayly and Edw. Burford(?); father of Dan., John and Wil. Carter.

*Gent. Mag.*, lxiv (1794), p. 189; no. 10; East, p. 380; nos 35, 105; East, p. 331; Bonham-Carter, pp. 8, 21; P.C.R.O. 22A/2/1/1/5; Y.T.T. Corporation Proceedings 1710–85, f. 54; *Turnpike Minute Book*, p. 177; B.L. Add. MS. 35603, f. 130; East, pp. 317–18; *Poll for Hants., 1734*, p. 134; *Poll, 1779*, p. 94; Sandwich MS. 380; P.C.R.O. 257A/1/9/3.

**36**
**Carter, John***

Born 16 Dec. 1741; d. 18 May 1808. Ad. 27 Oct. 1750. First son of John and Susanna, *née* Pike. Mar. Dorothy, dau. of Geo. Cuthbert, M.D., 9 Aug. 1770. Minor. Mayor of Portsmouth 1769, 1772, 1782, 1786, 1789, 1793, 1796, 1800, 1804; Sheriff of Hampshire 1784. Voted Whig 1779. Presbyterian. Son of Ald. John Carter; bro. of Dan. and Wil. Carter.

Everitt, 'Pedigrees', vol. iv; no. 164; East, p. 383; Bonham-Carter, *passim*; East, pp. 318–19; *Poll, 1779*, p. 88.

**37**
**Carter, William***

Born 22 July 1745; d. 5 Apr. 1798. Ad. 27 Oct. 1750. Second son of John and Susanna, *née* Pike. Mar. Sarah, dau. of Adam Jellicoe. Minor. Mayor of Portsmouth 1773, 1784, 1787, 1790. Voted Whig 1779. Presbyterian. Son of Ald. John Carter; bro. of Dan. and John Carter.

Everitt, 'Pedigrees', vol. iv; no. 164; East, p. 383; Bonham-Carter, p. 17; East, pp. 318–19; *Poll, 1779*, p. 95.

**38**
**Champneys,
Richard**

D. by 18 May 1751. Ad. 27 Oct. 1750. Gentleman; Sheriff of Somerset 1729–30. Father-in-law of Ald. Tho. Missing.

No. 164; East, p. 382; *Cal. T.B. & P. 1729–30*, p. 271; Everitt, 'Pedigrees', ii, pp. 933–4.

**39**
**Chandler, Samuel**

Bur. 21 Dec. 1752. Ad. 10 Apr. 1728; Ald. 13 Sept. 1744. Son of Sam., dissenting minister. Mar. Elizabeth — before 1717. Attorney: acted for the Crown 1731 to death. Free Burgess of Yarmouth, I.W., 1732 (dismissed 1741); Free Burgess of Newport, I.W., 1733; Freeman of Chichester 1739; election agent to Duke of Richmond; Turnpike Commissioner under 1742 Act (resigned 1744.) Voted Whig 1734. Father of Sam. Chandler.

P.C.R.O. 22A/2/1/1/6; East, p. 379; no. 105; East, p. 331; B.L. Add. MS. 40001, f. 137; P.C.R.O. 22A/2/1/1/4; Hants.R.O. C/1/A–8/7; C. & E. 58/143; Y.T.T. Corporation Proceedings 1710–85, ff. 26, 49–51; N.B.A. 45/16b, p. 698; W.Suss.R.O. C.C.A. C.2, f. 9; B.L. Add. MS. 32698, f. 357; *Turnpike Minute Book*, pp. 177, 130, 133; *Poll for Hants., 1734*, p. 135.

**40**
**Chandler, Samuel**

Bapt. 13 Nov. 1725; d. by 16 Sept. 1765. Ad. 29 Sept. 1747. Son of Sam. and Elizabeth. Purser. Turnpike Commissioner 1747; Clerk and Assistant to Turnpike Trust 1748. Son of Ald. Sam. Chandler.

P.C.R.O. 22A/2/1/1/4; P.C.R.O. CE1/14, p. 188; no. 140; East, p. 381; P.C.R.O. S2/26; *Turnpike Minute Book*, pp. 143, 146.

**41**
**Chute, Anthony**

Born 6 Mar. 1691/2; d. 20 May 1754. Ad. 17 Sept. 1733. First son of Edw. and Katharine, *née* Keck. Unmarried. Gentleman. Free Burgess of Yarmouth, I.W., 1733 (dismissed 1741); Free Burgess of Newport, I.W., 1733. M.P. for Yarmouth, I.W., 1737–41, Newport, I.W., 1741–7. Bro. of Fra. Chute.

C. W. Chute, *A history of The Vyne in Hampshire* (1888), p. 83; *Gent. Mag.*, xxiv (1754), p. 244; no. 15; East, p. 380; Chute, op. cit., pp. 82–3; Y.T.T. Corporation Proceedings 1710–85, ff. 26, 49–51; N.B.A. Class 2, Admissions 1717–1833; Sedgwick, i, p. 553.

**42**
**Chute, Francis**

Born c. 1696; d. Apr. 1745. Ad. 5 Oct. 1744. Son of Edw. and Katharine, *née* Keck. Unmarried. Chancery barrister: K.C. 1736. Free Burgess of Newport, I.W., 1734; Recorder of Portsmouth 1743. M.P. for Hedon 1741–2. Bro. of Ant. Chute.

C. W. Chute, *A history of The Vyne in Hampshire* (1888), p. 96; *Lond. Mag.*, xiv (1745), p. 205; no. 110; East, p. 381; Chute, op. cit., p. 89; N.B.A. Class 2, Admissions 1717–1833; Sedgwick, i, pp. 553–4.

**43**
**Clarke, George\***

D. by 19 Sept. 1768. Ad. 27 Oct. 1750; sw. 8 Nov 1750. Merchant; carrier, working for Customs, Portsmouth to London, 1748; innkeeper. Presbyterian: High Street Chapel.

P.C.R.O. CE1/14, p. 206; no. 164; East, p. 382; no. 168; *V.C.H. Hants.*, iii, pp. 70–1; C. & E. 58/1; P.C.R.O. 257A/1/9/3.

**44**
**Clevland, John**

Born 1707(?); d. 19 June 1763. Ad. 4 Aug. 1749; sw. 5 Aug. 1749; hon. First son of Capt. Wil., R.N., and Anne, *née* Davie. Mar. (1) Elizabeth, dau. of Sir Caesar Child, 2nd Bt; (2) Sarah, dau. of Ric. Shuckburgh, 1747. Clerk in Navy Office c. 1723–31; Clerk of Cheque, Plymouth, 1731–43; Commissioner of Navy 1743–6; Joint Secretary of Admiralty 1746–51; Secretary of Admiralty 1751 to death. M.P. for Saltash 1741–3, Sandwich 1747–61, Saltash 1761–3.

Sedgwick, i, p. 559; *Gent. Mag.*, xxxiii (1763), p. 314; no. 150; East, p. 381; no. 151; Murrell & East, p. 351; Sedgwick, i, pp. 559–60.

**45**
**Clinch, Edward**

D. by 15 Sept. 1755. Ad. 27 Nov. 1732. Master boat builder, Portsmouth Dockyard. Voted Whig 1705 (at Alverstoke), 1734. Presbyterian: trustee and subscriber, High Street Chapel, 1735.

P.C.R.O. CE1/14, p. 126; no. 10; East, p. 380; P.C.R.O. S2/25; *Poll, 1705*, p. 7; *Poll for Hants.*, *1734*, p. 131; P.C.R.O. 257A/1/9/3.

**46**
**Cockburne, James**

Ad. 27 Nov. 1732. Secretary to the Envoy-Extraordinary to Savoy-Sardinia 1710–11; secretary to Duke of Argyll 1736(?); agent and (from 1753) paymaster to Royal Regiment of Artillery 1752.

No. 10; East, p. 379 (ad. 6 Nov. 1732); D. B. Horn, *British diplomatic representatives, 1689–1789* (Camden 3rd Ser., vol. xlvi; 1932), p. 121; *Cal. T.B. & P. 1735–8*, p. 191; P.R.O. W.O.46/8, passim.

**47**
**Collins, Joseph\***

D. by 19 Sept. 1763. Ad. 27 Oct. 1750; sw. 8 Nov. 1750. Mar. Euphonia Richards 30 Apr. 1734. Clerk, Portsmouth Dockyard, by 1715(?). Voted Whig 1734.

P.C.R.O. CE1/14, p. 178; no. 164; East, p. 382; no. 168; P.C.R.O. 83A/1/1/2; P.C.R.O. S1/31; *Poll for Hants.*, *1734*, p. 130.

**48**
**Colliss,**
**Cornelius\***

D. Apr. or May 1746. Ad. 27 Dec. 1726; Ald. 22 Mar. 1732/3. Mar. (1) Sarah Jones, widow, 2 Jan. 1689/90(?); (2) Sarah Langrish, widow, 9 Sept. 1734. Joiner. Turnpike Commissioner under 1726 and 1742 Acts. Presbyterian 1716.

P.R.O. Prob.11/746, f. 144; no. 11; East, pp. 378, 330; P.C.R.O. 381A/1/1; P.C.R.O. S1/31; *Turnpike Minute Book*, pp. 173, 177, 143; P.C.R.O. 257A/1/9/1.

**49**
**Compton, John\***

Bur. 13 Mar. 1761. Ad. 27 Oct. 1750. Mar. Elizabeth Chappell, 14 Apr. 1744. Rope maker, tallow-chandler; dismissed as contractor 1749. Possibly Leet juror 1732. Presbyterian: trustee and subscriber, High Street Chapel, 1735(?); Church-warden, St Thomas's, 1742, 1743.

P.C.R.O. 100A/1/1/1/5; nos. 164, 167; East, p. 382; P.C.R.O. 100A/1/1/1/3; no. 161; N.M.M., POR/F/7; P.C.R.O. L1; P.C.R.O. 257A/1/9/3; P.C.R.O. 22A/2/1/12/1.

**50**
**Corbett, Thomas**

Born c. 1687; d. 30 Apr. 1751. Ad. 18 June 1733. First son of Wil. and Eleanor, *née* Jones. Admiral's clerk 1704–5; admiral's secretary 1705–11; Admiralty official: clerk 1715, chief clerk 1723, Deputy Secretary 1728, Joint Secretary 1741, Secretary of Admiralty 1742 to death. M.P. for Saltash 1734 to death.

Sedgwick, i, p. 578; *Gent. Mag.*, xxi (1751), p. 236; no. 12; East, p. 380; *D.N.B.*; *Corrections and additions to the D.N.B.* (Inst. of Historical Research, 1966), pp. 50–1.

**51**
**Davers, Thomas**

D. Dec. 1746. Ad. 28 Dec. 1743; hon. Naval officer: Capt. 1713, Commodore 1739, Rear-Adm. of Red 1743, Vice-Adm. of White 1744.

*Gent. Mag.*, xvi (1746), p. 668; Charnock, iv, pp. 39–40 (d. 16 Sept. 1747); no. 101; East, p. 381; Murrell & East, p. 350; Baugh, p. 133.

**52**
**Deacon, James***

Bur. 20 Jan. 1748/9. Ad. 29 Sept. 1739 (not in Book of Original Entries); Ald. 13 Sept. 1744. Mar. Elizabeth —. Wine merchant. Turnpike Commissioner under 1742 Act; recommended as Justice of the Peace for Hampshire 1749. Father of Wil. Deacon.

P.C.R.O. 22A/2/1/1/6; no. 105; East, pp. 381, 330; P.R.O. Prob.11/767, f. 37; *Turnpike Minute Book*, p. 177; B.L. Add. MS. 35603, f. 130.

**53**
**Deacon, William***

Ad. 27 Oct. 1750. Son of James and Elizabeth. Mar. Elizabeth Judson 25 Mar. 1761. Brewer, supplying beer to Russian men-of-war at Spithead 1775. Voted Whig 1779. Son of Ald. James Deacon.

No. 164; East, p. 383; P.R.O. Prob.11/767, f. 37; P.C.R.O. 22A/2/1/3/1; Sandwich MS. 380; *Poll, 1779*, p. 88.

**54**
**De La Fontaine, Elias Benjamin**

Ad. 27 Oct. 1750. Son of Ben. and Mary, *née* Missing. Minor(?). Stockbroker; Barrack Master of the Savoy 1775(?). Grandson of Tho. Missing (d. 1733); nephew (by marriage) of Ald. Wil. Rickman.

No. 164; East, p. 382; P.R.O. Prob.11/660, f. 204; Sandwich MS. 380.

**55**
**Eddowes, John***

Born 1693 or 1694; d. 3 June 1777. Ad. 29 Sept. 1744. Son of Rob. Ordnance official (?). Son of Rob. Eddowes.

Everitt, 'Misc. collns', i, p. 113; *Gent. Mag.*, xlvii (1777), p. 295; no. 109; P.R.O. W.O.55/1996; P.R.O. W.O.46/8, p. 2.

**56**
**Eddowes, Robert***

D. 7 Oct. 1765(?). Ad. 27 Nov. 1732; Duke of Argyll wished him to be made Ald. 1733. Storekeeper to Ordnance Board, Portsmouth. Turnpike Commissioner under 1742 Act. Father of John Eddowes.

*Gent. Mag.*, xxxv (1765), p. 491; P.C.R.O. CE1/14, p. 192; no. 10; East, p. 379 (ad. 6 Nov. 1732); B.L. Add. MS. 19030, ff. 170–1; P.C.R.O. S2/24; *Turnpike Minute Book*, p. 177.

**57**
**Eyer, Thomas***

Bur. 7 Oct. 1772. Ad. 27 Oct. 1750. Mar. Elizabeth Bartlett 20 Aug. 1746. House-carpenter; timber merchant by 1731. Sidesman, St Thomas's, 1741.

P.C.R.O. 100A/1/1/1/7; nos 164, 167; East, p. 382; no. 173; P.C.R.O. CD10/43/9; N.M.M. POR/F/5; P.C.R.O. 22A/2/1/12/1.

**58**
**Finch, Daniel, 8th Earl of Winchilsea and 2nd Earl of Nottingham**

Born 24 May 1689; d. 2 Aug. 1769. Ad. 11 Sept. 1744; hon. First son of Dan., 7th Earl of Winchilsea and 1st Earl of Nottingham, and Anne, dau. of Chr. Hatton, 1st Viscount Hatton. Mar. (1) Frances, dau. of Basil Feilding, 4th Earl of Denbigh, 28 Dec. 1729; (2) Mary, dau. of Sir Tho. Palmer, 4th Bt, 18 Jan. 1737/8. Gentleman of Bedchamber to Prince of Wales 1714–16; Lord of Treasury 1715–16; Controller of Royal Household 1725–30; First Lord of Admiralty 1741–4, Apr.–June 1757; Lord President of Council 1765–6. M.P. for Rutland 1710–11, 1730.

Sedgwick, ii, pp. 30–2; no. 102; East, p. 381; Murrell & East, p. 350; G.E.C. xii, pt ii, pp. 786–7.

**59**
**Fitzgerald, James, 20th Earl of Kildare**

Born 29 May 1722; d. 19 Nov. 1773. Ad. 14 May 1747; hon. Second son of Rob., 19th Earl of Kildare, and Mary, dau. of Wil. O'Brien, 3rd Earl of Inchiquin. Mar. Emilia, 2nd dau. of Cha. Lennox, 2nd Duke of Richmond, 7 Feb. 1746/7. Army officer: Master General of Ordnance in Ireland 1758–66, Col. of Royal Irish Regiment 1760, Maj.-Gen. 1761, Lieut.-Gen. 1770; Irish Privy Councillor 1746; Lord Deputy of Ireland 1756. Freeman of Chichester 1747. M.P. (Irish Parliament) for Athy 1741–4. Son-in-law of Duke of Richmond.

*D.N.B.*; no. 136; East, p. 381; Murrell & East, p. 350; G.E.C., vii, pp. 573–5; W.Suss.R.O. C.C.A. C.2, f. 36.

**60**
**Franckland,**
**Sir Thomas, 3rd Bt**

Born c. 1683; d. 17 Apr. 1747. Ad. 18 June 1733. First son of Sir Tho. Franckland, 2nd Bt. Mar. (1) Diana, dau. of Fra. Topham, 5 June 1715; (2) Sarah Moseley, 9 July 1741. Clerk of Deliveries in Tower 1714–15; secretary to Master General of Ordnance and Clerk of Deliveries in Ordnance 1715–22; Commissioner of Revenue 1724–8; Commissioner of Trade and Plantations 1728–30; Lord of Admiralty 1730–42. M.P. for Harwich 1705–13, Thirsk 1713–47.

Sedgwick, ii, pp. 50–1; no. 12; East, p. 380; *Gent. Mag.*, xvii (1747), p. 200.

**61**
**Francklin, Michael**

D. by 18 Sept. 1752. Ad. 27 Oct. 1750. Merchant. Mayor of Poole, Dors., 1736, 1737, 1738.

P.C.R.O. CE1/14, p. 105; no. 164; East, p. 382; C. & E. 58/143, p. 198; J. Sydenham, *The history of the town and county of Poole* (1839), p. 23.

**62**
**Frederick Louis,**
**Prince of Wales**

Born 6 Jan. 1706/7; d. 20 Mar. 1750/1. Ad. 6 Aug. 1742; hon. First son of Geo. II and Caroline of Ansbach. Mar. Princess Augusta of Saxe-Gotha, 26 Apr. 1736. Free Burgess of Newport, I.W., 1750; Free Burgess of Lymington, Hants., 1750. Bro. of Wil. Augustus, Duke of Cumberland.

*D.N.B.*; no. 92; East, p. 381 (ad. 6 Apr. 1742); N.B.A. 45/16b, p. 857; E. King, *Old times re-visited in the Borough and parish of Lymington, Hants.* (2nd edn, 1900), p. 194.

**63**
**Friend, Henry***

Bur. 22 Dec. 1761. Ad. 27 Oct. 1750. Son of Henry (rope maker) and Mary. Vinegar merchant, general dealer. Voted Whig 1734. Feoffee for St George's, Portsea, 1751. Nephew (by marriage) of John Vining.

P.C.R.O. 100A/1/1/1/5; nos 164, 167; East, p. 382; Hants.R.O. A Wills 1736; *Cal. T. B. & P. 1742–5*, p. 109; P.R.O. W.O.55/1996; N.M.M. POR/F/7; *Poll for Hants., 1734*, p. 134; no. 171.

**64**
**Gardner, Joseph***

Bur. 10 Sept. 1736. Ad. 27 Nov. 1732. Mar. Margaret —. Postmaster, distiller. Voted Whig 1734. Presbyterian: trustee and subscriber, High Street Chapel, 1735.

P.C.R.O. 22A/2/1/1/5; Hants.R.O. A Wills 1738; no. 10; East, p. 380; P.C.R.O. S2/23; P.C.R.O. CD8/29/15; *Poll for Hants., 1734*, p. 130; P.C.R.O. 257A/1/9/3.

**65**
**Gashry, Francis**

Born 14 Nov. 1702; d. 19 May 1762. Ad. 5 Aug. 1740. Son of Fra. and Susanna Gascherie, both of La Rochelle, France. Mar. Martha Goldsworthy before 1747. Secretary to Sir Cha. Wager 1732–42; Commissioner of Sick and Hurt Seamen 1737; Assistant Secretary to Admiralty 1738; Commissioner of Navy 1741–7; Controller of Victualling Accounts 1744–7; Treasurer and Paymaster of Ordnance. M.P. for Aldeburgh 30 Mar.–27 Apr. 1741, East Looe 1741–62. Nephew (by marriage) of Sir Cha. Wager; bro.-in-law of Burrington Goldsworthy.

Sedgwick, ii, p. 60; *Gent. Mag.*, xxxii (1762), p. 242; no. 74; East, p. 381; Namier & Brooke, ii, p. 492.

**66**
**Gawler, John**

D. 1777. Ad. 29 Sept. 1749. Son of John and Rebecca, *née* Franklin(?). Attorney. Presbyterian: trustee and subscriber, High Street Chapel, 1735.

W. Musgrave, *Obituary prior to 1800*, ed. G. J. Armytage (Harleian Soc., vols xliv–xlix; 1899–1901), iii, p. 18; no. 154; East, p. 381; *Hants. Allegns*, i, p. 296; Sandwich MS. 380; P.C.R.O. 257A/1/9/3.

**67**
**Godwin, Robert***

Bapt. 11 Nov. 1698; d. by 17 Sept. 1764. Ad. 27 Nov. 1732. Mar. Susan Brasted. Son of Rob. and Sarah. Merchant. Leet juror 1736; Turnpike Commissioner 1743. Voted Whig 1734. Churchwarden, St Mary's, Portsea, 1718–19, 1732–3.

P.C.R.O. 210A/1/1/1/1; P.C.R.O. CE1/14, p. 182; no. 10; East, p. 380; Everitt, 'Pedigrees', ii, p. 784; C. & E. 58/151, pp. 11–12; P.C.R.O. L1; *Turnpike Minute Book*, p. 125; *Poll for Hants., 1734*, p. 140; P.C.R.O. 100A/1/1/7/1.

**68**
**Goldsworthy,**
**Burrington**

D. by 19 Sept. 1774. Ad. 27 Nov. 1732. Mar. Philippia, dau. of Capt. Phil. Vanbrugh, R.N. Commissioner of Stamps before 1736; Receiver-General of Revenues arising by Rights and Perquisites of the Admiralty 1733; victualling correspondent and agent for prizes at Leghorn and then Cadiz. Nephew of Sir Cha. Wager; bro.-in-law of Fra. Gashry.

P.C.R.O. CE1/14, p. 255; no. 10; East, p. 379 (ad. 6 Nov. 1732); Namier & Brooke, ii, p. 509; *Cal. T.B. & P. 1735–8*, p. 285; *Cal. T.B. & P. 1731–4*, p. 521; Baugh, p. 397; C.U.L. C(H) Correspondence 1881.

F*

**69**
**Gore, Thomas**

Born 1694(?); d. 17 Mar. 1777. Ad. 28 Feb. 1745/6; hon. Third son of Sir Wil. Mar. Mary, dau. of Sir Wil. Humphreys, 1st Bt, 15 Sept. 1748. Commissary General of Musters 1746 to death. M.P. for Cricklade 1722–7, Amersham 1735–46, Portsmouth 1746–7, Bedford 1747–54, Cricklade 1754–68.

Namier & Brooke, ii, pp. 520–1; *Gent. Mag.*, xlvii (1777), p. 148; no. 121; East, p. 381; Murrell & East. p. 350; Sedgwick, ii, p. 71.

**70**
**Green, William***

Bur. 11 Feb. 1763. Ad. 27 Oct. 1750; sw. 8 Nov. 1750. Mar. Elizabeth Hughes 6 Mar. 1760. Tanner(?). Voted Tory 1734. Baptist: trustee, Orange Street Chapel, 1750.

P.C.R.O. 100A/1/1/1/5; nos 164, 168; East, p. 382; N.M.M. POR/F/5; *Poll for Hants.*, *1734*, p.140; P.C.R.O. 3A/3/1.

**71**
**Haddock, Nicholas**

Born 1686; d. 26 Sept. 1746. Ad. 12 Sept. 1734; sw. 30 Sept.; hon. Third son of Sir Ric. and Elizabeth, *née* Hurleston. Mar. Frances — before 1717. Naval officer: entered Navy 1699, Midshipman 1702, Lieut. 1704, Capt. 1707, C.-in-C. the Nore 1732, Rear-Adm. 1734, C.-in-C. Mediterranean 1738, Vice-Adm. 1741, Adm. 1744. M.P. for Rochester 1734–46. Bro. of Ric. Haddock.

*D.N.B.*; *Gent. Mag.*, xvi (1746), p. 497; no. 25; East, p. 380 (ad. 16 Sept. 1734); no. 25; Murrell & East, p. 349; Sedgwick, ii, pp. 93–4.

**72**
**Haddock, Richard**

D. 11 Apr. 1751. Ad. 28 May 1735; hon. First son of Sir Ric. and Elizabeth, *née* Hurleston. Naval officer: Lieut. 1692, Capt. 1695; Controller of Navy 1734–49. Bro. of Nic. Haddock.

*Lond. Mag.*, xx (1751), p. 189; no. 30; East, p. 380; Murrell & East, p. 349; Charnock, iii, pp. 103–5.

**73**
**Hardy, Sir Charles**

Born c. 1680; d. 27 Nov. 1744. Ad. 18 Dec. 1742; hon. Son of Phil. and Mary (*née* Filleul) le Hardy. Mar. Elizabeth, dau. of Josiah Burchett. Naval officer: entered Navy 1695, Lieut. 1701, Capt. 1709, Rear-Adm. 1742, Vice-Adm. 1743; Lord of Admiralty 1743–4. M.P. for Portsmouth 1743–4.

Sedgwick, ii, p. 109; *Gent. Mag.*, xiv (1744), p. 619; no. 96; East, p. 381; Murrell & East, p. 350; *D.N.B.*

**74**
**Hawke, Chaloner**

Born 1750; d. 17 Sept. 1777. Ad. 27 Oct. 1750. Third son of Sir Edw. and Catherine, *née* Brooke. Minor. Son of Ald. Sir Edw. Hawke; bro. of Edw., Mar. Bladen and Wil. Hawke.

Mackay, pp. 108, 343; no. 164; East, p. 383.

**75**
**Hawke, Sir Edward***

Born 21 Feb. 1710; d. 17 Oct. 1781. Ad. 21 Dec. 1747; sw. 28 Dec. 1747; Ald. 27 Sept. 1749; sw. 13 Oct. 1749. Son of Edw. and Elizabeth, *née* Bladen. Mar. Catherine, dau. of Walt. Brooke, 1737. Naval officer: entered Navy 1720, Capt. 1734, Rear-Adm. 1747, Vice-Adm. 1748, Adm. 1757, Rear-Adm. of Great Britain 1762–5, Vice-Adm. of Great Britain 1765 to death, Adm. of Fleet 1768 to death; First Lord of Admiralty 1766–71. M.P. for Portsmouth 1747–76. Nephew of Mar. Bladen; father of Chaloner, Edw., Mar. Bladen and Wil. Hawke.

Mackay, passim; *Gent. Mag.*, li (1781), p. 492; no. 142; East, p. 381; no. 143; no. 153; East, p. 331; no. 155; Namier & Brooke, ii, pp. 596–8; G.E.C., vi, p. 414.

**76**
**Hawke, Edward**

Born 1746; d. 2 Oct. 1773. Ad. 27 Oct. 1750. Second son of Sir Edw. and Catherine, *née* Brooke. Minor; Army officer: Lieut.-Col. by 1773. Son of Ald. Sir Edw. Hawke; bro. of Chaloner, Mar. Bladen and Wil. Hawke.

Mackay, pp. 108, 334; no. 164; East, p. 383; *D.N.B.*, under Hawke, Edw., Lord Hawke.

**77**
**Hawke, Martin Bladen**

Born 20 Apr. 1744; d. 27 Mar. 1805. Ad. 27 Oct. 1750. First son of Sir Edw. and Catherine, *née* Brooke. Mar. Cassandra, dau. of Sir Edw. Turner, 2nd Bt, 6 Feb. 1777. Minor. M.P. for Saltash 1768–74. Son of Ald. Sir Edw. Hawke; bro. of Chaloner, Edw. and Wil. Hawke.

Mackay, p. 108; no. 164; East, p. 383; Namier & Brooke, ii, p. 598; G.E.C., vi, p. 414.

**78**
**Hawke, William**

D. by 1753. Ad. 27 Oct. 1750. Fourth son of Sir Edw. and Catherine, *née* Brooke. Minor. Son of Ald. Sir Edw. Hawke; bro. of Chaloner, Edw. and Mar. Bladen Hawke.

No. 164; East, p. 383.

**79**
**Heron, Benjamin**

Born 21 Dec. 1722; d. 18 June 1770. Ad. 29 Sept. 1739; sw. 15 Sept. 1746. Fifth son of Capt. Pat. and Anne, *née* Vining. Mar. (1) Mary How; (2) Alice Mardon. Army(?) officer: Lieut. by 1739. Grandson of Ald. John Vining; bro. of John Vining Heron.

Everitt, 'Pedigrees', i, p. 78; ibid., iii, p. 1165; no. 69; East, p. 381; no. 131; P.C.R.O. CE1/13, p. 271.

**80**
**Heron, John**

Bapt. 23 June 1744; d. 1805. Ad. 27 Oct. 1750. Second son of John Vining Heron and Frances, *née* Leeke. Mar. Anne Douglas. Minor. Grandson of Ald. John Leeke; son of John Vining Heron.

P.C.R.O. 100A/1/1/1/3; Everitt, 'Pedigrees', i, p. 78; ibid., iii, p. 1163; no. 164; East, p. 383; Sandwich MS. 380.

**81**
**Heron,**
**John Vining***

Born 1713; d. 4 Nov. 1772. Ad. 27 Oct. 1750. First son of Capt. Pat. and Anne, *née* Vining. Mar. Frances, dau. of John Leeke, 27 Nov. 1738. Mercer. Grandson of Ald. John Vining; bro. of Ben. Heron; son-in-law of Ald. John Leeke; father of John Heron.

Everitt, 'Pedigrees', i, pp. 78–9; ibid., iii, p. 1163; nos 164, 167; East, p. 382.

**82**
**Hervey, William**

Born 25 Dec. 1699; d. Jan. 1776. Ad. 25 Dec 1746 (not in Book of Original Entries). Fourth son of John, 1st Earl of Bristol, and Elizabeth, dau. of Sir Tho. Felton, Bt. Mar. Elizabeth, dau. of Geo. Ridge of Kilmeston, Hants., 27 Nov. 1729. Naval officer: Capt. 1727, court-martialled and cashiered for excessive cruelty 1742, 'and was declared incapable of holding any subsequent command in the navy'.

*Burke's Peerage*, p. 355; East, p. 381; Charnock, iv, pp. 180–1; Everitt, 'Pedigrees', iii, pp. 1109–10.

**83**
**Hewett, John**

Bapt. 3 June 1719. Ad. 27 Oct. 1750; sw. 8 Nov. 1750. Son of Tho. Yeoman; possibly same man described as a Titchfield, Hants., farmer and 'rich' in 1775. Related to White family.

P.C.R.O. 100A/1/1/1/3; no. 164; East, p. 382; no. 168; P.C.R.O. 16A/1/2; Sandwich MS. 380.

**84**
**Hoadly, Benjamin,**
**Bishop of**
**Winchester**

Born 14 Nov. 1676; d. 17 Apr. 1761. Ad. 14 Sept. 1737; hon. Second son of Rev. Sam. and Martha, *née* Pickering. Mar. (1) Sarah Curtis; (2) Mary, dau. of John Newey, D.D., 1745. Cleric: lecturer, St Mildred's Poultry, London, 1701–11; rector, St Peter Le Poor, Broad Street, London, 1704; rector of Streatham 1710; chaplain to Duke of Bedford 1710; royal chaplain 1715; Bishop of Bangor 1715, Hereford 1721, Salisbury 1733, Winchester 1734.

*D.N.B.*; *Gent. Mag.*, xxxi (1761), p. 189; no. 48; East, p. 380; Murrell & East, p. 350.

**85**
**Honywood,**
**Philip**

D. June 1752. Ad. 22 Oct. 1740; hon. Second son of Cha. Ludovic and Mary, *née* Clements. Army officer: Capt. 1696, Col. 1709, Brig.-Gen. 1710, Maj.-Gen. 1727, Gen. 1743; Governor of Portsmouth 1741–52.

*Salis. Journ.*, 29 June 1752; no. 79; East, p. 381; Murrell & East, p. 350; Sedgwick, ii, p. 147; *English army lists and commission registers 1661–1714*, ed. C. Dalton (5v., 1892–6), v, p. 30n; Sheffield Central Library, Wentworth Woodhouse Muniments, M. 25.

**86**
**Hood, Samuel**

D. by May 1751. Ad. 27 Oct. 1750. Son of Sam. and Susanna, *née* Linzee. Minor. Grandson of Ald. Edw. Linzee.

No. 164; East, p. 382.

**87**
**Hooke, Edmund**

D. by 16 Sept. 1745. Ad. 13 Dec. 1731. Naval officer: Capt. 1712.

P.C.R.O. CE1/14, p. 43; Charnock, iv, p. 136; no. 4; East, p. 379.

**88**
**Huish, Henry**

Born 13 Apr. 1713; d. by 19 Sept. 1763. Ad. 27 Nov. 1732; sw. 16 Aug. 1737. Son of Geo. and Barbara. Naval officer: 2nd Lieut. 1715, Commander 1746, Commander and Purser 1748. Voted Whig 1734. Son of Geo. Huish (d. 1747); bro. of Geo. Huish (d. 1788).

P.C.R.O. 22A/2/1/1/4; P.C.R.O. CE1/14, p. 177; nos 10, 47; East, p. 380; P.R.O. Prob.11/752, f. 11; P.C.R.O. S2/16, 25; P.R.O. Adm.110/15; *Poll for Hants.*, *1734*, p. 116.

**89**
**Hunt, John***

Bur. 15 May 1752. Ad. 27 Nov. 1732. Mar. Mary —. Goldsmith: fined for selling sub-standard gold and silver wares 1718. Turnpike Commissioner under 1726 and 1742 Acts. Voted Whig 1734. Churchwarden, St Thomas's, 1725.

P.C.R.O. 22A/2/1/1/6; no. 10; East, p. 380; P.C.R.O. 22A/2/1/1/4; P.C.R.O. 11A/1/110; Goldsmiths' Company, London, Court Books, xi, p. 448; *Turnpike Minute Book*, pp. 173, 177; *Poll for Hants.*, *1734*, p. 128; B.L. Add. MS. 8153, f. 119.

**90**
**Jones, Richard**

Bapt. 26 Aug. 1742. Ad. 27 Oct. 1750. Second son of Rev. Nic. and Sarah, *née* Mounsher. Mar. Sarah Hewett 22 Apr. 1764. Minor. Grandson of Ald. John Mounsher; bro. of Tho. Jones.

P.C.R.O. 22A/2/1/1/5; no. 164; East, p. 382; P.C.R.O. 210A/1/1/3.

**91**
**Jones, Thomas**

Bapt. 1 Apr. 1738. Ad. 27 Oct. 1750. First son of Rev. Nic. and Sarah, *née* Mounsher. Mar. Jane Street 16 Mar. 1760. Minor. Free Burgess of Yarmouth, I.W., 1766 (resigned 1771). Grandson of Ald. John Mounsher; bro. of Ric. Jones.

P.C.R.O. 22A/2/1/1/5; no. 164; East, p. 382; Sandwich MS. 380; P.C.R.O. 22A/2/1/3/1; Y.T.T. Corporation Proceedings 1710–85, ff. 108, 134.

**92**
**Kirkpatrick, James**

D. 1770(?). Ad. 27 Oct. 1750. Mar. Ann —. Mercer; described as among 'three of the principal inhabitants' of Newport, I.W., 1756. Voted Whig 1734.

*Lond. Mag.*, xxxix (1770), p. 110; no. 164; East, p. 382; P.C.R.O. 22A/2/1/1/5; I.W.R.O. NPT/12/9; N.B.A. 45/16b, p. 927; *Poll for Hants.*, *1734*, p. 156.

**93**
**Laugharne, Richard***

D. by 20 Sept. 1762. Ad. 27 Oct. 1750. Mar. Mary Postlethwaite 23 Mar. 1730/1. Attorney by 1725. Clerk and Assistant to Turnpike Trust 1732–48; Turnpike Commissioner 1743. Voted Whig 1734 (at Merston, Suss.). Had business dealings with Dan. Smith's widow 1737.

P.C.R.O. CE1/14, p. 171; nos. 164, 167; East, p. 382 ('Langharne'); P.C.R.O. 100A/1/1/1/3; B.L. Add. MS. 40001, f. 239; *Turnpike Minute Book*, pp. 86, 88, 146, 124; *Poll for Suss.*, *1734*, p. 57; I.W.R.O. SW/276, 935.

**94**
**Leeke, John***

Born 1676 or 1677; bapt. 27 Mar. 1681; d. 20 Apr. 1765. Ad. 23 June 1713; Ald. 27 Sept. 1749. Son of John and Elizabeth. Mar. Mary — of Alverstoke 28 Mar. 1711. Goldsmith: fined for selling sub-standard gold and silver wares 1718; citizen and Freeman of London. Turnpike Commissioner under 1742 Act. Voted Tory 1734. Churchwarden, St. Thomas's, 1717–21. Father of Sam. Leeke; father-in-law of John Vining Heron.

Hants.R.O. C/10/A/456; Everitt, 'Pedigrees', ii, pp. 785–6; no. 153; East, pp. 376, 331; Goldsmiths' Company, London, Court Books, xi, p. 448; P.R.O. Prob.11/909, f. 225; *Turnpike Minute Book*, p. 177; *Poll for Hants.*, *1734*, p. 133; B.L. Add. MS. 8153, f. 119.

**95**
**Leeke, Samuel***

Born 4 Oct. 1713; d. 20 Mar. 1775. Ad. 27 Oct. 1750. Son of John and Mary. Mar. Mary, dau. of Rev. Ric. Bingham of Havant. Merchant; agent for various French prizes, Portsmouth, 1748. Son of Ald. John Leeke.

P.C.R.O. 22A/2/1/1/4; Everitt, 'Pedigrees', ii, pp. 785–6, 1187; C. & E. 58/149; nos 164, 167; East, p. 382.

**96**
**Legge, Edward**

Born c. 1710; d. 19 Sept. 1747. Ad. 13 Nov. 1747. Fifth son of Wil., 1st Earl of Dartmouth, and Anne, dau. of Heneage Finch, 1st Earl of Aylesford. Unmarried. Naval officer: entered Navy 1726, Lieut. 1734, Capt. 1738, Commodore 1747, C.-in-C. Leeward Is 1747. Elected M.P. for Portsmouth, before his death known, Dec. 1747.

Sedgwick, ii, p. 206; *Gent. Mag.*, xvii (1747), p. 592; no. 141; East, p. 381; *D.N.B.*

**97**
**Lennox, Charles, 3rd Duke of Richmond**

Born 22 Feb. 1734/5; d. 29 Dec. 1806. Ad. 27 Oct. 1750; hon. Third son of Cha., 2nd Duke of Richmond, and Sarah, dau. of Wil. Cadogan, 1st Earl Cadogan. Mar. Mary, dau. of Cha. Bruce, 3rd Earl of Aylesbury. Minor; Army officer: Ensign, 2nd Foot Guards, 1751, Capt. 1753, Lieut.-Col. 1756, Col. 1758, Maj.-Gen. 1761, Lieut.-Gen. 1770, Gen. 1782, Field-Marshal 1792; Lord of Bedchamber 1760; Lord Lieutenant of Sussex 1763 to death; Ambassador to France 1765–6; Secretary of State, Southern Dept, 23 May–21 Aug. 1766; Master General of Ordnance 1782–95. Bro. of Lord Geo. Henry Lennox.

G.E.C., x, pp. 840–2; *D.N.B.*; East, p. 382; Murrell & East, p. 351.

**98**
**Lennox, Lord George Henry**

Born 29 Nov. 1737; d. 22 Mar. 1805. Ad. 27 Oct. 1750; hon. Son of Cha., 2nd Duke of Richmond, and Sarah, dau. of Wil. Cadogan, 1st Earl Cadogan. Mar. Louisa, dau. of Wil. Henry Kerr, 4th Marquis of Lothian, 1758. Minor; Army officer: Ensign, 2nd Foot Guards, 1754, Aide-de-camp to Duke of Cumberland c. 1757, Lieut.-Col. 1758, Col. 1762, Brig. 1763, Maj.-Gen. 1772, Gen. 1793; Chargé d'affaires and Minister-Plenipotentiary to France July–Oct. 1766; Constable of Tower of London 1783; Governor of Plymouth 1784 to death. M.P. for Chichester 1761–7, Sussex 1767–90. Bro. of Cha. Lennox, 3rd Duke of Richmond.

*D.N.B.*; *Gent. Mag.*, lxxv (1805), pp. 294, 580; no. 164; East, p. 382; Murrell & East, p. 351; Namier & Brooke, iii, pp. 35–6.

**99**
**Lestock, Richard**

Born 22 Feb. 1679(?); d. 13 Dec. 1746. Ad. 3 Dec. 1741. Second son of Capt. Ric., R.N. Mar. Sarah ——. Naval officer: Lieut. 1701, Vice-Adm. 1743, Adm. 1746. Turnpike Commissioner under 1742 Act (replaced 1744). Father-in-law of James Peers.

*D.N.B.*; *Gent. Mag.*, xvi (1746), p. 668; no. 86; East, p. 381; *Turnpike Minute Book*, pp. 177, 133.

**100**
**Linzee, Edward***

Bapt. 3 June 1700; d. 14 or 15 May 1782. Ad. 10 Apr. 1728; Ald. 13 Sept. 1744. Son of Tho. and Mary, *née* Albeck. Mar. Anne Newnham of Portsmouth. Apothecary; desired to be excused knighthood 9 May 1778. Turnpike Commissioner under 1742 Act; Mayor of Portsmouth 1753, 1758, 1761, 1766, 1771, 1777, 1779, 1780. Voted Whig 1734. Presbyterian; subscribed to repair gates of meeting-house 1732 (? as Linsley). Son-in-law of Rob. Newnham; father of Rob. and Edw. Linzee; father-in-law of John Amherst and Ald. Tho. Monday.

P.C.R.O. 100A/1/1/1/2; P.C.R.O. 22A/2/1/1/7; Linzee, ii, p. 467; *Gent. Mag.*, lii (1782), p. 163; no. 105; East, pp. 379, 331; *Turnpike Minute Book*, p. 177; East, pp. 318–19; *Poll for Hants., 1734*, p. 133; P.C.R.O. 257A/1/9/3; P.R.O. Prob.11/1092, f. 299.

**101**
**Linzee, Edward***

Bapt. 8 Aug. 1738; d. Apr. 1796. Ad. 27 Oct. 1750. First son of Edw. and Anne, *née* Newnham. Minor; surgeon, apothecary. Voted Whig 1779. Grandson of Rob. Newnham; son of Ald. Edw. Linzee; bro. of Rob. Linzee.

Linzee, ii, p. 483; no. 164; East, p. 382; Sandwich MS. 380; *Poll, 1779*, p. 86; Everitt, 'Pedigrees', i, pp. 231–2.

**102**
**Linzee, Robert**

Bapt. 13 Feb. 1740/1; d. 4 Oct. 1804. Ad. 27 Oct. 1750. Second son of Edw. and Anne, *née* Newnham. Mar. (1) Ann, dau. of Tho. and Penelope Redsten, 9 Oct. 1771; (2) Mary Grant 2 Feb. 1792. Minor; naval officer: Lieut. 1761, Commander 1768, Capt. 1770, Col. of Marines 1793, Rear-Adm. 1794, Vice-Adm. 1795, Adm. 1801. Grandson of Rob. Newnham; son of Ald. Edw. Linzee; bro. of Edw. Linzee.

P.C.R.O. 22A/2/1/1/5; Linzee, ii, pp. 490–2; no. 164; East, p. 382; Sandwich MS. 380; Everitt, 'Pedigrees', i, pp. 231–2.

**103**
**Lock, Peirson***

D. by 20 Sept. 1756. Ad. 28 Sept. 1742. Shipwright: second assistant 1718, first assistant 1722, master by 1742. Presbyterian.

P.C.R.O. CE1/14, p. 131; no. 94; East. p. 381; P.C.R.O. S2/21; Baugh, p. 296; P.C.R.O. 257A/1/9/3.

**104**
**Lowe, John***

Bur. 24 Oct. 1774. Ad. 27 Oct. 1750. Mar. Mary Young 13 May 1719. Schoolmaster. Presbyterian: trustee and subscriber, High Street Chapel, 1735.

P.C.R.O. 22A/2/1/1/7; nos 164, 167; East, p. 382; P.C.R.O. 22A/2/1/1/4; P.C.R.O. 81A/3/20/21, no. 1; A. J. Willis, *Laymen's licences in the diocese of Winchester 1675–1834* (*A Hampshire Miscellany*, pt 2; 1964), p. 89; P.C.R.O. 257A/1/9/3.

**105**
**Lys, Henry***

D. 1791(?). Ad. 27 Oct. 1750. Son of Henry. Mar. Sarah Poulglass of Ryde, I.W., 10 Apr. 1751. Distiller. Turnpike Commissioner 1747; Gosport Paving Commissioner under 1763 Act. Voted Tory 1779.

*Gent. Mag.*, lxi (1791), p. 588; nos 164, 167; P.C.R.O. 81A/3/21/1; *Hants. Allegns*, i, p. 498; *Turnpike Minute Book*, p. 143; White, p. 78; *Poll, 1779*, p. 68.

**106**
**Martin, William**

Born 1696(?); d. 17 or 21 Sept. 1756. Ad. 7 Feb. 1743/4; hon. Son of Commodore Geo. Unmarried. Naval officer: entered Navy 1708, 2nd Lieut. 1710, Capt. 1718, Rear-Adm. 1743, Vice-Adm. 1744, Adm. 1747.

*D.N.B.*; *Gent. Mag.*, xxvi (1756), p. 451; Baugh, p. 133; no. 102; East, p. 381; Murrell & East, p. 350.

**107**
**Mathews, Thomas**

Born Oct. 1676; d. 2 Oct. 1751. Ad. 10 Apr. 1742; hon. First son of Brig.-Gen. Edw. and Jane, *née* Armstrong. Mar. (1) Henrietta Burgeois or Burges; (2) Millicent, dau. of John Fuller, Sheriff of London. Naval officer: entered Navy 1690, Lieut. 1699, Capt. 1703, Commissioner at Chatham 1736–42, Vice-Adm. 1742, C.-in-C. Mediterranean 1742–4, Adm. 1743, Rear-Adm. of Great Britain 1744–7, dismissed the service 1747; minister to Sardinia and Italian States 1742–4. M.P. for Glamorgan 1745–7, Carmarthen 1747 to death.

*D.N.B.*; *Gent. Mag.*, xxi (1751), p. 477; no. 90; East, p. 381 (ad. 6 Apr. 1742); Sedgwick, ii, pp. 246–7; Murrell & East, p. 350.

**108**
**Mathis, William**

D. by 19 Sept. 1763. Ad. 27 Nov. 1732. Mar. (1) Hannah Brice of Andover, Hants., 2 Feb. 1730/1; (2) Elizabeth — (d. 20 May 1766). Clerk of Survey, Portsmouth Dockyard, 1755. Voted Whig 1734 (at Alverstoke).

P.C.R.O. CE1/14, p. 177; no. 10; East, p. 379; *Hants. Allegns*, ii, p. 22; Everitt, 'Misc. collns', ii, p. 319; P.C.R.O. S2/26; *Poll for Hants.*, *1734*, p. 115.

**109**
**Medley, Henry**

D. 5 Aug. 1747. Ad. 13 Sept. 1744; sw. 17 Sept. 1744; hon. Naval officer: entered Navy 1703, Midshipman by 1706, Lieut. 1710, Commander c. 1720, Capt. of Channel Fleet 1742–4, Rear-Adm. of White 1744, Vice-Adm. 1745, C.-in-C. Mediterranean 1745.

*Gent. Mag.*, xvii (1747), p. 399; nos 106, 108; East, p. 381; Murrell & East, p. 350; *D.N.B.*

**110**
**Merac, John***

Bur. 22 Dec. 1783. Ad. 27 Oct. 1750. Mar. Alice Dowell 22 Dec. 1734. Rope maker. Leet juror 1749. Voted Tory 1779. Churchwarden, St Thomas's, 1742, 1743.

P.C.R.O. 100A/1/1/1/8; nos 164, 167; East, p. 382; P.C.R.O. 210A/1/1/1/2; no. 161; P.C.R.O. L.1; *Poll*, *1779*, p. 94; P.C.R.O. 22A/2/1/12/1.

**111**
**Metcalfe, Mathew***

Bur. 11 Mar. 1756. Ad. 27 Oct. 1750.

P.C.R.O. 22A/2/1/1/6; nos 164, 167; East, p. 382.

**112**
**Miller, Sir John, 4th Bt**

D. 19 Apr. 1772. Ad. 29 Sept. 1745; sw. 17 Oct. 1745. Son of Sir Tho., 3rd Bt, and Jane, *née* Gother. Mar. Susan, dau. of Mat. Combe, M.D., of Winchester, 1735. Politician, contractor. Member of Common Council of Chichester 1738; Free Burgess of Yarmouth, I.W., 1744; Steward of Chichester 1745; Mayor of Chichester 1748. Voted Whig 1734 (at East Lavant, Suss.).

G. E. Cockayne, *Complete baronetage* (5v. and index, 1900–9), iv, p. 194; *Burke's Peerage*, p. 1823; Sedgwick ii, pp. 258–9; no. 115; East, p. 381; no. 117; B.L. Add. MS. 32712, f. 63; W.Suss.R.O. C.C.A. C.2, f. 3; Y.T.T. Corporation Proceedings 1710–85, ff. 61–2; W.Suss.R.O. C.C.A. C.2, ff. 29, 41; *Poll for Suss.*, *1734*, p. 16.

**113**
**Missing, John**

Bapt. 26 Dec. 1734; d. July or Aug. 1793. Ad. 27 Oct. 1750. Son of John and Frances, *née* Higgins. Mar. Jane — (d. 1778). Barrister; Judge of Consistory Court, Winchester. Gosport Paving Commissioner under 1763 Act; Recorder of Portsmouth 1773–5, described in 1775 as 'very violent in patriotism'; Recorder of Romsey, Hants., 1780–93. Voted Whig 1779. Feoffee for St George's, Portsea, 1751. Great-nephew of Tho. Missing (d. 1733); cousin of Ald. Tho. Missing (d. 1772); uncle of Ric. Roy, jun., of Titchfield, Hants.

P.C.R.O. 22A/2/1/1/5; *Gent. Mag.*, lxiii (1793), p. 771; Everitt, 'Pedigrees', ii, pp. 933–4; nos 164, 167; East, pp. 382, 421; Sandwich MS. 380; Mrs Suckling, 'The Arms in the Town Hall at Romsey', *Papers and Proceedings of the Hampshire Field Club and Archaeological Society*, suppt. to vol. vi (1911–12), p. 30; White, p. 78; *Poll*, *1779*, p. 90; no. 171.

**114**
**Missing, Thomas**

Born after 1710; d. July or Aug. 1772. Ad. 27 Nov. 1732; sw. 16 Aug. 1736; Ald. 27 Sept. 1749. Son of Tho. and Rebecca, *née* Mitchen. Mar. (1) Anne, dau. of Geo. Streatfield of Stoke Newington, Mdx, 13 Nov. 1739; (2) Elizabeth, dau. of Ric. Champneys of Orchardleigh, Som., 2 Nov. 1744. Gentleman. Sheriff of Hampshire 1739–40; Turnpike Commissioner under 1742 Act; Deputy Vice-Admiral of Hampshire 1753; Mayor of Portsmouth 1756–7; Burgess of Poole, Dors., 1741. M.P. for Poole 1741–7. Son of Tho. Missing (d. 1733); cousin of John Missing; son-in-law of Ric. Champneys; bro.-in-law of Ald. Wil. Rickman, Ben. de la Fontaine and John Monday; father of Tho. Missing (d. 1788); uncle of John, Tho. and Wil. Rickman.

Sedgwick, ii, pp. 260–1; P.R.O. Prob.11/980, f. 302; nos 10, 42; East, p. 380; no. 153; East, p. 331; Everitt, 'Pedigrees', ii, pp. 933–4; *List of sheriffs*, p. 57; *Cal. T. B. & P. 1739–41*, pp. 596, 373; *Turnpike Minute Book*, p. 177; C. & E. 58/151, p. 131; East, p. 318; Poole Borough Archives, Record Book 1702–1816, f. 243.

**115**
**Missing, Thomas**

D. 25 Sept. 1788(?). Ad. 27 Oct. 1750. Son of Tho. and Elizabeth, *née* Champneys. Minor. Voted Whig 1779. Grandson of Ric. Champneys; son of Ald. Tho. Missing.

*Gent. Mag.*, lviii (1788), p. 934; no. 164; East, p. 382; Everitt, 'Pedigrees', ii, pp. 933–4; Sandwich MS. 380; *Poll, 1779*, p. 71.

**116**
**Monday, Thomas**

D. 9 May 1789. Ad. 27 Oct. 1750; Ald. 1775. Mar. Anne, eldest dau. of Edw. Linzee and widow of Adm. John Amherst, 8 Mar. 1778. Customs official: Land Surveyor, Portsmouth, 1755, Surveyor-General of Customs, by 1789 one of four for port of London. Mayor of Portsmouth 1775. Churchwarden, St Mary's, Portsea, 1734–9. Grandson of Tho. Missing (d. 1733)(?); son-in-law of Ald. Edw. Linzee.

*Gent. Mag.*, lix (1789), p. 471; nos 164, 166; East, p. 382; P.C.R.O. 22A/2/1/3/3; Sandwich MS. 380; C. & E. 58/152, p. 143; East, pp. 331, 318; P.C.R.O. 100A/1/1/7/1; Linzee, ii, pp. 459, 489; P.R.O. Prob.11/660, f. 204.

**117**
**Montagu, John, 2nd Duke of Montagu**

Born 29 Mar. 1690; d. 6 July 1749. Ad. 7 June 1736; hon. First son of Ralph, 1st Duke of Montagu, and Elizabeth, dau of Tho. Wriothesley, 4th Earl of Southampton. Mar. Mary, youngest dau. of John Churchill, 1st Duke of Marlborough, 20 Mar. 1704/5. Army officer: Capt. of Band of Gentlemen Pensioners 1734–40, Maj.-Gen. 1735, Col. of 1st Troop of Horse Guards 1737, Lieut.-Gen. 1739, Gen. 1746; Master of Great Wardrobe 1709 to death; Governor and Captain-General of St Lucia and St Vincent 1722; Master General of Ordnance 1740–Feb. 1741/2, Mar. 1742 to death. Governor of I. of Wight 1733–4; Free Burgess of Newport, I.W., 1733; Free Burgess of Yarmouth, I.W., 1733 (dismissed 1741). Father-in-law of Geo. Brudenell, 4th Earl of Cardigan.

G.E.C., ix, pp. 108–9; *Beaulieu: the abbey Palace House and Buckler's Hard* (1952), pp. 18–19; no. 35; East, p. 380; Murrell & East, p. 349; *Cal. T. B. & P. 1739–41*, p. 424; D.N.B.; N.B.A. Class 2, Admissions 1717–1833; Y.T.T. Corporation Proceedings 1710–85, ff. 32, 49–51.

**118**
**Montagu, John, 4th Earl of Sandwich**

Born 13 Nov. 1718; d. 30 Apr. 1792. Ad. 2 Aug. 1749; hon. First son of Edw. Montagu, Viscount Hinchingbrooke, and Elizabeth, dau. of Alex. Popham. Mar. Dorothy, dau. of Cha. Fane, 1st Viscount Fane, 3 Mar. 1740/1. Army officer: Col. 1745, Maj.-Gen. 1755, Lieut.-Gen. 1759, Gen. 1772; Lord of Admiralty 1744–6; Plenipotentiary at Breda 1746, at Aix-la-Chapelle Feb. 1747/8; First Lord of Admiralty 1748–51, Apr.-Aug. 1763, 1771–82; Vice-Treasurer of Ireland 1755–63; Secretary of State, Northern Dept, 1763–5, 1770–1; Joint Postmaster General 1768–70; Recorder of Huntingdon and Godmanchester, Hunts.

G.E.C., xi, pp. 435–7; *Gent. Mag.*, lxii (1792), p. 482; no. 148; East, p. 381; Murrell & East, p. 351; *D.N.B.*

**119**
**Mostyn, Savage**

Born 1713(?); d. 16 Sept. 1757. Ad. 4 Aug. 1749; sw. 5 Aug. 1749; hon. Third son of Sir Roger, 3rd Bt. Unmarried. Naval officer: Lieut. 1734, Capt. 1739, Rear-Adm. 1755, Vice-Adm. 1757; Controller of Navy 1749–55; Lord of Admiralty 6 Apr. –2 July 1757. M.P. for Weobley 1746 to death.

Sedgwick, ii, p. 280; *Gent. Mag.*, xxvii (1757), p. 436; no. 150; East, p. 381; no. 151; Murrell & East, p. 351; *D.N.B.*

**120**
**Mounsher, Andrew\***

Born 13 June 1686; d. 1767. Ad. 27 Oct. 1750. Third son of Abraham and Rebecca, *née* Blundy(?). Mar. Ann — . Sail maker; purser of sloop Saltash 1738; Leet juror 1739, 1742. Presbyterian: High Street Chapel 1739. Cousin of Ald. John Mounsher.

Everitt, 'Pedigrees', i, p. 44; Hants.R.O. A Wills 1767; nos 164, 167; East, p. 382; P.R.O. Adm.110/11, p. 473; P.C.R.O. L1; P.C.R.O. 257A/1/9/3.

**121**
**Mounsher, Eyles\***

Ad. 27 Oct. 1750. Son of James Mounsher. Minor(?). Grandson of Ald. John Mounsher; son of James Mounsher; bro. of John Mounsher.

No. 164; East, p. 382.

**122**
**Mounsher, James\***

Bapt. 22 Aug. 1723; d. 1797. Ad. 27 Nov. 1732; sw. 21 Aug. 1744. Third son of John and Sarah. Attorney ('distressed' 1775). Turnpike Commissioner Oct. 1744. Son of Ald. John Mounsher; father of Eyles and John Mounsher.

P.C.R.O. 22A/2/1/1/4; Everitt, 'Pedigrees', i, pp. 44–5; no. 10; East, p. 380; no. 103; Sandwich MS. 380; *Turnpike Minute Book*, p. 133.

**123**
**Mounsher, John***

Bapt. Aug. 1692; d. 1762. Ad. 10 Apr. 1728; Ald. 26 Feb. 1731/2. Son of John and Elizabeth. Mar. Sarah Henley 8 Dec. 1713. Rope maker, postmaster. Turnpike Commissioner under 1726 and 1742 Acts. Voted Whig 1734. Cousin of And. Mounsher; father of James, John and Tho. Mounsher.

Everitt, 'Pedigrees', i, pp. 44–5; P.C.R.O. 83A/1/1/2; East, p. 379; no. 6; East, p. 330; P.H. Ordnance MSS., passim; *Geese*, p. 9 (see Appendix II); *Turnpike Minute Book*, pp. 173, 177; *Poll for Hants.*, *1734*, p. 133.

**124**
**Mounsher, John***

Bapt. 4 June 1718; bur. 30 Apr. 1747. Ad. 27 Nov. 1732; sw. 29 May 1739. First son of John and Sarah. Mar. Rebecca Ayres of Southampton, at South Stoneham, 24 Feb. 1745/6. Gentleman. Turnpike Commissioner under 1742 Act. Son of Ald. John Mounsher; bro. of James and Tho. Mounsher.

P.C.R.O. 22A/2/1/1/4, 5; *Hants. Allegns*, ii, p. 52; Everitt, 'Pedigrees', i, pp. 44–5; no. 10; East, p. 380; no. 63; *Turnpike Minute Book*, pp. 177, 143.

**125**
**Mounsher, John***

Ad. 27 Oct. 1750. Son of James. Mar. Joannah Stodden 5 May 1757. Minor(?). Grandson of Ald. John Mounsher; son of James Mounsher; bro. of Eyles Mounsher.

No. 164; East, p. 382; P.C.R.O. 22A/2/1/3/1.

**126**
**Mounsher, Thomas**

Bapt. 28 Nov. 1735. Ad. 27 Oct. 1750. Fourth son of John and Sarah. Minor; described as 'Gone a private Seaman to America in a Merchant Ship' 1775. Son of Ald. John Mounsher; bro. of John and Tho. Mounsher.

P.C.R.O. 22A/2/1/1/5; no. 164; East, p. 382; Sandwich MS. 380.

**127**
**Munday, John***

D. by 17 Sept. 1764. Ad. 27 Nov. 1732. Mar. Mary Hammond 18 Aug. 1726. Contractor, brewer(?). Overseer of Poor, Kingston, 1724. Voted Whig 1734. Churchwarden, St Mary's, Portsea, 1734–8, 1747, 1748.

P.C.R.O. CE 1/14, p. 182; no. 10; East, p. 380; P.C.R.O. 22A/2/1/1/4; N.M.M. POR F/8; P.C.R.O. 100A/1/1/7/1; *Poll for Hants.*, *1734*, p. 131; P.C.R.O. 100A/1/1/7/2.

**128**
**Ogle, Sir Chaloner**

Born c. 1680; d. 11 Apr. 1750. Ad. 15 Sept. 1740; hon. Son of John and Mary, *née* Braithwaite. Mar.(1) Henrietta, dau. of Ant. Isaacson of Newcastle upon Tyne, c. 1726; (2) Isabella Ogle, his first cousin, 30 Oct. 1737. Naval officer: entered Navy 1697, Lieut. 1702, Capt. 1708, C.-in-C. Jamaica 1732–5, Rear-Adm. 1739, C.-in-C. West Indies 1742–5, Vice-Adm. 1743, Adm. 1744, Adm. of Fleet 1749. M.P. for Rochester 1746 to death.

Sedgwick, ii, p. 305; no. 76; East, p. 381; Murrell & East, p. 350; *Gent. Mag.*, xx (1750), p. 188.

**129**
**Orr, Robert***

Bur. 23 Feb. 1769. Ad. 27 Oct. 1750. Mar. Ann —.

P.C.R.O. 22A/2/1/1/6; nos 164, 167; East, p. 382.

**130**
**Paulet, Lord Harry**

Born 24 July 1691; d. 9 Oct. 1759. Ad. 17 Sept. 1733; hon. Second son of Cha., 2nd Duke of Bolton, and Frances, dau. of Wil. Ramsden. Lord of Admiralty 1733–42; Lord Lieutenant of Tower of London 1742–54. Free Burgess of Yarmouth, I.W., 1733 (dismissed 1741(?), re-admitted 1743); Free Burgess of Newport, I.W., 1733; Free Burgess of Lymington, Hants., 1745; Lord Lieutenant of Hampshire 1754–8. M.P. for St Ives 1715–22, Hampshire 1722–54.

G.E.C., ii, pp. 212, 214; Namier & Brooke, iii, p. 314; no. 15; East, p. 380; Murrell & East, p. 349; Y.T.T. Corporation Proceedings 1710–85, ff. 34, 58; N.B.A. Class 2, Admissions 1717–1833; St Barbe, p. 13.

**131**
**Peers, James**

D. 26 Nov. 1746. Ad. 2 Sept. 1735. Mar. (1) Elizabeth, eldest dau. of Wil. and Elizabeth(?) Harmond, June 1729; (2) — Lestock. Naval officer: Capt. by 1735. Voted Whig 1734. Son-in-law of Ric. Lestock; bro.-in-law of Ald. John White.

Charnock, v. pp. 111–12; no. 33; East, p. 380; Everitt, 'Pedigrees', i, pp. 411, 417; *Poll for Hants.*, *1734*, p. 129; *D.N.B.*, under Lestock, Ric.

**132**
**Pescod, William**

Born c. 1701; d. 26 Feb. 1760. Ad. 15 Apr. 1746. Son of Rob. and Mary. Mar. Jane, dau. of Sir Ric. Harris. Barrister. Recorder of Portsmouth 1745 to death; Recorder of Winchester by 1760 and Steward to College and Chapter.

Everitt, 'Pedigrees', ii, pp. 655–6; *Gent. Mag.*, xxx (1760), p. 153; no. 123; East, p. 381; no. 124; East, p. 421; T. F. Kirby, *Winchester scholars* (1888), p. 224.

**133**
**Philipson, John**

Born 28 Apr. 1698; d. 27 Nov. 1756. Ad. 11 Oct. 1740. Son of John and Rachel, *née* Lane. Mar. dau. of Ric. Burton, Commissioner of Navy, 29 Aug. 1717. Clerk in Navy Office 1727–39; chief clerk in Navy Ticket Office to 1739; Commissioner of Navy 1739–43; Lord of Admiralty 1743–4; Surveyor-General of Woods and Forests north and south of Trent 1745 to death. M.P. for New Shoreham 1734–41, Harwich 1741 to death.

Sedgwick, ii, pp. 345–6; no. 78; East, p. 381.

**134**
**Pike, Timothy***

Born 1725; d. 6 Mar. 1798. Ad. 27 Oct. 1750. Son of John. Mar. Mary — (d. 23 Oct. 1817). Brewer. Chamberlain of Portsmouth 1736–78. Nephew of Wil. Pike.

Everitt, 'Pedigrees', vol. iv; nos 164, 167; East, p. 382; P.C.R.O. CF1/5, 6.

**135**
**Pike, William***

Born 1691; d. 9 May 1777. Ad. 27 Nov. 1732. Son of Tho., of Poole, Dors., and Susanna. Mar. (1) Anne Bird 27 Feb. 1715/6(?); (2) Anne Rice of Gosport 1766. Maltster by 1723; brewer, worth £300 000–£400 000, by 1775. Overseer of Poor, Portsmouth, 1722; Justice of the Peace for Hampshire 1748–9(?); Gosport Paving Commissioner under 1763 Act. Voted Whig 1734 (in Hants., and at Westhampnett, Suss.). Presbyterian: member, High Street Chapel, 1716, trustee and subscriber 1735; subscribed 5 guineas to Orange Street Chapel (Baptist). Uncle of Tim. Pike; father-in-law of Ald. John Carter.

Everitt, 'Pedigrees', vol. iv; no. 10; East, p. 380; P.C.R.O. 11A/1/97; Sandwich MS. 380; P.C.R.O. 11A/1/94; B.L. Add. MS. 35603, f. 130; White, p. 78; *Poll for Hants., 1734*, p. 128; *Poll for Suss., 1734*, p. 93; P.C.R.O. 257A/1/9/1, 3; P.C.R.O. 3A/3/1.

**136**
**Poole, John***

D. 1769(?). Ad. 27 Nov. 1732. Assistant to master builder, Portsmouth Dockyard, 1726–48. Voted Whig 1734.

*Gent. Mag.*, xl (1770), p. 239; *Lond. Mag.*, xxxviii (1769), p. 688; no. 10; East, p. 379; P.C.R.O. S2/23; P.C.R.O. 67A/13: copy of Slight annotated by Sir Frederic Madden, p. 166; *Poll for Hants., 1734*, p. 138.

**137**
**Revell, Thomas**

D. 26 Jan. 1752. Ad. 18 June 1733. Mar. (1) — ; (2) — ; (3) Jane, dau. of Hon. Wil. Egerton, 12 May 1738. Victualling agent at Lisbon 1716; Commissioner of Victualling 1728–47; victualler for Minorca, Gibraltar and Georgia. M.P. for Dover 1734 to death.

*Gent. Mag.*, xxii (1752), p. 44; *Salis. Journ.*, 3 Feb. 1752; no. 12; East, p. 380; Sedgwick, ii, p. 381; *Cal. T. B. & P. 1735–8*, p. 540; *Cal. T. B. & P. 1739–41*, passim.

**138**
**Reynolds, James**

Born 6 Jan. 1686/7(?); d. 9 Feb. 1738/9. Ad. 1 June 1737; hon. Fourth son of James and Bridget, *née* Parker. Mar. (1) Mary Smith of Thrandeston Hall, Suff.; (2) Alicia Rainbird July 1737. Recorder of Bury St Edmunds 1712–25; serjeant at law 1715; Cambridge University Counsel 1718; Justice of King's Bench 1725–30; Chief Baron of Exchequer 1730–8. M.P. for Bury St Edmunds 1717–25.

Sedgwick, ii, p. 381; *Gent. Mag.*, ix (1739), p. 106; no. 44; East, p. 380; Murrell & East, p. 350.

**139**
**Rickman, James**

Bur. 4 Sept. 1766(?). Ad. 29 Sept. 1737 (not in Book of Original Entries). Mar. Helena —.

P.C.R.O. 22A/2/1/1/6; East, p. 380; P.C.R.O. S2/24.

**140**
**Rickman, John**

D. 22 Aug. 1787. Ad. 29 Sept. 1748. Son of John, of Yarmouth, I.W.,(?) and Anne. Mar. Mary Boulton 12 Dec. 1762. Customs official, Portsmouth: Landwaiter 1759, seeking promotion 1775, Surveyor of Customs 1776 to death.

C. & E. 58/180; no. 146; East, p. 138; P.C.R.O. 169A/2/3/1; C. & E. 58/154; Sandwich MS. 380; C. & E. 58/167.

**141**
**Rickman, John**

D. by 15 Sept. 1760. Ad. 27 Oct. 1750. Mar. Anne — 1728. Contractor, merchant. Free Burgess of Yarmouth, I.W., 1733 (dismissed 1741); Turnpike Commissioner 1747. Churchwarden, St James's, Yarmouth, 1747. Nephew of Ald. Wil. Rickman.

P.C.R.O. CE1/14, p. 158; nos 164, 166; East, p. 382; Everitt, 'Pedigrees', i, p. 22; N.M.M. POR/F/7; C. & E. 58/144; *Turnpike Minute Book*, p. 143; Y.T.T. H. Guy, 'Historical notes on Yarmouth, Isle of Wight', pt xiii.

**142**
**Rickman, John**

Bapt. 10 Dec. 1741; d. by May 1751. Ad. 27 Oct. 1750. Son of Wil. and Rebecca, *née* Missing. Minor. Grandson of Tho. Missing (d. 1733); son of Ald. Wil. Rickman; nephew of Ald. Tho. Missing; bro. of Tho. and Wil. Rickman.

P.C.R.O. 22A/2/1/1/5; no. 164; East, p. 383.

**143**
**Rickman, Thomas**

Ad. 27 Oct. 1750. First son of Wil. and Rebecca, *née* Missing. Minor(?); cleric by 1775. Grandson of Tho. Missing (d. 1733); son of Ald. Wil. Rickman; nephew of Ald. Tho. Missing; bro. of John and Wil. Rickman.

No. 164; East, p. 383; P.R.O. Prob.11/916, f. 74; Sandwich MS. 380.

**144**
**Rickman, William**

D. 1764. Ad. 27 Dec. 1726; Ald. 8 Aug. 1733. Mar. Rebecca, dau. of Tho. Missing, before 1731. Merchant, brewer, contractor; agent for Spanish prisoners 1739–48; agent of London owners of privateer 1743. Turnpike Commissioner under 1742 Act; Deputy Lieutenant of Hampshire 1745; Sheriff of Hampshire 1747–8. Presbyterian: trustee and subscriber, High Street Chapel, 1735. Son-in-law of Tho. Missing (d. 1733); bro.-in-law of Ald. Tho. Missing; father of John, Tho. and Wil. Rickman; uncle (by marriage) of Elias Ben. de la Fontaine.

Everitt, 'Pedigrees', i, p. 22; East, p. 378; no. 13; East, p. 330; P.R.O. Prob.11/660, f. 204; N.M.M. POR/F/5, 6; N.M.M. ADM/F/3; C. & E. 58/146; *Turnpike Minute Book*, p. 177; P.C.R.O. S2/25; *List of sheriffs*, p. 57; P.C.R.O. 257A/1/9/3.

**145**
**Rickman, William**

Ad. 27 Oct. 1750. Second(?) son of Wil. and Rebecca, *née* Missing. Minor; 2nd Lieut., 63rd Company of Marines, 1756; half-pay Capt. 1775. Grandson of Tho. Missing (d. 1733); son of Ald. Wil. Rickman; nephew of Ald. Tho. Missing (d. 1772); bro. of John and Tho. Rickman.

No. 164; East, p. 383; P.R.O. Prob.11/916, f. 74; P.C.R.O. S2/26; Sandwich MS. 380.

**146**
**Robinson, William***

D. by 19 Sept. 1763. Ad. 27 Nov. 1732. Mar. Rachel Mason, at Portsea, 25 Dec. 1701. Shipwright, 1715; Customs Boatman, Portsmouth, 1744. Turnpike Commissioner under 1742 Act. Voted Whig 1734.

P.C.R.O. CE1/14, p. 177; no. 10; East, p. 380; P.C.R.O. 100A/1/1/1/2; P.C.R.O. S1/31; *Cal. T. B. & P. 1742–5*, p. 654; C. & E. 58/147; *Turnpike Minute Book*, p. 177; *Poll for Hants., 1734*, p. 136.

**147**
**Rowley, William**

Born c. 1690; d. 1 Jan. 1768. Ad. 28 Jan. 1745/6; hon. Son of Wil. Mar. Arabella, dau. of Capt. Geo. Dawson, before 1729. Naval officer: entered Navy 1704, Lieut. 1708, Capt. 1716, Rear-Adm. 1743, Vice-Adm. 1744, Adm. 1747, Adm. of Fleet 1762; Lord of Admiralty 1751–56, Apr.–July 1757. M.P. for Taunton 1750–4, Portsmouth 1754–61.

Sedgwick, ii, pp. 393–4; no. 120; East, p. 381; Murrell & East, p. 350; *Gent.Mag.*, xxxviii (1768), p. 47.

**148**
**Roy, Richard**

D. by 20 Sept. 1756. Ad. 27 Nov. 1732. Mar. Jane Cleversley, Dec. 1701(?). Salesman(?). Bro.-in-law of John Missing.

P.C.R.O. CE1/14, p. 132; no. 10; East, p. 380; *Hants. Allegns*, ii, p. 175.

**149**
**Royston, James**

D. by May 1751. Ad. 27 Oct. 1750.

No. 164; East, p. 382.

**150**
**Russell, John, 4th Duke of Bedford**

Born 30 Sept. 1710; d. 14. Jan. 1771. Ad. 28 Feb. 1745/6; hon. Second son of Wriothesley, 2nd Duke of Bedford, and Elizabeth, dau. of John Howland. Mar. (1) Diana, dau. of Cha. Spencer, 3rd Earl of Sunderland, 11 Oct. 1731; (2) Gertrude, dau. of John Leveson-Gower, 1st Earl Gower, 2 Apr. 1737. Army officer: Col. 1745, Maj.-Gen. 1755, Lieut.-Gen. 1759; First Lord of Admiralty 1744–8; Secretary of State, Southern Dept, 1748–51; Lord Lieutenant of Ireland 1756–61; Ambassador to France 1762–3; Lord President of Council 1763–5. Warden of New Forest 1746 to death.

*D.N.B.*; no. 122; East, p. 381; Murrell & East, p. 350; G.E.C., ii, pp. 82–4.

**151**
**St John, Hollis**

Born 1708 or 1709; d. 6 Oct. 1738. Ad. 7 June 1736. Third son of Henry, 1st Viscount St John, and Angelica Magdalena, dau. of Geo. Pelissary (Treasurer-General of the Marine under Louis XIV). Unmarried. Chief Burgess of Newport, I.W., 1733; Free Burgess of Yarmouth, I.W., 1733.

*Gent. Mag.*, viii (1738), p. 547; no. 35; East, p. 380; *Burke's Peerage*, p. 297; N.B.A. Class 2, Admissions 1717–1833; Y.T.T. Corporation Proceedings 1710–85, f. 32.

**152**
**Shales, Henry***

Ad. 5 Aug. 1740. Son of John and Susannah. Victualling clerk, Clarence Yard, Gosport, 1736; victualling agent, Portsmouth, 1745 onwards. Turnpike Commissioner under 1742 Act.

No. 74; East, p. 381; Everitt, 'Pedigrees', i, pp. 94–5; Everitt, 'Misc. collns', i, p. 224; V.M. Clarence Yard Pay Book no. 4; P.R.O. Adm.110/15, p. 50; *Turnpike Minute Book*, p. 177; P.C.R.O. 22A/2/1/1/4.

**153**
**Shephard, John***

D. by 20 Sept. 1762. Ad. 27 Nov. 1732. Son of Sam. and Susanna. Mar. Elizabeth Coles 5 July 1719(?). Merchant(?). Leet juror 1733, 1735, 1737; Turnpike Commissioner under 1742 Act; Chamberlain of Portsmouth 1747–63; Surveyor of Turnpike 1752. Voted Whig 1734. Presbyterian: trustee of meeting-house 1742.

P.C.R.O. CE1/14, p. 171; no. 10; East, p. 380; P.C.R.O. 22A/2/1/1/5,4; C. & E. 58/145, p. 85; P.C.R.O. L1; P.C.R.O. CE1/14, pp. 64–5; *Turnpike Minute Book*, pp. 177, 156; *Poll for Hants.*, *1734*, p. 132; P.C.R.O. 257A/1/9/3.

**154**
**Shepherd, John**

Ad. 17 Sept. 1733. Treasury official: bookranger 1725–45, deputy messenger of receipt 1743, 1745; Receiver-General of House Duties for Hampshire 1737, renewed 1744. Free Burgess of Yarmouth, I.W., 1733 (dismissed 1741); Free Burgess of Newport, I.W., 1733.

No. 15; East, p. 380; J. C. Sainty, *Treasury officials 1660–1870* (1972), pp. 37, 150; *Cal. T. B. & P. 1735–8*, p. 386; *Cal. T. B. & P. 1742–5*, p. 574; Y.T.T. Corporation Proceedings 1710–85, ff. 34, 49–51; N.B.A. Class 2, Admissions 1717–1833.

**155**
**Shepherd, Jonathan***

Bur. 10 May 1762. Ad. 27 Oct. 1750. Mar. Elizabeth Trattle 19 Nov. 1741. Baker, contracting to supply bread to Portsmouth workhouse 1751–6. Leet juror 1739, 1742, 1747; Overseer of Poor, Portsmouth, 1742.

P.C.R.O. 22A/2/1/1/5; nos 164, 167; East, p. 382; P.C.R.O. 22A/2/1/1/6; A. J. Willis, 'Hampshire guardianships', *Genealogists' Magazine*, xiv (1964), p. 329; P.C.R.O. PL12/1; P.C.R.O. L1; P.C.R.O. PL1/2.

**156**
**Smith, Daniel**

D. 1736. Ad. 27 Dec. 1726; Ald. 8 Apr. 1735. Mar. Elizabeth Fitchett of Brading, I.W., 8 Jan. 1729. Brewer. Turnpike Commissioner 1735. Voted Whig 1734.

P.R.O. Prob.11/680, f. 254; East, p. 378; no. 29; East, p. 330; *Hants. Allegns*, ii, p. 215; P.R.O. Adm. 110/11, p. 62; *Turnpike Minute Book*, p. 100; *Poll for Hants.*, *1734*, p. 133.

**157**
**Spence, Thomas**

D. 29 June 1737. Ad. 18 June 1733. Mar. Ann — . Under-clerk at Treasury 1707–14; Controller of Lotteries 1729 to death; Serjeant-at-Arms, House of Commons.

*Gent. Mag.*, vii (1737), p. 451; no. 12; East, p. 380; J. C. Sainty, *Treasury officials 1660–1870* (1972), p. 37; *Cal. T. B. & P. 1739–41*, p. 85; *Cal. T. B. & P. 1729–30*, p. 170.

**158**
**Spicer, Samuel***

Born 11 Oct. 1722; d. 28 Feb. 1774. Ad. 27 Oct. 1750. Son of John and Margaret, *née* Pike. Mar. Sarah, dau. of David Lucas of Gosport, 10 June 1755. Distiller, brewer. Presbyterian 1745; subscribed 3 guineas to Orange Street Chapel (Baptist) 1750. Nephew of Wil. Pike; business associate of Tim. Pike.

Everitt, 'Pedigrees', i, pp. 66–7; nos 164, 167; East, p. 382; P.C.R.O. 100A/1/1/1/5; P.C.R.O. 257A/1/9/3; P.C.R.O. 3A/3/1.

**159**
**Stanhope, Charles**

Born 1673; d. 16 Mar. 1760. Ad. 7 June 1736. Second surviving son of John and Dorothy, *née* Agard. Unmarried. Treasury official: Under-Secretary of State, Southern Dept, 1714–17; Secretary to Treasury 1717–21; Treasurer of Chamber 1722–7. M.P. for Milborne Port 1717–22, Aldborough 1722–34, Harwich 1734–41.

Sedgwick, ii, pp. 433–4; *Gent. Mag.*, xxx (1760), p. 154; no. 35; East, p. 380.

**160**
**Stanyford, George***

Bapt. 7 Apr. 1715; d. 3 Oct. 1754. Elected 10 Apr. 1728; ad. 16 Aug. 1736. Son of Henry and Mary, *née* Ryley. Mar. Ann — . Turnpike Commissioner under 1742 Act. Bro. of Ald. Tho. Stanyford.

P.C.R.O. 22A/2/1/1/4, 6; East, p. 379; no. 42; Everitt, 'Pedigrees', i, p. 42; *Turnpike Minute Book* p. 177.

**161**
**Stanyford, Thomas**

Bapt. 2 June 1703; d. 18 Apr. 1765. Ad. 27 Dec. 1726; Ald. 2 Aug. 1735. Son of Henry and Mary, *née* Ryley. Unmarried. Serjeant at law; Solicitor to Board of Ordnance 1754; business at St Clement's Dane, London. Turnpike Commissioner under 1726 and 1742 Acts; Freeman of Chichester 1744. Bro. of Geo. Stanyford.

Everitt, 'Pedigrees', i, p. 42; *Lond. Mag.*, xxxiv (1765), p. 266; East, p. 378; no. 32; East, p. 330; P.C.R.O. S2/26; P.R.O. W.O.55/1988; *Turnpike Minute Book*, pp. 173, 177; W.Suss.R.O. C.C.A. C.2, f. 25.

**162**
**Stares, James**

D. by 20 Sept. 1762. Ad. 27 Oct. 1750; sw. 8 Nov. 1750. Mar. Jane Green 2 June 1715. Yeoman. Father of James Stares.

P.C.R.O. CE1/14, p. 171; nos 164, 168; East, p. 382; *Hants. Allegns*, ii, p. 240.

**163**
**Stares, James**

D. 1784. Ad. 27 Oct. 1750; sw. 8 Nov. 1750. Son of James and Jane, *née* Green. Yeoman. Voted Whig 1779 (at Titchfield, Hants.). Son of James Stares.

Hants.R.O. A Wills 1784; nos 164, 168; East, p. 382; *V. C. H. Hants.*, iii, pp. 204–5; *Poll, 1779*, p. 69.

**164**
**Stewart, Charles**

Born 1681; d. 5 Feb. 1740/1. Ad. 28 Aug. 1733; hon. Fifth son of Wil., 1st Viscount Mountjoy, and Mary, dau. of Ric. Coote, 1st Baron Coote of Coloony. Unmarried. Naval officer: entered Navy before 1697, Capt. 1704, commanded squadron against Salé, Morocco, 1720–1, Rear-Adm. 1727, C.-in-C. Jamaica 1729–32, Vice-Adm. 1734, second in command under Norris in Channel 1734. M.P. for Malmesbury 1723–7, Portsmouth 1737–41.

*Gent. Mag.*, xi (1741), p. 108; no. 14; East, p. 380; Murrell & East, p. 349; Sedgwick, ii, pp. 447–8.

**165**
**Stewart, James**

D. 30 Mar. 1757. Ad. 28 Sept. 1742; hon. Son of John. Mar. Mary, dau. of John Taylor of Portsmouth, before 1744. Naval officer: Capt. 1709, Rear-Adm. 1742, Vice-Adm. 1743, Adm. 1747, Adm. and C.-in-C. of Fleet 1750 to death. M.P. for Weymouth and Melcombe Regis 1741–7.

*Gent. Mag.*, xxvii (1757), p. 436; no. 93; East, p. 381; Murrell & East, p. 350; Sedgwick, ii, p. 446.

**166**
**Strode, Edward**

D. by 19 Sept. 1768. Ad. 29 Sept. 1742. Mar. Mary — . Army officer: Capt. 1724, Town Major of Portsmouth 1727; Maj. in Regiment of Invalids commanded by Col. Wardour 1751.

P.C.R.O. CE1/14, p. 206; no. 95; East, p. 381; P.C.R.O. 22A/2/1/1/4; P.C.R.O. S2/23, 26.

**167**
**Taylor, Henry***

Born May 1711; d. 25 Apr. 1785. Ad. 27 Oct. 1750. Second son of Wil. and Anna, *née* Crispe. Mar. Christian, dau. of Fra. Fox, M.A., 16 June 1740. Cleric: priest 1735, Vicar of Portsmouth 1743–85, Rector of Ovington, Hants., 1753, Rector of Crawley with Hunton, Hants., 1755.

Everitt, 'Pedigrees', i, p. 70; *Gent. Mag.*, lv (1785), pp. 402–3; nos 164, 166; East, p. 382; A. J. Willis, *Winchester ordinations 1660–1829* (2 v., 1964–5), i, p. 3; P.C.R.O. 22A/1/1, p. 77; P.C.R.O. S2/26.

**168**
**Thompson, William**

Born 1680(?); d. June 1744. Ad. 18 June 1733. Son of Fra. and Arabella, *née* Alleyn. Unmarried. Warden of Mint 1715–29; Governor of Scarborough Castle 1715 to death; Commissioner of Victualling 1729 to death. M.P. for Scarborough 1701–22, 1730 to death.

Sedgwick, ii, p. 467; *Lond. Mag.*, xiii (1744), p. 308; no. 12; East, p. 380.

**169**
**Thompson, Sir William**

Born 1676(?); d. 27 Oct. 1739. Ad. 16 July 1734; hon. Second son of Sir Wil. and Mary, *née* Stephens. Mar. (1) Joyce Brent, widow, 16 Feb. 1700/1; (2) Julia, dau. of Sir Cha. Conyers, 2nd Bt, 1711. Recorder of Ipswich 1707 to death; Recorder of London 1715 to death; Solicitor-General 1717–20; Cursitor Baron of Exchequer 1726–9; serjeant at law 1729; Baron of Exchequer 1729 to death. M.P. for Orford 1709–10, Ipswich 1713–14, 1715–29.

Sedgwick, ii, pp. 467–8; *Gent. Mag.*, ix (1739), p. 554; no. 24; East, p. 380; Murrell & East, p. 349.

**170**
**Townshend, Isaac**

Born c. 1685; d. 21 or 22 Nov. 1765. Ad. 27 Nov. 1732. Mar. Elizabeth, dau. of Wil. Larcum, surgeon. Naval officer: entered Navy c. 1698, Capt. 1720, Rear-Adm. 1744, Vice-Adm. 1746, Adm. of White 1747; Governor of Greenwich Hospital 1754 to death. Freeman of Chichester 1747. M.P. for Portsmouth 1744–54, Rochester 1757 to death.

Sedgwick, ii, p. 471; *Gent. Mag.*, xxxv (1765), p. 539; no. 10; East, p. 379 (ad. 6 Nov. 1732); W.Suss. R.O. C.C.A. C2, f. 36.

**171**
**Trenchard, George**

Born c. 1684; d. 31 Mar. 1758. Ad. 18 June 1733. First son of Sir John and Philippa, *née* Speke. Mar. Mary Trenchard of Wolfeton, Dors., his cousin. Army officer: Ensign, Earl of Monmouth's Foot 1693, Col. Henry Mordaunt's Foot 1695; out by 1702. Free Burgess of Yarmouth, I.W., 1731. M.P. for Poole 1713–41, 1747–55.

Sedgwick, ii, p. 480; no. 12; East, p. 380; Y.T.T. Corporation Proceedings 1710–85, f. 17.

**172**
**Turvin, Robert**

Bur. 6 Dec. 1771. Ad. 27 Nov. 1732. Mar. Ann Roberts 4 Oct. 1758. Customs official: controller of duties on coals 1731, deputy to Patent Controller, Portsmouth, 1731, Controller of Customs c. 1739.

P.C.R.O. 22A/2/1/1/7; no. 10; East, p. 379; P.C.R.O. 22A/2/1/3/1; C. & E. 58/145, p. 9; B.L. Add. MS. 33283, ff. 160–1; *Cal. T. B. & P. 1739–41*, p. 65.

**173**
**Varlo, Philip***

Bapt. 31 Dec. 1721; d. 6 Apr. 1778. Ad. 27 Oct. 1750; Ald. 1763. Second son of John and Elizabeth, *née* Weston. Mar. Mary, dau. of Mic. Atkins, 1775. Contractor for ships' blocks. Mayor of Portsmouth 1764, 1768, 1770, 1774, 1776. Son-in-law of Ald. Mic. Atkins; bro.-in-law of Wil. Atkins and Ald. Tho. White.

P.C.R.O. 22A/2/1/1/4; Everitt, 'Pedigrees', i, pp. 420–1; nos 165, 167; East, pp. 382, 331; P.R.O. Prob.11/792, f. 27; Sandwich MS. 380; East, p. 318.

**174**
**Vernon, Edward**

Born 12 Nov. 1684; d. 30 Oct. 1757. Ad. 19 July 1739; hon. Second son of James and Mary, *née* Buck. Mar. Sarah, dau. of Tho. Best of Chatham, Kent, c. 1729. Naval officer: entered Navy 1700, Lieut. 1702, Capt. 1706, Vice-Adm. 1739, Adm. 1745. M.P. for Penryn 1722–34, Portsmouth 21 Feb. 1740/1–27 Apr. 1741 (put up again May 1741), Ipswich 1741 to death.

Sedgwick, i, pp. 497–8; *Gent. Mag.*, xxvii (1757), p. 531; no. 64; East, p. 381; Murrell & East, p. 350; *D.N.B.*; P.C.R.O. PE2/5c.

**175**
**Villiers, Thomas**

Born 1709; d. 11 Dec. 1786. Ad. 2 Aug. 1749. Second son of Wil., 2nd Earl of Jersey, and Judith, *née* Herne. Mar. Charlotte, dau. of Wil. Capel, 3rd Earl of Essex, 30 Mar. 1752. Envoy to Poland 1738–43, 1744–6; Minister to Austria 1742–3; Minister to Prussia Feb.–Sept. 1746; Lord of Admiralty 1748–56; Joint Paymaster-General 1763–5, 1786; Chancellor of Duchy of Lancaster 1771–82, 1783–6. M.P. for Tamworth 1747–56.

Sedgwick, ii, p. 500; no. 149; East, p. 381; *D.N.B.*

**176**
**Wallop, John,**
**1st Viscount**
**Lymington**

Born 15 Apr. 1690; d. 22 Nov. 1762. Ad. 29 Sept. 1733 (not in Book of Original Entries); hon. Third son of John and Alicia, *née* Borlase. Mar. (1) Bridget, dau. of Cha. Bennett, 1st Earl of Tankerville, 20 May 1716; (2) Elizabeth, dau. of James Griffin, 2nd Baron Griffin, 9 June 1741. Lord of Treasury 1717–20; Chief Justice in Eyre north of Trent 1732–4. Freeman of Lymington, Hants., 1713; Free Burgess of Yarmouth, I.W., 1733 (dismissed 1741); Lord Lieutenant and Vice-Admiral of Hampshire 1733–42; Free Burgess of Newport, I.W., 1734; Governor and Vice-Admiral of I. of Wight 1734–42, 1746 to death. M.P. for Hampshire 1715–20.

G.E.C., x, pp. 610–11; Sedgwick, ii, p. 507; *Lond. Mag.*, xxxi (1762), p. 627; East, p. 380; Murrell & East, p. 349; St Barbe, p. 12; Y.T.T. Corporation Proceedings 1710–85, ff. 33, 49–51; N.B.A. Class 2, Admissions 1717–1833.

**177**
**Walton, George**

Bur. 8 June 1788. Ad. 27 Oct. 1750. Son of John. Mar. Anne Johnston 15 Jan. 1770. Minor; Customs official, Portsmouth: Landwaiter 1762, Deputy Searcher 1779.

No. 164; East, p. 383; Sandwich MS. 380; P.C.R.O. 22A/2/1/3/3; C. & E. 58/173, p. 228; B.L. Add. MS. 8135, f. 139.

**178**
**Warren, Sir Peter**

Born c. 1703; d. 29 July 1752. Ad. 25 Dec. 1746, in recognition of the reduction of Louisburg; hon. Third son of Mic. and Catharine, dau. of Sir Chr. Aylmer, 1st Bt. Mar. Susanna, dau. of Step. de Lancey, of New York, July 1731. Naval officer: entered Navy 1716, Midshipman 1719, Lieut. 1723, Capt. 1727, Rear-Adm. 1745, C.-in-C. Western Squadron 1747, Vice-Adm. of Red 1747. M.P. for Westminster 1747 to death.

Sedgwick, ii, p. 522; *Gent. Mag.*, xxii (1752), p. 384; no. 133; *Salis. Journ.*, 5 Jan. 1746/7; Murrell & East, p. 350; *D.N.B.*

**179**
**West, John,**
**7th Baron**
**De La Warr**

Born 4 Apr. 1693; d. 16 Mar. 1766. Ad. 7 June 1736; hon. Son of John, 6th Baron De La Warr, and Margaret, *née* Freeman. Mar. (1) Charlotte, dau. of Donough MacCarthy, 4th Earl of Clancarty, 25 May 1721; (2) Anne, widow of Geo. Nevill, Lord Bergavenny, 15 June 1744. Army officer: standard bearer to Gentlemen Pensioners 1712–14, Maj. and guidon of 1st Troop of Horseguards 1715, Lieut.-Col. 1717, Col. 1737, Brig.-Gen. 1743, Maj.-Gen. 1745, Lieut.-Gen. 1747, Governor of Tilbury 1747–52, Governor of Guernsey 1752 to death, Gen. of Horse 1765; clerk extraordinary of Privy Council 1712–23; verderer, Windsor Forest, 1718; Treasurer of Household 1731–7. M.P. for Grampound 1715–22.

*D.N.B.*; no. 35; East, p. 380; Murrell & East, p. 349; G.E.C., iv, p. 162; Sedgwick, ii, pp. 530–1.

**180**
**White, Charles***

Bapt. 28 Apr. 1733; d. by May 1751. Ad. 27 Oct. 1750. Second son of John and Anne, née Hammond. Minor. Son of Ald. John White; bro. of John, Ald. Tho. and Ald. Wil. White.

P.C.R.O. 22A/2/1/1/5; no. 164; East, p. 383; P.C.R.O. 22A/2/1/1/4; Everitt, 'Pedigrees', i, pp. 134-5.

**181**
**White, John***

Ad. 27 Nov. 1732 (noted as 'dead'). First son of John and Anne, née Hammond. Minor(?). Son of Ald. John White; bro. of Cha., Ald. Tho. and Ald. Wil. White.

No. 10; East, p. 380.

**182**
**White, Thomas***

Bapt. 21 May 1726; d. 14 Feb. 1797. Ad. 10 Apr. 1728; sw. 1 July 1747; Ald. 27 Sept. 1749. Third(?) son of John and Anne, née Hammond. Mar. Sarah, dau. of Mic. Atkins, 3 Sept. 1753. Attorney, described as 'independent with a moderate fortune' 1775. Turnpike Commissioner 1747; Mayor of Portsmouth 1752, 1757, 1760, 1763, 1774, 1791. Son of Ald. John White; bro. of Cha., John and Ald. Wil. White; son-in-law of Ald. Mic. Atkins; bro.-in-law of Wil. Atkins and Ald. Phil. Varlo.

P.C.R.O. 22A/2/1/1/4; Everitt, 'Pedigrees', i, pp. 134-5; ibid., vol. iv; East, p. 379; nos 138, 153; East, p. 331; P.C.R.O. 22A/2/1/1/6; Sandwich MS. 380; *Turnpike Minute Book*, p. 143; East, pp. 318-19.

**183**
**White, Thomas***

D. by 20 Sept. 1756. Ad. 27 Oct. 1750. Mar. Elizabeth Rogers, 12 Feb. 1743/4.

P.C.R.O. CE1/14, p. 131; nos 164, 167; East, p. 382; P.C.R.O. 22A/2/1/1/5.

**184**
**White, William***

Born 2 Aug. 1730; d. 31 Dec. 1812. Ad. 27 Nov. 1732; Ald. 1761. Fourth son of John and Anne, née Hammond. Unmarried. Minor. Voted Whig 1779(?). Baptist: trustee, Orange Street Chapel, 1750. Son of Ald. John White; bro. of Cha., John and Ald. Tho. White.

Everitt, 'Pedigrees', i, pp. 134-5; ibid., vol. iv; no. 10; East, pp. 380, 331; *Poll, 1779*, p. 91; P.C.R.O. 3A/3/1.

**185**
**Whithed, Francis**

Born 1719(?); d. 30 Mar. 1751. Ad. 27 Oct. 1750. Second son of Alex. and Mary (née Whithed) Thistlethwayte. Unmarried, with one dau. Gentleman. Hereditary ranger of Bere Forest. M.P. for Hampshire 1747 to death.

Sedgwick, ii, pp. 534-5; *Lond. Mag.*, xx (1751), p. 189; no. 164; East, p. 382;

**186**
**Wildman, William, 2nd Viscount Barrington**

Born 15 Jan. 1716/7; d. 1 Feb. 1793. Ad. 2 Aug. 1749; hon. Son of John, 1st Viscount Barrington, and Anne, dau. of Sir Wil. Daines. Mar. Mary, dau. of Henry Lovell, 16 Sept. 1740. Lord of Admiralty 1746-54; Master of Great Wardrobe 1754-5; Secretary at War 1755-61, 1765-8; Chancellor of Exchequer 1761-2; Treasurer of Navy 1762-5; Joint Postmaster General Jan.-Apr. 1782. M.P. for Berwick-upon-Tweed 1746-54, Plymouth 1754-78.

Sedgwick, i, p. 439; *Gent. Mag.*, lxiii (1793), p. 187; no. 149; East, p. 381; Murrell & East, p. 351; G.E.C., i, p. 433.

**187**
**Wilkinson, James***

D. 10 July 1772(?). Ad. 27 Oct. 1750. Mar. Rebecca Millard 9 Oct. 1711. Bookseller, stationer. Overseer of Poor, Portsmouth, 1717, 1718; Turnpike Commissioner 1747. Churchwarden, St Thomas's, 1724; Presbyterian: trustee and subscriber, High Street Chapel, 1735.

*Lond. Mag.*, xli (1772), p. 345; nos 164, 167; East, p. 382; P.C.R.O. 381A/1/1; P.C.R.O. CF1/5, f. 17; P.C.R.O. 11A/1/88-90; B.L. Add. MS. 8153, f. 119; P.C.R.O. 257A/1/9/3; *Turnpike Minute Book*, p. 143.

**188**
**William Augustus, Duke of Cumberland**

Born 15 Apr. 1721; d. 31 Oct. 1765. Ad. 25 July 1739; hon. Third son of Geo. II and Caroline of Ansbach. Unmarried. Army officer: Col. of Coldstream Guards 1740, Maj.-Gen. 1742, Lieut.-Gen. 1743, Capt.-Gen. of British Forces 1745-57. Free Burgess of Newport, I.W., 1740. Bro. of Fred. Louis, Prince of Wales.

*D.N.B.*; no. 65; East, p. 381; Murrell & East, p. 350; N.B.A. 45/16b, p. 750.

**189**
**Wills, Sir Charles**

Bapt. 23 Oct. 1666; d. 25 Dec. 1741. Ad. 29 Sept. 1732 (not in Book of Original Entries). First son of Ant. and Jenofer or Guinevere. Unmarried. Army officer: Ensign, Col. Tho. Erle's Regiment of Foot, 1689, Capt., 19th Foot, 1691, Maj. 1694, Lieut.-Col. 1697, Col. 1705, Brig.-Gen. 1707, Maj.-Gen. 1709, Lieut.-Gen. 1715, Governor of Berwick-upon-Tweed 1715, Governor of Portsmouth 1718–20, Lieut.-Gen. of Ordnance 1718 to death, Gen. 1730, Gen. of Foot, 1739; Privy Councillor 1719. M.P. for Totnes 1718–41.

Sedgwick, ii, p. 547; P.R.O. W.O.46/7; East, p. 379; D.N.B.; East, p. 638; *Cal. T. B. & P. 1729–30*, p. 553.

**190**
**Winnington,**
**Thomas**

Born 31 Dec. 1696; d. 23 Apr. 1746. Ad. 18 June 1733. First son of Salwey and Anne, *née* Foley. Mar. Love, dau. of Sir James Reade, 2nd Bt, 6 Aug. 1719. Lord of Admiralty 1730–6; Lord of Treasury 1736–41; Cofferer of Household 1741–3; Paymaster-General 1743 to death; Recorder of Worcester by 1746. M.P. for Droitwich 1726–41, Worcester 1741 to death.

Sedgwick, ii, pp. 500–2; *Gent. Mag.*, xvi (1746), p. 222; no. 12; East, p. 380; D.N.B.

**191**
**Yorke, Philip,**
**1st Baron**
**Hardwicke**

Born 1 Dec. 1690; d. 6 Mar. 1764. Ad. 22 Aug. 1739; hon. Son of Phil. and Elizabeth, *née* Gibbon. Mar. Margaret, dau. of Cha. Cocks, 16 May 1719. Barrister 1715; Recorder of Dover 1718 to death; Solicitor-General 1720–4; Attorney-General 1724–33; Chief Justice of King's Bench 1733–7; Speaker, House of Lords, 1734, 1736; Lord Chancellor 1737–56; High Steward of Cambridge 1749 to death. M.P. for Lewes 1719–22, Seaford 1722–3, Nov. 1733. Father-in-law of Geo. Anson, 1st Baron Anson.

Sedgwick, ii, p. 569; no. 66; East, p. 381; Murrell & East, p. 350; G.E.C., vi, pp. 305–6.

**192**
**Young, Edward**

D. by 19 Sept. 1763. Ad. 7 June 1736. Commissioner of Taxes 1729–41. Free Burgess of Newport, I.W., 1733; Free Burgess of Yarmouth, I.W., 1733 (dismissed 1741). Client of Duke of Montagu.

P.C.R.O. CE1/14, p. 177; no. 35; East, p. 380; N.B.A. Class 2, Admissions 1717–1833; Y.T.T. Corporation Proceedings 1710–85, ff. 32, 49–51; Historical MSS. Commission, *MSS. of Lord Montagu of Beaulieu* (1900), p. 202; *Cal. T. B. & P. 1729–30*, p. 242; *Cal. T. B. & P. 1739–41*, p. 625.

# Appendix VI

Table of government contracts awarded to resident Aldermen and Burgesses 1731-1751

The information is taken from the following sources:

N.M.M. POR/F/5 (for 1732–8), 6 (for 1738–42), 7 (for 1742–6), 8 (for 1746–9), 9 (for 1751–4);

P.R.O. Adm.110/10 (for 1727–32), 11 (for 1732–9), 12 (for 1739–41), 13 (for 1741–4), 14 (for 1744–6) 15 (for 1746–9), 16 (for 1749–51);

P.R.O. W.O.55/1986 (for 1727–32), 1987 (for 1732–5), 1988 (for 1735–9), 1989 (for 1739–40), 1990 (for 1740–1), 1991 (for 1741–2), 1992 (for 1743–4), 1993 (for 1744–6), 1994 (for 1746–7), 1995 (for 1747–9), 1996 (for 1749–53).

Ald. = Alderman      D = Dockyard      F = Fleet      O = Ordnance

| Date | Contractor | Subject | Use |
|---|---|---|---|
| June 1732 | Dan. Smith (Ald.) | Painting ship's gun carriages | O |
| 29 June 1732 | Dan. Smith (Ald.) | Beer | F |
| 26 Nov. 1732 | John Vining (Ald.) | Charcoal, oak, 7 fir laths | D |
| 18 Feb. 1732/3 | John Vining (Ald.) | Purbeck scappled paving-stone for the Academy | D |
| Mar. 1733 | Dan. Smith (Ald.) | Painting ship's gun carriages | O |
| 1 June 1733 | Wil. Rickman (Ald.) | Portland block, ashlar stone for Plymouth Yard | D |
| 12 Aug. 1733 | Mic. Atkins (Ald.) | Timber | D |
| 3 Dec. 1733 | Wil. Rickman (Ald.) | Portland stone for Plymouth | D |
| Apr. 1734 | Tho. Bowerbank | Bricks for the Channel Is | O |
| 21 May 1734 | John Vining (Ald.) | Heart laths | D |
| 15 Aug. 1734 | Mic. Atkins (Ald.) | Timber; ash and oak knees | D |
| July 1734 | Henry Stanyford (Ald.) | Wagon for transporting arms | O |
| 31 Aug. 1734 | James White, on behalf of Mary Carter | Fir rafters | D |
| 30 Oct. 1734 | Wil. Rickman (Ald.) | Portland stone for Plymouth and Portsmouth | D |
| 10 Nov. 1734 | John Vining (Ald.) | Charcoal, slates | D |
| 15 Jan. 1734/5 | James White, on behalf of Mary Carter | Fir rafters | D |
| 26 Jan. 1734/5 | Tho. Appleford | Candles | D |
| 5 Apr. 1735 | John Vining (Ald.) | Charcoal | D |
| 4 June 1735 | John Vining (Ald.) | Sea mark at Ashey Down, I.W. | D |
| 15 Oct. 1735 | John Vining (Ald.) | Slates, laths | D |
| 28 Nov. 1735 | Tho. Bowerbank | Barrack bedding | O |

| Date | Contractor | Subject | Use |
|---|---|---|---|
| 20 Dec. 1735 | Tho. Till, on behalf of the Duke of Richmond | Beech plank | D |
| 18 Mar. 1735/6 | John Vining (Ald.) | Welsh culm | D |
| 26 Mar. 1736 | Wil. Rickman (Ald.) | Portland stone for Plymouth Yard | D |
| 5 Oct. 1737 | John Vining (Ald.) | Slates, laths, tiles | D |
| 1 Nov. 1737 | Wil. Green, on behalf of John Green | Tanner's wares | D |
| 28 Nov. 1737 | Tho. Appleford | Tallow candles | D |
| 20 Apr. 1738 | John Vining (Ald.), in succession to Elizabeth Tuggery | Tiles | D |
| 4 July 1738 | Tho. Stanyford | Axle-trees, trucks | O |
| 29 Nov. 1738 | Wil. Atkins | Elm and oak timber knees | D |
| 26 Apr. 1739 | Tho. Appleford | Candles | D |
| 16 Mar. 1739/40 | John Vining (Ald.) | Isle of Wight rubble and stone for North Dock basin | D |
| 26 Mar. 1740 | Wil. Rickman (Ald.) | Portland stone | D |
| 28 Apr. 1740 | Wil. Rickman (Ald.) | Small beer for the Dockyard smithy | D |
| 19 June 1740 | Wil. Rickman (Ald.) and others | Beer | F |
| 12 July 1740 | John Carter (Ald.) and James White, in succession to Mary Carter | Wainscot board | D |
| 30 Aug. 1740 | John Vining (Ald.) | Rape vinegar | D |
| 19 Sept. 1740 | Mr Stanyford | Fir planks, fir balks | O |
| 19 Sept. 1740 | Mic. Atkins (Ald.) | Fir planks, fir balks | O |
| 3 Oct. 1740 | Wil. Atkins | Elm and oak timber | D |
| 11 Mar. 1740/1 | Wil. Green, John Green and John Clements | Ballast, baskets, birch brooms | D |
| 24 Apr.–7 May 1741 | Wil. Rickman (Ald.) | Portland stone for Plymouth Yard | D |
| 14 June 1741 | John White (Ald.) | Timber | D |
| 12 Aug. 1741 | Wil. Rickman (Ald.) | Portland stone for Plymouth and Portsmouth | D |
| 22 Jan. 1741/2 | John Carter and James White | Dutch wainscot board | D |
| 1 July 1742 | Wil. Rickman (Ald.) | Pitch | D |
| 7 July 1742 | John White (Ald.) | Oak timber, plank, treenails | D |
| 2 Nov. 1742 | John Compton | Candles | D |
| 19 Mar. 1742/3 | Mic. Atkins (Ald.) | Block maker's wares | D |
| 13 July 1743 | Elizabeth Vining and Henry Friend, in succession to John Vining | John Vining's contracts as above | D |
| 8 Apr. 1744 | John Carter (Ald.), on behalf of Messrs Young, Green and Carter, all of Poole | Cable, cordage | D |
| 23 Apr. 1744 | John Compton | Tallow | D |

| Date | Contractor | Subject | Use |
|---|---|---|---|
| 23 July 1744 | Elizabeth Vining and Henry Friend | Lime (in lieu of culm 'on account of the French war') | D |
| 1 Feb. 1744/5 | John Compton | Candles | D |
| 18 Nov. 1745 | John Rickman, on behalf of Tho. Bryen and others | Portland stone | D |
| 28 Jan. 1745/6 | John Rickman | Portland stone | D |
| 28 Jan. 1745/6 | Mic. Atkins (Ald.) | Barrack bedsteads for Portchester Castle | O |
| 7 Mar. 1745/6 | Henry Friend | Slate, tiles | D |
| 4 June 1746 | John White (Ald.) | Timber knees | D |
| 2 July 1746 | Henry Friend | Plantation pitch | D |
| 26 Nov. 1746 | John White (Ald.) | Sloop (Sally) for use in the port | D |
| 10 Dec. 1746 | John Rickman | Brigantine (Molly) for transporting soldiers to Jersey and Guernsey | F? |
| 11 Dec. 1746 | John Compton | Candles | D |
| 11 Feb. 1746/7 | John Rickman | Train oil | D |
| Dec. 1747 | John White (Ald.) | Timber | D |
| 16 Jan. 1747/8 | Fra. Whithed | Timber | D |
| 27 Mar., 2 Apr. 1748 | John Rickman | Train oil | D |
| 29 Mar., 7 Apr. 1748 | John Compton | Candles | D |
| 3 June 1748 | John Rickman | Portland stone | D |
| 24 June 1748 | Mic. Atkins (Ald.) | Carriages for ships' guns | O |
| 23 May 1749 | John Rickman, on behalf of Tho. Bryen and others | Portland stone | D |
| 25 July 1750 | John Rickman | Portland stone for Plymouth Yard | D |
| Mar. 1750/1 | Henry Friend | Soap | O |

# Appendix VII

Table of Statutes referred to in the Introduction, notes and Appendices

For individual references see the Index, under Acts of Parliament. The titles of Acts down to 1714 are those given in *The Statutes of the Realm* (9v. and index, 1810–28); those of later Acts are from *The Statutes at large*. The years are those of the parliamentary sessions.

## PUBLIC ACTS

| | | |
|---|---|---|
| 1605–6 | 3 James I, c.4 | An Act for the better discovering and repressing of popish recusants. |
| 1673 | 25 Cha. II, c.2 | An Act for preventing dangers which may happen from popish recusants. |
| 1678 | 30 Cha. II, st.2, c.1 | An Act for the more effectual preserving the King's person and government by disabling papists from sitting in either House of Parliament. |
| 1708–9 | 7 Anne, c.26 | An Act for appointing Commissioners to treat and agree for such lands, tenements and hereditaments as shall be judged proper to be purchased for the better fortifying Portsmouth, Chatham and Harwich. |
| 1709–10 | 8 Anne, c.23 | An Act for vesting certain lands, tenements and hereditaments in trustees for the better fortifying and securing the harbours and docks at Portsmouth, Chatham and Harwich. |
| 1710–11 | 9 Anne, c.33 | An Act for repairing the highways from Sheet Bridge in the parish of Petersfield to the town of Portsmouth in the county of Southampton. |
| 1726 | 12 Geo. I, c.19 | An Act for enlarging the term granted by an Act passed in the 9th year of the reign of Her late Majesty Queen Anne, entitled An Act for repairing the highways from Sheet Bridge in the parish of Petersfield to the town of Portsmouth in the county of Southampton, and for making the said Act more effectual. |
| 1732 | 5 Geo. II, c.18 | An Act for the further qualification of Justices of the Peace. |
| 1740–1 | 14 Geo. II, c.43 | An Act to enable Thomas Smith, esq., lord of the manor of Farlington in the county of Southampton, to supply the town of Portsmouth and parts adjacent with good and wholesome water at his own proper costs and charges. |

| 1741–2 | 15 Geo. II, c.14 | An Act to explain and amend two Acts of Parliament, one made in the 9th year of Her late Majesty Queen Anne, entitled An Act for repairing the highways from Sheet Bridge in the parish of Petersfield to the town of Portsmouth in the county of Southampton, and another Act made in the 12th year of the reign of His late Majesty King George the First, for enlarging the term in and by the said Act granted and for other purposes therein mentioned, and for enlarging the term and powers by the said last-mentioned Act granted. |
| 1762–3 | 3 Geo. III, c.56 | An Act for the better paving of the streets and for preventing nuisances and other annoyances in the town of Gosport in the county of Southampton. |
| 1835 | 5 & 6 Wil. IV, c.76 | An Act to provide for the regulation of municipal corporations in England and Wales. |

# Appendix VIII

Concordance with other manuscripts

This concordance is designed to show which items in the Book of Original Entries also appear in the Election and Sessions Books (P.C.R.O. CE1/13, 14) or the Register of Grants (P.C.R.O. CF20/1).

| Book of Original Entries, no. | Other manuscript | Book of Original Entries, no. | Other manuscript | Book of Original Entries, no. | Other manuscript |
|---|---|---|---|---|---|
| 1 | CE1/13, p. 211 | 65 | CE1/13, p. 267 | 117 | CE1/14, p. 47 |
| 2 | CE1/13, p. 212 | 66 | CE1/13, p. 267 | 118 | CE1/14, p. 48 |
| 3 | CE1/13, p. 213 | 67 | CE1/13, p. 271 | 119 | CE1/14, p. 48 |
| 4 | CE1/13, p. 213 | 69 | CE1/13, p. 271 | 120 | CE1/14, p. 49 |
| 6 | CE1/13, p. 215 | 70 | CE1/13, p. 273 | 121 | CE1/14, p. 50 |
| 7 | CE1/13, p. 218 | 74 | CE1/13, p. 274 | 122 | CE1/14, p. 49 |
| 10 | CE1/13, p. 220 | 76 | CE1/14, p. 4 | 123 | CE1/14, p. 51 |
| 11 | CE1/13, p. 222 | 77 | CE1/14, p. 4 | 124 | CE1/14, p. 52 |
| 12 | CE1/13, p. 223 | 78 | CE1/14, p. 6 | 125 | CF20/1, p. 194 |
| 13 | CE1/13, p. 223 | 79 | CE1/14, p. 6 | 128 | CE1/14, p. 52 |
| 14 | CE1/13, p. 224 | 80 | CF20/1, p. 192 | 131 | CE1/14, p. 53 |
| 15 | CE1/13, p. 227 | 82 | CE1/14, p. 10 | 132 | CE1/14, p. 56 |
| 17 | CF20/1, p. 185 | 84 | CE1/14, p. 13 | 133 | CE1/14, p. 58 |
| 18 | CF20/1, p. 185 | 86 | CE1/14, pp. 15–16 | 134 | CE1/14, p. 59 |
| 20 | CE1/13, p. 232 | 88 | CF20/1, p. 192 | 136 | CE1/14, p. 59 |
| 21 | CF20/1, p. 186 | 89 | CF20/1, p. 193 | 138 | CE1/14, p. 60 |
| 22 | CF20/1, p. 187 | 90 | CE1/14, p. 17 | 140 | CE1/14, p. 64 |
| 23 | CF20/1, p. 186 | 91 | CF20/1, p. 193 | 141 | CE1/14, p. 66 |
| 24 | CE1/13, p. 232 | 93 | CE1/14, p. 20 | 142 | CE1/14, p. 68 |
| 25 | CE1/13, p. 41 | 94 | CE1/14, p. 21 | 143 | CE1/14, p. 69 |
| 28 | CF20/1, p. 189 | 95 | CE1/14, p. 21 | 144 | CF20/1, p. 195 |
| 29 | CE1/13, p. 240 | 96 | CE1/14, p. 23 | 145 | CF20/1, p. 195 |
| 32 | CE1/13, p. 242 | 97 | CE1/14, p. 24 | 146 | CE1/14, p. 73 |
| 33 | CE1/13, p. 242 | 98 | CE1/14, p. 28 | 148 | CE1/14, p. 75 |
| 35 | CE1/13, p. 247 | 100 | CE1/14, p. 28 | 149 | CE1/14, p. 76 |
| 36 | CF20/1, p. 190 | 101 | CE1/14, p. 32 | 150 | CE1/14, p. 76 |
| 38 | CF20/1, p. 190 | 102 | CE1/14, p. 33 | 151 | CE1/14, p. 76 |
| 39 | CF20/1, p. 162 | 103 | CE1/14, p. 33 | 153 | CE1/14, p. 79 |
| 42 | CE1/13, p. 248 | 104 | CE1/14, p. 33 | 154 | CE1/14, p. 79 |
| 44 | CE1/13, p. 254 | 105 | CE1/14, p. 34 | 155 | CE1/14, p. 81 |
| 47 | CE1/13, p. 255 | 106 | CE1/14, p. 34 | 157 | CF20/1, p. 196 |
| 48 | CE1/13, p. 255 | 107 | CE1/14, p. 35 | 161 | CF20/1, p. 196 |
| 49 | CF20/1, p. 190 | 108 | CE1/14, p. 35 | 162 | CE1/14, p. 84 |
| 56 | CF20/1, p. 191 | 109 | CE1/14, p. 38 | 164 | CE1/14, p. 86 |
| 57 | CE1/13, p. 264 | 110 | CE1/14, p. 40 | 165 | CE1/14, p. 87 |
| 58 | CF20/1, p. 191 | 113 | CF20/1, p. 193 | 166 | CE1/14, p. 87 |
| 59 | CE1/13, p. 266 | 114 | CF20/1, p. 194 | 167 | CE1/14, p. 87–8 |
| 63 | CE1/13, p. 266 | 115 | CE1/14, p. 45 | 168 | CE1/14, p. 88 |
| 64 | CE1/13, p. 267 | 116 | CF20/1, p. 194 | 169 | CE1/14, p. 88 |
|  |  |  |  | 172 | CF20/1, pp. 200–2 |

# Index

1 References to the Introduction are by pages, in roman numerals; all other references are to entry numbers.
2 No attempt is made to differentiate between persons bearing the same name, except where a person is identified by a description in italics.
3 Outside the vicinity of Portsmouth, place-names are normally entered under the parishes existing at the time of the record. Cross-references to these are given from the name of the county (for England and Wales) or country.
4 The following subject headings are used in the Index, as well as others to which cross-references are given: administration, local; administration, national; administration, private; aliens; antiquities; Army; articles of utility; arts; buildings and grounds; Church, clergy and religion; documents and diplomatic; drainage; education; fauna; flora; folklore and customs; food and drink; games and entertainments; industry and production; languages; law and justice; medicine; natural phenomena; Navy; political activity; science and learning; trade and commerce; transport and communications; war and rebellion.

Aldershot, *Hants.*, p. xxviii.

ale, *see* beer and ale.

aliens: French, pp. xxxvii, l; Spanish, p. l.

Allen (Alleyn, Allin), —, 112n.
    Arabella, App. V 168.
    Tho., App. IV 8.

Alverstoke, *Hants.*, 54n, App. V 45, 94, 108; *see also* Bury; Forton; Gosport; Haslar.

America, p. lv, App. V 126; *places indexed,* Annapolis; Canso; Georgia; Jamaica; Leeward Is., Louisburg; Newfoundland; New Hampshire; New York; Nova Scotia; Placentia; Port Royal; St Lucia; St Vincent; West Indies.

Amersham, *Bucks.*, App. V 69.

Amherst, Anne, App. V 1, 116.
    Elizabeth, App. V 1.
    Jeffery, App. V 1.
    John, *admiral*, 132, 169, App. V 1, 100, 116.

Amsterdam, *Netherlands*, p. lviii.

Andover, *Hants.*, p. xxxvii, App. V 108.

Andrews, Ann, App. V 2.
    Ric., pp. xxxiv, lixn, App. V 2.

Annapolis, *Nova Scotia*, p. xxv.

Anne, *Queen*, pp. xvii, xxiv, xxvii, xlv.

annuities: Consolidated annuities, p. xliv; South Sea Company, p. xliv.

Anson, Elizabeth (*née* Yorke), *Lady Anson*, App. V 3.
    Geo., *admiral, 1st Baron Anson*, pp. xxviii, l, liiin, liv–lv, lvii, no. 128, App. 1, App. V 3, 191.
    Isabella, App. V 3.
    Wil., App. V 3.

antiquities, *see* heraldry; seals; stamps.

Antwerp, *Netherlands*, App. V 17.

Appleford, Humf., App. V 4.
    Mary, App. V 4.
    Tho., pp. xxxiv, lvii, no. 164, App. V 4, App. VI.

apprenticeship: enforcement of Statute, p. xxxivn; apprentice to attorney, p. lxi; apprentice's absence, p. lxi.

architecture: description of Portsmouth Guildhall, p. xviii, App. I; construction of Guildhall, p. xlix, nos 40, 41, 45, 59, 68, 71, 72, 85; of Royal Naval Academy, p. xxii; of boat-houses, p. xxvn; porches, porticos, of houses, etc., 17, 19n, 39n, 72, 85, App. I; steps, 36, 38; stucco work, 68; *see also* building materials; occupations; windows.

Argyll, Duke of, *see* Campbell, John.

Arians, p. xlvi.

arms and armour: ammunition, App. I; battery, p. xvii; cannon, p. xxiin, App. I; firelock, p. xxii; gun-carriages and gun-stocks, pp. xxv, xxvi, xliii, App. II 1, App. VI; gunpowder, App. I.

Armstrong, Jane, App. V 107.

Army: Secretary at War, App. V 186; Paymaster-General of the Forces, App. V 190; Muster-Master General, p. xxviii, no. 121, App. V 69; state, cost, of Portsmouth Garrison, p. xxiii, App. I; relations between the Army and the town, pp. xx, xxiii, xxvii–xxx; barracks, p. xxiii;

barrack yard, p. xxiv; guardhouse, p. xxiv; magazine, p. xxv; stores, p. xxvii, App. VI.

— Governor of Portsmouth, pp. xx, xxiii, xxix, xxxix, xlvi, xlviii, lix, no. 79, App. I, App. V 85, 189; his position in the town, pp. xxvii–xxviii, lv; Lieut.-Governor, p. xxn; Town Major, p. xxviii, App. V 166; physician to the Garrison, pp. xxxvii–xxxix, l, lv.

— other garrisons and their commanders: Berwick-upon-Tweed, App. V 189; Gibraltar, p. xxv; Guernsey, App. V 179; Minorca, p. xxvi; Plymouth, App. V 98; St Lucia and St Vincent, App. V 117; Scarborough, App. V 168; Tilbury, App. V 179; Tower of London, App. V 98, 130; I. of Wight, App. V 117, 176.

— other officers, pp. xxn, xxviii, ln, lxi, nos 79, 131n, App. I, App. V 14, 17, 59, 76, 79, 85, 97, 98, 107, 117, 118, 150, 166, 171, 179, 188, 189; Barrack Master of the Savoy, App. V 54; regimental agent, paymaster, App. V 46.

— particular corps: Band of Gentlemen Pensioners, App. V 117, 179; Col. Tho. Erle's Regiment, p. xxxix, App. V 189; Coldstream Guards, App. V 188; Foot Guards, App. V 97; 2nd Foot Guards, App. V 98; Horse Guards, App. V 117, 179; Earl of Monmouth's Foot, App. V 171; Henry Mordaunt's Foot, App. V 171; 19th Foot, App. V 189; Royal Irish, App. V 59; Col. Wardour's Regiment of Invalids, App. V 166; company, regiment, of Foot at Portsmouth, pp. xxxix, lxi; *see also* Artillery.

— *see also* engineers; fortifications; occupations; Ordnance; War Office.

Arney, Mary, App. V 7.

Arnold, —, 31, 161.
    John, pp. xxx, xli, xliv, lviii, nos 1–5, 174, App. III, App. IV 12.
    Sarah, p. lviii.
    Wil., App. IV 9.

Arreton, *I.W.*: East Standen, p. xlvn.

articles of utility:
    axle trees, p. xliii.
    badge, p. xxxvi.
    ballast baskets, App. VI.
    ballot box, p. xxx.
    blocks, p. xxvi.
    bottle, App. I.
    buckets, p. xxiv.
    candles, p. xxvi, App. I, App. VI.
    cane, p. lxi.
    casks, p. xxv.
    net, App. II 1.
    piping, p. xxi.
    rivets, p. xxvin.
    ropes, pp. xxv, xxvi.
    sign-post, 43, 174.
    soap, p. xxiv, App. VI.
    tallow, p. xxvi, App. VI.
    tree nails, App. VI.
    trucks, p. xliii, App. VI.
    umbrella, p. xi.

vases, 72.

— *see also* arms and armour; bells; books; brass; bricks; carriages; carts and wagons; clocks and watches; cloth; clothes; coaches; coal; copper; flags; food and drink; furnishings; iron; jewels and plate; lead; lime; paper; parchment; ships' stores; slates; stones and quarries; tiles; tobacco; tools and implements; woods and timber.

Artillery, Royal, App. V 46.

arts, *see* architecture; diaries; engravings; epitaphs; music; obituaries; occupations; pamphlets; pictures; poetry; portraits; sermons; sculpture.

Arundel, *Suss.*, p. xxx.

Ashbourne, *Derb.*, pp. xxxvii, xl.

Ashey Down, *in Newchurch, I.W., see* Newchurch.

Assizes: for Hants., 135, 174.

Athy, *Ireland*, App. V 59.

Atkins (Attkins), Ann, App. V 6.

  Elizabeth, App. V 5.

  Jane, App. V 5, 6.

  Mary, App. V 173.

  Mic., pp. xx, xxvi, xxx, xxxvii, xxxviii, xl, xli, xliv, l, li, lvi, lvii, nos 29–41, 43, 44, 47–58, 60, 61, 63–67, 69, 73–85, 87–98, 100–109, 111, 114–117, 119, 125–132, 135–141, 143, 145, 148–153, 155, 156–158, 160, 163, 165, 174, App. III, App. IV 12, App. V 5, 6, 173, 182, App. VI.

  Sarah, App. V 182.

  Wil., 57, 82, 163n, 174, App. V 5, 6, 173, 182.

Attweek, Ric., App. IV 8.

Aubery, Ric., p. xxxin.

Auditors, *see* administration, local.

Augusta of Saxe-Gotha, *Princess of Wales*, App. V 62.

Austria, App. V 175.

Austrian Netherlands, *see* Netherlands, Austrian.

Aylesbury, Earls of, *see* Bruce.

Aylesford, Earl of, *see* Finch, Heneage.

Aylmer, Catharine, App. V 178.

  Sir Chr., *1st Bart*, App. V 178.

  Mat., *1st Baron Aylmer*, p. xxviii.

Ayres, Rebecca, App. V 124.

Bailey, *see* Bayly.

Baker, —, 18.

Bailiffs, *see* administration, local.

Ballard, Elizabeth, App. V 7.

  Mary, App. V 7.

  Rachel, App. V 7.

  Wil., 77, App. V 7.

Bangor, *Caerns.*, App. V 84.

banks: banknotes, 51; Bank of England, p. xliv.

Baptists, App. V 70, 184; meeting-house, minister, p. xlv; trustees, subscribers, of Orange St. Chapel, Portsea, App. V 70, 135, 158, 184; *see also* nonconformists.

Barlow, Geo., App. IV 8.

Barrington, Lords and Ladies, *see* Wildman.

Bartlett, John, App. IV 8.

  Elizabeth, App. V 57.

Wil., 83, 87, 111.

Barton, Edw., p. xlivn, nos 10, 67, 85n, 174, App. V 8, 9.

  Lewis, pp. xxvi, xxx, xli, xliv, xlvii, xlviii, nos 1–13, 15, 16, 18, 19, 22, 24–29, 31–34, 37–43, 47–55, 57–60, 62, 63, 68, 70–73, 76–119, 123–125, 127, 128, 130–132, 134–139, 142–145, 153, App. III, App. IV 12, App. V 8.

  Mary, App. V 8.

  Miriam, App. V 8.

  Tho., p. xlivn, nos 47, 174.

Bates, Mary, App. V 30.

Baverstock, Dan., App. IV 9.

Baxter, —, p. xlivn.

  John, 10, App. V 10.

Bayly, Geo., pp. lv, lvii, nos 10, 164, App. V 11, 12, 35.

  John, p. lvii, no. 164, App. V 11, 12, 35.

  Mary(?), App. V 12.

  Sarah, App. V 11.

  Tho., App. IV 8.

Beadles, *see* administration, local.

Beale, Step., App. IV 8.

Beauclerk, Cha., *1st Duke of St Albans*, App. V 13.

  Diana (*née* De Vere), *Duchess of St Albans*, App. V 13.

  Mary (*née* Chambers), *Lady Vere*, App. V 13.

  Vere, *1st Baron Vere*, p. lix, App. V 13.

Bedford, *Beds.*, p. xxxii, App. V 69.

Bedford, Dukes and Duchesses of, *see* Russell.

Bedfordshire, *place indexed*, Bedford.

Bedwyn, Great, *Wilts.*, App. V 29.

beer and ale: ale, App. I; beer, p. xxvi, App. VI; small beer, App. I, App. VI; suppliers of beer, pp. xxiv, xxv, App. V 53; discrepancy in supply, p. xxv; *see also* inns and public houses; occupations.

Belfield (Belfeild), Henry, pp. xxvi, xxviii–xli, xlvi, xlviii, nos 2, 3, 5–9, 11–14, 17, 22–32, 34, 37–42, 47, 116, 157.

Belle Île-en-Mer, *France*: battle of Belle Isle (1747), p. lv.

bells, pp. xxii, xxxvi.

Bennett, Bridget, *see* Wallop.

  Camilla (*née* Colville), *Countess of Tankerville*, App. V 14.

  Cha., *1st Earl of Tankerville*, App. V 14, 176.

  Cha., *2nd Earl of Tankerville*, 20, 174, App. V 14.

Benson, Edw., App. IV 9.

  Fra., 171, 172.

Bensted, *see* Binsteed.

Bere Forest, *Hants.*, App. V 185.

Bergavenny, Lord, *see* Nevill, Geo.

Berkeley, *Glos.*, p. xxxiiin.

Berkeley, Lord Geo., p. xxxvi.

Berkshire, App. V 13; *places indexed*, Windsor; Windsor Forest.

Berwick-upon-Tweed, *Northumb.*, p. xxxvii, no. 60n, App. V 186, 189.

Best, Sarah, App. V 174.

Bettesworth, Nic., App. IV 9.

Beven, Sam., p. xxxii, nos 1, 8, 73, 174, App. IV 4.
Bevis, Tho., App. IV 8.
Bingham, Ric., App. V 95.
Binsteed, Geo., p. xliii.
   Mary, App. V 15.
   Wil., p. lix, nos 10, 28, 38, 68, App. V 15.
Birch, Ric., 171, 172.
Bird, Anne, App. V 135.
   Elizabeth, p. xxxvin.
   Henry, App. IV 8.
   John, p. xxxvin.
birds: eagle, App. II 1–3; hawk, App. II 1, 2; heron, p. lvin, App. II 1; *see also* poultry.
Bishop's Waltham, *Hants.*, see Waltham, Bishop's.
Bissell, Cha., *Town Clerk of Portsmouth*, p. xlvi, no. 19, App. V 16.
   John, 19, 111, 164, 167, 174, App. V 16.
   Jos., 19.
   Mary, App. V 16.
Blackley, James, pp. xxxn, xxxviii, xli.
   Tho., p. lxi, no. 28.
Bladen, Elizabeth, App. V 75.
   Frances, App. V 17.
   Isabella, App. V 17.
   Martin, *soldier and politician*, 81, App. V 17, 75.
   Mary, App. V 17.
   Nat., App. V 17.
Blagden, Geo., App. IV 8.
Blanckley, Anne, App. V 18, 19.
   Stanyford, 162, App. V 18, 19.
   Tho., 33, 53, 174, App. V 18, 19.
Bliss, Ant., p. xlvi, no. 48.
Blose, Jos., App. IV 8.
Blundy(?), Rebecca, App. V 120.
Boldre, *Hants.*, p. xl.
Bolton, Dukes of, *see* Paulet.
Bolton (Boulton), Ann, App. V 6.
   John, App. IV 8.
   Mary, App. V 140.
Bond, John, App. IV 9.
bonds, 16, 27, 58, 62, 75, 83, 87, 88, 127, 130, 145.
books: law books, pp. xxxix, lxi, nos 137, 158, 174; shop books, 126; books belonging to Aldermen, p. xli; *see also* documents and diplomatic.
Borlase, Alicia, App. V 176.
Boston, *Lincs.*, p. xxxiv.
Bottom, Edw., App. IV 8.
Boulton, *see* Bolton.
Bowden, James, 171, 172, App. IV 9.
Bowerbank, Cathrine, App. V 20.
   Chr., p. xxviin.
   Tho., pp. xxviin, xxvii, xlix, nos 10, 45, App. V 20, App. VI.
Bowes, John, 36, 174.
Bowyer, Amos, 111.
Boxgrove, *Suss.*: Goodwood, pp. xlixn, lvn.
Boyes, John, App. IV 8.
Boyfield, Ric., 164, App. V 21.
Brading, *I.W.*, App. V 156; Sandown, p. xl.
Brady, Anne, App. V 22, 23, 25.
   Cha., 10, App. V 22–26.

Cuthbert, p. lixn, App. V 22–26.
   Elizabeth, App. V 24, 26.
   Jane, App. V 24.
   Matteate, 70, 174, App. V 22–26.
   Phil., 84, App. V 22–26.
   Rachel, App. V 26.
   Sam., pp. xxxiin, xxxvii, xli, xliv, xlvii, xlviii, l, lv, nos 1, 2–4, 6–30, 32–37, 39, 41, 43, 44, 46–53, 55–59, 61–72, 74–130, 132–134, 144n, App. III, App. IV 12, App. V 22–26.
Braithwaite, Mary, App. V 128.
Bramble, Ric., 161.
Brand, John, App. IV 4.
brandy shops, p. xviii.
brass: candlesticks, sconces, p. xlvi; *see also* occupations.
Brasted, Susan, App. V 67.
bread, pp. xxxix, xliii, nos 5, 39, App. I, App. II 1; contractors for, pp. xxv, xxvi, App. V 155; bake-house in Gosport, p. xxii; *see also* occupations.
Breda, *Netherlands*, App. V 118.
Brent, Joyce, App. V 169.
Brice, Hannah, App. V 108.
bricks, p. xxi, no. 172, App. I; *see also* occupations.
Bridger, Jos., App. IV 8.
bridges: drawbridges, pp. xx, xxiiin; *see also* Petersfield.
Bristol, *Glos.*, p. xxxin.
Bristol, Earl and Countess of, *see* Hervey.
British Library: Anson Papers, p. l; Newcastle Papers, p. l; Wager Papers, p. xlviii.
Brockenhurst, *Hants.*, p. xl.
Bromley, Jane, App. V 5, 6.
Brooke, Catherine, App. V 74–78.
   Pusey, p. l, no. 10, App. V 27.
   Walt., App. V 75.
Brouncker, —, 144.
Brown (Browne), James, 85n, App. IV 8.
   Rob., App. IV 8.
Bruce, Cha., *3rd Earl of Aylesbury*, App. V 97.
   Elizabeth, *see* Brudenell.
   Mary, *see* Lennox.
   Tho., *2nd Earl of Aylesbury*, App. V 28, 29.
Brudenell, Anne, App. V 29.
   Elizabeth, App. V 29.
   Elizabeth (*née* Bruce), *Countess of Cardigan*, App. V 28, 29.
   Geo., *3rd Earl of Cardigan*, App. V 28, 29.
   Geo., *4th Earl of Cardigan*, 35, App. V 28, 29, 117.
   James, p. lixn, App. V 28, 29.
   Mary (*née* Montagu), *Countess of Cardigan*, App. V 28.
Bryen, Tho., App. VI.
Buck, Mary, App. V 174.
Buckinghamshire, *place indexed*, Amersham.
Buckland, *on Portsea I., Hants.*, p. xxxiii, no. 144n, App. IV 9.
Bucknall, James, 164, 167, App. V 30.
   Jane, App. V 30.
   Mary, App. V 30.

G*

building materials: mud, p. xviii, App. I; stucco, 68; *see also* bricks; lead; lime; slates; stones and quarries; tiles; woods and timber.

buildings and grounds: outhouses, p. lx; stores, storehouses, pp. xviii, xx, xxviin, no. 39n; yards, 17, 173; costs of construction, pp. xxii, xxvn, xxxvi, lix; encroachments, 17, 19, 36, 38, 39, 56, 80, 91, 113, 114, 125, 126, 156; beach land, 18, 23, 28, 89, 116, 157; waste land, 21, 34, 144, 161, 171–173; *see also* architecture; brandy shops; bridges; building materials; cemeteries; charity; Church, clergy and religion; coffee-houses; fairs and markets; fences; fires; gardens; houses; inns and public houses; mortgages; occupations; rents; schools; shops; stables; wells; windows.

Bull, Tho., App. IV 9.

Burchett, Elizabeth, App. V 73.
  Josiah, App. V 73.

Burford, Edw., 7, 174, App. V 31, 35.
  Mary, App. V 31, 35.
  Sarah, App. V 31.

Burgeois (Burges), Henrietta, App. V 107.

Burgesses, *see* administration, local.

Burnet, Gilb., *Bishop of Salisbury*, p. xli.

Burrard, John, 100, 107, App. V 32.

Burton, Ric., App. V 133.

Bury, *in Alverstoke, Hants.*, 10.

Bury St Edmunds, *Suff.*, App. V 138.

Bussey, John, App. IV 9.

Butler, John, App. IV 8.
  Mary, App. V 8.
  Wil., p. l, App. IV 8.

Byng, Geo., *1st Viscount Torrington*, p. xxii, App. V 33.
  John, *admiral*, 134, App. V 33.
  Margaret (*née* Master), *Lady Torrington*, App. V 33.
  Rob., 22.

Cadiz, *Spain*, App. V 68.

Cadogan, Sarah, *see* Lennox.
  Wil., *1st Earl of Cadogan*, App. V 97, 98.

Caernarvonshire, *place indexed*, Bangor.

Calbourne, *I.W.*: Newtown, p. xxix.

Calshot Castle, *in Fawley, Hants.*, *see* Fawley.

Cambridge, *Cambs.*, p. xxxii; University, App. V 138, 191; Queens' College, p. xlvi; University Library, Cholmondeley (Houghton) manuscripts, pp. xxv–xxvii, xlviii, xlixn, no. 89n.

Cambridgeshire, *places indexed*, Cambridge; Wisbech.

Campbell, John, *2nd Duke of Argyll*, pp. xxviii, xlviii, xlix, liii, App. V 46, 56.
  Peter, *Lieut.-Governor of Portsmouth*, p. xxn.

Canso, *Nova Scotia*, p. xxv.

Capel, Charlotte, *see* Villiers.
  Wil., *3rd Earl of Essex*, App. V 175.

Cardigan, Earls and Countesses of, *see* Brudenell.

Carlos, Greg., 80, 174.

Carmarthen, *Carms.*, App. V 107.

Carmarthenshire, *place indexed*, Carmarthen.

Caroline of Ansbach, *Queen*, App. V 62, 188.

carriages, p. xli; *see also* coaches; occupations.

Carrier, Isabella, App. V 3.

Carter, —, App. VI.
  Dan., 164, App. V 34–37.
  Dorothy, App. V 36.
  John, pp. xxvi, xxxi, xxxviii, xxxix, xli, xliv, xlvii, l, liv–lvii, nos 10, 35, 36n, 99, 105, 107–125, 127–134, 136–138, 140–146, 148–150, 152–158, 160–170, 174, App. III, App. IV 11, 12, App. V 11, 31, 34–37, 135, App. VI.
  Jos., App. IV 7, 8.
  Mary, App. V 35, App. VI.
  Sarah, App. V 11, 35, 37.
  Susanna, App. V 34–37.
  Wil., 164, App. IV 8, App. V 34–37.

Carter family, pp. xxxviii, lvi, lviin.

carts and wagons: wagons, p. ln; *see also* articles of utility; occupations.

Cathray, Desborow, p. xxvii.

cattle, App. I; cattle trade, p. xxxv.

Cavendish, Phil., pp. xlviii, xlix, li–livn, nos 41, 81n.

cemeteries: burial ground, 172.

censuses: Compton Census, p. xlv.

Chamberlains, *see* administration, local.

Chambers, Mary, *see* Beauclerk.
  Tho., App. V 13.

Champneys, Elizabeth, p. liii, App. V 114, 115.
  Ric., p. liii, no. 164, App. V 38, 114, 115.

Chancery: decree, p. lxi; enrolment of charters, p. xxix.

Chandler, Elizabeth, App. V 39, 40.
  Rachel, App. V 7.
  Sam., pp. xxx, xxxvii, xli–xliii, xlvii, xlix, liv, lvii, nos 99, 105, 107, 108, 110–119, 121–146, 148–150, 152, 153, 155–157, 160–170, 174, App. III, App. IV 12, App. V 39, 40.

Channel, English, *see* English Channel.

Channel Is, *places indexed*, Guernsey; Jersey.

Chappell, Elizabeth, App. V 49.

charity: charitable gifts by Corporation, p. xxxvi; by Aldermen, pp. xx, xxxix, xliv–xlv; almshouse, p. xx; bequests to the poor, pp. xxxix, xlixn; gifts to St Thomas's Church, pp. xxxix, xlvi; bequest to Orange St. Chapel, p. xlv.

Charles V, *Holy Roman Emperor*, p. xli.

Charles, James, App. IV 9.

Charles I, *King*, pp. xxxiv, xxxv, nos 1, 55, 135, 174, App. III.

Charles II, *King*, p. xxix.

Charlotte of Mecklenburg, *Queen*, p. xxxn.

Charlton, *in Singleton, Suss.*, *see* Singleton.

Charminster, *Dors.*: Wolfeton, App. V 171.

Chatham, *Kent*, pp. xviiin, xxii, App. V 107, 174, App. VII.

cheese, App. I.

Cheesman, James, App. IV 8.

Chetwynd, Walt., p. xxxn.

Chichester, *Suss.*, pp. xxviin, lv, no. 164, App. V 11, 14, 39, 59, 98, 112, 161, 170; West Sussex Record Office, Goodwood manuscripts, pp. xlix, livn, lv, lvi.

Child (Childe), Sir Caesar, *2nd Bart*, App. V 44.
  Cha., 114, 174.
  Elizabeth, App. V 44.

Chitty, Henry, App. IV 9.

Church, clergy and religion: Dissolution of monasteries, p. xx; latitudinarian views, p. xlvi; test against transubstantiation, 3, 6, 11, 13, 29, 32, 99, 105, 123, 129, 153, 155; appointment and character of Portsmouth clergy, p. xlvi, App. I; church furnishings and repairs, pp. xxxix, xlvi; Corporation pew, pp. xlvi, lvii, nos 170, 174; action against perturbation of seat, 147, 158, 159; foundation of St George's, Portsea, p. xx, nos 171, 172, App. V 63, 113.

— clergy: Archbishop of Canterbury, p. xli; Bishop of Bangor, App. V 84; of Hereford, App. V 84; of Salisbury, App. V 84; of Winchester, 147, 159, 171, App. V 84; Dean and Chapter of Christ Church, Oxford, p. xlvn; of Winchester, App. V 132; of Windsor, p. xlvi; Rector of Crawley with Hunton, App. V 167; of St Peter le Poor, London, App. V 84; of Ovington, App. V 167; of Streatham, App. V 84; Vicar of Portsmouth, p. xlvi, App. V 167; of Weyhill, p. xxviin; royal chaplain, App. V 84; others, App. II 2, App. V 84, 143.

— Churchwardens and sidesmen: of St Mary's, Portsea, App. V 67, 116, 126; of St Thomas's, Portsmouth, App. V 5, 7, 15, 16, 30, 49, 57, 89, 94, 110, 187; of St James's, Yarmouth, App. V 142.

— *see also* Acts of Parliament; Arians; Baptists; cemeteries; censuses; charity; Congregationalists; Consistory Court; epitaphs; funerals; nonconformists; Presbyterians; sermons.

Churchill, John, *1st Duke of Marlborough*, App. V 117.
  Mary, *see* Montagu.

Chute, Ant., p. xlviin, no. 15, App. V 41, 42.
  Edw., App. V 41, 42.
  Fra., *Recorder of Portsmouth*, pp. xxxi, lix, nos 98, 99, 110, 118, 174, App. IV 1, App. V 41, 42.
  Katharine, App. V 41, 42.

Civil Wars (1642–51), p. xxxiv.

Clancarty, Earl of, *see* MacCarthy, Donough.

Clapham, Ric., p. xxxii, no. 28, App. IV 4.

Clarendon, Earl and Countess of, *see* Villiers.

Clarke, Geo., 164, 168, App. V 43.
  Saul, p. xli.

Clements, John, App. VI.
  Mary, App. V 85.

Clement's Inn, *see* Inns of Court.

clergy, *see* Church, clergy and religion.

Clerks of the Market, *see* administration, local.

Clerks of the Peace, *see* administration, local.

Cleversley, Jane, App. V 148.

Clevland, Anne, App. V 44.
  Elizabeth, App. V 44.
  John, *Secretary of the Admiralty*, pp. lviii, lvii, nos 150, 151, 160, App. V 44.
  Sarah, App. V 44.
  Wil., App. V 44.

Clinch, Edw., 10, App. V 45.

clocks and watches: watches, pp. xl, xli.

cloth: silk, App. I; velvet, p. xlvi, App. I; black cloth, p. lvii, no. 170; green broad cloth, 85n; *see also* occupations.

clothes: women's clothes, App. I; mourning clothes, p. xxxix; mayoral robes, p. xli; Corporation officers' uniforms, p. xxix; gloves, App. I; shoes, App. I; *see also* household, royal; occupations.

Clungeon, James, App. IV 8.

coaches, p. xxxvi; *see also* carriages.

coal: coal trade, p. xxxv; charcoal, p. xxiv, App. VI; culm, p. xxiv, App. VI.

Cobden, —, 144.

Cockburne, James, 10, App. V 46.

Cocks, *see* Cox.

coffee-houses, p. xviii, App. II 3.

Cofferers, *see* administration, local.

Colby(?), Anne, App. V 22, 23, 25.

Cole, Wil., App. IV 9.

Coleman, Mary, App. V 15.

Coles, Elizabeth, App. V 153.
  Ric., 171, 172.

Collins, Cha., App. IV 8.
  Euphonia, App. V 47.
  Jos., 164, 168, App. V 47.

Colliss (Collis), Cornelius, pp. xxx, xxxix–xli, xliv, xlvi–xlviii, nos 11–42, 44, 46–48, 50–114, 116, 118–124, 127, 174, App. III, App. IV 12, App. V 48.
  Elizabeth, p. xl.
  Sarah, App. V 48.

Colville, Camilla, *see* Bennett.
  Edw., App. V 14.

Combe, Mat., App. V 112.
  Susan, App. V 112.

commerce, *see* trade and commerce.

Common Pleas, Court of: attorney of Common Pleas, p. lx, no. 39n.

communications, *see* transport and communications.

Compton, Elizabeth, App. V 49.
  John, p. lvii, nos 161, 164, 167, 174, App. V 49, App. VI.

Congregationalists: minister at Andover and Fareham, p. xxx, App. V 39; *see also* nonconformists.

Consistory Court: at Winchester, 147, 158, 159, 174.

Constables, *see* administration, local.

Conyers, Sir Cha., *2nd Bart.*, App. V 169.
  Julia, App. V 169.

Cook, Rob., 28n.

Coote, Mary, *see* Stewart.
  Ric., *1st Baron Coote of Coloony*, App. V 164.

copper: plate, 59n; rivets, p. xxviin; *see also* brass.

Corbett, Eleanor, App. V 50.
  Tho., *Secretary of the Admiralty*, p. lviii, no. 12, App. V 50.
  Wil., App. V 50.

Corbin, Nic., App. IV 8.

Felton, Elizabeth, *see* Hervey.
  Sir Tho., *Bart*, App. V 82.
fences: fences, pales, palisades, pp. xvii, xxi,
  nos 17, 19n, 38, 39n, 56, 91, 161, 172; iron rails,
  85; walls, p. xxi, no 172.
Field, Rob., App. IV 8.
Fielding, *see* Feilding.
Filleul, Mary, App. V 73.
Finch, Anne, *see* Legge.
  Ann (*née* Hatton), *Countess of Winchilsea*, App.
    V 58.
  Dan., *7th Earl of Winchilsea*, App. V 58.
  Dan., *8th Earl of Winchilsea*, 104, App. V 58.
  Frances (*née* Feilding), *Countess of Winchilsea*,
    App V 58
  Heneage, *1st Earl of Aylesford*, App. V 96.
  Mary (*née* Palmer), *Countess of Winchilsea*,
    App. V. 58.
Findon, *Suss.*, p. xl.
fires, p. xxiv, App. I.
fish: gudgeon, App. II 1, 3; oysters, p. xxxiiin;
  trout, App. II 1, 3; fishing, p. xxxiiin; fish
  market, 163.
Fisher, Step., App. IV 9.
Fitchett, Elizabeth, App. V 156.
Fitzgerald, Emilia (*née* Lennox), *Duchess of Leinster*,
  p. xlixn, App. V 59.
  James, *20th Earl of Kildare and 1st Duke of
    Leinster*, p. xxviii, no. 136, App. V 59.
  Mary (*née* O'Brien), *Countess of Kildare*, App. V
    59.
  Rob., *19th Earl of Kildare*, App. V 59.
flags, p. xlviii, no. 64n; flagstaff, p. xxv.
Fleet, Wil., 171, 172.
flora: seeds, App. II 1; *see also* corn; food and
  drink; gardens; woods and timber.
Foche, Frances, App. V 17.
Foley, Anne, App. V 190.
folklore and customs, *see* myths; Saturn.
Fontaine, de la, *see* De la Fontaine.
food and drink, pp. xlii, l; Corporation feasts,
  p. xxxvi, no. 64n; biscuits, pp. xxv, xxvi;
  brandy, p. xliv; cakes, App. I; chocolate, App. I;
  cider, p. xxiiin; coffee, App. I; gin, App. I;
  herbs, App. II 1; liquors, App. I; meat, p. xxxv,
  App. I; peas, p. xxiv; rum, p. xliv; salt, pp. xxiv,
  xxvi; tea, App. I; vegetables, p. xxxivn;
  vinegar, p. xxivn, App. VI; *see also* beer and ale;
  brandy shops; bread; cheese; coffee-houses;
  corn; fish; inns and public houses; occupations;
  poultry; water; wine.
fortifications: at Portsmouth, pp. xvii–xviii, no. 66n,
  App. I, App. VII; at Gosport, App. I; *see also*
  bridges; Portsmouth.
Forton, *in Alverstoke, Hants.*, p. xxviin; Hospital,
  pp. xxii, l, lv.
Foster, James, *divine*, p. xli.
  Rob., App. IV 9.
foxes, App. II l; *see also* hunting.
Fox, Christian, App. V 167.
  Fra., App. V 167.

France, App. V 65, 97, 98, 150, 151, App. VI;
  Treasurer-General of the Marine, App. V 151;
  *places indexed*, Belle Île-en-Mer; Paris; Rochelle,
  La.
Franckland, Diana, App. V 60.
  Sarah, App. V 60.
  Sir Tho., *2nd Bart*, App. V 60.
  Sir Tho., *3rd Bart*, 12, 174, App. V 60.
Francklin, Mic., 164, App. V 61.
Franklin(?), Rebecca, App. V 66.
Frankville, *see* Newtown.
Fraser, Simon, *11th Lord Lovat*, p. xliii.
Frederick Augustus, *Duke of York and Albany*, App.
  V 28.
Frederick Louis, *Prince of Wales*, p. lviii, nos 92,
  170, App. V 14, 62, 188.
Freeman, —, 39n.
  Margaret, *see* West.
Friend, Henry, pp. xxiv, li, nos 164, 167, 171, 172,
  App. V 63, App. VI.
  Mary, App. V 63.
Fripp, *see* Phripp.
Frith, Jos., App. IV 9.
Fry, John, App. IV 8, 9.
Fuller, John, 22, App. V 107.
  Millicent, App. V 107.
funerals, p. xlv, no. 52n.
Furmidge, Fra., App. IV 9.
furnishings: beds, pp. xviii, xxii, xxvii, App. VI;
  carpet, 85; cushions, p. xlvi, no. 85; desks,
  p. xlvi, no. 126; seats, 147, 158, 159, 170, 174;
  tables, p. xxxix, no. 85; *see also* brass; occupations.
furs: beaver skins, p. xxvi; fur trade, p. xxvi.


Gale, John, App. IV 9.
games and entertainments: Corporation feasts,
  p. xxxvi, no. 64n; unspecified entertainments,
  p. ln; *see also* hunting; occupations.
Gard, du, *see* Du Gard.
gardens, pp. li, lx, nos 17, 21.
Gardner, Jos., p. xlviiin, no. 10, App. V 64.
  Margaret, App. V 64.
Garrett, Dan., App. IV 8.
  Kilbury, 21.
Gashry (Gascherie), Fra., 74, App. V 65, 68.
  Martha, App. V 65.
  Susanna, App. V 65.
Gateshead, *co. Dur.*, p. xxxv.
Gattrell, Tho., 28.
Gawler, John, 154, App. V 66.
  Rebecca, App. V 66.
George I, *King*, pp. xxi, xxxn, xlv.
George II, *King*, p. xxii, no. 147, App. I, App. V
  58, 62, 188.
George III, *King*, p. xxxn, App. V 29.
George IV, *King*, App. V 28.
Georgia, *America*, App. V 137.
Germany, *places indexed*, Aachen; Dettingen;
  Prussia.
Gibbon, Elizabeth, App. V 191.
Gibbs, Mary, App. V 17.

Tho., App. IV 9.

Gibraltar, pp. xxv, xxvi, App. V 18, 137.

Gibson, Edmund, *Bishop of London*, p. xlvi.
Sir John, *Lieut.–Governor of Portsmouth*, pp. xxviii, xlvi.

Gilbert, Jos., App. IV 8.

Gill, Tho., 171, 172.

Glamorgan, App. V 107.

Gloucestershire, 66; *places indexed*, Berkeley; Bristol.

Godden, Geo., App. IV 9.

Godman, Geo., App. IV 8.

Godmanchester, *Hunts.*, App. V 118.

Godshill, *I.W.*: Whitwell, p. xl.

Godwin, Rob., 10, App. V 67.
Sarah, App. V 67.
Susan, App. V 67.

Goldsworthy, Burrington, 10, App. V 65, 68.
Martha, App. V 65.
Philippia, App. V 68.

Gomme, de, *see* De Gomme.

Good, John, App. IV 9.

Goodeve, James, p. xxxiii, App. IV 10.
John, App. IV 8.

Goodwood, *in Boxgrove, Suss.*, *see* Boxgrove.

Gordon, John, App. IV 9.

Gore, Mary, App. V 69.
Tho., *Commissary General of Musters*, p. xxviii, no. 121, App. V 69.
Sir Wil., App. V 69.

Gosport, *in Alverstoke, Hants.*, pp. l, liii, lvi, lxin, nos 91, 114, App. V 105, 113, 135, 152, 158, App. VII; Carver's Wharf, p. liiin; Clarence Yard, pp. xxii, xxiv, App. V 152; Priddy's Hard Ordnance Depot records, p. xliv; state of fortifications, App. I.

Gother, Jane, App. V 112.

Goven, James, 174.
John, pp. xxxvin, xlvi, nos 147, 158, 159.

Gover, Peter, App. IV 9.

Gower, Earl, *see* Leveson-Gower, John.

Gower, Wil., App. IV 9.
— *see also* Leveson-Gower.

Graham, —, p. xliiin.

Grampound, *Cornw.*, App. V 179.

Grant, Mary, App. V 102.
Peter, App. IV 9.

Great Bedwyn, *Wilts.*, *see* Bedwyn, Great.

Green, —, App. VI.
Elizabeth, App. V 70.
Jane, App. V 162, 163.
John, App. VI.
Paul, 62, 127, 130.
Wil., 164, 168, App. V 70, App. VI.

Greenwich, *Kent*, p. xlix; Royal Naval College, p. xxii; Hospital, App. V 170; *see also* National Maritime Museum.

Griffin, Elizabeth, *see* Wallop.
James, *2nd Baron Griffin*, App. V 176.

Grigg, Dan., p. xxxiii, App. IV 6.
Henry, App. IV 6.
Rob., 38, 174.

Wil., App. IV 8.

Gringo, John, p. liii.

Gristock, Emanuel, App. IV 8.

Grossmith, Wil., 171, 172.

Grove, Hugh, pp. xxxii, xxxvi, nos 19, 31, 50, 73, 81n, App. IV 3.

Grover, Dan., 39n.

Guernsey, *Channel Is*, App. V 179, App. VI.

Gulston, Jos., p. lvn.

Haddock, Elizabeth, App. V 71, 72.
Frances, App. V 71.
Nic., *admiral*, 25, 174, App. V 71, 72.
Sir Ric., App. V 71, 72.
Ric., *Controller of the Navy*, 22, 30, 174, App. V 71, 72.

Hague, The, *Netherlands*, p. lvn.

Hain, Jos., App. IV 8.

Halsey (Hallsey), Henry, App. IV 8.

Hammond (Hamond), Anne, App. V 180–182, 184.
Geo., App. IV 9.
Mary, App. V 127.

Hampshire, pp. xxxi, xl, ln, App. V 27, 32, 35, 52, 114, 130, 135, 154, 176, 185; *see also* administration, local; Assizes; *places indexed*, Aldershot; Alverstoke; Andover; Bere Forest; Boldre; Brockenhurst; Bury; Cosham; Crawley; Droxford; Fareham; Fareham Creek; Farlington; Fawley; Forton; Gosport; Haslar; Havant; Hayling I.; Kilmeston; Lymington; New Forest; Ovington; Penton Grafton; Petersfield; Portchester; Portsea I.; Portsmouth; Portsmouth Harbour; Romsey; Sherborne St John; Soberton; Southampton; Southwick; Spithead; Stockbridge; Stoneham, South; Titchfield; Warblington; Waltham, Bishop's; Wickham; Winchester; Worthy, Martyr; Wymering.

Hancock, Tho., 111.

Hanway, Jonas, *philanthropist*, p. xvii.
Tho., p. lxi.

Harbour Masters, *see* administration, local.

Hardwicke, Earl and Countess of, *see* Yorke.

Hardy (Le Hardy), Sir Cha., *admiral (d. 1744)*, 96, App. V 73.
Elizabeth, App. V 73.
Mary, App. V 73.
Phil., App. V 73.

Harley, Rob., *statesman, 1st Earl of Oxford*, p. xxviii.

Harmond, Elizabeth(?), App. V 131.
Wil., App. V 131.

Harris, Jane, App. V 132.
Sir Ric., App. V 132.

Hart (Heart), Rob., p. xxviin, nos 22, 80n.

Hartman, John, App. IV 8.

Harvey, *see* Hervey.

Harwich, *Essex*, p. xviiin, App. V 60, 133, 159, App. VII.

Haslar, *in Alverstoke, Hants.*: Haslar Hospital, pp. xxii, l, li, no. 80n.

Hastings, *Suss.*, App. V 29.

Hastings, Henry, p. xliiin.
   Theophilus, *9th Earl of Huntingdon*, p. xliiin.
Hattam, John, 161.
Hatton, Anne, *see* Finch.
   Chr., *1st Viscount Hatton*, App. V 58.
Havant, *Hants.*, p. xlin, App. V 2, 95.
Hawke, Catherine, App. V 74–78.
   Cassandra (*née* Turner), *Lady Hawke*, App. V 77.
   Chaloner, 164, App. V 74–78.
   Sir Edw., *admiral, 1st Baron Hawke*, pp. lv–lvii, nos 142, 143, 153, 155, 164, 174, App. I, App. II, App. V 17, 74–78.
   Edw., 164, App. V 74–78.
   Elizabeth, App. V 75.
   Mar. Bladen, *2nd Baron Hawke*, 164, App. V 74–78.
   Wil., 164, App. V 74–78.
Hawkins, John, App. IV 8.
Hayling I., *Hants.*, p. xxxin.
Haywards, *see* administration, local.
Heart, *see* Hart.
Hedges, Sir Cha., *politician and lawyer*, p. xviin.
Hedon, *Yorks.*, *E. R.*, App. V 3, 42.
Hellyer, John, App. IV 9.
Henley, Sarah, App. V 123.
heraldry: Portsmouth armorial crest, p. xviii; armorial watermark, p. lviii; grant of arms, p. xxxix; *see also* flags.
Hereford, *Herefs.*, App. V 84.
Herefordshire, *places indexed*, Hereford; Ludlow; Weobley.
Herne, Judith, *see* Villiers.
Heron, Alice, App. V 79.
   Anne, App. V 79–81.
   Ben., 69, 131, 174, App. V 79, 81.
   Frances, p. xxxviii, App. V 80, 81.
   John, p. xlixn, no. 164, App. V 80, 81.
   John Vining, pp. xxxviii, lvin, nos 126, 164, 167, 174, App. V 79–81, 94.
   Mary, App. V 79.
   Pat., App. V 79, 81.
Herring, John, App. IV 8.
Hervey, Elizabeth, App. V 82.
   Elizabeth (*née* Felton), *Countess of Bristol*, App. V 82.
   John, *1st Earl of Bristol*, p. xxxiv, App. V 82.
   Wil., pp. xxxiv, lixn, App. V 82.
Hewett, John, 164, 168, App. V 83.
   Sarah, App. V 90.
   Tho., App. V 83.
Hewson, *see* Huson.
Hibberd, John, App. IV 9.
Higgins, Frances, App. V 113.
Higgs, Ric., App. IV 11.
High Constables, *see* administration, local.
Hill, Tho., pp. xlix, lvi.
Hillyer, *see* Hellyer.
Hilsea, *on Portsea I., Hants.*: Hilsea Barracks, p. xxiiin.
Hinchingbrooke, Lord and Lady, *see* Montagu.

Hoadly, Ben., *Bishop of Winchester*, p. xlvi, nos 48, 147, 159, App. V 84.
   Martha, App. V 84.
   Mary, App. V 84.
   Sam., App. V 84.
   Sarah, App. V 84.
Hodges, D. R., p. xlin.
Hodgkin, Wil., 145, 174, App. IV 8.
Hodgson, James, App. IV 9.
Hogarth, Wil., *artist*, p. xlin.
Holland, *see* Netherlands.
Holles, *see* Pelham-Holles.
Honywood, Cha. Ludovic, App. V 85.
   Mary, App. V 85.
   Sir Phil., *Governor of Portsmouth*, pp. xxviii, lv, no. 79, App. V 85.
Hood, Sam., 164, App. V 86.
   Sam., *admiral, 1st Viscount Hood*, p. xxxviii.
   Susanna (*née* Linzee), *Baroness Hood*, p. xxxviii, App. V 86.
Hooke, Edm., 4, App. V 87.
Hooker, Edw., 159.
Horace (Q. Horatius Flaccus), *poet*, App. II 3.
horses, pp. xviiin, xxxv, xli, ln, lvn; teams, pp. xxiv, li; *see also* coaches; household, royal; stables.
Horsfill, Wil., App. IV 8.
Horton, Wil., App. II 1, 3.
Horwood, Wil., App. IV 9.
House, Geo., App. IV 8.
household, royal: Gentleman of Bedchamber, App. V 58; Lord of Bedchamber, App. V 14, 97; Master of Buckhounds, App. V 14; Treasurer of Chamber, App. V 159; Cofferer of Household, App. V 190; Deputy Cofferer, App. V 29; Controller, App. V 58; Master of Horse, App. V 28; Keeper of Privy Purse, App. V 29; Master of Robes, App. V 29; Governor of Royal Princes, App. V 28; Treasurer, App. V 179; Master of Great Wardrobe, App. V 117, 186.
houses: in general, in Portsmouth, pp. xviii, xx, liii, lx, lxi, no. 89; elsewhere, p. xl; particular houses, messuages, in Portsmouth and Portsea, pp. xxv, xxviii, xxxvi, xxxix, lvn, lvi, lvii, nos 3, 10, 17, 28, 36, 38, 39n, 43, 48, 56, 66n, 80, 91, 111, 113, 114, 116, 125, 126, 129, 155–157, 161, 164–166, 169, 173, 174.
Howard, —, 111n.
   Dan., App. IV 9.
Howe (How), John, App. IV 8.
   Mary, App. V 79.
Howland, Elizabeth, *see* Russell.
   John, App. V 150.
Howlett, Ric., App. IV 8.
Hughes, Elizabeth, App. V 170.
   Ric., *Navy Board resident Commissioner at Portsmouth*, pp. xxx, xxxiin, xxxivn, xxxix, li–liv, nos 22, 75.
Hugley, Laramore, App. IV 8.
Hugony, John, App. IV 7, 8.
Huish, Barbara, App. V 88.
   Geo., *Town Clerk of Portsmouth (d. 1747)*, pp.

Larcum, Elizabeth, App. V 170.
  Wil., App. V 170.
La Rochelle, *France, see* Rochelle, La.
Laugharne, Mary, App. V 93.
  Ric., 164, 167, App. V 93.
Lavant, *Suss.*: East Lavant, App. V 112.
law and justice: actions, against Mayor, 5, 39;
  against Sergeants-at-Mace, 39; for arrears of
  quit rent and capon money, 111; for arrears of
  town rents, 39n; for obstruction, 52, 54, 174;
  for recovery of local customs rates and dues,
  26n, 111, 159; Blackley and Huish v. Leeke and
  Hanway, p. lxin; Huish v. Varlo, p. xxxixn;
  Portsmouth Corporation v. Goven, pp. xxxvi,
  xlvin, nos 147, 158, 159; Rex v. Solgard, pp.
  xxxvi, liii, no. 52n; Toll v. Pigott and others,
  135.
— judges and law officers: Lord Chancellor, 66,
  174, App. V 191; Chief Justice of King's Bench,
  App. V 191; Chief Justice in Eyre, App. V 28,
  176; Chief Baron of Exchequer, 44, 174, App. V
  138; other judges, 24, 174, App. V 113, 138,
  169; Attorney-General, App. V 191; Solicitor-
  General, p. xxxi, no. 52n, App. V 169, 191.
— other lawyers: master extraordinary in Chancery,
  p. lxi; sergeants at law, pp. xxxvii, xli–xliii,
  l–li, App. V 138, 161, 169; other barristers,
  p. xxxi, nos 118, 119, App. V 42, 113, 132, 191;
  attorneys, pp. xxx, xli–xliii, lx, lxin, no. 39n,
  App. II 2, App. V 7, 16, 39, 66, 93, 122, 182;
  proctor, syndic, 147, 158n, 159; notary public,
  147; Solicitor to the Queen, p. xxxin; to the
  Board of Ordnance, p. xliii, App. V 161;
  Counsel to Cambridge University, App. V 138;
  lawyers as members of Portsmouth Corporation,
  pp. xlii–xliii.
— Portsmouth courts, p. xxxiv, no. 59n; Court
  Leet, pp. xxix, xxxii, nos 39, 59n, 174; Court of
  Pie Powder, p. xxixn; Court of Record, pp.
  xxix, xxxii, no. 67n; Coroner's Inquest, 52;
  Leet jury, pp. xxix, xxxiii, xxxv; Leet jurors,
  App. V 7, 15, 49, 67, 110, 120, 153, 155; other
  juries, p. xxxii; court fees, p. xxx.
— other courts, *see* Admiralty; Assizes; Chancery;
  Common Pleas; Consistory Court; Exchequer;
  King's Bench; Petty Sessions; Quarter Sessions.
— sentences: death, 34n, App. V 33; amerce-
  ments, fines, pp. xxix, xxx, xxxv, xxxvi, li, nos
  39, 112, 174, App. V 9, 89, 94; expulsion from
  Parliament, p. xxv; dismissal, p. l, App. V 82,
  107.
— *see also* Acts of Parliament; administration,
  local; crimes; documents and diplomatic; Inns
  of Court; Justices of the Peace; prisons; wills;
  writs.
lead, pp. xxiv, liii.
leases: of Corporation property, pp. xxxv, lix, nos
  17, 18, 21–23, 28, 34, 36, 38, 56n, 80, 89, 91,
  113, 114, 116, 125, 126, 144, 156, 157, 161,
  172–174; of dung and soil, 5; counterparts of
  leases, 1n, 22, 36n, 46, 58, 83, 87, 88, 145;

surrender of leases, 28, 56, 87.
Lee, Jos., 171, 172.
  Rob., App. IV 8.
Leeds, *Yorks., W.R.,* p. xxx.
Leeke, Elizabeth, App. V 94.
  Frances, App. V 80, 81.
  John, pp. xxxvii, xxxviii, xl–xlii, xliv, xlvin,
    lvii, lxi, nos 126, 153–158, 160–170, 174, App.
    III, App. V 80, 81, 94, 95.
  Mary, App. V 94, 95.
  Sam., 164, 167, App. V 94, 95.
Leeward Is, *West Indies,* App. V 96.
Legge (Legg), Anne, App. V 29.
  Anne (*née* Finch), *Countess of Dartmouth,* App.
    V 96.
  Edw., 141, App. V 96.
  Geo., *Viscount Lewisham,* App. V 29.
  Henry, *Chancellor of the Exchequer,* pp. liiin, livn.
  Wil., 157, 174.
  Wil., *1st Earl of Dartmouth,* App. V 96.
Leghorn (Livorno), *Italy,* App. V 68.
Le Hardy, *see* Hardy.
Leinster, Duke and Duchess of, *see* Fitzgerald.
Lennox (Lenox), Cha. *2nd Duke of Richmond,* pp.
    xxvii, xliii, xlix, livn, lv, lvi, App. V 39, 59,
    97, 98, App. VI.
  Cha., *3rd Duke of Richmond,* p. lvii, no. 164,
    App. V 97, 98.
  Emilia, *see* Fitzgerald.
  Lord Geo. Henry, p. lviin, no. 164, App. V 97, 98.
  Louisa, App. V 98.
  Mary (*née* Bruce), *Duchess of Richmond,* App. V
    97.
  Sarah (*née* Cadogan), *Duchess of Richmond,* App.
    V 97, 98.
Lesso, de, *see* De Lesso.
Lestock, —, App. V 131.
  Ric., *admiral,* 86, 91, App. V 99, 131.
  Sarah, App. V 99.
Levermore, Peter, 18.
Leveson-Gower, Gertrude, *see* Russell.
  John, *1st Earl Gower,* App. V 150.
Lewes, *Suss.,* App. V 191.
Lewis, Tho., pp. xxxvi, xlviii, xlix, lviii, nos 31,
    37, 41, 174.
Lewisham, Lord, *see* Legge, Geo.
Leyden, *Netherlands:* University, p. xxxvii.
Light, Tho., 23, 174, App. IV 8.
lime, App. VI.
Lincolnshire, *place indexed,* Boston.
Linzee (Linsley), Ann *or* Anne, App. V 1, 100–102,
    116.
  Edw., pp. xxviiin, xxxn, xxxvii, xxxviii, xli,
    xliv, lvin, nos 99, 105, 108–111, 113–138,
    140–142, 144–146, 148–150, 152–158, 160–
    167, 169, 170, 174, App. III, App. IV 12,
    App. V 86, 100–102, 116.
  Mary, App. V 100, 102.
  Rob., 164, App. V 100–102.
  Susanna, *see* Hood.
  Tho., App. V 100.

136

Lipscombe, James, p. xxxiii, App. IV 6.
  Kempster, App. IV 8.
  Ric., App. IV 8.
Lisbon, *Portugal*, App. V 137.
Littlefield, James, 26, 49, 58, 174, App. IV 8.
Liverpool, *Lancs.*, p. xxxi.
Livorno, *Italy, see* Leghorn.
Lloyd, *see* Loyd.
Lock (Locke), John, *philosopher*, p. xli.
  Peirson, 94, App. V 103.
London: pp. xviii, xxiv, xxviin, xlivn, xlvi, lv,
  lvi, nos 39n, 164, App. V 22, 30, 43, 94, 107,
  144, 169; port of London, App. V 116; St
  Mildred's Poultry, App. V 84; St Peter Le Poor,
  Broad St., App. V 84; Savoy, App. V 54; Tower
  of London, p. xxiii, no. 55, App. V 60, 98, 130;
  White Hart, Paternoster Row, App. I; *see also*
  British Library; Inns of Court; National Mari-
  time Museum; Public Record Office.
Loney, John, 171, 172.
Long, Ric., App. IV 8.
Longcroft, C., p. xlin.
  Rob., 83, 87, 88.
Looe, East, *Cornw.*, App. V 65.
Lothian, Marquis of, *see* Kerr, Wil. Henry.
Louis XIV, *King of France*, App. V 151.
Louisburg, *Nova Scotia*, App. V 178.
Lovat, Lord, *see* Fraser, Simon.
Lovell, Mary, *see* Wildman.
Lowe, John, 164, 167, App. V 104.
  Jos., App. IV 9.
  Mary, App. V 104.
Loyd, Cha., App. IV 8.
Lucas, David, App. V 158.
  Sam., App. IV 9.
  Sarah, App. V 158.
Ludlow, *Herefs.*, p. xxxiv.
Luke, Tho., App. IV 11.
Lumley, Ric., *2nd Earl of Scarborough*, p. xxvii.
Lunn, —, 19n.
  Jos., App. IV 8.
Lymington, *Hants.*, p. xxxiii, App. V 32, 62, 130,
  176.
Lymington, Lord and Lady, *see* Wallop.
Lys, Henry, 164, 167, App. V 105.
  Sarah, App. V 105.

MacCarthy, Charlotte, *see* West.
  Donough, *4th Earl of Clancarty*, App. V 179.
MacKenzie, Geo., *3rd Earl of Cromartie*, p. xliii.
Madden, Sir Fred., *antiquary*, p. xlvin, App. II.
Maidlow, Tho., 81n.
Maine, Ric., App. IV 9.
  Wil., 171, 172.
Maldon, *Essex*, App. V 17.
Mallard, Tho., App. IV 9.
Malmesbury, *Wilts.*, App. V 164.
Manchester, *Lancs.*, p. xxxv.
maps and plans: plan of Portsmouth Guildhall, 41,
  45.
Mardon, Alice, App. V 79.

Marines, Royal, p. lviin, App. V 102, 145.
markets, *see* fairs and markets.
Marlborough, *Wilts.*, App. V 29.
Marlborough, Duke of, *see* Churchill, John.
Marsh, Dan., 18, 174.
Martin, Geo., App. V 106.
  James, 145.
  John, App. IV 8.
  Step., pp. xvii, xx.
  Wil., *admiral*, 102, App. V 106.
Martyr Worthy, *Hants., see* Worthy, Martyr.
Marvell, John, App. IV 9.
Mason, Rachel, App. V 146.
Master, Margaret, *see* Byng.
Mathews, Edw., App. V 107.
  Henrietta, App. V 107.
  Jane, App. V 24, 107.
  Millicent, App. V 107.
  Tho., *admiral*, p. xlix, no. 90, App. V 107.
  Wil., 58, 83, 87, 88, 112n, 145, 174.
Mathis, Elizabeth, App. V 108.
  Hannah, App. V 108.
  Wil., 10, App. V 108.
Maynard, Jacob, App. IV 8.
Mayors, *see* administration, local.
Mears (Mearus), And., App. IV 10.
  David, App. IV 9.
Measurers, *see* administration, local.
measures, *see* weights and measures.
medicine: broken ribs, p. xxxiin; gout, App. II 1;
  lameness, pp. xliii, livn; lunacy, pp. xxxn,
  xxxviii; inoculation against smallpox, p. xliv;
  bleeding of patients, App. II 1; surgeon of
  Dockyard, p. l; physician to Garrison, pp.
  xxxviii, l, lv; Commissioners, Agents, for Sick
  and Wounded Seamen, p. l, no. 18n, App. V 65;
  medical care of prisoners of war, p. ln; hospitals,
  pp. xx, xxii, lv, App. V 170; ships' medical
  chests, p. l; education of physician, 8on; thesis,
  *De renum et vesicae calculo*, p. xxxvii; Doctor of
  Medicine, *see* Bayly, John; Bayly, Geo.; Bowes,
  John; Brady, Sam.; Combe, Mat.; Smith,
  Wil.; Stepney, Geo; *see also* occupations.
Mediterranean Sea, 86, App. V 33, 71, 107, 109.
Medley, Henry, *admiral*, 106, 108, App. V 109.
Melcombe Regis, *in Weymouth, Dors., see* Wey-
  mouth.
Mellish, John, 39n.
  Ric., App. IV 8.
Merac, Alice, App. V 110.
  John, 161, 164, 167, 174, App. IV 8, App. V 110.
Merston, *Suss.*, App. V 93.
Metcalfe, Mat., 164, 167, App. V 111.
Mew, Rob., App. IV 9.
Middlesex, *places indexed*, Newington, Stoke; West-
  minster.
Milborne Port, *Dors.*, App. V 159.
Miles, Jos., App. IV 8.
Miletus, *King of Ireland*, p. xxxvii.
Millard, Rebecca, App. V 187.
Miller, Jane, App. V 112.

Nevill, —, 39n.
   Anne, *see* West.
   Geo., *Lord Bergavenny*, App. V 179.
New, Ric., 91, 174.
Newcastle, Duke of, *see* Pelham-Holles, Tho.
Newcastle upon Tyne, *Northumb.*, p. xxxiv, App.
   V 128.
Newchurch, *I.W.*: Ashey Down, App. VI; Ryde,
   App. V 105.
Newey, John, App. V 84.
   Mary, App. V 84.
New Forest, *Hants.*, App. V 150.
Newfoundland, *America*, pp. xlviii, lv, lvi, lviin;
   *place indexed*, Placentia.
New Hampshire, *America*, p. lvn.
Newington, Stoke, *Mdx*, App. V 114.
Newland, *in Titchfield, Hants.*, *see* Titchfield.
Newman, John, App. IV 8.
Newnham (Newnam), Anne, App. V 100–102.
   John, 171, 172.
   Rob., pp. xxxviii, xlii, xliv, nos 1–44, 46–50, 52–
     56, App. III, App. IV 12, App. V 100–102.
Newport, *I.W.*, pp. xxixn, xxxvii, no. 164, App. V
   14, 39, 41, 42, 62, 92, 117, 130, 151, 154, 176,
   188, 192.
Newton, Dan., App. IV 9.
Newtown, *in Calbourne, I.W.*, *see* Calbourne.
New York, *America*, App. V 178.
Nicholls, Jos., 171, 172.
nonconformists, Protestant, pp. xxxix, xlv, no. 36n,
   App. V 15; *see also* Baptists; Congregationalists;
   Presbyterians.
Nore, The, *coast of Kent*, App. V 71.
Norris, James, App. IV 8.
   Sir John, *admiral*, pp. xxvii, xlviii, liii, App. V
     164.
   Wil., 113, 174, App. IV 8.
North, Wil., *6th Baron North*, p. xlvi.
Northumberland, App. V 14; *places indexed*,
   Berwick-upon-Tweed; Newcastle upon Tyne.
Norton, Ric., p. xlviiin.
Norton family, p. xlivn.
Nottingham, *Notts.*, p. xxixn.
Nottinghamshire, *place indexed*, Nottingham.
Nova Scotia, *America*, p. lvi; *places indexed*, Anna-
   polis; Canso; Louisburg.
Nunn, Ric., App. IV 9.

Oades, —, 39n.
   Wil., App. IV 8.
Oakshott, John, App. IV 9.
oaths: of allegiance, supremacy and abjuration, 3,
   6, 11, 13, 29, 32, 99, 105, 123, 129, 153, 155;
   Burgess's oath, p. xxxiv, no. 64.
obituaries, pp. xxn, xxvn, xxviiin, xxxviiin, lxin;
   *see also* epitaphs.
O'Brien, Mary, *see* Fitzgerald.
   Wil., *3rd Earl of Inchiquin*, App. V 59.
occupations:
   actor, pp. xxiiin, xlin.
   agent, pp. xlviii, lxin, App. V 30, 68, 95, 144.

apothecary, pp. xli, xliv, App. V 100, 101.
architect, p. xlix.
baker, 5, App. V 155.
blacksmith, 23.
block maker, pp. xxx, xxxviii, xli, App. V 5,
   173, App. VI.
boat builder, App. V 45, 136.
boatman, 43n, App. V 146.
bookseller, App. II 3, App. V 187.
brazier, 83, 87.
brewer, pp. xxiv, xxv, xxxiv, xxxviii, xli, xlii,
   xliv, xlvi, no. 21, App. V 5, 53, 127, 134, 135,
   144, 156, 158.
bricklayer, p. li.
butcher, pp. xxxii, xxxv, no. 113.
carpenter, p. livn, nos 38, 52, App. II 1, App.
   V 15, 31.
carriage maker, p. xlii.
carrier, App. V 43.
carter, 26, 49, 58, 145.
clerk, pp. xxviii, lx, App. V 47.
cobbler, App. I.
contractor, pp. xxv, xxvii, xxx, xxxviii, xli–xliii,
   xlvii, l, li, no. 83n, App. V 20, 49, 112, 127,
   142, 144, 155, 173, App. VI
cooper, p. xxii.
cordwainer, 125.
distiller, 157, App. V 64, 105, 158.
draper, App. V 8.
farmer, p. xxxv, App. V 2, 83.
gaoler, p. xxxii.
general dealer, App. V 4, 30, 63.
goldsmith, pp. xxxvii, xli, xlii, xlivn, lxi, App.
   V 9, 89, 94.
grocer, p. xlii, nos 16, 27, 38, 171, 172.
gunner, pp. xxviii, xxxvi, lvi, App. I.
headmaster, 164.
house-carpenter, pp. xxvn, xlii, nos 17, 22n, 71n,
   139, 171–173, App. V 57.
housekeeper, App. V 31.
hoyman, p. xxiv.
husbandman, 58n, 87, 88, 144.
innkeeper, App. V 43.
joiner, pp. xxx, xli, xlii, no. 34, App. V 48.
labourer, pp. xxi–xxiv, xxviii, li, no. 58.
liquor merchant, p. xliv.
maltster, 62, 127, App. V 135.
mason, App. V 15.
master of ship, pp. li, lxi.
mercer, p. xlivn, no. 126, App. V 8, 81, 92.
merchant, pp. xxv, xxix, xli, xlii, xlivn, l, lvn,
   nos 83, 87, 88, 114, 145, App. V 2, 30, 35, 43,
   61, 67, 95, 142, 144, 153.
physician, pp. xxxviii, lv, no. 80n, App. I.
postmaster, pp. xlii, xlviiin, lviin, App. V 64,
   123.
printer, App. I, App. II 1, 3.
purser, 75n, App. II, App. V 40, 88, 120.
rat-catcher, p. xxiii.
rope maker, p. xlii, no. 161, App. V 49, 63, 110,
   123.

sail maker, 116, App. V 120.
salesman, App. V 148.
sawyer, p. li, no. 113.
scavenger, p. li.
schoolmaster, App. V 104.
seaman, p. l, App. V 126.
secretary, 75, App. V 46, 50, 65.
sergeant, App. I.
servant, pp. xxn, xxxix, ln, lx.
ship owner, p. xxxii.
shipwright, pp. xxiiin, xxxivn, li, nos 18, 22n, 94, 171, 172, App. V 103, 146; assistant ship-wright, App. V 103.
shop-maid, App. I.
smith, p. xxv.
soldier, App. I, App. VI.
stationer, p. xxxiin, App. V 187.
stockbroker, App. V 54.
surgeon, pp. xlii, l, nos 28, 80, App. V 101, 170.
tallow-chandler, pp. xxxiv, xli, nos 171, 172, App. V 4, 49.
tanner, App. V 70, App. VI.
timber merchant, pp. xxx, xlii, App. V 6, 57.
turnkey, 60, 61, 174.
upholder, 139.
upholsterer, 85n.
victualler, 156, App. V 137.
vinegar merchant, p. xxiv, App. V 63.
warrant officer, p. xxviii.
watchman, p. liii.
waterman, p. liii.
wine merchant, pp. xli, xliv, App. V 52.
yeoman, App. V 83, 162, 163.
— see also administration, local; administration, national; apprenticeship; Army; Church, clergy and religion; Customs and Excise; industry and production; law and justice; medicine; Navy; Ordnance; Victualling.
Ogle, Sir Chaloner, admiral, 76, 174, App. V 128.
Henrietta, App. V 128.
Isabella, App. V 128.
John, App. V 128.
Mary, App. V 128.
Onslow, Arthur, Speaker of the House of Commons, 22.
Orchardleigh, Som., App. V 114.
Ordnance, Board of, p. xxiii; debentures, p. xliv; office, Tower of London, pp. xxiii, xxiv; Master General, pp. xxviii, xlix, App. V 60, 97, 117; Lieut.-General, App. V 189; Surveyor-General, p. xxiii; Treasurer and Paymaster, App. V 65; other central officers, App. V 60.
— at Portsmouth: local office, p. xxiv; storehouse, p. xx; supplies for Garrison, p. xxv; contracts, contractors, pp. xxv–xxvii, xliii, App. VI; labour opportunities for civilians, p. xxiii; local political influence, pp. xxx, xxxiv, xlvi, xlviii, lvii; political rivalry with Admiralty, p. xxvi.
— officers at Portsmouth: Barrack Master, p. xxvii, App. V 20; Clerk of Cheque, pp. xxvi, xxx, xli, xliv, xlvii, App. V 5; Clerk of Stores, p. xli; Clerk of Survey, pp. xxvii, xlix, App. V 20;

Overseer of Gunwharf, p. xxvii, App. V 20; Overseer of Works, p. xxiv; Solicitor to Board, p. xliii, App. V 161; Storekeeper, pp. xxiii–xxv, xlviiin, App. V 10, 56; others, App. V 55; leave of absence, p. xxvin; alleged fraud, p. xxvin.
— see also Artillery; engineers; Gosport; Ireland; Public Record Office.
Orford, Suff., App. V 169.
Orford, Earl of, see Walpole, Sir Rob.
Orr, Ann, App. V 129.
Rob., 164, 167, App. V 129.
Ovington, Hants., App. V 167.
Owen, Wil., App. IV 8.
Oxford, Oxon.: University, p. xxxvii; Christ Church, p. xlvn.
Oxford, Earls of, see De Vere, Aubrey; Harley, Rob.
Oxfordshire, place indexed, Oxford.

Pafoot, James, 34.
Pafford (Paffard), Tho., App. IV 8.
Wil., App. IV 8.
Palmer, Mary, see Finch.
Sir Tho., 4th Bart, App. V 58.
pamphlets: anon., The geese in disgrace, pp. xlii, xliii, lvin, App. II; Martinus Scriblerus, Annotations on The geese in disgrace, App. II 3; R. Wilkins, The borough, pp. xviii, xxi, xlv, App. I.
paper: stamped paper, 2; see also watermarks.
parchment, p. lviii.
Paris, France, p. lvn.
Parker, Bridget, App. V 138.
Parliament: case before House of Lords, p. lxi; Speaker of House of Lords, App. V 191; debates on municipal reform, p. xlvin; committee on victualling abuses, p. xxv; elections, pp. xxviii, xlvi–xlviii, liii, lv, lviin, no. 81n, App. I; Members of Parliament, pp. xxiv, xxv, xxvii, xxxix–xl, liii, lv, lvi, App. V 3, 13, 17, 29, 33, 41, 42, 44, 50, 58, 60, 65, 69, 71, 73, 75, 77, 96, 98, 107, 114, 119, 128, 130, 133, 137, 138, 147, 159, 164, 165, 168, 171, 174–176, 178, 179, 185, 186, 189–191; type of Member for Portsmouth, pp. xxvii, xlviii, App. I, App. II 1; expulsion of Member, p. xxv; Sergeant-at-Arms of House of Commons, App. V 157; see also Acts of Parliament; documents and diplomatic; Ireland.
Parsons, James, App. IV 9.
Patten, John, App. IV 8.
Paulet (Pawlett), Cha., 2nd Duke of Bolton, App. V 130.
Cha., 3rd Duke of Bolton, p. xxxi.
Frances (née Ramsden), Lady Winchester, App. V 130.
Lord Harry, 4th Duke of Bolton, pp. xxvi, xlvin, nos 15, 174, App. V 130.
Payne, M., App. I.
Rob., App. IV 10.
Peel, Sir Rob., stateman, 2nd Bart, p. xlvin.
Peers, —, 111, App. V 131.
Elizabeth(?), App. V 131.

Thrandeston, *Suff.*: Thrandeston Hall, App. V 138.

Threlkeld, Rob., 23.

Tilbury, *Essex*, App. V 179.

tiles, p. xxiv, App. VI.

Till, Tho., p. xxvii, App. VI.

Tillotson, John, *Archbishop of Canterbury*, p. xli.

timber, *see* woods and timber.

Titchfield, *Hants.*, pp. xxv, xxix, no. 164n, App. V 83, 113, 163; Crabthorn, 164; Crofton, 164; Newland, 164; Posbrook, p. xl; Stubbington, p. xl.

tobacco: pipe, App. I.

Toll, —, 135.

Tollery, Tho., App. IV 8.

tools and implements:
    birch broom, App. VI.
    crane, p. xxxiiin.
    mathematical instruments, App. I.
    pickaxe, p. li.
    pulley, p. xxv.
    pump, p. xxiiin, nos 152, 163, 174.
    scavel, p. xxiiin.
    shovel, p. li.
    wheelbarrow, pp. xxv, li.
— *see also* arms and armour; carts and wagons.

Topham, Diana, App. V 60.
    Fra., App. V 60.

Tories: Tory voters, p. xlvin, nos 38n, 114n, 171n, App. V 4, 16, 18, 70, 94, 105, 110.

Torrington, Lord and Lady, *see* Byng.

Totnes, *Devon*, App. V 189.

Town Clerks, *see* administration, local.

Townshend, Elizabeth, App. V 170.
    Isaac, *admiral*, p. lviin, no. 10, App. V 170.

trade and commerce: decline of trade gilds, p. xxxiv; gild merchant at Portsmouth, p. xxxiv; combination of employers, p. li; trade within Portsmouth, App. I; Portsmouth coastal and overseas trade, pp. xxxv, xlii, lv, App. I; Commissioners of Trade and Plantations, 81, App. V 17, 60; *see also* administration, local; annuities; apprenticeship; banks; beer and ale; bonds; brandy shops; coffee-houses; crimes; Customs and Excise; fairs and markets; fish; furs; inns and public houses; prices; roads and road transport; ships and shipping; shops; stocks and shares; wages; weights and measures; woods and timber.

transport and communications, *see* Acts of Parliament; carriages; carts and wagons; coaches; horses; occupations; roads and road transport; ships and shipping; turnpikes.

Trattle, Elizabeth, App. V 155.
    Jos., App. IV 8.
    Wil., App. IV 6.

Treasury: Lords of Treasury, App. V 58, 176, 190; Secretary, App. V 159; Under-clerk, App. V 157; bookranger, App. V 154; deputy messenger of receipt, App. V 154; Controller of Lotteries, App. V 157; Commissioner of Revenue, App. V 60; Receiver-General of Revenues arising by

Rights and Perquisites of the Admiralty, App. V 68; complaint to Treasury, p. xxvi; warrant, p. xxxviii; *see also* Exchequer.

Trenchard, Geo., 12, App. V 171.
    Sir John, App. V 171.
    Mary, App. V 171.
    Philippa, App. V 171.

Tribe, Dan., App. IV 8.

Trotten, Ric., App. IV 9.

Tucker, John, App. IV 8.

Tuggery, Elizabeth, App. VI.

Turner, Cassandra, *see* Hawke.
    Sir Edw., *2nd Bart*, App. V 77.
    John, 71, 72.

turnpikes: Commissioners, trustees, Portsmouth and Sheet Turnpike Trust, p. xxxi, nos 56n, 83n, App. V 2–187 *passim*; Clerks and Assistants, App. V 40, 93; Surveyors, App. V 5, 153; *see also* Acts of Parliament.

Turvin, Ann, App. V 172.
    Rob., p. xxxiv, nos 2, 10, App. V 172.

Twilford, Sam., p. li.

universities, *see* Cambridge; Edinburgh; Leyden; medicine; Oxford; Southampton; Utrecht.

Uphill, John, p. li.

Utrecht, *Netherlands*: University, p. xxxvii.

Vanbrugh, Phil., App. V 68.
    Philippia, App. V 68.

Varlo, Elizabeth, App. V 173.
    John, App. V 173.
    Mary, p. xxxviii, App. V 173.
    Phil., pp. xxviiin, xxxviii, xxxixn, xlii, lvii, nos 16, 27, 165, 167, App. V 5, 6, 173, 182.

Vere, de, *see* De Vere.

Vere, Lord and Lady, *see* Beauclerk.

Vernell, Henry, App. IV 9.

Vernon, Edw., *admiral*, pp. xlviin, xlix, liii, nos 64, 81n, 174, App. V 174.
    James, App. V 174.
    Mary, App. V 174.
    Sarah, App. V 174.

Victualling, Board of, p. xxiin, nos 26n, 111, App. I; Commissioners, App. V 137, 168; Controller of Victualling Accounts, App. V 65; agent at Portsmouth, p. xxi, App. V 152; other agents, correspondents, App. V 68, 137; clerk at Gosport, App. V 152; arrears of pay, p. xxii; bills, contracts, pp. xxvi, xlv.

Villiers, Charlotte (*née* Capel), *Countess of Clarendon*, App. V 175.
    Judith (*née* Herne), *Countess of Jersey*, App. V 175.
    Tho., *1st Earl of Clarendon*, p. xxviii, nos 149, 160, App. V 175.
    Wil., *2nd Earl of Jersey*, App. V 175.

Vining, Anne, App. V 79, 81.
    Elizabeth, p. xxiv, App. VI.
    John, pp. xix, xxiv–xxvi, xxxviii–xlii, xliv, xlvi–xlviii, l, nos 1–6, 11–13, 19, 20, 24, 28, 29, 31, 37–41, 46–52, 54–74, 76, 78–81, 83–

Whitehead (Whithed), Fra., 164, App. V 185, App. VI.
  James, 87, 88, 145.
  Mary, App. V 185.
Whiteing, Ben., App. IV 8.
Whittle, *see* Wittell.
Whitwell, *in Godshill, I.W., see* Godshill.
Wickham, *Hants.*, p. xxxvii.
Wight, I. of, pp. xl, xlii, App. V 117, 176; *places indexed*, Arreton; Brading; Calbourne; Godshill; Newchurch; Newport; Yarmouth.
Wildman, Anne (*née* Daines), *Lady Barrington*, App. V 186.
  John, *1st Viscount Barrington*, App. V 186.
  Mary (*née* Lovell), *Lady Barrington*, App. V 186.
  Wil., *2nd Viscount Barrington*, p. xviii, nos 149, 160, App. V 186.
Wilkins, Rob., pp. xviii, xxi, xxiin, xlv, App. I.
Wilkinson, James, 137n, 164, 167, App. II 1, App. V 187.
  Rebecca, App. V 187.
  Tate, p. xxiiin.
William III, *King*, pp. xvii, xxi, xxxvii.
William Augustus, *Duke of Cumberland*, 65, 174, App. V 62, 98, 188.
Williams, Wil., App. IV 9.
wills, pp. xxn, xxxviiin, xxxix, xli, xliin, xliii, xlivn, xlixn, no. 127; executor, legacy, p. lxi.
Wills (Willis), Ant., App. V 189.
  Sir Cha., *Governor of Portsmouth*, pp. xxiv, xxviii, lix, App. V 189.
  Guinevere *or* Jenofer, App. V 189.
Wilmoth, Walt., 28.
Wilshire, Ric., App. IV 8.
Wiltshire, *places indexed*, Bedwyn, Great; Cricklade; Malmesbury; Marlborough; Salisbury.
Winchester, *Hants.*, pp. xxixn, xxxi, xxxiv, xlvi, l, nos 118, 119, 158, App. V 84, 112, 113; Cathedral, App. V 132; College, App. V 132; *see also* Consistory Court.
Winchester, Lady, *see* Paulet, Frances.
Winchilsea, Earls and Countesses of, *see* Finch.
windows, pp. xix, xxviii, no. 125, App. I; shop windows, p. xxix; cellar windows, 36, 38, 39n, 56, 80, 113.
Windsor, *Berks.*, p. xlvi, App. V 13; Castle, App. V 28, 29.
Windsor Forest, *Berks.*, App. V 179.
wine, p. xlii, App. I; French, p. xxxv; port, sherry, p. xxxin.
Winnington, Anne, App. V 190.
  Love, App. V 190.
  Salwey, App. V 190.

Tho., *politician*, 12, App. V 190.
Winter, —, p. li.
  Wil., App. IV 8.
Wisbech, *Cambs.*, p. xxxiii.
Wittell, Wil., App. IV 9.
Wolfeton, *in Charminster, Dors., see* Charminster.
wolves, p. xlii, App. II 1, 3.
Wood, Paul, App. IV 9.
Woodman, Joshua, 161.
woods and timber: timber, pp. xxii, xxvi, xxvii, xxx, xlii, App. VI; from New Hampshire, p. lvn; firewood ('firing'), App. I; charcoal, p. xvii, App. VI; ash knees, App. VI; beech plank, p. xxvii, App. VI; elm blocks, App. II 3; elm knees, App. VI; other elm, App. II; fir balks, laths, plank, rafters, App. VI; oak blocks, p. xliii, App. II 1, 3; oak knees, laths, App. VI; other oak, App. II, App. VI; other laths, heart laths, App. VI; wainscot board, App. VI; attempted theft of wood, p. liii; Surveyor-General of Woods and Forests, App. V 133; *see also* Bere Forest; New Forest; occupations; Windsor Forest.
Woodyer, Wil., App. IV 4.
Worcester, *Worcs.*, App. V 190.
Worcestershire, *places indexed*, Droitwich; Kidderminster; Worcester.
Worthy, Martyr, *Hants.*, 159.
Wriothesley, Elizabeth, *see* Montagu.
  Tho., *4th Earl of Southampton*, App. V 117.
writs: issued by Corporation, p. xxxii; mandamus, p. lviin.
Wyatt, Wil., 2.
Wymering, *Hants.*, p. xviii; *see also* Cosham; Hilsea.

Yarmouth, *I.W.*, 89n, 164, App. V 27, 35, 39, 41, 91, 112, 117, 130, 140(?), 142, 151, 154, 171, 176, 192.
York, *Yorks.*, p. lviiin.
York and Albany, Duke of, *see* Frederick Augustus.
Yorke, Elizabeth, App. V 191; *see also* Anson.
  Jos., 66n.
  Margaret (*née* Cocks), *Countess of Hardwicke*, App. V 191.
  Phil., *1st Earl of Hardwicke*, pp. xxxin, xlvin, livn, nos 66, 174, App. V 3, 191.
Yorkshire, *places indexed*, Aldborough; Hedon; Leeds; Scarborough; Sheffield; Thirsk; York.
Young, —, App. VI.
  Edw., 35, App. V 192.
  John, App. IV 9.
  Mary, App. V 104.
  Ric., p. liii.

148

# Portsmouth Record Series

## PUBLICATIONS

The Portsmouth Record Series began publication in 1971. Primarily it is intended to make the written sources for Portsmouth's history widely available. But beyond this it is hoped that the Series may help to set a new pattern for the publication of local records in Great Britain. For well over a hundred years record societies and other bodies have been publishing documents that are the sources of local history. But during the last twenty-five years the establishment of local record offices has made the majority of manuscripts easily available to research, while cheap photographic methods enable the searcher to use records from scattered repositories without recourse to printed texts. It is with this in mind that the Portsmouth Record Series has been planned. It is proposed to print complete texts only of three types of record: first, a very few documents that are of basic importance to the history of the City; second, any records of Portsmouth that are sufficiently unusual to give their publication more than purely local interest; and, third, records of types found elsewhere but hitherto unpublished. For the rest the Series will consist of calendars, catalogues, indexes and bibliographies.

The volumes already published in the Series are:

1 *Borough Sessions Papers 1653–1688*: a calendar compiled by Arthur J. Willis and edited by Margaret J. Hoad with an Introduction by Margaret J. Hoad and Robert P. Grime (1971).

2 *Portsmouth and Sheet Turnpike Commissioners' Minute Book 1711–1754* edited by William Albert and P.D.A. Harvey (1973).

## LIST OF SUBSCRIBERS TO THE SERIES

*December 1975*

### INDIVIDUALS

Ashton, Miss M.A., 9 Kiln Road, Fareham
Attrill, J.R., 5 Masefield Avenue, Paulsgrove
Aylen, Mrs D.R., 50 Lower Drayton Lane, Portsmouth
Bainbridge, Mrs J.L., 8 Gannet House, Eastern Parade, Southsea
Barrett, Revd P.L.S., The Little House, Deeford Road, Pershore, Worcestershire
Bloomfield, J.C., 185/187 Fratton Road, Portsmouth
Bromley, Professor J.S., Department of History, The University, Southampton
Butler, D.J., 5 St David's Way, Whitley Bay, North Tyneside, Tyne and Wear
Clark, C.H., Dursley, Garden Lane, Southsea
Dowdeswell, G.P., 51 Hulbert Road, Waterlooville
Dymond, Miss D., CBE, 15a Festing Grove, Southsea
Emery-Wallis, Councillor F.A.J., 5 Craneswater Park, Southsea

Groves, W.E.S., 95 Elm Grove, Southsea
Haslegrave, J.R., CBE, 27 Eastern Parade, Southsea
Haycocks, Mrs J.E., 48 Andrew Crescent, Waterlooville
Keeping, S.F., 80 Chaveney Road, Quorn, Loughborough, Leicestershire
Linington, J.G., 5 Pembroke Road, Portsmouth
Lock, J.F., 41 Seafront, Hayling Island
McCarthy, Mrs J., Ewhurst, Robertsbridge, East Sussex
MacDonald, G.A., 8 King Street, Emsworth
Ommanney, Lt-Col. C.L., South Court, Crondall, Farnham, Surrey
Partridge, Miss T.C., 66 Prince Albert Road, Southsea
Patterson, Professor A.T., The Sele, Stoughton, Chichester, Sussex
Pilkington, J.L.L., 8 Emsworth Road, Havant
Read, Mrs P., 19 Broad Street, Portsmouth
Rickman, C.D., 87 Rothesay Road, Gosport
Rogers, P.M., 6 Blackmoor Walk, Havant
Smart, J.A.G., 153 Manners Road, Southsea
Stace, H.J.A., 62 Park Lane, Bedhampton
Stowell, Mrs H.M., Durley Lodge, Durley, Southampton
Surry, N.W., Department of Historical and Literary Studies, Portsmouth Polytechnic, Bellevue Terrace, Southsea
Taplin, Councillor E.H., 10 St Ronan's Road, Southsea
Tweed, R.B., Guildhall, Portsmouth
Wade, R.B., New Clements, Sandringham Road, Fareham
Wadey, Mrs J.M., 1 Bramble Way, Finningley, Doncaster, South Yorkshire
Wall, Mrs R.M., 80 Orchard Road, Southsea
Webb, J. G., 11 Blount Road, Pembroke Park, Portsmouth
Willis-Fear, M.J.W., Pembrokeshire Record Office, The Castle, Haverfordwest, Dyfed
Wooden, F.E., 32 Miller Drive, Fareham

### INSTITUTIONS (Great Britain and Ireland)

Birmingham, Reference Library
Cambridge, University Library (copyright library)
Chester, City Record Office
Dublin, Trinity College Library (copyright library)
Edinburgh, National Library of Scotland (copyright library)
Gosport, Museum
London, British Library (copyright library)
          Institute of Historical Research
          Public Record Office
          Society of Antiquaries of London
          University Library
Manchester, University Library
          Public Libraries
Norwich, East Anglia University Library
Oxford, Bodleian Library (copyright library)
Portsmouth, City of Portsmouth Boys' School
          City Record Office
          College of Education
          Friendship Link
          Grammar School
          Polytechnic
          Priory School
Reading, University Library
Southampton, University Library
Winchester, Hampshire County Library
          Hampshire Record Office

### INSTITUTIONS (overseas)

*United States of America*

Ann Arbor (Mich.), Michigan University Library
Chicago (Ill.), Newberry Library
Los Angeles (Calif.), California University Research Library
Princeton (N.J.), University Library

The GOTHAMITES in Council. — Humbly Inscribed to the

*In the Porch the Emblems of Disapointment, Malice, Envy, Covetousness &c &c.*

*\* The Envied Contract.*

Two Black Crown'd Geese of middle Age.
By some thought Cunning, few thought sage,
Who oft had smother'd Discontent,
And Long on Mischief been intent:

Publish'd according to Act of Parliament Feb. 21. 1761 by Dan Job. Stat